P9-EFG-928

WASHINGTON EXPOSÉ

By Jack Anderson

Public Affairs Press, Washington, D.C.

FOR MY WIFE OLIVIA

Published by Public Affairs Press
419 New Jersey Avenue, S.E., Washington, D.C. 20003

Printed in the United States of America
Library of Congress Catalog Card No. 67-14902

PREFACE

First let me warn that I am no pundit. I do not observe the Washington scene from Olympian heights. I am neither historian nor scholar. I like to think I am an investigative reporter. I poke into the shadows of government, searching with a small light for the facts that officials would prefer to keep in the dark. I have a tendency to stray from orthodox news trails, and I blunder into many dead ends. But while others are occupied with the imposing view out front, I catch an occasional glimpse behind the scenes.

Investigative reporting isn't, of course, the best way to make friends. I have been booed, sued, accused, assaulted, denounced, blackballed, and investigated. I have been hauled before Congress, hounded by the FBI, bawled out by Presidents, threatened by gangsters. The Minutemen have issued an order for my execution.

The first time I met Senator Kenneth McKellar (D.-Tenn.), he greeted me with a flurry of flying fists. The late Senator Joseph McCarthy (R.-Wis.) once commandeered a Senate elevator to keep me from riding with him. Not long ago, I received a letter addressed to "Jack Anderson, liar, louse, ring-tailed rat and yellow-bellied skunk." No street number; no city or state. Although a Census official has estimated there are at least 14,000 Jack Andersons in this country, the Post Office delivered the letter unerringly to my door.

Through it all, I have held to the old-fashioned notion that the fourth estate has a special calling to oppose and expose. The Washington chronicler, above all, should keep his pencil sharp to prick the powerful and deflate the pompous.

Personally, I have never found the stuff for an expose in an official press release. I have never broken a scandal by waiting for the offenders to call a press conference to confess their wrongdoing. I have never met a government spokesman who would pull back the rug and point out the hidden facts that might embarrass the government. Nor have I ever scored a news beat by waiting until those facts were safely recorded in the privileged transcripts of Congress or the courts. A muckraker simply has to follow his suspicions where they lead him, maintaining a determined irreverence for the sacred cows and the political bulls.

For close to 20 years, I have stumbled around the Washington maze, asking many questions, getting fewer answers, learning a little here and there. In these pages I try to throw some light on the hidden side of Washington, the side the public is seldom shown. Scholars will look in vain for the sources. I have named only those bold enough to speak on the record. Most of my information comes to me confidentially, often from people who have an intense aversion to publicity.

I don't mean to suggest that my informants are furtive figures who meet me in back alleys and whisper cryptic facts. The best stuff has come from Presidents, Cabinet officers, members of Congress, Generals, and Admirals. The higher they are, the least anxious they are usually to be quoted.

The first tip that started me on the trail of Senator Thomas J. Dodd (D.-Conn.) came from a former Congressman. An Internal Revenue agent, who had been investigating the tax write-off on President Eisenhower's farm and had been sworn to secrecy, told me how three oil millionaires were paying Ike's farm bills. In breaking the Sherman Adams-Bernard Goldfine scandal I received unexpected help from one of Goldfine's many attorneys, one who didn't admire his rich client. At first, he routinely denied that his client had given valuable gifts to President Eisenhower's chief aide. Then the lawyer leaned forward and confided in a hushed voice: "I'll deny I ever told you this, but Sherman Adams has never bought a stitch of clothing, a stick of furniture, or a bottle of liquor since he met Goldfine."

On another story, Richard Mack himself gave me the information, albeit inadvertently, that forced him to resign from the Federal Communications Commission.

Sometimes I've been more lucky than adroit. Once, I got the details of a grain storage scandal because I happened to have the same name as a White House aide. A high Agriculture Department official, mistaking me for this more eminent Jack Anderson, took my call and answered my questions with refreshing frankness.

The stories I've missed, alas, have been more impressive than those I've broken. Back in April, 1960, I was tipped off that Bobby Baker, then right-hand man to Senator Lyndon B. Johnson, was worth more than $300,000, although he had been working on Capitol Hill on a government salary ever since he was a Senate page. I learned, too, that Bobby had some unusual business connections.

When I confronted Baker about his backdoor enterprises, he pulled open a desk drawer, hauled out his tax returns going back five years, spread them on his desk, and invited me to inspect them. "You know I wouldn't be foolish enough to lie on my tax returns," he said. I examined the returns carefully, found little income above his official wages. He reported less than $3,000 a year from his law firm, virtually no income at all from his other businesses. What I had overlooked was his paper worth. It is quite possible to own a fortune on paper and not report it in your returns until you cash in your chips. Someone else broke the Bobby Baker story four years later.

This book is by no means my work alone. My staff—Opal Ginn, Sam Segal, and William Curtis—helped with the research. Donald Ludlow, the wise correspondent for the London Daily Mirror, assisted me with parts of the manuscript. Parade's Fred Blumenthal, a valued friend, joined me in interviewing Andy Evans. Fred's sensitive questioning, more than my own, drew out Evans' remarkable story.

I owe a special debt to Parade for permitting me to use material written for that publication. Jess Gorkin, certainly one of the sharpest editors in the business, guided many of my investigations. Most of all, I am indebted to that master news sleuth, Drew Pearson, who taught me all I know about investigative reporting.

JACK ANDERSON

Washington, D. C.

CONTENTS

1

BEHIND THE HEADLINES

Most Americans will acknowledge, if pressed, that they are the most enlightened people on earth. There is scarcely a home in the country that doesn't keep its fires blazing in the winter with the late editions. Nowhere else can so many men tell you precisely how many baseballs Willie Mays has slammed over the fence. Only in America are the ladies so steeped in the problems of the lovelorn. And the whole nation is absorbed in the latest escapades of Batman.

Of course, fewer men can tell you how many metal balls have been knocked into outer space or which nation is ahead in the great race to the worlds beyond our world. Fewer women can discuss domestic problems, if these happen to be national rather than marital. And more newspaper readers follow the action in the comic strips than the real thing in Vietnam. Public interest in Congressional debates is so low that a legislator simply cannot count upon the voters to re-elect him for championing their cause. All too often, he is obliged to support the pressure groups and special interests, which pay far closer attention to what goes on in Congress. If Americans would concern themselves with tax legislation enough to compel Congress to close the loopholes, for example, they probably could reduce federal income taxes by half.

Why are so many people starved for information in a land of plenty, where news is available on the doorstep each morning or at the turn of a television knob? For one thing, they have come to expect their news mediums to entertain rather than inform. They take their information in small, sugared capsules, scanning the headlines with only half an eye, listening to the news broadcasts with half an ear.

Accordingly, most newspapers serve up the day's events in easy-to-take doses. They report who, what, when, and where; *seldom do they explain why.* They reduce great complexities to simplicities. They may sum up a peace-or-war issue, for example, in one punchy paragraph or condense a deep debate into a couple of colorful quotes. *Most big-city dailies give the public only a sniff of foreign news.* Even the local columns are devoted more to police reports, politics, and puffery than to the racial ferment, say, that may be about to explode just a few blocks from the editorial rooms. *Too few papers dare to print exposes before they are safely recorded in privileged documents or, for that matter, bother to probe behind the daily press hand-outs.*

Some publishers have trouble recognizing news when it conflicts with their preconceptions. Republican publishers found it easy to believe, for example, that there was something corrupt about President Harry Truman's accepting a deep freeze from his military aide and President Lyndon Johnson's taking a stereo set from his Senate aide. Stories splashed across the front pages made the deep freeze in 1952 and the stereo set in 1964 symbolic of Washington corruption.

Yet in between these celebrated gifts, *Dwight Eisenhower accepted more presents than any other President in history.* Among them was no mere deep freeze but a huge, walk-in freezing compartment—not to mention a full electric kitchen given to Ike by the AVCO corporation, which made millions from government contracts while he occupied the White House. He also received a free stereophonic set as part of a $4,000 Black Hawk tractor, which, in addition, was equipped with push buttons, a cigarette lighter, and power steering. Indeed, it contained so many gadgets that two factory representatives had to come to the Gettysburg farm to show Ike's helpers how to operate it.

But these were small items in Ike's great gift collection. He also accepted a $3,000 putting green complete with a

$1,000-a-year maintenance policy from the Professional Golfers Association, a three-wheeled golf cart from Cushman Motors of Lincoln, Nebraska, a television set with elaborate antenna from Radio Corporation of America, a painting of Custer's Last Stand from American Airlines, a white marble fireplace from the White House staff, and 40 trees and shrubs from Nikita Khrushchev, then the Soviet Premier.

Less easy to identify were the donors of an orchid-filled greenhouse, a 30-foot flagpole, a 60-foot wall, pine bedroom furniture, antique birch spice cupboards, a large brass sundial mounted on a 120 mm. shell, a farm runabout with fringed canopy, and three hand-tooled saddles—not to overlook the mink-lined pigskin gloves he used to drive his gift tractor. He also received a barnyard full of expensive livestock, including at least 20 purebred Angus cattle, a purebred Arabian stallion and filly, three ponies, two quarter horses, an assortment of heifers, calves and pigs, and a flock of Rhode Island Red hens.

But the same newspapers which had headlined Truman's deep freeze, found nothing newsworthy in Ike's fabulous gifts. Perhaps it was his open face, the blue eyes as clear and guileless as the sky above his native Kansas, that compelled confidence. He had the look of a leader who could be trusted to clean up corruption in government. Or perhaps the publishers simply believed the great build-up they gave him. From pages of friendly print arose a public image called Ike, whom few could fail to like. His warmth was projected like a spring thaw upon voters, for 20 years cold to the Republican ticket.

If newspapers don't always present the news in depth, most radio and television stations are even less concerned about news content. Their shining goal is to broadcast enough news to satisfy the Federal Communications Commission that they have performed their public service. *"When it comes to covering the news in any kind of detailed way," says television reporter David Brinkley, "we are just almost not in the ball game."* As for radio, 15-minute newscasts have all but disappeared from the air; the surveys show that most listeners get bored after five minutes. This is time for about as much information as they could glean from driving slowly past a well-lighted news stand.

Thus, many Americans, under-exposed to colorful reality, are left to grope in a subterranean world of half light. It is a bleak world of black and white, of shadows that take on weird, even grotesque shapes. Those who inhabit it become prey for the demagogues. Gullible, they are easily taken in by snap-finger solutions. They accept simple, yes-or-no answers, and take comfort from political cure-alls.

Nor can they cope with the sophisticated propaganda of the times. *The world has been thrust into the age of "double-speak" and "double-think" forecast by the late George Orwell in his farseeing novel, "1984."* Such words as freedom and democracy, peace and justice have been debased in the communist language mint. Thus dictatorships pose as "people's democracies"; aggressors are called liberators, and the defenders are called aggressors. *Still other words, like loyalty and patriotism, have been corrupted by the radicals of the right who, in the name of democracy, seek to destroy it.*

The soap box patriots are exceeded only by the political pitchmen who would rather exploit than explain the issues. *They have a language of their own, spoken out of both sides of the mouth.* It is a curious double talk, which often accentuates the positive in order to accentuate the negative. They can defend the indefensible—racial discrimination, say, or war profiteering—in language so lofty as to sound believable. What is good for themselves, they portray as good for America.

Not even the government of, by, and for the people can always be trusted to tell the truth. Though most government statements are straightforward enough, the public should

Progress Reported in Dominican Talks

SANTO DOMINGO, July 24 (AP) A little progress was reported this week and a little presure was applied by the Organization of American States in negotiations to end the Dominican rebellion. It is three months old today.

The progress concerned the possibility that military representatives of the junta and the rebel regime might sit down together at the bargaining table. For more than two months an OAS team has been shuttling between the two sides.

The pressure was low-keyed. Informed sources said Ellsworth Bunker, chief of the mediating team, discussed the "facts of life." These sources said Bunker mentioned the country's deteriorating economy and reminded people the OAS mediators "can't stay forever."

Pressure is increasing among the population for an end to the debilitating crises. A number of sources in both junta and rebel camps say this is bringing flexibility to previously rigid positions.

After returning Monday night from Washington, Bunker met separately with the junta and with the rebel faction.

The talks proceed in constant danger of a setback.

The rebels complain daily of what they describe as police repression and political arrests. A spokesman for the OAS Human Rights Commission says the Commission receives an average of 28 complaints a day of political arrests by junta authorities. The spokesman said the majority of those arrested are imprisoned for one or two months before their cases are investigated. In comparison, he said, there are two or three complaints a day of political arrests by rebel authorities.

Santo Domingo Talks Produce Little Progress

SANTO DOMINGO, Dominican Republic (AP)—A little progress was reported last week and a little pressure was applied by the Organization of American States in negotiations to end the Dominican rebellion. It was three months old yesterday.

The progress concerned the possibility that military representatives of the junta and the rebel regime might sit down together at the bargaining table. It would be the first face-to-face talks. For more than two months, an OAS mediating team has been shuttling back and forth between the two sides.

The pressure was low-keyed and almost indirect. Informed sources said Ellsworth Bunker, chief of the mediating team, discussed the "facts of life." These sources said Bunker mentioned the country's "deteriorating economy" and reminded people the OAS mediators "can't stay forever."

Pressure is increasing among the population for an end to the debilitating crisis. A number of sources in both junta and rebel camps say this is bringing flexibility to previously rigid positions.

One rigid position has been the key issue of the military. Should rebel officers be allowed to rejoin the armed forces? Should the chiefs of the junta's military organization be removed? How long should the Inter-American force, made up mostly of U.S. soldiers, remain in the country once a compromise provisional government is established?

A rebel source says his side is considering the idea of sending "second-level" officers to the bargaining table to talk over military problems with similar representatives from the other side and the OAS mediators.

The same Associated Press story was used by two newspapers, but their headlines are quite different. Small wonder that the public finds it difficult to figure out what's really going on.

beware of tricky wording. Many an embarrassing fact has been spread over with verbal camouflage. Other facts have been filtered out in the bureaucratic process—neatly condensed for quick comprehension, sometimes reduced down to mere catchwords and cliches. Officials who have hestitated to spread falsehood have also accomplished the same result simply by sweeping the truth under a secrecy label. Half a story, or no story at all, can be a subtle form of misrepresentation.

All Presidents have sought to present the best possible face to the public. Lyndon Johnson not only preens and poses; he also wants to operate the cameras. He keeps the curtain closed on what his Administration is doing until all the facts are in and the final decisions are reached. Only then is he inclined to inform the public. Seldom does he let them in on the decision process, and the doubters and dissenters usually are silenced. *His directives to subordinates are often accompanied with stern admonitions about secrecy. His tantrums over unauthorized news leaks have terrorized the few sources who once talked freely.*

Yet it must be said that no past President has been more accessible to reporters. He shovel-feeds information to them, though it is more often what he wants to say than what they want to hear. He even expropriates announcements that normally are put out by government agencies. During a four-day week-end at the LBJ Ranch, for example, President Johnson issued 42 separate announcements, including one on the survival of the whooping cranes. He avoids critical questions, however, as if they were hypodermic needles.

Under his leadership, most government departments have centralized their public information operations—the better to control the outflow of news. *Though most officials tell the truth, they are increasingly inclined to mold the facts as the Administration would like them to appear.* Within the government, they offer little opposition to the official line. They would rather play it safe than play it right. They are devoted to the principle that they can't get into trouble over decisions they don't make. There is no matter too trivial for them to buck up to a superior or to refer to a committee. They put nothing into writing without plenty of handy escape clauses.

The pressures for conformity, the preference for entertainment over information, the tolerance for every point of view—these have combined to suppress controversy. It has become the fashion for writers to be high-minded and carefully objective, presenting every view but taking stands only on safe subjects. Radio and television producers shy away from controversy as if it were unpatriotic. They hire motivational researchers, statisticians, sociologists, psychologists, and pollsters to make sure they never offend the mass mind.

This blandness is dictated, in part, by the advertising agencies, which don't like to ruffle the unseen audience. Radio-TV stations, more than newspapers, bow toward Madison Avenue, the advertising Mecca. Even the great networks take care not to offend sponsors who might withdraw a multimillion-dollar account over a political comment not to their liking. The few telecasters, who once may have risked a little controversy, were set back by the outcry over Howard K. Smith's documentary, "The Political Obituary of Richard Nixon." The ABC network was struck by a storm of protest, not because the political obituary may have been premature, but because Smith had the impudence to interview Alger Hiss as one of the figures who had played a role in Nixon's life. James Hagerty, ABC's vice president in charge of news, went before the cameras to warn solemnly: "If we are weakened, you are weakened, for if through fear or intimidation, we fail to provide all the news—favorable or unfavorable—then you, the citizens of the nation, cannot be properly informed." *But when a couple of right-wing sponsors threatened to take their money and go elsewhere,* ABC *suddenly forgot all about its duty to inform the citizens of the nation.* The front office kicked Hagerty upstairs, ended Smith's experiment in bold journalism, and began censoring the news more closely.

Thanks to such shyness, we are fast becoming a nation of conformists—of thinking men who smoke Viceroys (though true thinkers, familiar with the lung cancer reports, wouldn't smoke at all), who brush with Pepsodent and wonder where the yellow went, who worry about what their best friends won't tell them. Too many Americans, if not brain-washed, have had their gray tissue thoroughly rinsed. They have succumbed to the techniques of the advertising agencies, whose pitchmen in pinstripes seem able to promote laxatives, deodorants, and presidential candidates with equal know-how. They deal in slogans and simplicities, pap for the public, which the more simple souls swallow cheerfully. Now the advertising men are even experimenting with subliminal advertising, so they can plant slogans in the subconscious without distracting the viewers from "Gunsmoke" or "Batman."

There is a subtle menace in too much conformity, in the government's Uncle-knows-best attitude. The democratic machinery should never run so smoothly and silently that the rumble of opposition becomes muffled. Let there be a few cogs that grate against the massive wheels of Big Government, Big Business, and Big Labor.

2

GOVERNMENT COVER-UP

Uncle Sam's word, once as good as his gold, no longer is trusted around the world. Too many times U.S. spokesmen have resorted to deception which, inevitably, has produced more embarrassment than would have resulted from the incidents they tried to hide. They have been caught in one awkward lie after another *until world confidence in Uncle Sam has been severely shaken.* This has produced a crisis in credibility, which has reduced America's effectiveness in world affairs.

Some people contend that the President, for the protection of the nation, sometimes must withhold the whole truth about foreign affairs. *But domestic officials have also played loose with the truth to cover up blunders, hide corruption and make bad policies look good.*

The public can be excused for wondering occasionally whom and what to believe. Defense Secretary Robert McNamara's optimistic reports on the war in Vietnam, for example, have been regularly contradicted by events on the battlefront. The Defense Department's credibility has sunk so low, charges aviation writer Robert Hotz, *"that most Pentagon reporters really don't believe a story until it has been officially denied."*

Pentagon spokesman Arthur Sylvester contends that "information is a weapon, a very important weapon, to be used or withheld." Though he denies any intent to "phony up" the news, *he defends the government's inherent right to "lie to save itself when it's going up into a nuclear war."* At a meeting with war correspondents in Vietnam, he complained: "I can't understand how you fellows can write what you do while American boys are dying out there." U.S. correspondents had a patriotic duty, he said, to make their country look good. Asked whether he seriously expected the American press to be "the handmaiden of government," he retorted: "That's exactly what I expect." Later, the correspondents complained that government spokesmen sometimes lied to them. Snapped back Sylvester: *"Look, if you think any American official is going to tell you the truth, then you're stupid. Did you hear that, stupid!"*

This attitude raises the question whether a democracy, in the war of words, should get down on the communist level and trade lies. Not only are communist leaders better liars, but they have no free press to contradict them. In a democracy, the truth has a habit of bubbling to the surface. *Democracy's strength lies in the free flow of accurate information to its citizens.* Of course, security information must be withheld from the public, so it won't reach an enemy. In this case, a simple "no comment" is better than a lie.

Yet increasingly, American policymakers have engaged in the disturbing practice of concocting "cover stories," as official lies are delicately called, to keep the communists guessing about our moves. Unhappily, the covers repeatedly have been ripped off these stories. Six days after a U-2 spy plane disappeared over Russia in 1960, the State Department blandly announced: "There was no deliberate attempt to violate Soviet airspace, and there has never been." The world soon learned that U-2's had been winging over Russia for several years, and the *cover story exploded in the faces of those who had invented it.*

The following year, the late Adlai Stevenson, relying on information from Washington, lied to the United Nations about the Bay of Pigs invasion. Another who helped spread misinformation about this debacle was White House aide Arthur Schlesinger, Jr., who, in his recent memoirs, presents a different set of facts from those he gave to the New York

CONFIDENTIAL

LIMITED OFFICIAL USE

TOP SECRET

RESTRICTED

FOR ADMINISTRATIVE USE ONLY

FOR STAFF USE ONLY

FOR UNITED STATES GOVERNMENT USE ONLY

SUBMITTED IN CONFIDENCE

Limited to Official U. S. Government Use

ADMINISTRATIVELY CONFIDENTIAL

CONFIDENTIAL (F.R.)

FOR SUBCOMMITTEE USE ONLY NOT FOR RELEASE

FOR OFFICIAL USE ONLY

NOT TO BE REFERENCED, OR GIVEN FURTHER DISTRIBUTION WITHOUT APPROVAL

ADMINISTRATIVE CONFIDENTIAL

NOT FOR PUBLICATION

MEDICAL - PRIVATE

Administratively restricted to

NOT RELEASABLE TO

OFFICIAL USE ONLY

"NOT FOR PUBLIC INSPECTION"

CONFIDENTIAL
THIS PAPER IS AN ORIGINAL DOCUMENT

COPY OF DECISION NOT TO BE RELEASED TO APPELLANT
EXEC. ORDER V.R. NO. 11

Limited to Official Bureau of the Budget Use

LIMITED OFFICIAL USE

FOR U.S. GOVERNMENT USE ONLY

SECRET

ADMINISTRATIVELY RESTRICTED

LIMITED OFFICIAL USE

Some of the secrecy stamps which government officials use to conceal information from the public and Congress.

Times in 1961. When his book disclosed the size of the invasion force was 1400 men, the Times reminded him of his claim to them that no more than 200 to 300 men were involved. *"Did I say that?" blurted Schlesinger. "Well, I was lying. This was a cover story."*

During the Cuban missile crisis a year later, government information was tightly controlled and carefully coordinated to give a false picture. Five days after aerial photographs were taken of Soviet missiles in Cuba, for example, the Pentagon issued the following statement to newsmen: "A Pentagon spokesman denied tonight that any alert has been ordered or that any emergency measures have been set in motion against communist-ruled Cuba. Further, the spokesman said the Pentagon has no information indicating the presence of offensive weapons in Cuba." *Though not a word of this was true, press chief Sylvester still insisted three months later: "There has been no distortion, no deception, and no manipulation of the news released by the Defense Department during the Cuban crisis."*

Again in 1965, when Singapore's Prime Minister Lee Kuan Yew claimed a CIA agent had offered him a $3.4 million bribe, State Department spokesman Robert McCloskey indignantly announced: "We deny that allegation." *Not until Lee threatened to produce the proof, in the form of tape recordings and a 1961 letter from State Secretary Dean Rusk, did McCloskey backtrack.* "Those who were consulted yesterday," he said sheepishly, "were not fully aware of the background of the incident, which occurred four and a half years ago."

In the 1965 Dominican Republic uprising, a whole series of conflicting stories were put out. At first Washington announced that U.S. forces had been sent to protect the lives of American citizens. Later, it was admitted that the purpose was to prevent a communist takeover. The government released a list of 58 Reds said to be active on the rebel side.

Reporters quickly found that the list not only included duplications, but contained the names of men then in prison or out of the country.

"If a government repeatedly resorts to lies in crises where lies seem to serve its interests best, it will one day be unable to employ the truth effectively when the truth would serve its interests best," warns J. Russell Wiggins, editcr of the Washington Post. "A government that too readily rationalizes its right to lie in a crisis will never lack for either lies or crises."

Government statements have also shed more smoke than light upon the Vietnam War. *At the same time that President Johnson has appealed to the people to support his Vietnam policies, his Administration has not been frank about what's going on.*

In August, 1964, for example, the White House denied a report that UN Secretary-General U Thant had forwarded a peace feeler from North Vietnam. A year later, the President himself told a press conference: "Candor compels me to tell you that there has not been the slightest indication that the other side is interested in negotiation." *The President's candor, it turned out, was less than complete.* Three months later, there was official acknowledgment that the United States had rejected three negotiation bids from North Vietnam, including one relayed by U Thant in August, 1964. Perhaps these offers were insincere, as the Administration contended after the facts were smoked out, *but if the President would lie about them once, how can he expect the world to believe him later?*

Indeed, *official obfuscation appears to be the policy in Vietnam.* A 1962 State Department cable, still classified, as are most embarrassing government documents, directed U.S. commanders in Vietnam not to take reporters on missions that might result in bad publicity. "Ambassador has over-all authority for handling of newsmen, in so far as U.S. is concerned," the cable read. "He will make decisions as to when newsmen permitted to go on any missions with U.S. personnel . . . Correspondents should not be taken on missions whose nature such that undesirable dispatches would be highly probable."

The cable also ordered suppression of the fact that Americans, in 1962, were already directing combat missions against the Viet Cong. "We recognize that American newsmen will concentrate on activities of Americans," the cable noted. "It not repeat not in our interest, however, to have stories indicating that Americans are leading and directing combat missions against Viet Cong . . . Sensational press stories about children or civilians who become unfortunate victims of military operations are clearly inimical to national interest." The confidential cable also warned sternly: "U.S. military and civilian personnel must see that [these instructions] are adhered to scrupulously and that Ambassador given complete cooperation if we to avoid harmful press repercussions on both domestic and international scene."

Though this cable has been superseded by others, containing noble language about the public's right to non-security information, *the original guidelines are still followed.* Long after the alleged policy change, for instance, Lt. Col. George Brown, an official briefing officer, gave an imaginative account of an ambush northwest of Saigon. Guerrillas had struck at the second half of a First Infantry Division truck column, he said. He told dramatically how the troops had dismounted to fight off the attack.

Survivors later complained about the way newspapers "get things fouled up." The trucks had been sent, they said, to pick up foot soldiers who had been attacked while they were milling around preparing to board. *"The report was totally misleading," said an officer, "even though it did make us look better than we deserved."*

Helicopters were destroyed at a base near Danang, accord-

THE AMERICAN UNIVERSITY • SPECIAL OPERATIONS RESEARCH OFFICE

A QUARTERLY JOURNAL of Revolution and Social Change

5010 WISCONSIN AVENUE, N. W. • WASHINGTON, D. C., 20016
AREA CODE 202-244-7300

26 February 1965

Public Affairs Press
419 New Jersey Avenue, S.E.
Washington, D.C.

Gentlemen:

On July 1st 1965 The American University's Special Operations Research Office (SORO) will begin publication of a quarterly journal designed to explore the many facets of a major preoccupation of U.S. political and military planners. This is the anticipation, prevention, or resolution of tensions within countries which adversely affect international peace or the national interests of the United States.

Entitled CONFLICT, this new journal will be an unclassified quarterly review of the "state-of-the-art" in what is now called counter-insurgency. It will reflect progress in the scientific study of revolutionary behavior as well as operational innovations to cope with such behavior.

CONFLICT will be produced by SORO's Counterinsurgency Information Analysis Center (CINFAC), a facility established under contract between The American University and the Department of Army to service the specialized needs of the Defense Department and other Federal agencies for societal information in today's politico-military world environment.

Contributors to CONFLICT will include government officials, scholars of national and international repute, and scientists from the staffs of SORO and similar agencies active in counterinsurgency research.

Initial distribution of CONFLICT will be limited to a selected list of government officials, scientists, scholars, and other civilian specialists. This is an audience whose professional needs CONFLICT is designed to fill.

One of the most important features of this magazine will be an extensive Book Review section. Arrangements have been made to have books reviewed by men of assured professional standing in the fields of Political Science, International Relations, Military Affairs, Economics, Contemporary History, and other related fields.

We would appreciate being put on the list to receive your catalogues from which we shall request such books as we may be required to review.

Sincerely,

James R. Price
Editor

JRP/bah

A letter announcing plans for the publication of "Conflict" by the Army's Counterinsurgency Information Analysis Center at American University. This quietly subsidized journal has been suppressed.

ing to another briefing officer, by mortar shells fired from afar. After newspapers had headlined this story, reporters discovered that the helicopters were blown up by demolition charges carried on to the base in satchels and planted on the helicopters under the noses of the Marine guards.

Casualty figures are subtly misrepresented to make American losses appear less than they really are. An entire company might be wiped out in an ambush, for example, but the casualties will be described as "light" on the theory that one company is only a small part of the full force in the battle zone. Information officers also put out a weekly "kill ratio" contrasting the Viet Cong and U.S.-Vietnamese casualties. *But the Vietnamese casualties from distant battlefields habitually come in too late to be included, thus the weekly report often gives a falsely favorable picture.* One weekly report, showing a ratio of 814 Viet Cong killed for every American or Vietnamese casualty, was widely promoted by spokesmen of the U.S. Information Agency to show that the war was going well. Yet the figures did not include the Vietnamese casualty count from one major battle, which would have lowered the favorable ratio considerably. When reporters brought this up, a spokesman scolded them for acting "like certified public accountants."

At least one spokesman added high drama to a casualty report by claiming, after an attack on a Special Forces camp at Pleime, that 90 enemy bodies had been counted, many of them draped grotesquely on the barbed wire around the camp. A reporter managed to reach the camp to photograph the grisly scene, but the besieged defenders denied ever seeing any bodies on the barbed wire. In fact, the 90 casualties were counted, not by soldiers at the scene but by desk officers back in Saigon.

Stories claiming that the individual GI is superior in combat to the VC, are also somewhat exaggerated. *Though quick to adapt, American troops simply aren't as experienced at jungle fighting as the Viet Cong.* At first, the Americans went into the jungle loaded down with heavy equipment. Many had to be carried back out after collapsing from heat exhaustion. Combat units still must be constantly rotated to give the troops frequent rest intervals. Meanwhile, they have abandoned their hot bullet-proof vests, heavy 106 mm. anti-tank weapons, and other cumbersome equipment. They are slowly learning from the Viet Cong that lightweight rifles and knives are the best weapons in the jungle.

The GIs also aren't as popular in South Vietnam as their public relations men would like to pretend. Though the GIs carry pocket instructions on how to get along with the Vietnamese, their free spending has stirred resentment. They have the money to take over the best restaurants, monopolize the taxicabs, and attract the prettiest girls. This fraternization has produced other problems that the public relations men don't talk about. Many of the girls are Viet Cong agents, who trade romance for information. They have introduced venereal disease into the ranks, despite medical precautions.

The raw facts about the Vietnam war go through a filtering and flavoring process, which can be ascribed partly to a natural desire to make American troops look as heroic as possible, partly to President Johnson's determination to portray the war as he wants the world to see it. To this end, he keeps careful control of the flood gates, releasing torrents of favorable information but holding back unfavorable information. *Thus, the Johnson Administration has achieved the remarkable feat of being, at the same time, the most open-mouthed and also the most close-mouthed in history.*

The President, a master of the subtle art of flattery and an expert in the use of the calculated leak, seeks to influence the news by influencing the men who write it. But when flattery fails, he is fully capable of brow-beating recalcitrant newsmen. He has brought all the pressures of the presidency to bear on them. More than once, he has ordered investigations of correspondents whose writings displeased him.

Increasingly, the government has turned the tables on reporters who have dug too deeply into its activities. The Defence Department has even called in the FBI to investigate such distinguished writers as columnist Joseph Alsop, the New York Times' Hanson Baldwin, Newsweek's Lloyd Norman, and the Washington Star's Richard Fryklund. *Once Fryklund was investigated for writing an article he didn't even publish.* He showed it to Arthur Sylvester, the Pentagon press chief, who set off the probe. Gumshoes tailing Fryklund reported he was distributing copies of his new book mainly to Air Force officers. When Defense Secretary Robert McNamara slyly mentioned this at a Joint Chiefs of Staff meeting, General Curtis LeMay, then Air Force chief, grumbled he was tired of having the Air Force accused of news leaks and suggested maybe McNamara's own office might have been responsible. Shot back the Secretary: "All right, you investigate my office."

I have had government bloodhounds sniffing my own trail many times. Once, a Pentagon security officer told me he had been asked to assign plainclothesmen to follow me every time I entered the Pentagon. He got out of it only by pleading it would tie up the entire security force posting them at all the Pentagon entrances to watch for me. Another time, a friend inside the FBI showed me an investigative file that the FBI had started on me. I copied down enough details to prove I had seen it, then called upon the FBI for an explanation. *J. Edgar Hoover confessed privately that the White House had ordered the investigation.*

Perhaps the most unusual retaliation was ordered by the late President Kennedy during his celebrated pique against the now defunct New York Herald-Tribune. His angry cancellation of White House subscriptions received wide publicity and inspired such slogans-around-town as: "Billions for defense but not ten cents for the Herald-Tribune." However,

88th Congress, 1st Session - - - - - House Report No. 354

THE MYSTERIOUS DISAPPEARANCE OF $7.5 MILLION OF U.S. SECURITIES FROM VAULT OF THE FEDERAL RESERVE BANK AT SAN FRANCISCO, CALIF.

REPORT BY

THE

COMMITTEE ON BANKING AND CURRENCY

HOUSE OF REPRESENTATIVES

88th Congress

TRANSMITTING

A REPORT OF A SPECIAL SUBCOMMITTEE

MAY 29, 1963.—Committed to the Committee of the Whole House on the State of the Union and ordered to be printed

---

U.S. GOVERNMENT PRINTING OFFICE

★ 85006 WASHINGTON : 1963

This intriguing document contains an incredible story of ineptitude that the Treasury Department tried to suppress.

there was an untold sequel to the incident. President Kennedy asked Carmine Bellino, a private investigator who handled secret White House assignments, to check on publisher John Hay Whitney's involvement in a stockpile contract and pass along the information to Senate investigators. But the chairman of the investigating committee, Senator Stuart Symington (D-Mo.), refused to call Whitney on the Congressional carpet.

From the White House down to the most obscure government agencies, newsmen have been pressured, pampered, and deceived. All too often, outright lies have been told to make bureaucrats look good. *Once a lie has been launched, there is a great reluctance inside the government to confess it.* Any challenge is passed down through the bureaucratic layers to the man who told the original lie. Since he isn't likely to admit he was wrong, an elaborate justification is usually bucked back up, endorsed by a series of superiors. More than once, an agency head has put the full weight of the U.S. government behind some foolish statement by a low-rung bureaucrat.

A Food and Drug report on "Nutritional Quackery," for example, made the flat statement: "Research has demonstrated that the nutritional values of our crops are not significantly affected by either the soil or the kind of fertilizer used." This was contradicted by the National Health Federation, which submitted some impressive scientific evidence to the contrary. *Yet not even Congress could get the Food and Drug Administration to retract.*

Congressional pressure forced the agency, however, to order a review. Dr. Homer Hopkins, who was asked to re-examine the question, reported back: "The statement that 'the nutritional values of our crops are not significantly affected by either the soil or kind of fertilizer used,' cannot be defended." Nevertheless Assistant Commissioner W. B. Rankin continued to insist in a letter to Congressman David King (D-Utah)

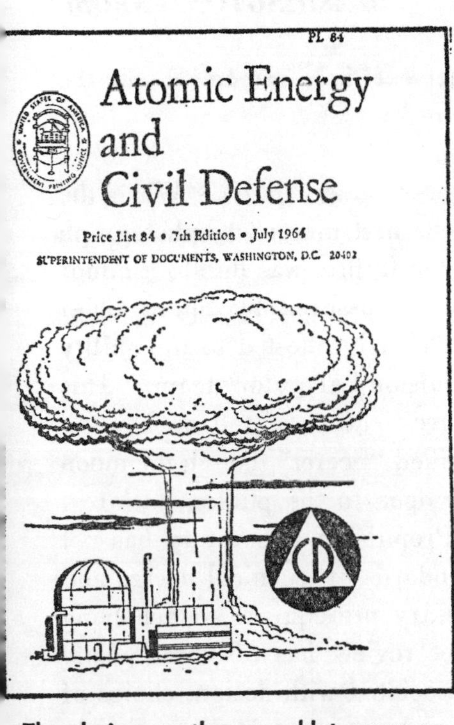

The design on the pamphlet cover reproduced at the top was changed to the one shown at the bottom after Representative Craig Hosmer cautioned the Pentagon against reminding people of the destructive power of atomic energy.

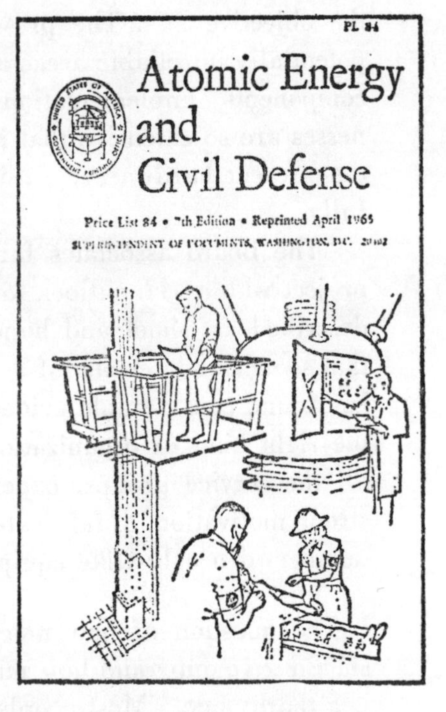

that the original erroneous statement "is in agreement with the views of our Dr. Homer Hopkins."

Secrecy is often used to cover up deception. When the Ranger-6 spacecraft failed in its first mission to photograph the moon, the public was told the failure was due to a minor malfunction. Even Congress was assured by Space Chief James Webb that the mission "clearly attested to the ability and competence of the Jet Propulsion Laboratory team." This was hardly what his secret investigation of the mishap divulged. The report, still classified "Secret" though the moon shot was supposed to be wide open to the public, declares:

"The Board finds that Jet Propulsion Laboratory has not applied to Ranger the high standards of technical design and fabrication which are a necessary prerequisite to achieving the objective . . . The present review has disclosed many potentially unreliable areas associated with design, choice of components, implementation and processes. These weaknesses are so extensive that in combination they suggest that the present hardware . . . is unlikely to perform successfully . . .

"The Board associates failure to perform on the Ranger project with a JPL outlook towards the project which may be described as 'shoot and hope,' i.e., shoot enough and hope that sooner or later one of a series will work . . . The Board has found considerable evidence that JPL does not now have the right kind of organizational management and structure, all the service groups, experience and techniques, nor the strong motivation, to fabricate, procure, and assemble a large number of nearly-alike equipments."

The question of how much truth government spokesmen should give out—and how much the people are entitled to—is a thorny one. Most people probably would agree that the government, for the protection of its citizens, need not always

January 18, 1964

Background Information
on the
President's Economic Message
for Use in Sunday Papers.

In his Economic Message tomorrow, President Johnson:

1. Would announce that in the last quarter of 1963

-- the U.S. economy hit a $600 billion rate of gross national product (GNP) for the whole quarter, capping a record $100 billion rise in less than 3 years;

-- the GNP was about $2 billion above earlier estimates, and enough to pull up the GNP for 1963 as a whole to $585 billion;

-- profits and labor earnings both hit new highs, well above the third quarter.

2. Would express the conviction

-- that new records are not enough;

-- that early action on the tax cut is vital

(a) to create enough jobs to end, at long last, the intolerable 5-1/2% unemployment and

(b) to get our factories operating well above their current unsatisfactory rate of 87% of capacity

3. Would view 1964 prospects, given the tax cut, with optimism:

a. With the tax cut, the Federal Government will give the economy a greater fiscal stimulus in 1964 than in any previous year in our peacetime history.

b. With the tax cut, the rate of expansion will exceed that of 1963 by a substantial margin.

4. Would specify his views on the price, wage, and monetary policies that can keep the economy on an even keel as it speeds up its pace of expansion in response to the tax cut.

5. Would present some of his further thinking on

-- the problem of poverty and how to strike at its roots;

-- America's economic challenges today.

Managing the news is expedited by material of this sort. Background information is usually given off the record.

tell every last detail about every situation. On the other hand, it should not lie or mislead lest it lose the trust of the very persons it is seeking to protect. *In a democracy, when the government cannot tell the whole truth, it should stand by its privilege to shut up.*

October 27, 1962

MEMORANDUM FOR DEPARTMENT OF DEFENSE PERSONNEL

SUBJECT: Procedures for Handling Media Representatives

Increasing responsibilities have been placed on the public information offices throughout the Department in the current world situation to avoid the disclosure of information affecting the national security. Accordingly, it becomes increasingly important to disclose all information which can be appropriately released to the public in an expeditious and equitable manner. To accomplish this objective, it is necessary that these offices be kept fully informed as to information made available to media representatives by both military and civilian officials of the Department. To this end, the following procedure will be adhered to:

> The substance of each interview and telephone conversation with a media representative will be reported to the appropriate public information office before the close of business that day. A report need not be made if a representative of the public information office is present at the interview.

This procedure applies to all Department of Defense personnel in the Washington area.

Arthur Sylvester

Arthur Sylvester
Assistant Secretary of Defense
(Public Affairs)

Still in effect, this directive discourages Pentagon personnel from giving newsmen information other than the official line.

3

THE GREAT PROTECTION RACKET

Freshman Congressman Joseph Resnick, eager, energetic, idealistic, received permission to address the House of Repsentatives for one minute. He had spoken precisely 26 seconds when Speaker John McCormack, glowering, lowered the gavel on him. The bewildered Resnick, a half uttered participle still stuck in his throat, was compelled to take his seat. He looked around beseechingly; colleagues turned away. "What did I do?" pleaded the Congressman from Ellenville, New York.

He soon learned that he had violated the First Commandment of Congress: "*Thou shalt not take the name of a colleague in vain.*" *Though the commandment is nowhere recorded, it is as binding as if it were etched on a tablet of stone.* The unhappy Resnick, taking the House floor to plead for a code of ethics, had made the mistake of illustrating his case. "I have been shocked," he declared, "to read a series of columns by Drew Pearson and Jack Anderson which have made serious charges against the alleged activities of Senator Thomas J. Dodd . . ."

That was as far as Resnick got. The mention of Dodd's name brought down the gavel with a resounding crash. Advised of his unpardonable sin, Resnick hastily deleted Dodd's name from his remarks and inserted the sanitized text in the Congressional Record. This explained cautiously that "a Member of the other body" had been accused of carrying out assignments for a registered foreign agent. "I found the stories related in these columns so hard to believe, as a matter of fact, that I telephoned Jack Anderson and demanded to see evidence of these charges," added Resnick. "Mr. Anderson invited me to his office to inspect his files. I sent a member of my staff, who spent over three hours going through Mr. Anderson's files. My assistant saw all the original material quoted in the columns, all of which he told me was unquestionably authentic. He also saw material which has not yet appeared in print, and which he assures me is even stronger and more sensational than what has already been printed in the newspapers."

Congress has focused the white light of truth on many a scandal. *For turning the spotlight inward and catching a Senator in its glare, however, Resnick suddenly found himself a pariah.* Colleagues, who formerly had been cordial, became cold; House leaders made their displeasure known; he was shut off from the camaraderie of the cloakroom. "I am not the most popular fellow in class," he confessed ruefully to his aides, "but I'm not sure I understand why."

Across the Capitol, on the Senate side, Tom Dodd was receiving sympathetic back-pats from his fellow Senators. "I'll stick by you," comforted Senator Russell Long (D-La.), "even if you are guilty." Senator Birch Bayh (D-Ind.) wrote Dodd a solicitous letter, calling the charges against him "a yellow attack," and pledging that "we're all behind you." Dodd stood accused of the gravest improprieties. He had delivered speeches, signed letters, entertained clients, and run errands for a registered foreign agent. He had diverted to his personal use huge sums that had been collected to pay his election expenses. He had accepted gifts of cash, free airplane rides, and the use of an automobile from businessmen for whom his Senate office had interceded. *Yet the powers on Capitol Hill were indignant, not over Dodd's misconduct but over Resnick's speech calling attention to it.*

The Select Committee on Standards and Conduct, which is supposed to oversee Senate ethics, held a meeting at the height of the Dodd revelations. Afterward, Chairman John Stennis (D-Miss.) solemnly announced that the committee had nothing to investigate because no one had filed any complaints. To rectify this, I shot off a letter to the committee. "I had assumed that the committee could act on its own initiative once improprieties had been made public," I wrote, speaking also for Drew Pearson. "If you require a formal complaint, please consider this as such." The letter spelled out Dodd's offenses, then offered: "We are prepared to turn over to the committee full documentation of all these charges and to suggest witnesses who, under oath, can give many more details."

Back came a two-line acknowledgment from Chairman Stennis: "Receipt of your letter of February 11, 1966, is acknowledged. The Select Committee on Standards and Conduct will communicate further with you if there is need for the information which you offer."

It is no light matter to investigate the transgressions of a Senator—particularly if he happens to be a member of The Establishment with friends in high places, more so if these friends happen to include the President of the United States and the legendary director of the FBI.

This was impressed upon Drew Pearson and myself soon after we began writing about Senator Dodd. Suddenly the story developed an O. Henry twist. *We the investigators found ourselves being investigated.* Out of J. Edgar Hoover's establishment swarmed a posse of FBI agents, pencils at the ready, seeking out our news sources. *A private eye, steeped in boudoir rumors, made more delicate inquiries. Our informants were subjected to relentless grilling and personal harassment; one after another lost his job.*

We had spent six months on the story, running down leads, interviewing witnesses, collecting documentation. We had developed evidence of apparent federal violations, which we had handed over to the FBI. Agents lugging equipment had spent hours in my home photographing copies of the Senator's private papers, which we had obtained from his former employees. When these people began to receive visits from the FBI, we innocently assumed the agents wanted to verify the charges against Senator Dodd. But astonishingly, they didn't ask a single witness a single question about the Senator. Instead they examined our informants about their part in securing the documents, thus giving the impression that the government intended to protect Dodd and prosecute his detractors. Less sure witnesses would have been scared into silence before the Senate could have heard their testimony.

It is not a federal crime, incidentally, to copy a Senator's "private" papers. This has been verified by no less than Dodd himself, who asked the Library of Congress to search the statutes for some violation he could charge against his ex-employees. Back came the reply: "*No violation of United States law seems to be involved.*" At worst, they might be accused of a petty misdemeanor; the Library's legal expert, Johnny H. Killian, found an applicable statute (Title 22-1211) in the District of Columbia Code. Because the ex-employees had returned the papers after copying them, however, he suggested to Dodd that it would be difficult to obtain a conviction. "It appears that the statute has been applied to instances," advised Killian, "where the intent to take permanently has been present."

In the past, the FBI has refused to investigate the most heinous crimes outside its jurisdiction. Even the assassination of the late President Kennedy was left to the Dallas police to prosecute. Yet when we documented our charges against Dodd out of his personal files, a dozen agents were assigned to find out who had given us the information.

This raises questions that may be more important than the Dodd scandals themselves. Should a high official, whose conduct is questioned, be permitted to use federal police to intimidate the witnesses against him? Should FBI *agents be allowed to investigate newsmen for no crime at all unless*

Testimonial for U. S. Senator Thomas J. Dodd — No. 158

April 6 1964 — 51-57/111

PAY TO THE ORDER OF Mr. Edward Lockett $

Two Thousand five hundred dollars and 00/100 DOLLARS

THE CONNECTICUT BANK AND TRUST COMPANY
HARTFORD, CONNECTICUT 18

E. J. Sullivan

⑆0111⑈0057⑆ 131079 8⑈

This $2500 check was paid to free-lance writer Edward Lockett for ghost-writing a book for Senator Dodd, who pocketed the advance royalty paid by a publisher. Note that the check was drawn on an account designated "Testimonial for U.S. Senator Thomas J. Dodd." Most speeches by Dodd are ghost-written.

THIS CHECK IS IN PAYMENT OF THE FOLLOWING ACCOUNT ENDORSEMENT BY PAYEE CONSTITUTES RECEIPT IN FULL
IF INCORRECT PLEASE RETURN

DATE	PARTICULARS	AMOUNT

S. P. A. D.
675 FOURTH AVENUE
BROOKLYN 32, N. Y.

No. 549

October 29 1965 — 1-12/210 20

PAY TO THE ORDER OF Senator Thomas J. Dodd $1,000.00

The sum of $1000 and 00 ct. DOLLARS

CHEMICAL BANK NEW YORK TRUST COMPANY
38TH STREET & BROADWAY
NEW YORK

AUTH. SIG.
AUTH. SIG.

⑆0210⑈0012⑆ 020⑈005695⑈

Senator Dodd received this check from the Maritime Union. Later he supported the union's opposition to shipping wheat to Soviet Russia in foreign vessels.

it has become a crime to accuse a Senator of improprieties? An answer has been given to at least one question. Whose idea was it to go after Dodd's accusers and make a federal case of a minor misdemeanor? The FBI said the order came from Nicholas Katzenbach, then Attorney General.

We had expected Senator Dodd to fight back. He is an extraordinary man, silver haired, with a classic profile recalling the toga-clad Roman Senators of old. The red leather chair in his office is built up to display his broad shoulders and heavy torso to best advantage. His office is dimly lit (the overhead lights have been removed and only the most feeble illumination is provided by table lamps) in order to hide the ravages of wear and worry on his distinguished face. He is a man of quick temper and passionate convictions that amount almost to phobias. With his family and his staff, he can switch from tolerance to tyranny in an instant. He can be a boon companion or a dreary bore, depending upon his mood.

A lawyer who failed his bar examination and was admitted to practice in Connecticut by special dispensation, he has a passion for gumshoes dating back to his own brief service with the FBI in 1933. He stayed with the FBI for less than a year, but these were his heroic days. By his own account, he took part in the famous shoot-out with the Dillinger gang at the Little Bohemia Roadhouse in Rhinelander, Wis. He had other heroic days when, as a Justice Department attorney, he acted as a prosecutor during the Nuremberg trials of the Nazi leaders. But the FBI is still his first love.

FBI agents have always had the run of Dodd's Senate office. If anyone said an unkind word about J. Edgar Hoover, the Senator was usually the first on his feet to defend his old chief. If a stubborn subversive refused to talk to the FBI, Senator Dodd could be relied upon to haul him before the Senate Internal Security Subcommittee and put him through the wringer. More than one citizen, whose loyalty was never in question, was sweated out by Dodd merely for criticizing the FBI.

In return for Dodd's devotion to the FBI, *the* FBI *has always been willing to do a little extra-curricular investigating on his behalf.* Once the Senator wanted to check on the after-hours movements of his administrative assistant, James Boyd. For two weeks agents trailed Boyd, then submitted a report typed on plain white paper. This was merely one of many unmarked reports that Dodd received from the FBI. Of course, there is nothing in the books that authorizes the FBI to engage in private snooping for members of Congress.

The Senator also used the Internal Security Subcommittee to handle his personal investigations. Late in the evening of September 28, 1962, he received a telephone call from his sister, Mary Dwyer, in Willimantic, Connecticut. She told him that a guest speaker at Windham High School had dared to criticize him in his own bailiwick. Angrily, Dodd buzzed his secretary, Mrs. Marjorie Carpenter, and told her to get the school's principal on the phone. With Mrs. Carpenter still on the line, the Senator gave Principal H. Chester Nelson a merciless tongue lashing for ten minutes. Then Dodd called in Internal Security staff aide, David Martin, and ordered him to run an investigation of the offending speaker. The lecturer turned out to be a Hungarian freedom fighter with anti-communist credentials as good as Dodd's.

Another time, when the Senator's son, Tom jr., brought home a "D" in a course at Georgetown University, the irate father sensed something unAmerican about the low mark and ordered the professor investigated. The finding was that Tom Jr. had not been doing his home work.

Perhaps a great FBI agent was lost when Dodd forsook Hoover's tough discipline and plunged into Connecticut politics. He won appointment as state director of the National Youth Administration and became friendly with a lanky, energetic fellow who headed the program in Texas—Lyndon B. Johnson.

A quarter of a century later, Dodd was to nominate Johnson for President at the 1960 Democratic convention. At the next convention, Johnson was to summon Dodd to the White House along with Hubert Humphrey to decide which of them would be his running mate in 1964. LBJ also considered Dodd as a possible successor to Robert Kennedy as Attorney General.

With Johnson in the White House and Hoover, apparently immortal, still firmly in command of the FBI, Dodd no doubt felt he was above the kind of investigation he had so often conducted on others. For a time it looked as if his confidence was not ill placed.

After our first columns questioning his conduct appeared, Senator Dodd made a great gesture. He called on the Senate and the FBI to investigate him, presumably confident of not one but two whitewashes. The next thing we knew, the FBI was hot on our trail. They not only tried to find out who had helped us with the Dodd story but with other stories. For instance, they tried to discover how I had obtained the unpublished manuscript written in his cell by Cosa Nostra informer Joe Valachi.

Informants in the Justice Department told us that our telephones were being tapped. The Attorney General invited us to his office and politely warned that we might be prosecuted. A cabinet officer even sent friendly word that indictments had been drawn against us in connection with the theft of the Dodd papers.

But our troubles were small compared to those of our informants who had supplied us with the documentation. I can identify here only the four who have already admitted under oath that they copied documents from the

JULIUS KLEIN
UNITED OF AMERICA BUILDING
CHICAGO 1, ILLINOIS

August 15, 1964

Senator Thomas J. Dodd
1407 - 31st Street, N. W.
Washington, D. C.

PERSONAL

Dear Tom:

I have your letter of August 13.

It appears that the Westrick letter was never sent. I regret this very much because the Chancellor went on vacation for the month of August.

When I returned from Europe early in July you were good enough to say that you would write such a letter. I remember you dictated a note to your secretary to remind you to write next morning. I took it for granted that you did -- because, in the meantime, some of your colleagues have already written to Dr. Westrick.

To save you time, I am enclosing herewith a rough draft. Maybe you want to paraphrase it and add a little bit about the President's stand on Viet Nam, especially since Westrick is a 100% believer in your strong policy. This also includes the Congo.

Both Westrick and Speaker McCormack have the same decoration from the Vatican. They are good friends. The Speaker too went out of his way with Westrick to give me a big boost.

"Please destroy this letter. I made NO copy," General Klein assured Senator Dodd. The remainder of the letter is on the next page.

You remember you met Westrick at Ambassador McGhee's party in Bonn and also again in Washington when he was there with Chancellor Erhard. If I am not mistaken Mrs. Dodd sat next to Westrick at the White House affair. Maybe you want to include her good wishes in your letter to Westrick.

Please get the letter out on Monday. You can say that you were so burdened with various foreign relations problems and are only now trying to catch up with your correspondence, before you adjourn to go to the Democratic Convention. This will explain your letter at this late time.

With kind regards and many thanks,

Sincerely yours,

Julius

Julius Klein:dh
encl.

Please destroy this letter - I made NO copy

Continuation of Klein's letter to Senator Dodd.

Senator's files and turned them over to me.

It was not an easy decision for these four people to make. They could not accept payment for their stories—even if we had been willing to offer it—without putting their motive in a bad light. Rather than any financial gain, they became subject to economic retaliation. They also knew that in American society the informer is more likely to be damned than praised, even if the information is in a good cause. Nor were they the sort of people who like to see their names in the newspapers. They were sophisticated without being cynical, well aware of the dirty pool that can be played on Capitol Hill when the career of a powerful political figure is at stake.

Their motive? They belong to a vanishing breed who put the public weal before their personal welfare.

It was Senator Dodd's misuse of campaign funds that finally turned James Boyd against the man he had served faithfully for 12 years. A cum laude graduate of Boston University, Boyd had stars in his sky blue eyes when he joined Dodd to fight against Connecticut's boss-controlled Democratic machine. He almost worshipped the Senator, despite some trying idiosyncrasies, because he felt Dodd was a man of caliber and courage. But when his idol proved to have feet of clay, Boyd threw everything aside to expose what he considered to be a betrayal of trust. He knew that he risked prosecution for copying evidence from Dodd's files. He knew that he faced unemployment, perhaps for a long period. He was giving up the prestige of being chief of staff to a United States Senator. But he accepted all these challenges.

Shapely, blonde Mrs. Marjorie Carpenter, a modest but quietly determined young woman, became disillusioned after only two years as the Senator's personal secretary. She had a closer view into Dodd's private affairs than other staff members. Probably more than the others, she detested the glare of the spotlight, but she would not be deterred from what she believed to be her duty.

Mike O'Hare, the Senator's bookkeeper and office manager, came to him as an apprentice office worker straight from Catholic University. O'Hare's intimate knowledge of the Senator's finances has made him a key witness, and Dodd has lashed out at him bitterly. But the Senator has yet to learn that when O'Hare finally made his soul-wracking decision to hand over the damaging documents, the young man had tears in his eyes. "I have been protecting these books with my life," he told me. "Now I am giving them to you to publish for the world to read." O'Hare did not leave the Senator's office until January, 1966, about the time the first Dodd columns were published.

Terry Golden, a pretty, red-haired secretary, worked in an outer office and was not as exposed to the Senator as the others. But she became aware of wrongdoing and decided her duty was not to the Senator who hired her but to the taxpayers who paid her salary.

Months earlier, Dodd got wind of our inquiries into his affairs and sent intermediaries to speak to us in his behalf. Yet curiously, he ignored phone calls from me requesting an interview, face to face. An intermediary explained that his staff must not have given him my messages, but the intermediary also failed to arrange an interview.

Meanwhile, a weird game of cops and robbers began in the Senator's office. Suggesting darkly that the Communists were out to get him, Dodd began cleaning out files and changing locks on doors. Once Mike O'Hare, who has a pixyish sense of humor and who was fed up with the antics, playfully hid some papers belonging to the Senator's anti-Communist specialist, David Martin, a furtive fellow who takes a conspiratorial view of the most mundane events. Martin flew into a frenzy when he found the papers missing. He was ready to call in the FBI and the Marines if need be.

Congressional Country Club, Inc.

8500 River Road
Washington, D. C. 20034

Hon. Thomas J. Dodd 3135
354 Senate Office Bldg.
Washington, D.C.

PLEASE DETACH AND RETURN THIS STUB WITH YOUR REMITTANCE

THIS BILL MUST BE PAID ON OR BEFORE THE 20TH OF THE MONTH

DATE	CHARGES	DATE	CREDITS	BALANCE
JUN 30 64 HC	8.93			8.93 *
JUL 5 64 HC	12.18			21.11 *
JUL 11 64 HC	2.08			23.19 *
JUL 25 64 HC	.46			23.65 *
JUL 1 64 AR	11.06			34.71 *

THIS BILL MUST BE PAID ON OR BEFORE THE 20TH OF THE MONTH

DATE	CHARGES	DATE	CREDITS	BALANCE
JAN 1 64 D	90.00			90.00 *
DEC 1 63 AR	25.48			115.48 *

THIS BILL MUST BE PAID ON OR BEFORE THE 20TH OF THE MONTH

DATE	CHARGES	DATE	CREDITS	BALANCE
		AUG 1 64 AR	34.71 ◇	
		AUG 5 64 CK	50.84	16.13 CR
AUG 16 64 HC	5.19			10.94 CR
AUG 23 64 HC	1.34			9.60 CR

These personal bills were among those paid with funds raised for Senator Dodd's political campaigning.

When O'Hare confessed the prank, Martin had to be restrained from hitting him.

The reaction to our first revelations about the strange doings of Senator Dodd was rather ho hum. There was buzzing in the Capitol cloakrooms, of course, but Dodd's colleagues carefully refrained from public comment. *Members of the exclusive senatorial club are most reluctant to touch a tarbrush.*

In the Connecticut press, our columns were almost totally blacked out. Only the courageous little Waterbury Republican published them, despite a barrage of letters from readers protesting that a fine man was being persecuted. The Hartford papers took no notice of the columns until Dodd began to issue denials. This required some explanation, of course, of what he was denying.

Then the process of intimidation began. The Senator, striking back as expected, went after his former employees with amazing vindictiveness. A word to Speaker John McCormack brought an abrupt cancellation of James Boyd's new job with the House Public Works Committee. Dodd also tried to get the Civil Rights Committee, associated with the American Bar Association, to fire Mrs. Marjorie Carpenter. Though the committee did not dismiss her, Mrs. Carpenter sensed that her new bosses were embarrassed and submitted her resignation. She found a job with the law firm of Arnold and Porter after scrupulously identifying herself and explaining her role in the Dodd affair. She kept the job precisely one week; a phone call from the Senator's office persuaded the law partners to change their minds about her employment.

Another phone call from Dodd convinced Judge David Bazelon that he should drop Terry Golden as his secretary. And Mike O'Hare, blackballed wherever he sought a job, became desperate.

At the same time, FBI agents were calling upon our informants and warning them that anything they said might be used in evidence against them. Some were questioned politely, others grilled relentlessly. Some of the questioning actually took place in Dodd's Senate office, thus giving witnesses the impression that the FBI was working for Dodd. One of the Senator's employees, Doris O'Donnell, seven months pregnant, was cross-examined for more than two hours in an anteroom just off the Senator's private office.

Typical of the FBI's terse and tough attitude was the way agent Phil King handled Mrs. Carpenter. "We can't have people breaking into a Senator's office and taking his files," he began sharply. Then he asked for her height, weight, and the color of her eyes and hair—as if taking these details down for a criminal description.

Clearly, the FBI was pulling out all the stops to help the embattled Dodd. Drew Pearson and I have been around Washington long enough to know that J. Edgar Hoover is reluctant to investigate either Senators or newspapermen. Anxious as he was to do Dodd a favor, it is most unlikely that he would investigate our news sources without pressure from the very top. Officially, the FBI notified us that the investigation had been ordered by Attorney General Katzenbach; theirs was not to reason why.

It is worth recording that Hoover has his own private phone link with the President. When Lyndon Johnson was in Congress, Hoover lived across the street from him. Now Hoover remains in office past the retirement age by special dispensation of LBJ. Obviously, the FBI would do nothing to displease the President nor act in delicate areas without his consent. *From sources inside the White House, we have learned that the President personally received the* FBI *reports on the Dodd case for his bedtime reading.* It is safe to assume he did what he could—within reason—to protect his old Senate comrade, Tom Dodd.

One day we received a polite invitation to meet with

Attorney General Katzenbach at the Justice Department. He was flanked by Fred Vinson Jr., chief of the criminal division, and Jack Rosenthal, the information director. Technically, the meeting was called to discuss a query from us as to whether the Justice Department had shown the same diligence in investigating a number of Senators and Congressmen who themselves had obtained copies of forbidden documents. They included Dodd himself, who had received unauthorized State Department papers from Otto Otepka.

Katzenbach looked stern but spoke softly. The FBI, he said, was merely trying to discover whether any documents had been stolen. "There is no corpus dilecti," I replied. "The documents in question are in the Senator's office right where he has always kept them." While we admitted having copies of the documents, we rejected any charge of theft and asked to be shown any federal law against copying a Senator's "private" papers. Indeed, we pointed out that the FBI had copied the same papers.

We suggested to Katzenbach that Senator Dodd, in loudly protesting his papers had been "stolen," was obviously laying groundwork for a later claim that the evidence against him was "tainted." We charged that the Justice Department was playing into his hands. Katzenbach assured us that the evidence secured against Senator Dodd could be used in court. He also did not question our right to quote the documents in print. No action was contemplated, he insisted gently, against Drew Pearson or myself. The only people being investigated were the Senator's former employees.

"In other words," I said, "if we will throw these people to the wolves, you will leave us alone. Let me make this clear, if you are going to indict them, you will have to indict us along with them."

"I don't enjoy indicting anybody," said the Attorney General.

"I don't think I would enjoy being indicted," I said, "but this is one indictment I would be willing to fight. I would like to find out whether a jury of American citizens would recognize the right of newspapermen to document charges of corruption against a United States Senator."

The conversation was long, inconclusive, and sometimes unpleasant. It ended with the impression that everybody, except Senator Dodd, was still under investigation.

The FBI's efforts were supplemented by those of a private eye, James J. Lynch, of Wantagh, Long Island, a big bluff former FBI agent who had done work for Lewis Rosenstiel, head of Schenley Liquors. Interesting facts: (1) Dodd has been Rosenstiel's attorney; (2) Lou Nichols, a former FBI official, is now a Schenley vice president; (3) Dodd and an FBI official flew in a Schenley plane to a speaking engagement which the FBI man had asked Dodd to make.

While the FBI had the run of Senator Dodd's front office, private eye Lynch was working the back doors. He was looking for dirt that might discredit Drew or myself, but more particularly our witnesses. He called upon Marjorie Carpenter's former husband and asked frankly for unfavorable information against her. Lynch secured an affidavit from Mrs. Rose Marie Lambkin by threatening: "If you don't talk here we can have our conversation in the jailhouse." He gave Judith Burling, another former Dodd employee, the impression that he was a federal agent. When she challenged him, he admitted he was a former FBI man. Then he hinted ominously that unless she cooperated her father might lose his job.

When Lynch failed to persuade Boyd's former wife to say anything against him, a subtler pressure was brought to bear. The former Mrs. Boyd received a telephone call from Mrs. Dodd's sister, Helen Farley, who had been friendly with the Boyds.

"Everybody is going to be hurt by this," confided Helen

Farley. "Can't we do anything to stop it?" She then asked the former Mrs. Boyd for an appointment to talk things over. During this conversation, the Senator himself could be heard in the background prompting: "Any time at her convenience." Mrs. Boyd politely declined. Later she received a letter from Mrs. Farley's daughter-in-law, Betty Farley, pressing her to get in touch "if she ever felt she needed someone to talk to."

The Senator himself spread smear stories suggesting that his former employees were immoral and would certainly go to prison. One of Dodd's attorneys, Walter J. Kenny, telephoned Mike O'Hare. "We just want you to know," he said, "we have a complete check on Terry Golden. It would be a shame for a lovely girl like her to have her reputation hurt in any way. Maybe after you hear the kind of questions we throw at Jim Boyd, you will get the flavor of it."

Kenny also pressed another former Dodd employee, Glen Cooper, for derogatory information against the witnesses. When Cooper refused to cooperate, Kenny murmured darkly: "*These four are finished. Do you want to be finished, too?*"

After the Senate Ethics Committee's hearings opened, Dodd's son Jeremy, a combative young man, did a little pressuring in the Dodd tradition. He poked a finger in Mike O'Hare's chest and threatened: "I just want to tell you one thing. When this is over I am going to follow you to your . . . grave!" This incident hit the headlines and drew an apology from the Senator. But there were no apologies for the dirty work going on behind the scenes.

The Senator's defense was undertaken by the world's largest law firm—Cahill, Gordon, Reindel and Ohl. Dodd's colleagues began to raise their eyebrows at the appearance of such big guns. A task force of seven lawyers descended on Washington, ensconced themselves in the Sheraton-Carlton Hotel, and began a thorough review of all the evidence in the case. At the Senate hearings, Dodd's attorneys outnumbered the committee members. Their desk was piled high with documents and transcripts which they scoured for information to be slipped to chief attorney John F. Sonnett.

So insulting was Sonnett's questioning that Senator Stephen Young (D., Ohio), complained on the Senate floor about "the sinister type of interrogation conducted by Mr. Sonnett. He has attempted to attack the reputations of young women witnesses by innuendo, even indulging in improper inquiry as to whether they intend to marry certain persons. Mr. Sonnett should know this is improper and irrelevant to the issue and is a course of conduct unbecoming a gentleman or a good trial lawyer."

Our own lawyers estimated that Dodd's array of legal beagles must be costing at least $3,000 a day. The obvious question, since Dodd claimed to be poor: who was footing the bill? The Senator declared on television that the firm was donating its services, a most thoughtful and generous gesture.

It may be only a coincidence that the firm of Cahill, Gordon, Reindel, and Ohl happens to represent Radio Corporation of America. It may be a coincidence, too, that the senior partner, John Thomas Cahill, a director both of RCA and its subsidiary NBC, personally represented NBC before Dodd's Juvenile Delinquency Subcommittee during the early 1960's. Senator Dodd spared NBC great embarrassment during his investigation of violence on television. He suppressed evidence against NBC which could have been damaging.

I asked Sonnett whether RCA was, in fact, paying for Dodd's defense. "You're a fresh kid," he snapped. I wrote down his answer and asked him if that was the way he wanted it recorded. He grunted in the manner of a great man annoyed by someone beneath his attention. Then I asked if he was speaking for himself or for his firm. "I am a senior partner in the firm," he said. A few hours later, RCA's chairman, General David Sarnoff, telephoned Drew

Pearson and denied that his firm was paying Dodd's legal expenses.

Like the FBI, the Senate Ethics Committee at first seemed to be more interested in protecting than probing Dodd. The real object of their investigation, committee members leaked to the Chicago Tribune, was to find out who had "stolen" the damning documents from his offices. Only the deepening public outrage persuaded the Committee, and eventually the FBI, to concentrate on Dodd rather than his detractors.

Dodd's standing as a Senator must be decided, in the end, by his peers in the Senate. The Justice Department may have something to say about his alleged law violations. It is natural that a man should fight for his freedom, for his name and for his career. But how a man fights is also a measure of the man and his worthiness to remain a United States Senator.

The Dodd-go-round wasn't the first time I had been caught in the Capitol's revolving door. In a Parade article, published in 1963, I wrote about "Congressmen Who Cheat," who sell influence, misuse funds, and pad payrolls. The revelations kicked up a flurry on the House floor; a dozen Members angrily leaped to their feet to deny it all. No one was more indignant than Congressman Omar Burleson (D-Tex.) whose Administration Committee is responsible for policing the House. "We invite Mr. Anderson or anyone else who can support these charges," he challenged, "to come before us in public hearing and reveal all or any part of the allegations in the article. My committee is willing and ready on short notice to convene itself for a public hearing on these matters."

"Is it proper to inquire of the chairman," demanded Congressman William Avery (R-Kans.), "what is his view if the author of this article declines this invitation?" Burleson replied in ringing tones: "I would conclude either that there was no fact or else that he did not respond to the call to exhibit good citizenship." Not wishing to have my good citizenship questioned, I hastily offered to testify.

I showed up at the appointed hour with a 14-page statement which I never got a chance to read. Burleson announced that the committee was interested only in the identity of my source, something he knew no newsman would divulge. *I assured him my statement contained all the names and details he would need to document several cases of Congressional misconduct.* But the pressed and pomaded Burleson, who had raised such a cry for my testimony, now refused to listen to it. Beating out a staccato with his gavel, he dismissed the meeting and stalked grandly out of the room, leaving the witness with no hearing.

Perhaps Burleson feared his own name might be included in the statement; for he once had collected expense money from his committee for "official business" while he celebrated Thanksgiving and Christmas at his Texas home. There was one name in my statement that later made headlines: Bobby Baker. But the irrepressible Bobby was not the leading figure in the story I had intended to tell the committee.

My testimony would have dealt with Congressman John McMillan (D-S.C.), who stood at the center of a little clique of bright young men from South Carolina who liked to make a fast buck. This tight little circle included Bobby Baker of Pickens, Ralph Hill of Greensea, and Don Reynolds of Lamar.

I had been prepared to testify: (1) that the Congressman had loaned Hill $3,000 to start the Capitol Vending Company and used his political influence to arrange locations in government buildings for Hill's cigarette, candy, and coffee machines; (2) that the Congressman had sent insurance business to Don Reynolds who, in turn, had arranged the bank mortgage on McMillan's home in Arlington, Virginia, and had obtained a Ford convertible for him as far back as 1950; and (3) that Reynolds, during a brief hitch in the foreign service, had sneaked a mistress out of Germany and had sent her to the Congressman's home. A confidential State Department report on the matter charges that Reynolds "made unauthorized use of his Berlin consulate's standing to obtain an exit visa for his mistress. His action was discovered and an effort made to stop the visa, but Congressional pressure on the State Department was great. The girl's destination was Congressman McMillan's home in South Carolina."

But the most significant incident, that I had intended to call to the committee's attention, would have thrown light on the award of a $21 million contract to build Washington's new sports coliseum. Philadelphia construction tycoon Matt McCloskey, one of the Democratic Party's celebrated sugar daddies, came to see Bobby Baker about the contract in 1960. Baker obligingly arranged a private meeting with Congressman McMillan who, as chairman of the House District Committee, not only was responsible for authorizing the construction but had a powerful influence on the contracting authorities. Also present: Don Reynolds.

In return for giving his political blessing to the McCloskey contract, McMillan made clear he wanted Don Reynolds to get the insurance on the stadium. It turned out exactly as the South Carolinians had schemed. McCloskey won the contract, and Reynolds wrote the performance bond. The grateful Reynolds gave Baker $4,000 and bought a $5,100 Cadillac for McMillan. *Not until the Washington Post began snooping into the Cadillac purchase did McMillan hastily send Reynolds two belated checks repaying the $5100.*

Later, there was a falling out among the bright young men from South Carolina. Hill filed a lawsuit and Reynolds turned informer against Baker. Their revenge blew the lid off the Bobby Baker scandals, causing political repercussions that echoed all the way to the White House. It was typical of the Senate investigation of Baker, however, that Congressman McMillan was never mentioned. Though he was the key figure in the little South Carolina cabal, the investigating Senators courteously kept his name out of it. They investigated everyone connected with the stadium deal, for example, except the Congressman with the Cadillac.

Republican Senators did a lot of shouting about suppressing evidence in the Baker investigation. Yet they conspired with the Democrats to suppress evidence that might have embarrassed their fellow Senators. There were angry political recriminations over the conduct of the investigation. But when it came to shielding Senators, a remarkable bipartisan spirit prevailed. The Senate Rules Committee investigated Bobby Baker with one eye shut, unwilling to look at the Senators who had set the example for him since he came to the Senate as a 14-year-old page boy.

Baker was virtually raised by the U.S. Senate. Its members were his closest friends, his constant associates, his counselors and confessors. He played politics with Senators, borrowed money from them, participated in business ventures with them. When he built his famous Carousel Motel, so many Senators showed up for the opening that the Senate could have called a quorum in Ocean City. The committee sent investigators into 32 states and two foreign countries chasing down information on Baker. They interviewed over 200 witnesses and took sworn testimony from 60. His most casual acquaintances were cross-examined. *But not a single Senator was asked a single question.*

The committee suddenly lost interest in Baker's dealings with Spiegel, Inc., the Chicago mail order house, for example, after discovering he had taken a group of Democratic Senators to talk to Modle Spiegel, the board chairman, about campaign contributions. To fly the Senators to Chicago, Baker wangled a free plane from Fairchild Aviation. The committee also looked into Baker's relationship with Freight Forwarders, but discreetly omitted the fact that the company had picked up Senator Everett Dirksen's bills at the Carousel

Motel and that Maurice Forgash, the company president, had entertained Senate Commerce Chairman Warren Magnuson (D-Wash.) aboard his yacht.

No one was louder in his accusations against Baker than was Senator Hugh Scott (R-Pa.). He castigated Baker for feathering his nest while he was supposed to be working full time as a Senate employee, condemned Baker for using political influence as if this were something the Senator would never think of doing, raised questions about Baker's political fund-raising activities. The same Hugh Scott was a full-time Senator before he joined the Philadelphia law firm of Obermayer, Rebmann, Maxwell, and Hippel. Among the firm's clients are a number of banks; it may be merely a coincidence that Scott has lodged repeated inquiries with the Comptroller of the Currency about banking matters. As for political contributions, Scott still hasn't divulged the list of those who paid $100-a-plate to attend a fund-raising dinner for him at the Army-Navy Club on September 17, 1963. At least one full table, I have learned, was purchased by Jimmy Hoffa's Teamsters Union.

Senator Carl Curtis (R-Neb.) also cross-examined Baker sternly about using his government phone to transact private business. He demanded whether Baker had ever sent his secretary, the late Carole Tyler, on private errands while she was on the government payroll. The public could have been more impressed if Curtis had produced a list of his own Senate phone calls. His secretary, Mildred Kenny, also goes to Miden, Nebraska, at the taxpayers' expense to work in his old law office.

Many bills have been introduced to correct Congressional abuses; some have been passed overwhelmingly by both the Senate and House. But with rare efficiency, they have managed never to act in tandem. The House may cast a rousing vote for some improvement which, unfailingly, will get hung up in the Senate—an unspoken arrangement by which one

SILVER SPRING, MD. OCTOBER 18 1957 No. 785

SUBURBAN TRUST COMPANY

WOODMOOR OFFICE
SILVER SPRING, MD.

65-201

KTBC RADIO AND TELEVISION STATION AND
THE MID-ATLANTIC STAINLESS STEEL CO. INC.

CERTIFIED
$1000.00

ONE THOUSAND AND NO/100 DOLLARS

DON REYNOLDS ASSOCIATES, INC.

PRESIDENT.

This $1000 check signed by Don B. Reynolds paid for advertising on the television station owned by the Lyndon Johnson family. Reynolds testified during the Bobby Baker investigation that the advertising was a kickback on an insurance policy he sold to LBJ.

DUPLICATE INVOICE

The Magnavox Company

Fort Wayne, Indiana

U. S. A.

BILL TO: DON REYNOLDS, 8484 FENTON ST, SILVER SPRINGS MD

SHIP TO: SEN LYNDON JOHNSON, 4921 30TH PLACE N W, WASHINGTON D C

INVOICE NUMBER: 55496 PAGE: 1

6-26-59

TERMS: NET

LINE ITEM	REL. LOC	QUANTITY	NUMBER	NAME		PACK. LIST	UNIT	EXTENSION
1		1			6/25		382.50	382
		1						382.

Seller represents that with respect to the production of the articles and/or the performance of the services covered by this invoice, it has fully complied with Section of the Fair Labor Standards Act of 1938, as amended.
The seller warrants that the prices charged herein are not in excess of the maximum ceiling prices established under applicable regulations issued pursuant to the Defense Production Act of 1950, or any other applicable law, order or regulation.

An invoice indicating that goods purchased by Don B. Reynolds were shipped to Senator Lyndon Johnson at his home address.

house pigeonholes the other's unwanted reforms. When the legislative slate is wiped clean again in the next session, it will be the Senate's turn to pass reforms and the House's turn to ignore them. *Thus, both Senators and Representatives can vote for reforms with full assurance none will be enacted.*

But, if reforms get nowhere, Members of Congress are more diligent about boosting their own benefits. In 1965 they voted themselves a pay increase that pushed their salary from $22,500 up to $30,000. Of this, they set aside $3,000 as tax exempt, thus widening their own tax loophole while the Treasury Department was begging them to close loopholes. They also voted themselves a yearly stationery allowance of $2,400 each, another $2,400 for field office rental, and an indeterminate amount for "clerk hire." *A Congressman who knows how to squeeze the green ink out of a dollar bill can double his salary from these three funds.*

Some Members scrounge letterheads from Congressional committees so they can pocket their stationery allowance. When Senator Thomas Dodd's daughter, Martha, was married, he not only charged his official stationery account for the gold, embossed wedding invitations but ordered an expensive desk set as a birthday gift from Martha to her new husband. Even millionaire Senator Hiram Fong (R-Hawaii) paid his office rent to his own company, Finance Factors Building, Ltd.

A few unscrupulous Congressmen have bought liquor, clothes, refrigerators, television sets, and automobiles by putting the salesmen on the Congressional payroll until the purchases were paid off. Representative William Cramer (R-Fla.) used to send his printing to Art Press, a commercial firm. He paid his bills by putting the owner's wife, Caroline Baron, on the public payroll. Later, he also arranged for the owner, Carl Baron, to draw a government salary. Carl's brother, Paul, was placed on the public payroll by another Congressman who wanted to economize on his printing bills, E. Y. Berry (R-S.D.).

ITED STATES SENATE STATIONERY ROOM

Date 8-12, 1963

unt Dodd

Delivered to [illegible]

105

350	Wedding Invitation + Plate #983	78	75
350	Reception Cards + Plate #984	38	30
350	Outside Envl. stamped + Plate #985	3	50
		120	55

Att M. Carpenter

DUPLICATE

No. 7207

[illegible], Clerk.

16—8803-1 U. S. GOVERNMENT PRINTING OFFICE

As this receipt shows, Senator Dodd obtained wedding invitations and reception cards from the Senate Stationery Room. His daughter needed the cards; the taxpayers were stuck with the bill.

The legislators have also provided for themselves fringe benefits undreamed of by the most imaginative union leaders. Congressmen who voted against medical benefits for the elderly, for example, call regularly at the Capitol dispensary for free flu shots, vitamins, and tranquilizers. They can also have a tooth filled or an appendix removed for cut rates at any military hospital of their choice. *The taxpayers pick up the tab for Senators' parking, haircuts, steambaths, massages, snuff and Mountain Valley Water.* Members of the House, being less privileged, must pay 75 cents for a haircut. But both can stock up on maps, pamphlets, and other official literature issued at public expense.

For a bargain $10.83 a month, Members of Congress can buy $20,000 worth of life insurance without going through the formality of a medical examination. They can also qualify for pensions after serving only five years as legislators. Senators are permitted six, Congressmen four round trips a year to their home states at the taxpayers' expense. *But for those who like to commute, some big corporation usually provides private plane transportation.* Ling-Temco-Vought often flies Texas Congressmen home for the week-end in its $300,000 Lear Star. United Aircraft operates a 2-passenger Convair, eight-passenger Jet Star, and four-passenger King Air between Washington, D.C., and Hartford, Conn.; New England Congressmen frequently hitch free rides. Tennessee Gas Transmission, Armco Steel, Sears Roebuck, and a host of other companies also fly Congressmen around.

The Ford Motor Company sternly refuses to haul Congressmen in company planes, but it sometimes helps solve their transportation problems on the ground. For a token $750 a year, the chairman of any Congressional committee can drive a gleaming, new Lincoln Continental. Even a lesser Senator, whose vote on auto matters also counts, can keep a Chrysler Imperial LeBaron in his garage for the same $750 annual rental. One who snapped up this bargain, Senator

June 7, 1965

MEMORANDUM TO: Senator Dodd

FROM: Gerry Zeiller

Before calling Dave Dunbar, I talked with Tom Scott of the Appropriations Committee regarding the new building for the Government Printing Office. He told me that the House Committee had denied funds for the project for this year, and that he expected a great deal of debate on the project both in the Senate Appropriations Committee and on the Floor when the legislation appropriation is taken up.

While it is still possible for the money to be approved in fiscal year 1966, there is also a good chance that it won't be. At the present time there is 2½ million dollars which was appropriated in FY 65 for plans and specifications for the building, but this does not have anything to do with the moving of its equipment.

I told Mr. Dunbar this, and I also told him that I would discuss the matter with you and you would then decide whether or not there would be any need for you talking to the Public Printer, James Harrison.

This memorandum shows how Senator Dodd's office tried to help David Dunbar, a Connecticut businessman, get a government contract. At about the same time, Dunbar turned over a brand new Oldsmobile to Dodd. It is against the law for a member of Congress to accept payment or gratuities for helping a constituent in Washington.

Vance Hartke (D., Ind.), must have been a disappointment to Detroit. He led the Senate fight to impose safety regulations on the auto industry, no doubt planning strategy as he drove to Capitol Hill in his low-rental Imperial LeBaron. Senator Dodd saves even the $750; he was put behind the wheel of a Jet 88 Oldsmobile by a thoughtful Connecticut contractor. The car carries the Connecticut license tag, "U.S. SEN. 1," but the registration is made out to Dunbar Associates, Inc., of Newington, Connecticut.

How long can Congress go on pretending that abuses of the public trust are found only in the Executive Branch? The public is beginning to see through the sanctified curtain members of Congress have drawn around themselves. But the public is still waiting for Congressmen to submit to the same code of ethics that they impose upon others.

4

SENIORITY, SENILITY, AND SUCCESS

L. Mendel Rivers, the white-maned, bourbon-imbibing chairman of the House Armed Services Committee, is held in such high esteem in his native South Carolina that he has already been cast in heroic bronze to take his place alongside Robert E. Lee, Pierre Beauregard, and other Southern heroes who have been immortalized in granite and metal. The latter were obliged to wait until they were dead and gone to have monuments erected in their honor. But grateful businessmen, who have benefited from the military bases Rivers has brought to South Carolina, have rushed history for him.

A noble, life-size bronze bust of Rivers now gazes majestically down from a seven-foot, solid granite shaft upon Rivers Avenue in North Charleston. The road, known elsewhere as Route 52, had previously been named in his honor. The Rivers monument was unveiled on a gloomy October afternoon in 1965. As the Citadel band struck up a martial air, a sudden downpour drenched the glittering assemblage of Admirals, Generals, and top civilians. Daintily, Mrs. Rivers cut the ribbon, and the Congressman touched a finger to his eye.

The main eulogy was delivered by Congressman F. Edward Hébert (D-La.), who noted that never before had he seen so many top defense officials gathered in one place. *He never mentioned that they had come at the taxpayers' expense in three separate planes. Nor did he say that an equally impressive group had turned up a year earlier in the tiny South Carolina town of St. Stephen to help celebrate "L. Mendel Rivers Day."*

Thus, twice had the Joint Chiefs of Staff, the secretaries of the three services, and assorted other brass hats taken time out from the Vietnam war to pay homage to the House drunk. *For Rivers is best known in Washington circles for his alcoholic escapades.* There was the time in London, for example, that he was caught chasing through a hotel corridor in his BVD's. More than once the Navy has discreetly loaded him into an ambulance and whisked him off to the Bethesda Naval Hospital to dry out. Five times during May and June, 1966, the Armed Services Committee was obliged to postpone action on a $17.8 billion military authorization bill while the genteel chairman was taking the cure.

On more sober occasions, Rivers has championed military pay raises, a widening of the Vietnam war, and the John Birch Society. He extolled the society on the House floor as "a nationwide organization of patriotic Americans" and praised "its courageous and perceptive founder, Robert Welch"—who, parenthetically, has often expressed his contempt for democracy.

Rivers has also involved himself in curious causes, such as his strange intervention in behalf of the Power Equipment Corporation over a ship repair contract. He applied both pressure and praise in an attempt to influence Vice Admiral John Will, then commander of the Military Sea Transport Service, to pay the firm an extra $177,150.61. *First, Rivers praised the Admiral on the House floor, then telephoned him to demand that the claim be paid.*

Yet, despite his curious conduct, the Congressman's influence is such that the top brass would drop everything to stand through a downpour while his bronze likeness was unveiled. Indeed, one of the nation's largest defense contractors, Lockheed Aircraft, offered to make up the balance if North Charleston's businessmen failed to raise enough money for the celebrated Rivers monument. It turned out that they collected all but $200, which Lockheed cheerfully coughed up. At Rivers' beck, the Air Force also will furnish him with

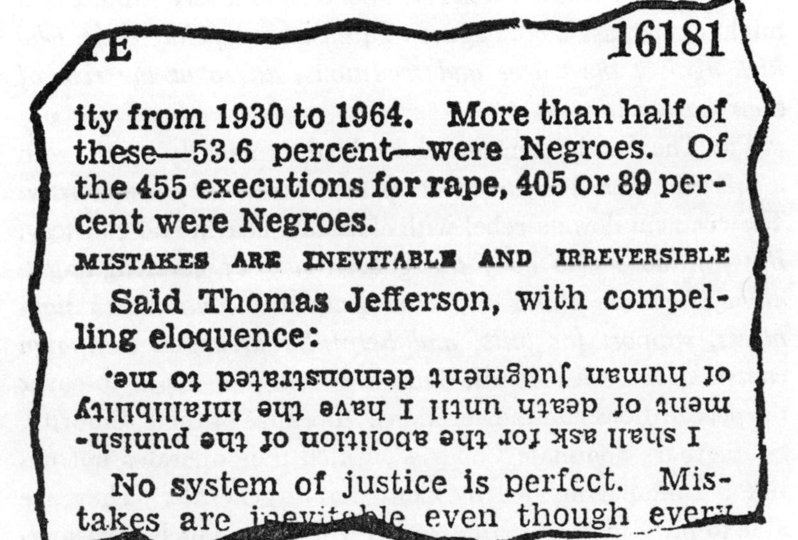

E 16181

ity from 1930 to 1964. More than half of these—53.6 percent—were Negroes. Of the 455 executions for rape, 405 or 89 percent were Negroes.

MISTAKES ARE INEVITABLE AND IRREVERSIBLE

Said Thomas Jefferson, with compelling eloquence:

I shall ask for the abolition of the punishment of death until I have the infallibility of human judgment demonstrated to me.

No system of justice is perfect. Mistakes are inevitable even though every

Oops! Here is how the Congressional Record for July 25, 1966, inadvertently printed remarks by Senator Philip Hart about the inevitability of mistakes.

an airplane any time he wants to fly home for the week-end.

Mendel Rivers owes his remarkable stature (1) to the seniority system and (2) *to the protection racket on Capitol Hill.* For members of Congress are under the discipline of The Establishment, sort of a gentlemen's Cosa Nostra, which enforces its own code of omerta: silence about any subject that might embarrass a colleague. *Those who defy the code, who kick against the traces and traditions, do so at the risk of their careers.*

For The Establishment, whose leaders usually speak with a soft Southern drawl, can be as ruthless as they are courtly. They can cut down a rebel with elaborate charm and courtesy. *But for those who obey the golden rule of go-along-to-get-along, there are plums of patronage, choice committee assignments, support for bills, and helpfully arranged campaign contributions.* Above all, there is a sheltering cloak to cover the peccadilloes and indiscretions. Because of their seniority, Southerners dominate Congress, which thus operates not unlike a Union Army led by Confederate generals. They are able to bury bills and stifle action without so much as a hearing. Often one man, such as the House Rules Chairman, can thwart the will of the majority.

Certainly no member of the Senate is more beloved than kindly, 87-year-old Carl Hayden, who has represented Arizona in Congress ever since it became a state. Yet he illustrates how the Senate seniority system often places the biggest burdens on the frailest shoulders. As the Senate's President pro tempore and Appropriations chairman, he is the most powerful of Senators. But because of age, his immense power falls largely upon assistants and advisers who have never run for office and who could take advantage of the old man if they wished.

Other times, Hayden simply goes along with Senators who are old friends or who butter him up. Once he claimed his

Ready Reference Guide To Senate Press Aides

STATE	SENATOR	PRESS CONTACT
ALA.	Lister Hill (D.)	Don Cronin
	John J. Sparkman (D.)	Grover C. Smith
ALASKA	E. L. Bartlett (D.)	Miss Mary Lee Council
	Ernest Gruening (D.)	George Sundborg
ARIZ.	Carl Hayden (D.)	Spencer Oliver
	Barry Goldwater (R.)	Tony Smith
ARK.	John L. McClellan (D.)	Ralph Matthews
	J. William Fulbright (D.)	Pat Fleming
CALIF.	Thomas H. Kuchel (R.)	Warren Francis
	Clair Engle (D.)	Fred Asselin
COLO.	Gordon L. Allott (R.)	Jack Ware
	Peter H. Dominick (R.)	Frank Lee
CONN.	Thomas J. Dodd (D.)	James P. Boyd
	Abraham A. Ribicoff (D.)	Mrs. Natalie Spingarn
DEL.	John J. Williams (R.)	Miss Eleanor R. Lenhart
	J. Caleb Boggs (R.)	James A. Flood
FLA.	Spessard L. Holland (D.)	Oscar Elder
	George A. Smathers (D.)	Miss Natalie Martin
GA.	Richard B. Russell (D.)	Earl Leonard
	Herman E. Talmadge (D.)	Gordon Roberts
HAWAII	Hiram L. Fong (R.)	Miss Leila Villada
	Daniel K. Inouye (D.)	Jack Teehan
IDAHO	Frank Church (D.)	Porter Ward
	Len B. Jordan (R.)	Mrs. Jody Baldwin
ILL.	Paul H. Douglas (D.)	Howard E. Shuman
	Everett M. Dirksen (R.)	John Gomien
IND.	Vance Hartke (D.)	John Munger
	Birch Bayh (D.)	Paul Danaceau
IA.	Bourke B. Hickenlooper (R.)	Don O'Brien
	Jack Miller (R.)	Andrew Montgomery
KANS.	Frank Carlson (R.)	Miss Betty Rosness
	James B. Pearson (R.)	Joe McConkey
KY.	John S. Cooper (R.)	Geoffrey Drummond
	Thruston B. Morton (R.)	Stephen Lord
LA.	Allen J. Ellender (D.)	C. B. Morrison
	Russell B. Long (D.)	William E. Leonard
ME.	Margaret C. Smith (R.)	Bill Lewis
	Edmund S. Muskie (D.)	Chapman Stockford
MD.	J. Glenn Beall (R.)	Ben Whitehurst
	Daniel B. Brewster (D.)	William Townsend
MASS.	Leverett Saltonstall (R.)	Charles Clapp
	Edward M. Kennedy (D.)	Jeremiah Marsh
MICH.	Pat McNamara (D.)	Edwin N. Winge
	Philip A. Hart (D.)	Jerry Kabel
MINN.	Hubert H. Humphrey (D.)	Winthrop G. Griffith
	Eugene J. McCarthy (D.)	Jerry Eller
MISS.	James O. Eastland (D.)	Courtney Pace
	John Stennis (D.)	Phil Stroupe
MO.	Stuart Symington (D.)	Fred McGhee
	Edward V. Long (D.)	Charles Hughes
MONT.	Mike Mansfield (D.)	Raymond Dockstader
	Lee Metcalf (D.)	Merrill Englund
NEB.	Roman L. Hruska (R.)	Dean Pohlenz
	Carl T. Curtis (R.)	Miss Doris Rook
NEV.	Alan Bible (D.)	Jack Carpenter
	Howard W. Cannon (D.)	Chester B. Sobsey
N.H.	Norris Cotton (R.)	Kenneth Roberts
	Thomas J. McIntyre (D.)	Norman Abelson
N.J.	Clifford P. Case (R.)	Sam Zagoria
	Harrison A. Williams Jr. (D.)	Miss Dorothy Sortor
N.M.	Clinton P. Anderson (D.)	Howard Bray
	Edwin L. Mechem (R.)	Robert Barnes
N.Y.	Jacob K. Javits (R.)	Richard Aurelio
	Kenneth B. Keating (R.)	Mrs. Eleanor Merrill
N.C.	Sam J. Ervin Jr. (D.)	W. Hall Smith Jr.
	B. Everett Jordan (D.)	William B. Whitley
N.D.	Milton R. Young (R.)	Chris U. Sylvester
	Quentin N. Burdick (D.)	William O. [illegible]
OHIO	Frank J. Lausche (D.)	Ray M. White
	Stephen M. Young (D.)	Herbert Jolovitz
OKLA.	A. S. Mike Monroney (D.)	Mrs. Beth Short
	J. Howard Edmondson (D.)	John Meek
ORE.	Wayne Morse (D.)	Miss Phyllis Rock
	Maurine B. Neuberger (D.)	Lloyd Tupling
PENN.	Joseph S. Clark (D.)	Bernard E. Norwitch
	Hugh Scott (R.)	Eugene S. Cowen
R.I.	John O. Pastore (D.)	C. J. Maisano
	Claiborne Pell (D.)	Raymond N. Nelson
S.C.	Olin D. Johnston (D.)	Thomas W. Chadwick
	Strom Thurmond (D.)	Harry S. Dent
S.D.	Karl E. Mundt (R.)	Walter Conahan
	George McGovern (D.)	George Cunningham
TENN.	Albert Gore (D.)	Jack W. Robinson
	Herbert S. Walters (D.)	Frank Brizzi
TEX.	Ralph W. Yarborough (D.)	Louie E. Mathis
	John G. Tower (R.)	R. Ken Towery
UTAH	Wallace F. Bennett (R.)	Tom Korologos
	Frank E. Moss (D.)	Grant W. Midgley
VT.	George D. Aiken (R.)	Charles Weaver
	Winston L. Prouty (R.)	Tom Hayes
VA.	Harry Flood Byrd (D.)	J. Heywood Bell
	A. Willis Robertson (D.)	William Foster
WASH.	Warren G. Magnuson (D.)	Carl Downing
	Henry M. Jackson (D.)	Brian Corcoran
W. VA.	Jennings Randolph (D.)	James W. Harris
	Robert C. Byrd (D.)	Louis I. Freed
WIS.	William Proxmire (D.)	Roy Meer
	Gaylord Nelson (D.)	William Beckel
WYO.	Gale W. McGee (D.)	Tom Wilson
	Milward L. Simpson (R.)	Doug Baldwin

Senators, like the federal agencies they like to criticize for employing press agents, also have assistants who help them get their names in the papers.

right to preside during some confusion over the rules. It was up to him to rule for or against an anti-filibuster motion. The Senate parliamentarian tried to explain the situation to him, but Hayden wouldn't listen. "I want to go with Russell," he insisted, "I want to go with Russell." (He referred to Senator Richard Russell (D-Ga.), the leader of the Southern bloc.) Hayden impatiently banged his gavel, mumbled a ruling, and shuffled out of the chamber, leaving the Senate in chaos. Several Senators rushed after him and urged him to return to the rostrum to clarify his ruling. "No," said the old man, "I am not going back."

Occasionally, the seniority system thrusts up a black sheep, such as Harlem's flamboyant Congressman Adam Clayton Powell, into a position of power. His global gallivanting—nightclubbing in Paris, deep-sea fishing at Acapulco, gambling on the Riviera, and yachting in the Caribbean—is uninhibited. His wife, the beautiful Marjorie Flores, collects a Congressional salary while sunning herself in Puerto Rico. She wound up 1965 with a salary of $19,444—*more than twice what the next highest paid member of Powell's staff collected and six times the $3,074 she received as a Congressional secretary before she married him in 1960.* Perhaps it is possible to shed some light on her duties in Puerto Rico. Once she ordered Powell's staff to prepare and mail her instructions in Spanish on how to play dominoes. At this writing, she is contemplating divorce, and her place on the public payroll may be taken by another beauty, Corinne Huff, who has been keeping Powell company on his escapades.

Powell has such sway with the Negro voters in New York City's Harlem that political leaders of both parties have been willing to overlook his deficiencies. *In the 1956 campaign three of President Eisenhower's aides—Sherman Adams, Max Rabb, and Charles Willis—arranged to deliver $50,000 to Powell in return for his support of the Republican ticket.* The money was paid on the flimsy pretext that he needed it to cover his campaign expenses in Ike's behalf. *But in 1958 the Democrats doubled the ante in order to get the Harlem vote for Governor Averell Harriman.* Tammany Hall's Carmine de Sapio put up $100,000 in campaign cash and got in return Powell's support for the Democratic state ticket.

Powell controls all health, labor, education, and welfare legislation in the House. It should be said, in fairness, that he has been an able committee chairman when he hasn't been off vacationing. Seniority has made him a power on Capitol Hill whom few dare defy. When his sports car was ticketed for parking in front of the Washington airport terminal at an angle that blocked two lanes of traffic, for example, the director of the airport, G. Ward Hobbs, cancelled the ticket and hurried over to the Congressman's office to apologize.

Sacred seniority makes some Congressmen so powerful that others must kowtow to them. Cantankerous Representative Mike Kirwan (D-Ohio), for one, has risen to such heights during his 30 years in the House that few lesser members ever cross him. When he encountered opposition in his 1964 Democratic primary for the first time in over 20 years, he herded 64 Congressmen upon the House floor to make flowery speeches endorsing him. Some of these same Congressmen bitterly criticized President Franklin D. Roosevelt for intervening in Democratic primaries. "In 40 years of public service," President Johnson has declared, "I have never supported anyone in a primary except myself." Yet 64 Congressmen ignored this time-honored rule.

One after another, they rose to eulogize one of their fellow members. Their lofty language made it sound like a funeral service. Not even the late, beloved Speaker Sam Rayburn received so many tributes after his death. The object of their praise, however, was not dead. He sat on the House floor listening to the tributes, apparently keeping score on how many Congressmen delivered proper encomiums. *What no one mentioned in all the rosy oratory was that all 64 Congress-*

men had pork barrel projects before Kirwan's appropriations subcommittee, and he held the veto over their pork.

One of the first on his feet was Congressman Carl Albert (D-Okla.), who unwittingly gave away his motive for singing Kirwan's praises. "Mike Kirwan has had an important influence upon countless reclamation and public works projects funded during the last two decades," declared Albert in admiration. "These have run the gamut from power and flood-control dams to fish hatcheries and game preserves. Name a project, and you can be sure that Mike Kirwan had a hand in its development." *Albert neglected to add that he hoped to get $3.5 million out of Kirwan as down payment on his pet $13.3 million Arbuckle Reclamation project in Oklahoma.*

Indeed, the loudest praise seemed to come from those who sought the most money from Kirwan to spend on vote-getting projects at home. Congressman Ed Boland (D-Mass.) called him "understanding, compassionate, kind, and sympathetic." But most of all, Boland hoped Kirwan would be generous in providing federal funds to complete the $16 million Cape Cod National Seashore. Cried Congressman Al Ullman (D-Ore.): "Mike Kirwan is made of the stuff that built America." What Ullman really wanted Kirwan to help build, of course, was the Mason dam a few miles up the Powder River from Ullman's home town of Baker, Oregon.

Even Republican Congressmen, who are no less eager for pork-barrel projects, joined in the tributes, though it provided campaign fodder for an encrusted Democrat. Congressman Seymour Halpern (R-N.Y.) described Kirwan as "humble, forthright, honest, good, understanding, and a fine gentleman"—words Halpern hoped would be worth an appropriation from Kirwan's subcommittee to establish Bowne House in Flushing, New York, as a national religious shrine. Amid all the hearts and flowers, perhaps the prevailing sentiment was best summed up by Congresswoman Martha Griffiths (D-Mich.), who wanted Kirwan to grant money for a national

SUGGESTED NEWS RELEASE TO ACCOMPANY TV SCRIPT ON BASE CLOSINGS

For Immediate Release   Date

WASHINGTON, D. C. — Congressman ____________________ said today that "imaginative businessmen" can make recently closed military bases "tax-payers instead of tax-eaters."

In a radio-TV interview prepared for WXYZ-TV (10 a.m., Sunday, Nov. 3) Congressman ____________________ said that many of these closed installations are "valuable properties and imaginative businessmen know it."

The Congressman reviewed steps taken by the federal government to help workers displaced by the base closings. "It is a significant sign of the times, I think, that people are being considered," he said, adding:

"It was not always so."

Congressman ____________________ praised the careful planning of Secetary of Defense Robert McNamara who has taken steps to work out displacement problems in the affected communities.

All Democratic Congressmen have to do is fill in their names in this type of do-it-yourself press release prepared by the Democratic National Committee. Speech material is also furnished.

cemetery at Fort Custer, Michigan. "In this century," she said solemnly, "the 19th district of Ohio will never again be represented by a man who has reached the power that Mike Kirwan has."

No doubt the nation's forefathers were wise in entrusting the power of the purse to Congress. *They did not, however, anticipate the influence this would give a few individual legislators in the back rooms of government.* The late Congressman Albert Thomas (D-Tex.), who handled space funds for the House Appropriations Committee, was able to move the nation's space center to his home town of Houston—an awkward distance from the launching pads at Cape Kennedy, Florida. When a special board was about to award the telephone contract at the Houston Space Center to General Telephone, which had offered the best deal, Thomas blocked it with a single telephone call.

Thomas' call, an important event at the Space agency, was taken by aide R. P. Young, who summed up the conversation in an urgent confidential memo: "Congressman Albert Thomas called me, and said he heard that there is a controversy developing between General Telephone and Bell Telephone in Texas as to who will provide service to the Houston Space Flight Center. He said he would like to provide some free, unsolicited and unbiased advice on this matter. He recommended that we go to Bell for the service."

Not long afterward, Southwestern Bell acknowledged its gratitude to Thomas in a confidential memo to employees: "The Southwestern Bell Telephone Company has been awarded the contract to provide communications for the NASA space lab, located in the Clear Creek area. There were two telephone companies in competition for the right to serve this important installation. Residents of the Houston area owe a debt of gratitude to Congressmen Albert Thomas and Bob Casey [Thomas' Houston colleague] for their efforts in getting the space lab located here. Mr. Thomas and Mr. Casey were also extremely helpful to our company—providing necessary information and other assistance—during the negotiations for the space lab communications contract."

It wasn't the first time Thomas had demonstrated a curious benevolence toward the Bell System. Once he issued an invitation, which had more the ring of a summons, to John Moore, then General Services Administrator, to attend a stag party for Bell's Board Chairman Frederick Kappel. This occurred at a time when Bell was competing with Western Union for the GSA contract to establish a nationwide telecommunications network for the civilian side of the government. Kappel sent word to me that he hardly knew Thomas and was puzzled over this hospitality. Nevertheless, both Kappel and Moore attended the party and discussed telecommunications problems over their martinis.

Probably nowhere under the American flag is the clamor louder than on Capitol Hill for clean, honest government. Congress compels officials to sell their stocks, lest in serving the government they might also serve themselves. Congress is severe with any employee, high or low, who is caught using the public trust for private gain. But unhappily, not all legislators submit to the same code of ethics they impose on others. Scandals have become so commonplace on Capitol Hill that public faith in Congress has been undermined.

Some members of Congress pad the public payroll and pocket government expense money. For those with more ingenuity—and less scruples—there are far greater opportunities. A few Senators and Representatives have discovered that well-heeled pressure groups, in their tireless quest for far more government benefits, are willing to pass around a few private benefits to the right people. For favors on Capitol Hill, corporations have been known to pay off in stock tips, business franchises and legal fees. Unions offer undercover help and financial support during political campaigns. The back door to many a Congressman's office can be reached through his law firm. A startling number are directors of banks, saving and loan associations, and other businesses. More than two dozen own shares in radio and television stations. Others operate farms which benefit substantially from agriculture legislation. Many Senators and Congressmen actively trade on the stock market, buying and selling shares of corporations that do business with the government. Some legislators conceal their stock holdings by registering it in other names.

Some of the most respected figures in Congress are the most accomplished backdoor dealers. Senator Everett Dirksen (R. Ill.), the Senate's lovable scallawag, whose sagging face, untamed hair and organ voice have made him one of Capitol Hill's favorite characters, has wheedled Democratic Presidents into appointing two of his political henchmen, Harold Woodward and Carl Bagge, to the Federal Power Commission, which makes billion-dollar decisions affecting the oil and gas industry. It is a coincidence worth recording that, far away in Peoria, Illinois, Dirksen's law firm—Davis, Morgan and Witherell—represents Panhandle Eastern Pipe Line, one of the giant gas wholesalers, whose economic well-being depends upon decisions of the Federal Power Commission. Another stalwart of the Senate, grimly stern John McClellan (D-Ark.), the embodiment of righteous wrath, held headlined hearings into bank scandals. He also appeared before the American Bankers Association convention to charge that "too many national banks are being unwisely chartered too fast and too freely." But at the same time he was investigating newly-chartered banks out of his front office, he was working out of his back office to block competition for his own banks. He forwarded letters to the Comptroller of the Currency opposing charters for banks that would compete with the First National Bank of Little Rock and the Bank of West Memphis, Arkansas. He happens to hold substantial holdings in both banks.

HOUSE OF REPRESENTATIVES
COMMITTEE ON BANKING AND CURRENCY
EIGHTY-NINTH CONGRESS
2129 RAYBURN HOUSE OFFICE BUILDING
WASHINGTON, D.C.

March 4, 1966

C O N F I D E N T I A L

MEMORANDUM

TO: Dr. Nelson

FROM: Ray C. Cole

SUBJECT: James J. Saxon Interview

Mr. Saxon was interviewed on this date in his office, 3120 Main Treasury.

The Comptroller was questioned relative to his knowledge of "black money" being invested in the banking field. Saxon stated that this activity was greatly exaggerated in its extent, that indeed such investment was miniscule because of the small amounts of money returnable. These small amounts coming from banks in the $1 million class do not have funds enough to justify "black money" investment.

Mr. Saxon stated that the entry of underworld figures or money into the Federal System was almost impossible and that the State System was carefully watched, thus prohibiting the entry of unsavory characters into banking circles.

Saxon stated that with very few exceptions, Bank of Miami Beach, Brighton, Colorado, Dania, Florida, and Five Points Bank in Florida, he knew of no serious wrong doing in the banks today. The Comptroller cites one Van Zamph affiliated with both the Miami Beach and Dania banks that was a real "bad apple" whom it is expected will be prosecuted.

Van Zamph has been in association with SalKolff and one Low Patten. The Comptroller's office is in the process of completely eliminating these individuals from U. S. banking.

The Comptroller's files relative to these banks and individuals was requested. Saxon stated that they were of a classified nature and, upon query, stated that he was not personally acquainted with the cases but that his Deputy, Bill Camp, was familiar with these cases and would contact the writer in the near future. Saxon did indicate a degree of familiarity with a state bank in Missouri that was headed toward receivership because of bad management. His office was successful in obtaining an

This confidential memo about the McClellan Committee's investigation of "black money" investments in banks reveals that Senator John McClellan has personal banking ties. His investigation was intended to discourage the chartering of new national banks which would compete with the old-line banks.

injunction that stopped the improper activities of the officers. Bill Camp has complete information on this and we shall attempt to secure same.

Relative to Saxon's testimony before the McClellan Committee (March 1965) and the Senate investigation, Mr. Saxon stated that in the San Francisco Bank case they had provided for the Committee their complete file. Further in the hands of the McClellan people, the context of the files was exaggerated, twisted and blown all out of proportion for publicity purposes. Mr. Saxon stated that copies of their files were even printed and sold on the West Coast by a Public Relations figure (not otherwise identified). Mr. Saxon stated that because of his unhappy experience with the San Francisco file and the McClellan Committee, he would not again provide such service to a Congressional Committee. At this point the writer assured Mr. Saxon of proper observance of the confidentiality of any material he might furnish this Committee. Saxon then stated that he would discuss the situation with his Deputy, Bill Camp, and Camp would contact the writer.

During the discussion, Saxon, appearing the aggrieved public servant, told of Senator McClellan's banking interest, his membership on the board of the Little Rock Bank, his association with the West Memphis Bank, and efforts McClellan had made to obtain three charters for his friends, one of which was successful.

Relative to savings and loan companies, Saxon stated that he believed "black money" investment here was probably more widespread in tha regulation was not so stringent as in banking. He stated that John Horne, Home Loan Bank Board, may have information relative to such investment. He stated that Home Loan Bank was or had been pretty much controlled by the Savings and Loan League, a problem not shared by his office and its association with the ABA.

John Horne's office will be contacted in the near future and review of his files will be attempted.

- - -oOo- - -

Continuation of the confidential memo about Senator McClellan's banking interests.

Even the most honest Congressmen cannot entirely escape doing business with the special interests. For with rare exceptions, a member of Congress cannot count upon the public to finance his campaign. *He must turn to the people with an ax to grind for the bulk of his money—the great unions and corporations, farm groups and other pressure groups.* And the plink of every donated coin, the rustle of every unfolding bill, or the scratch of pen on check adds emphasis to the need for reform of one of the greatest evils in the American system.

For the tragic truth is that political campaigns are financed by means that are not only antiquated but often corrupt. Even candidates, who could never be persuaded to take a questionable legal fee, are forced to accept shady money (or close their eyes while political bagmen collect in their behalf) in order to run for office. *The Pike's Peak cost of campaigning is so staggering today that only the well-heeled candidate can afford to run.* And to become well-heeled, he must take money from persons who expect him to do favors in return. In fact, it's a miracle of politics and a tribute to officeholders that the pressure groups don't wield more influence than they do. Here are the blunt comments of some political professionals, who spoke frankly to me on condition that their names be withheld:

• A veteran Democratic fund-raiser: "There isn't a major campaign that doesn't receive illegal contributions. The candidate may not know, or pretend he doesn't. But the Corrupt Practices Act is broken, bent, twisted, ignored and circumvented all the time."

• A Senator who investigated the subject in 1956: "The laws regulating political campaigns are not only hopelessly inadequate; they are meaningless. The only purpose they serve today is to demoralize the people in politics and breed contempt for the law."

• A Republican Congressman: "The average Congressman would throw out any lobbyist who offered him a $100 bribe yet accept a $1,000 campaign contribution from the same man without a qualm."

• A Senator from a small state: "It was impossible for me to raise enough money in my state for my campaign. I had no alternative but to accept out-of-state contributions. Seventy percent of my expenses were paid by outside interests."

It costs as much as $2 million to campaign for governor or senator in a big state. *A seat in the House can be won for $25,000, but may cost four or five times that much.* The Democrats came out of the 1960 Presidential campaign with a staggering $4.5 million deficit, causing the late President Kennedy to exclaim: "My God, what would we have done if we had lost?"

The biggest campaign bite goes for television. One big-state Senator described his $230,000 television bill as "expensive but essential." Another essential for the modern candidate is the private political poll. It costs $10,000 to $12,000 to run a first and second sampling, three times that much in a complex state like California.

Travel costs have soared with the airplane; so has the price of printing, staff salaries, campaign paraphernalia. Even fund-raising now costs almost a dollar to raise a dollar. Congressman William Ayres (R-Ohio) ran a newspaper ad ("Bill Ayres Needs Your Help") pleading for $1 contributions. The ad cost $200, brought in $51.

The campaign laws require candidates to report what they collect and spend. *But there are a thousand and one ways for candidates to avoid disclosure.* So enter the political bagmen, experts in the fine art of slipping money under the table. Their most frequent ruse is "double billing," by which a union or corporation pays certain campaign expenses directly but shows them on the books as "business expenses." A printing bill may be picked up or a campaign film paid for.

One group of New England corporations has contributed to both Republican and Democratic candidates by paying them "commissions." Still another dodge is to channel donations through friends, relatives, employees.

The high-sounding Committee for Economic Growth, lavish with campaign donations, turned out to be a group of restaurant owners who were fighting against tax tightening on expense accounts. Most of the committee's donations went to members of the Senate and House committees that write tax legislation. A $1,500 contribution went to Senator Russell Long (D-La.) who delivered a blistering Senate attack on the expense account rules. Another $1,000 went to Congressman John Dent (D-Pa.) who introduced a bill to cancel restrictions on expense account spending.

The Committee on American Leadership turned out to be a coal industry group fighting for an increase in its tax depletion allowance. Among the donations distributed by the committee were $500 to Congresswoman Elizabeth Kee (D-W. Va.) and $650 to Congressman John Saylor (R-Pa.). Both introduced bills to have the depletion allowance boosted. These members of Congress would be outraged at the suggestion that their votes could be influenced by campaign contributions. Long and Dent were opposed to expense account limitations before the contributions. Kee and Saylor represent coal districts and would have tried to help the coal interests anyway. Senators Warren Magnuson (D-Wash.) and Len Jordan (R-Ida.) both accepted $500 contributions from lumber interests in 1962, then teamed up to push through a lumber-labeling bill that would hamper competitive Canadian lumber. Both men represent lumber states and have lumber interests at heart.

Yet this raises a question of propriety: *which comes first, the contribution or the conviction?* Since a politician must have money to run for office—and he can't raise it from the public—he can only get funds from special interests. *Whose gifts should he accept?* It would seem the most ethical solution is to accept campaign contributions only from interests whose views he already shares. Yet if he serves their interests, how are the voters to know whether he is doing so out of conviction or for campaign cash?

In the desperate struggle to fill their campaign coffers without selling their souls, candidates keep dreaming up new fund-raising gimmicks. The most productive are the $100-a-plate dinners; some candidates start holding these dinners two years before the election. Other variations include $25-a-plate breakfasts, $50-a-plate luncheons, cocktails for cash. Senator Dodd, who tried them all and pocketed the proceeds, has raised a cloud over such affairs.

Though too many Congressmen operate on the shady side of Capitol Hill and need a little sunlight turned on them as the best disinfectant against corruption, *the readers should be reminded that the majority of Congressmen are honest.* They probably work longer hours and give more dedicated service than do the people who elect them. They likely also adhere to higher standards than their critics do. Private citizens, free to pursue their own ambitions, expect their elected representatives to put the public good ahead of personal welfare. It is heartening how many do.

High among the stalwarts stands Senator Mike Mansfield (D-Mont.), the 62-year-old Senate majority leader. He is one of those rarest of politicians who cares nothing for power or publicity. He is guided only by conscience and duty, and in politics, the demands of the one do not always coincide with the demands of the other.

The lean, six-foot Montanan with the gentle manner and quiet voice, whose tanned, lined face shows the somberness of his mood, has misgivings about the Vietnam War. Yet, as majority leader, he is the spokesman for the President's party in the Senate; duty and loyalty require that he give maximum support to Lyndon Johnson's policies. If Mansfield allows the voice of his conscience to speak too loudly, it might be interpreted abroad as a dramatic division in the top policy-making councils. But those who know Mike Mansfield are certain of this much: he will evade no decisions, and he will face them alone. He asks no man to share his responsibility with him. "If Mike knew he was going to lose every vote in Montana," asserts an intimate, "he would still do what he thought was right. He will not deviate from what he believes is his duty. But sometimes duty requires him to carry out policies in which he does not wholly believe. Long ago, Mike made up his mind to do what he must."

Though they may differ in style and occasionally in opinion, the President has the highest regard for Mansfield's integrity. For it was Lyndon Johnson, seeking a successor, who urged Mansfield to accept the Senate leadership. *"I didn't want the job," Mansfield later confided to a friend, "but I felt I couldn't say no."* However, he did say no—quietly but firmly—in 1964 when President Johnson began telling people that Mansfield was the best man for the Vice Presidency. The thought of becoming the man second in line for the White House was simply too much for the modest Montanan.

In contrast with the iron-fisted Senate rule of Lyndon Johnson, Mansfield relies on persuasion, accommodation, and understanding. He doesn't try to run the Senate himself, as Johnson did, but urges the committee chairmen to take the lead. He gives them all the credit and glory. When the flash bulbs begin to explode and the television cameras to whir, he literally steps back and pushes others to the front. He is sensitive about the feelings of other Senators. When Senator Ted Kennedy (D-Mass.) was troubled over charges that he had once cheated in a college exam, Mansfield rose on the Senate floor and confessed that as a young Marine he had twice been thrown in the brig.

He never indulges in invective, never opposes for opposition's sake. *He twists no arms, makes no deals.* Senators accept his leadership because they respect him. In every poll that has been taken, Mansfield has been voted by Democratic and Republican Senators alike as the colleague they most admire. "He doesn't have a single enemy in the place," says Louisiana Senator Russell Long, the No. 2 Democrat. And the dean of the Republicans, Vermont Senator George Aiken, declares: "There isn't a Republican Senator who would raise a finger to hurt Mike." In short, Mansfield is living evidence that in politics, if not in baseball, nice guys can win.

But this doesn't mean he is anybody's patsy. The late Senator Joe McCarthy (R-Wis.), campaigning against Mansfield in Montana, suggested he was a communist coddler. Later, back in Washington, McCarthy strode up to Mansfield, slapped him on the back and asked: "How are things in Montana, Mike?" Mansfield looked him in the eye and replied coldly: "Much better since you left."

Mansfield makes his decisions with great gravity. He never speaks on a subject without long and deep thought. He never rushes into any action. All important decisions are committed to paper. When he is called to the White House with other Congressional leaders, he pulls out a written statement and reads from it. Copies are filed away in a top-secret safe, so that the stand he has taken cannot be questioned later on.

If Mansfield had his choice, he would prefer to go down in Senate history as a foreign affairs expert rather than a great leader. That he reached the Senate at all is an accolade for the son of poor Irish immigrants. Born on the edge of New York's Hell's Kitchen, he didn't get his high school diploma until he was 30. Through extra courses, he obtained his college degree at the same time and became an assistant history professor at Montana University. If this was a sheltered life, he had already seen it in the raw. The least combative of men, he has served in three of the four armed forces.

During World War I, as a boy of 14, he lied about his age and enlisted in the Navy, seeing service on convoy duty in the submarine-infested Atlantic. By the time he was 19, he had also served in the Army and the Marines. He still wears the Marines' discharge button in his lapel.

In a Senate full of friends, Mansfield's closest companion is Senator George Aiken, and the contrast between the two men is dramatic. The Democrat from the West, tall, spare and solemn, towers over the Republican from the East, who is short and gnarled and has an elfish twinkle. The two have been eating breakfast together almost every morning for 15 years. They are so close that they have come to be known as the Damon and Pythias of the Senate.

Some men seek power, enjoy and employ it. Some have power thrust upon them, and accept it only from a sense of duty. Frequently they find its exercise painful in the extreme. Such a man is Mike Mansfield. Another like him is hulking, white-maned Senator Paul Douglas (D-Ill.), who, at age 50 gave up a professor's post to become a private in the Marines and slog through some of the Pacific's most ferocious fighting. But there have been fewer victories for Douglas, the politician, who fights for the little people without Washington influence. After losing one battle to the entrenched interests, standing unbowed against terrible pressure, he turned to an aide and sighed: "The Japanese were only after my body. These fellows are after my soul."

The scrupulous Douglas also instructed his campaign aides to accept no contributions from people with an interest in Senate legislation. Ignorant of this, a Textile Workers official plunked down $10,000 which the union had raised to help finance his campaign. Douglas shooed the startled official out of his office and told him to take his money with him. A campaign worker later cornered the union man, apologized for Douglas' naivete, and worked out a "double billing" arrangement under which the money could be spent on the Senator's campaign without his knowledge.

It took a special kind of courage for Southerners to stand up and be counted in favor of the voting rights bill. The evening before the vote, Congressman Hale Boggs (D-La.), told a few friends he had decided to vote for the bill. His daughter, "Cokie", walked over to her father and kissed him, saying she was proud of him. "I'm not only going to vote for it," said Boggs, "I'm going to make a speech for it."

Next day, his colleague from Louisiana, Congressman Joe Waggonner, Jr., leaped into the debate on the side of the segregationists, declaring that Louisiana was being maligned by this legislation and that there was little discrimination in his state. Boggs, born in Mississippi, reared in Louisiana, rose to reply. "I wish", he declared, "I could stand here as a man who loves his state, who has spent every year of his life in Louisiana since he was five years old, and say there has not been any discrimination. But unfortunately, it is not so . . . I shall support this bill because I believe the fundamental right to vote must be a part of this great experiment in human progress under freedom, which is America."

Political courage isn't always easy to measure. Sometimes it takes more courage to compromise than to cling stubbornly to a principle. For without compromise, our democratic processes would become brittle and shatter. A politician's first function is also to get elected; it would be naive to suppose he could stay in office without making some concessions to campaign contributors, local interests, pressure groups, and party leaders.

No doubt many would like to growl back at the people who pressure them, but their political instincts demand that they smile instead. A rare exception: waspish Senator Steve Young (D-Ohio), whose caustic letters to constituents have become famous. He has denounced just about every pressure group from the American Medical Association to the Daughters of the American Revolution. When an American Legion post suggested he shouldn't keep a scheduled speaking engagement, he called them "puffed-up patriots" and concluded fiercely: "I'll make that speech!"

Boyishly handsome Senator Frank Church (D-Idaho), another with political courage, defied the public opinion polls and called for negotiation of the Vietnamese conflict. This is not a popular stand in his native Idaho, a state of rugged individualists, who are always ready to spill red blood in defense of liberty. He could also have ducked the fight over the Wilderness Bill, which was opposed by the powerful lumber and mining interests in his home state. Instead, he led the fight for the bill.

In the push and press of the back rooms, Congressman John Blatnik (D-Minn.), whose gentle manner is merely the moss on a character of granite, has been as rugged a political in-fighter as he was a World War II commando parachuting behind enemy lines. The modest Blatnik, often working in his shirtsleeves late into the night, has handled the tedious, unspectacular legislation that seldom makes headlines.

A politician need not be right to be courageous. No one can be right all the time in this changing world. But those who fight for their convictions deserve respect. Here are a few more of them:

- SENATOR SPESSARD HOLLAND (D. Fla.) — A staunch Southerner, he believed the poll tax to be wrong and led the Senate battle against it, though it cost him several Southern friends.
- SENATOR TOM KUCHEL (R-Calif.) — When an unspeakable smear was circulated against him, accusing him of sex perversion, he was told that he would only advertise the charge by answering it. Yet he dared to fight back, as he has

dared to stand up to the extremists in a state where they have a clamorous voice.

• CONGRESSMAN CARL PERKINS (D-Ky.) — Scrupulously honest, he not only puts postage stamps on all personal letters but has been known to track down a letter at the House post office that mistakenly went out with the official mail and return it for a five-cent stamp. Once he helped a disabled veteran with three children obtain a disability allowance. The grateful vet knitted a white shawl and brought it by wheel chair to Perkins' office. When the Congressman later was shown the shawl, he smiled appreciatively but told an aide: "We'll have to send it back with a note of thanks."

• CONGRESSWOMAN EDITH GREEN (D-Ore.) — Though it is considered political folly for a Member of Congress to side against powerful local interests to help another state, she opposed the Morningside Hospital in her home town and supported a new mental hospital in Alaska. She based her decision on the merits.

• SENATOR CLIFFORD CASE (R-N.J.) — Rather than risk the slightest obligation that might conflict with his duty, he has turned down favors even from friends who might have an interest in Senate legislation. It has cost him money, taken from the dwindling holdings he had as an attorney, to be a Senator.

• CONGRESSMAN CHARLES BENNETT (D-Fla.) — Crippled by polio while serving in the infantry in the Philippines during World War II, he has renounced claim to more than $60,000 in veterans' disability benefits, turning the proceeds over to help develop Fort Caroline, Florida, as a park. He politely returns all gifts and gratuities, or turns them over, in the case of fruit and flowers, to a hospital.

There is no lack of worthy men on Capitol Hill. Though there may be chicanery, there is also courage and integrity. As an investigative reporter, I have poked into the back rooms of Congress for two decades seeking out corruption. I am convinced that Congress still belongs to the people. The vested interests would like to own Congress; while it is true that they have succeeded in buying some legislators, most Congressmen are not for sale.

6

LIVING IT UP AT PUBLIC EXPENSE

That ancient sightseer, Marco Polo, was renowned not only for his mileage but his literary output. Now his place in history has been challenged by a peppery, peripatetic Senator in his seventies—Allen Ellender, Democrat of Louisiana—who has been five times around the world and deep into many of its remote areas. Making allowances for nations formed within the past couple of years, only tiny, hostile Albania has been able to keep him out. But Premier Hoxha should be warned that Ellender is not easily deterred.

As for the impulse of the traveler to inflict his experiences upon others, Ellender unquestionably has the venturesome Venetian beat—in volume if not literary merit. Marco was a shrewd observer of peoples, places, and customs. Ellender runs to pompous statements of the obvious. Example: It's "very hot" on the equator at noon. Unlike Ellender, Marco did not have his works published at the expense of the U.S. taxpayer, nor his transportation furnished by the U.S. Air Force, nor his pocket money provided from Special Account No. 19FT561. The latter is the secret account from which members of Congress can draw local lucre at American Embassies throughout the world.

The idea that Congressmen should travel is sound: to widen their knowledge of the world, to act as ambassadors of good will, to keep a hawk-eye on how the taxpayers' dollars are spent abroad. But members of Congress, like lesser mortals, don't always fulfill their destiny. For a few the temptation to take a plush vacation at the taxpayers' expense has proved overpowering.

The most indefatigable tourist who ever strayed from Capitol Hill is the Senator from Louisiana. Unlike Harlem's globetrotting Congressman Adam Clayton Powell, Ellender is more sightseer than carouser. He totes a movie camera and takes dozens of reels for the wonderment of those at home who, out of respect for his Senate seniority, let themselves be collared into attending his illustrated lectures. He also packs a supply of little black notebooks in which he jots his more piercing impressions, later to be published as official Senate reports. When confronted with a new volume of *Ellender's Travels,* even his best friends wince.

On one "good will mission" to Africa, he succeeded in getting banned from three new nations, thus spoiling his record of keeping up with the map as fast as it is subdivided. He outraged African leaders, whose good will he had come to cultivate, by prating to the press that "the average African is incapable of leadership except through the assistance of Europeans." American diplomats, charged with his care and comfort, blanched. Secretary of State Dean Rusk had conniptions. But the Senator seemed only puzzled over the uproar he caused. On reading a New York Herald-Tribune editorial which said he had availed himself of a basic American freedom—the right to make a fool of himself—Ellender savagely scribbled in his notebook: "The pipsqueak who wrote that is uninformed."

Though the Senator ostensibly desired to learn about Africa, he was more disposed to lecture. Ambassadors, trying dutifully to brief him, were brushed aside. African leaders, no small talkers themselves, were stunned into silence by the jet stream of the Senator's voice. They were regaled with the Ellender success story, instructed on the intricacies of Congress, and, in the case of President Keita of Mali, formerly a French colony, treated to a discourse on satellite communication legislation delivered in Cajun French. President Keita, a polite man, sat with glazed eyes; the Senator's words, like Telstar, were way over Keita's head.

As a son of the bayous, Ellender is proud of his Cajun and uses it every chance he gets. After his arrival in Mali, where he announced he had come to see that American money wasn't being wasted, Ellender recorded in a notebook: "Most of those present were surprised to hear me talk French. I believe the Ambassador was pleased." Ambassador William Handley, reporting confidentially to the State Department, commented: "The Senator speaks an adequate but at times impenetrable French."

Keita's courtesy nearly encouraged the Senator, in a flush of Gallic garrulity, to promise Mali some economic aid, but he overcame the impulse and hinted instead for a handout for himself. Reported the Ambassador's confidential cable: "The Senator had asked the President to name some products typical of Mali that he could buy as souvenirs of his visit. The President ordered an aide to present some typical products as gifts to the Senator. These were given to him at the airport just prior to his departure." This aid-in-reverse included a wooden hippo, ivory carvings, necklaces woven from straw, and an alligator briefcase.

In setting out on his safari, Ellender was not merely content with a letter authorizing him to dip into "Special Account" funds. He also got on the phone to the Pentagon with a request that transport planes, assigned to air attaches, should be placed at his disposal. Defense officials groaned but anted up. The fact that Ellender would be the sole passenger in these expensive planes was no reason for turning down a member of the powerful Senate Appropriations Committee. Nor did anyone dare suggest that, in the interest of the economy he was preaching, the Senator could have saved the taxpayers some money by taking commercial flights.

The Senator also made it known that he didn't care for hotels, preferring to be accomodated in the homes of senior officials. So the word went out: "Ellender is on his way. Keep him happy." From Mauritania to Mozambique, diplomats paled beneath their tan. Many had encountered him before and were not looking forward to renewing the acquaint-

ROBERT T. STAFFORD
VERMONT

ROOM 138
HOUSE OFFICE BUILDING

MEMBER:
ARMED SERVICES COMMITTEE

NEAL J. HOUSTON
ADMINISTRATIVE ASSISTANT

Congress of the United States
House of Representatives
Washington, D. C.

Dear Senator [illegible]:

The Second Annual Congressional Flight Survey will take-off from Dulles International Airport, 6:00 p.m., Eastern Daylight Time, Thursday, June 11.

The subjects for study in 1964 are "Agriculture-Industry-Business Aviation in the Midwest". In addition, the FAA welcomes Members of Congress to an Aerial Open House Inspection of the Agency's working laboratories in the sky.

Including the late afternoon departure on Thursday, June 11, the Flight Survey will cover Friday, Saturday and Sunday, June 12, 13, and 14.

Through the cooperation of FAA, the Congressional Flying Club is proud to sponsor the Aerial Open House Inspection of FAA's airborne work platforms. A limited number of Members of Congress will have a firsthand look at important airways evaluation and inspection work performed aloft, as they fly from Dulles International to Oklahoma City. The working aircraft will be a Boeing KC-135 and a turboprop Convair. This is a rare opportunity for MC's to see how these aircraft and crews monitor the capabilities and the effectiveness of airways navigational aids and electronic services.

Upon arrival in Oklahoma City, the Flight Survey group will be honored at a special reception by civic leaders of the area. On Friday morning, members will receive an informal briefing and demonstration of the sonic boom tests now being conducted there. They are also invited to take a brief tour of the Aeronautical Center.

Following an early luncheon on Friday, the party will then become the guest of the International Flying Farmers and General Aviation organizations. It will be carried on economic survey flights for a close look at Midwest agriculture, industrial development trends and surface-air transportation operations. The itinerary will include stops at a Flying Farmer center at Wichita, Kansas, the hub of U. S. general aviation manufacturing, and at Cedar Rapids, Iowa, where industrial development is the prime topic for study. Chambers of Commerce and farm groups will host the members at each stop. Members will be returned to Kansas City, Missouri, for the return flight to Washington via working airways check aircraft. Anticipated arrival at Washington is approximately 8:00 p.m.

An invitation to a typical Congressional junket. It is signed by Representative Robert T. Stafford (R.-Vt.), the tour chairman. The Federal Aviation Agency wins friends among legislators by organizing such trips, especially during summer months.

As was the practice in 1963, members will pay a modest fee for lodging. They will be hosted by local groups at each stop, but breakfast and some luncheons will be at the individual's expense. Clothing should be informal, summer dress. Jackets and ties will be required at many affairs. Sports clothes are desirable for flying.

The number of seats available for all airplanes is limited. Therefore your CFC committee must limit Congressional reservations to 30. They are being assigned on a first-come, first-served basis.

Obviously, for the above reasons, Members of Congress must make the complete tour. It cannot be used as airlift for a weekend in the district.

However, it is recommended that Members of Congress utilize this Survey Flight as an opportunity to invite their associates from other areas of the U. S. to join them in this tour for a close look at the economic side of the Nation's "Breadbasket".

Please let me know immediately if you plan to make this flight.

Sincerely yours,

Robert T. Stafford
Chairman, Tour Program

R.S.V.P.
Ext. 4115

Continuation of Rep. Stafford's invitation to a Congressional junket.

ance. It was as if they had been told that a cranky but rich old uncle was about to descend upon them.

His first African stop was Morrocco where he was greeted by amiable but apprehensive Ambassador John H. Ferguson. Ellender was favorably impressed, noting in one of his notebooks that the Ambassador was "energetic and willing to learn." Ferguson learned all right—all about the Senator's favorite subject, Allen Ellender. Ferguson wasted no time in passing on his information; he got off a confidential cable alerting his colleagues far and near: "*Escort officer learned that Senator is a widower, a grandfather, that he neither drinks nor smokes, that he does not eat shellfish, that he drinks only tea with breakfast, that his relevant hobby is color movie photography, that he insists on going to his room not later than 10 p.m. no matter what is in progress, that he speaks Cajun French, that he likes early morning starts, that he started his political career under the auspices of Huey Long.*"

As Ellender moved across Africa, perspiring diplomats added to their knowledge of his eccentricities and clued each other in advance. They found that the Senator ignored their briefings but briefed them instead, lectured African leaders instead of listening to them. And there always remained the shadow of the little black book, where names and impressions were being noted. Again and again Ellender revealed his fascination over trivia. Of his meeting with President Moktar ould Daddah of Mauritania, he recorded that they watched a wrestling match, then ate a delicacy called "Coush-Coush" with their hands. Ellender duly reported to Congress: "I ate much more than I should and much more than I expected."

In Gabon the Senator finally was out-talked by President Leon Mba, whom he described ruefully as "quite a talker." When Ellender warned the local AID director against raising chickens in Gabon's hot, humid climate, he was informed that they were already being raised successfully. Somewhat sourly the Senator admitted that "it's probably worth a try."

During an overnight stop in the central African republic of Chad, Ellender cast a pall over a diplomatic reception. He got off to a typical start, according to Charge d'Affaires Richard Reddington, who cabled the State Department: "The Senator enumerated for President Tombalbaye all the places in Africa he was to stop on his current trip and spoke at length of his career in the Senate." Then Ellender encountered the French Charge d'Affaires and began lecturing him on French shortcomings. Reported Reddington woefully: "The Senator said forthrightly to the French Charge d'Affaires that France, Britain and other U. S. allies had failed to assume their share of the burden of the defense of the free world, leaving the whole job to the U. S. He expostulated on the danger of the U. S. public debt."

So the elderly Ellender shuttled around Africa for two months, carping here, quibbling there, demanding explanations but rarely, if ever, listening to them. His exercise in diplomacy in Chad was nothing compared to his performance in South Africa where he exchanged segregationist views with the late Prime Minister Verwoerd, architect of apartheid. But it was in Southern Rhodesia that the Senator really put his foot in his mouth with his disparagement of the Africans' capacity to govern themselves. His words were flashed across the continent, and a roar of anger arose from Black Africa. It caught up with him at Dar es Salaam, Tanganyika. As he stepped out of an Air Force plane, beaming at the large turnout he thought had come to welcome him, Ambassador William Leonhart raced up the ramp. Hastily, Leonhart explained that the crowd was hostile and the Senator was in danger. But Ellender, still uncomprehending, spotted the photographers and held the Ambassador off, barking: "Wait a minute. Come on, boys, take some more."

Then an immigration official arrived and handed the Senator a notice which read: *"To Mr. Allen Ellender, of Louisiana, U. S. Take notice that you are a prohibited immigrant on the ground that you have no pass or permit to enter Tanganyika. You are hereby ordered to leave the country immediately.*" Ellender, red-faced and flustered, argued that he had a visa. But the official ignored him and walked off. Not until then was Ambassador Leonhart able to explain to the Senator that he had been barred from Nganda, too, and that his reception elsewhere was doubtful. Ellender was obliged to remain in the plane until it could be cleared for take-off. While he waited, he managed to give the Ambassador and accompanying aides the standard lecture on economy and how to get along with Africans.

The Senator was allowed to spend the night on the clove-scented island of Zanzibar and make a brief stop at Usumbura, where he learned that Ethiopia would allow him to land only long enough for his plane to refuel and that the Council of Ministers in Kenya was debating his case. Kenya finally let him land briefly at a British military airbase where he could be protected. Ellender also was allowed to stay overnight at Somali but only on condition that he would remain in the home of AID director Alfred Hurt and depart the country by 6 a.m. The hegira among the heathen was over, rounded off with a stop in Paris. Winging home, the Senator was unable to land in New Orleans because of fog (a condition that some might say was ripe with symbolism). Eventually, he got back safely to his beloved Southland with all his prejudices and preconceptions perfectly intact.

What did Ellender learn from two months of senatorial research in Africa? He thought the prices in Dakar, capital of Senegal, were high and craftsmanship poor. He found the markets in Monrovia, capital of Liberia, and Lagos, capital of Nigeria, were both "dirty and smelly." But he got a good haircut in Lagos. In Yaounde, capital of Cameroon, he picked up a "fig leaf" worn by the native women. In Burundi he learned that virgins wear their hair long and non-virgins wear it short. In Durban, South Africa, he was delighted with the way the colorful Zulu rickshaw runners bound along while blowing whistles and horns. ("They're real comics.") In Togo, hc had some narrow shaves with the hot-rodding "mammy wagons," as the local buses are called. In Dahomey he saw the "Dance of the Amazons," which ended in a screaming frenzy that left him longing for a tape recorder. So went his official observations.

If Ellender has out-distanced all other Congressional wanderers, he cannot afford to slow his pace—not if he is to keep ahead of the world's most determined travelers. For each tourist season, dozens of Senators and Representatives set out from Capitol Hill to explore the world. This great game called junketing, played with the taxpayers' money, has reached such proportions that when President Johnson once considered calling a special session of Congress, an aide remarked wryly: "You'd better call it in Paris."

Indeed, one Congressional group penetrated deeper into Africa than even the intrepid Ellender. Four Congressmen —W. R. Poage (D-Tex.), D. R. Matthews (D-Fla.), Ralph Harvey, (R-Ind.), and Charles Hoeven (R-Iowa)—showed up in an Air Force Constellation at the fabled symbol of the end of nowhere: Timbuktu. *They came to inspect foreign agriculture, a difficult thing to do in Timbuktu which has had no agriculture since the slaves who tilled the parched soil fled in 1893.*

The four junketeers arrived at high noon, after circling for 90 minutes trying to contact Timbuktu's control tower. Attracted by the great plane, a curious crowd abandoned their siesta to inspect the foreigners who had come to inspect them. The regional governor, Babacar Maiga, greeted the visitors who presented him with a shining John F. Kennedy half dollar. He accepted it with polite puzzlement over American tipping customs, then returned gratefully to his siesta. The Congressmen proceeded into town where they encountered a group of barefoot children waving pictures of President Johnson—a brave pro-American demonstration which two advance men from the American Embassy in Bamako had thoughtfully arranged.

The investigators patted the children, posed for snapshots in front of a "Welcome to Timbuktu" sign, and inspected some U-drive-it-camels. Fowler West, a staff assistant, tried out a surly camel, which displayed a decidedly anti-American attitude. This discouraged the Congressmen from taking camel rides, so they toured a mosque in stocking feet instead. Seeking more tangible evidence of their visit, they were steered to a grinning merchant, known locally as *"Bon Prix,"* who sold them some souvenir swords, decorated ostrich eggs, and a bag of dates. Then, their "investigation" completed, they flew off to Bamako after less than three hours in Timbuktu.

Not all junketeers are glorified sightseers. Many follow grueling schedules, inspecting U. S. spending abroad, gathering information to shape future legislation, and spreading good will. But far too many enjoy plush vacations at the taxpayers' expense. One Senator's wife, while on an official trip with her husband, wrote with happy candor to friends: *"John is truly relaxing and having the time of his life. He and I are having a long-delayed honeymoon."*

Some junketeers behave so outrageously that, if the American taxpayers weren't already financing their travel, it would pay the Kremlin to foot the bill. One Southern Congressman almost literally drank his way across Europe a few seasons ago. In Paris he entertained himself yelling rebel war whoops and playing the harmonica. In Madrid he tore the dress off a frightened lady guide and stopped Spaniards on the street, demanding belligerently: "Why don't you like the United States?" Another gay Senator slapped the King of Greece on the back and squeezed the Queen in a bear hug. The same Senator grabbed West Germany's President and swung him around the floor in a heavy-footed version of a Viennese waltz.

At a Helsinki reception a Senator became mischievous after too much vodka and shocked the assembled dignitaries by smacking a prominent Finnish lady on her equally prominent *derriere.* Even at the Vatican a member of the Joint Congressional Atomic Energy Committee harassed the Pope with belligerent and irrelevant questions. When a colleague tried gently to silence him, the truculent Congressman snapped: "I don't want any answers from you. I want them from him." A thumb jerked in the direction of His Holiness made the situation embarrassing for everyone in the room.

Perhaps the biggest Congressional exodus in history followed the grueling 1965 session. Under President Johnson's whiplash, the legislators labored so strenuously that, once freed in November, they scattered joyfully like school boys on the last day of school. Many didn't stop until they got on the other side of the globe. The President's stern admonition to his fellow citizens to see America first and spend their money at home went unheeded. The fact that they were spending the taxpayers' money, not their own, didn't make matters any better. At least a third of Congress headed for overseas vacation spots. Of these, about 100 stopped off in South Vietnam long enough to pose for pictures with our fighting men. That they spent more time in Honolulu and Hongkong did not detract from the publicity value of their Vietnam visits. *The busiest man in the Pacific was Lieutenant Colonel Robert F. Blume, chief of the Army Visitors Bureau in Hawaii, who was kept in a frenzy meeting planes, arranging hotel reservations, and answering questions about bathing beaches and night clubs.*

Even before the final gavel fell in Congress, the great exodus had begun. Two of the old curmudgeons of Congress,

Representative H. R. Gross (R-Iowa) and Representative Howard Smith (D-Va.), who had become too creaky with age to enjoy traveling, preferred to attribute their immobility to a concern for the taxpayers' dollars. The disappearance of so many colleagues the last week of the session caused them to shake their heads over the junketing generation.

"With all the junketeers that are taking off these days," snorted Gross, "I note about 70 absentees this morning, and I know that some of them are off and running to foreign countries. I just wondered whether there is going to be enough funds to take care of all the trips. There have been meetings all over the place the last few days on who is to go where and how." So many were going to Rome that Gross worried aloud whether the United States had enough local currency on hand in Italy to take care of all the junketing Congressmen.

"I understand," Smith reassured him, "we have a bundle over there." He added piously that the House Rules Committee, which he then headed (he was defeated in the 1966 Virginia primary by a less creaky candidate), had been "very niggardly about granting" authorization for overseas travel. But Congressmen by the dozens easily got around Smith to inspect everything from post offices in Paris to water control in the Swiss Alps. Those who went to Paris to look at the Post Office were Congressmen Robert Corbet (R-Pa.), Dominick Daniels (D-N.J.), Edward Derwinski (R-Ill.), Thaddeus Dulski (D-N.Y.), William Green (D-Pa.), James Hanley (D-N.Y.), Albert Johnson (R-Pa.), James Morrison D-La.), and Arnold Olsen, (D-Mont.). To assist them in studying the mails from Bern to Berlin, they thoughtfully brought along their wives. Four Congressmen, accompanied by wives, visited the Swiss watersheds. They were Representatives William Cramer (R-Fla.), George Fallon (D-Md.), Robert Jones (D-Ala.), and John Kunkel (R-Pa.). They traveled by way of the Mediterranean aboard the S. S. Independence, a leisurely cruise made in the name of the House Public Works Committee.

Most junketeers, preferring to travel far and fast, chose jet transportation. Grumped Gross: "I have been hearing criticism that the government is not providing big enough and fast enough jets to get the junketeers over to Ouagandougou or wherever they are headed. They are also complaining that they have to take smaller planes to get to certain countries—which planes, they say, are not comfortable enough."

Congressional groups usually rate a special military plane, complete with Air Force stewards to serve meals and handle luggage, an escort officer to smooth out travel arrangements, and sometimes even a doctor to minister to aches and pains. Wives, children and assorted relatives are common free riders on these planes.

Legislators traveling alone often get free trips on Air Force planes or Navy ships going their way. They are supposed to travel on a space-available basis, but it's a bold transportation officer who gives a GI priority over a Congressman. Indeed, there isn't a general so bold as to turn down a Congressman of the influence of House Armed Services Chairman L. Mendel Rivers (D-S.C.), who has no trouble getting Air Force planes to fly him wherever he wants to go. While a Boeing 707 was being prepared for take-off at Andrews Air Force Base, the pilot told a friend of mine that he was heading for Madrid to bring Rivers home. The great jet, according to the pilot, was empty.

Traveling lawmakers, once abroad, are able to take all sorts of advantage of a peculiar money deal. Many countries, being short of dollars, are allowed by law to pay for U. S. supplies in their own currencies. In 1953 Congress slipped through a special amendment giving members free access to "counterpart funds," as this money is called, to pay their overseas expenses. These are the funds, kept in Special Account

No. 19FT561, that Senator Ellender used to finance his African safari. For a glorious decade, Congressmen on the go could stuff their pockets with counterpart funds, no accounting asked and none given except for vague totals. Abuses became so flagrant, however, that some restrictions were imposed.

Counterpart funds have been used to finance lavish entertainment, to purchase expensive gifts, even to redeem for U.S. dollars. Representative Victor Wickersham (D-Okla.) loaded up on fancy merchandise in Europe, then set up shop in his Congressional office to sell the goods to House employees at a profit. Senator Tom Dodd (D-Conn.) wound up a European vacation with a paper sack stuffed with counterpart currency. After he checked into the Paris airport for the return flight, an aide who was remaining behind started to leave with the sack of money. "What are you going to do with that?" Dodd demanded. The aide said he intended to return the money to the American Embassy. "Never mind returning anything," blustered Dodd. He expropriated the sack and spent its contents at the nearest airport gift shop.

But it was the well-publicized escapades of Representative Adam Clayton Powell (D-N.Y.) that brought the crackdown on counterpart spending. The Harlem globetrotter took off for Europe in September, 1962, with two glamorous secretaries to make a study, he said, "of employment opportunities for European women." Drew Pearson discovered that Powell had asked the State Department to secure for his swinging party tickets to the Vienna Film Festival, reservations at swank European night clubs, and tickets to the best plays in London. To top it off, he arranged a six-day cruise of the Aegean Sea with a leisurely side tour to the Greek Islands. Drew's story, followed by my Parade article on Congressional cheating in March, 1963, created such an uproar that the House stripped Powell of most of his travel money and Congress clamped stricter controls on counterpart funds.

The chastised Powell, a delegate to an international labor conference at Geneva in June, 1963, found himself limited to the paltry $22 per diem that ordinary government employees draw. This was scarcely enough to pay for his hotel room, let alone permit him to live overseas in the style to which he had become accustomed. Urgently, he cabled the State Department, pleading for more money; but he was obliged to dig into his own jeans to pay even his legitimate expenses. Before too much sympathy is lavished on poor Powell, however, it should be recorded that he managed to wangle enough per diem to take six vacations at the taxpayers' expense during the winter of 1964-65. He followed the sun from Puerto Rico to Hawaii and back. Later he stayed in Acapulco so long that he caught more marlins than any other sports fisherman that season. The taxpayers saved some money at least on his sixth vacation. He spent several days cruising around the Caribbean with a pretty secretary aboard the Teamster Union's yacht, the Sea Rose. To no one's particular surprise, since he is chairman of the House Labor Committee with jurisdiction over labor legislation, the Teamsters billed neither Powell nor the taxpayers for the use of their boat.

Bad publicity restrains some legislators on the loose overseas. The average Congressional traveler is more likely nowadays to head for the Quai d'Orsay than the Folies-Bergere. But the restrictions on counterpart funds hasn't noticeably reduced Congressional globe-trotting. With a limit of $50 per diem, most junketeers have forsaken counterpart money as the best means for financing their trips. *It has become the custom for Congressional committees to hit up the taxpayers each year for supplemental expense money, ranging from* $50,000 *to* $200,000 *apiece.* Many a junket is now financed out of this. Buried in the small print of the federal budget are also a number of confidential funds controlled by committee chairmen. Insiders tell me, for example, that Congressman John Rooney (D-N.Y.), chairman of a House Appropriations subcommittee, makes use of this money to take at least one unadvertised trip abroad each year.

But the biggest boodle, available for Congressional sightseeing, now comes straight out of executive department funds. Government agencies court the Congressmen who have jurisdiction over their legislation by taking them on all-expense-paid tours. The breakdown of how much is spent for this sort of clandestine Congressional travel is more closely guarded than our nuclear secrets. First, I tried the State Department, which is supposed to have the biggest fund for entertaining Congressmen *carte blanche.*

"I am not aware of such a fund," said one spokesman.

"I think there is a fund for emergencies but this is a diplomatic fund," said another.

"Ask the Treasury Department," suggested a third.

"That's the State Department's baby, talk to them," said the Treasury man.

"I tried to find out myself," responded another State Department employee, "but I was told I would be better off not asking any questions."

A confidential contact inside the State Department, glancing furtively to make sure no one was listening, confided: "The Pentagon is probably the all-time abuser with its unlimited resources and willingness to dip into them."

Through my Pentagon pipelines, I learned that the armed forces indeed seek to win friends and influence votes by taking Congressmen on joy rides (which they prefer to call "inspection trips") about the world. Deluxe travel service is provided out of Defense Department funds which I could find nowhere recorded. Secretary of Defense Robert McNamara, ever the watchdog over defense dollars, has set up a confidential point system to restrict this red-carpet travel to Congressmen who count. Each fiscal year he allots 300 points apiece to the Secretaries of the Army, Navy and Air Force. For each day that a Congressman is a military guest, one point is charged against the Secretary whose service invited him. Once the 300 points are used up, no more Congressmen are permitted to go on junkets. McNamara has also ruled that no freshman member of Congress can be invited on military junkets, presumably on the theory that freshmen aren't important enough to waste points on.

The Army, which operates the Panama Canal Zone Company, also offers a bargain, two-week cruise to sunny Panama for Congressmen. The government-owned S. S. Cristobal —fully equipped with a swimming pool, promenade deck, and well-stocked bar—sails between New Orleans and the Canal Zone. Almost any Congressman can take the free cruise for the asking and need pay only $150 round-trip for each extra guest. The ordinary citizen pays more than double that amount.

Reserve officers who are members of Congress customarily serve their active duty each year inspecting world pleasure spots, enduring the rigors of such outposts as Paris, Rome, Honolulu and Hong King. Senator Strom Thurmond (R-S.C.) who doubles as a Major General in the Army reserves, usually organizes two trips each year, so his Congressional "troops" can take their choice of Europe or Asia. When McNamara suggested abolishing the Army Ready Reserves, there were roars of outrage from the reservists on Capitol Hill. The loudest came from Thurmond, the Senate's most outspoken champion of states' rights, who opposes taking Army reservists out of federal control and putting them in the National Guard under state control.

Thurmond is a conservative Republican. His second in command of the Congressional reserve unit, Senator Ralph Yarborough (D-Tex.), is a liberal Democrat. They agree on hardly anything. Yarborough, a reserve colonel, has been particularly wary of his commanding officer ever since General Thurmond wrestled him to the floor in a Senate corridor in 1964. But both these soldier-solons forgot past differences and joined in a noisy duet, blasting McNamara for trying to break up their cozy Capitol Hill corps.

It needs to be borne in mind that many traveling Congressmen work hard overseas. Their junkets sometimes make sound studies and produce valuable results. In the world outside, where two-thirds of the U.S. budget is being spent, Congressional committees have uncovered and remedied waste and bumbling. They have learned firsthand of needed reforms and have written appropriate legislation. They have talked directly to the people of the world. Such trips, with split-second schedules and heavy work loads, are anything but glamorous.

So the American taxpayers pay their money and take—not their choice, but potluck as to whether junkets are worthwhile. Or as one legislator has put it: "Congressional visits are like muskmelons. The good ones are very good, and some are not so good."

Chester County ASCS Office
Henderson, Tennessee
February 21, 1966

Dear Mr. Farmer:

Do you want to work all summer while your neighbor is fishing? If not rent your corn and cotton to the Government.

Final date for signing up in the Feed Grain and Cotton Programs is April 1, 1966. So hurry.

Sincerely yours,

R. L. Plunk, Office Mgr.

Apparently laziness is now being encouraged officially—judging by the above postcard sent to farmers of Chester County, Tennessee, by a field agent of the Agriculture Department.

6

INSIDE THE WHITE HOUSE

Not since slavery was abolished has the nation known a tougher taskmaster than Lyndon B. Johnson. He drives his staff 12 to 16 hours a day, scourges them with a whiplash tongue, intrudes on their private lives without apology, demands their complete loyalty and utmost devotion. Indeed, there is only one man outside his staff whom he pushes harder, and that man is Lyndon B. Johnson. But if the President is a slave driver, he is a benevolent one. For he also overwhelms his staff with warmth, overpowers them with generosity, and treats them with a tenderness that is positively paternal. He invites them for intimate swims and repasts, includes them at White House parties, and flies them down to the LBJ Ranch for homey weekends. And he is perfectly capable of crying genuine tears over their sorrows.

In his pursuit of greatness, however, President Johnson spares no one. *He has a Caesar-sized complex which brooks no insubordination.* Behind his desk, he scribbles terse commands on staff papers or barks orders into the ozone, pushing buttons to direct his voice to the right assistants. Out of the air will come back subservient replies, usually: "Yes, Mr. President." He speaks to his subordinates like a Texan talking to a Rhode Islander. Usually, his voice is quiet, but he can raise it to a terrible crescendo when the volcano inside him is disturbed. Then he will berate anyone within bomb burst of his voice, letting the epithets and accusations fly like shrapnel. Some of his derogatory expressions would singe innocent ears. He keeps the doors to his oval sanctuary and outer offices closed — contrary to the late President Kennedy's open-door policy—less to protect his privacy than to provide insulation for his outbursts.

Understandably, his aides are more than a little gun shy of his voice. Yet the President denies most plaintively that he intimidates them. He has complained to newsmen: "Now won't you all quit writing these stories, 'Won't anybody say no to LBJ,' because I have more people running around here saying no." It is true that he seeks their opinions and encourages their dissents. He will listen to any suggestion that might help achieve a consensus. *But once he has made up his mind, consensus means the LBJ way. For a while, until it caused some embarrassing publicity, he even kept his staff under surveillance.* White House switchboard operators logged every phone call, and chauffeurs copied down every place staff aides were driven. Though these telephone and limousine checks were not initiated to enforce economy, as spokesman Bill Moyers blandly suggested, neither was the espionage system established for any sordid purpose. The President didn't mean to snoop on his aides, say insiders; he merely wanted to watch benevolently over their shoulders.

He has an insatiable craving for information, for knowing everything that's going on. No previous President, for example, ever took FBI reports to bed with him.

He likes to control all White House activity down to the most trivial detail. He decides personally how many chauffeurs should be on duty, who can use which limousines, who is entitled to White House mess and ground privileges, etc. And he is never content to entrust an assignment to an aide without instructing him precisely who to see, what to say, and how to respond. The President personally makes military and diplomatic decisions that past Presidents have left to officers and diplomats in the field. *He doesn't merely lay down the military policy in Vietnam, for example; he personally decides which targets should be hit in North Vietnam. "They don't bomb an outhouse without my approval," he once boasted happily to me.*

He is equally involved in domestic details. He passes on all changes in farm price supports, a matter that used to be trusted to the Agriculture Department. Every major price increase —aluminum, cars, coal, copper, steel—has found LBJ in the middle, directing how to combat it. Sometimes the most obscure labor dispute will have him reaching for the phone to tell Assistant Labor Secretary James J. Reynolds what to do about it. The President has been known to make as many as 30 phone calls to key Congressmen to help his legislative chief, Postmaster General Lawrence O'Brien, push a bill through Congress. Usually, O'Brien gives him a list of legislators on the fence. "The President acts like Larry O'Brien's assistant," says one White House aide.

The President's immediate staff includes 290 workers shoehorned into the White House west wing. Across the parking lot in the old, rococo Executive Office Building are another 1,365 workers. The lights in both buildings burn late into the night, despite the President's penchant for electrical economy. *It is not uncommon for him to poke his head into random offices late at night.* If he finds people working at 10 p.m., say, he will smile with satisfaction or make an approving comment. It seldom occurs to him to apologize for keeping them away from their families. Indeed, when family obligations interrupted the output of a couple of staff members, he grumbled to Vice President Humphrey: "What I need are more bachelors."

Aides know instinctively, when the phone rings at 7 a.m., that it must be the President. They aren't safe from his phone calls even while commuting; he makes frequent use of the two-way radios in White House limousines. And they have learned not to accept luncheon appointments outside the White House. "They don't sit around at Paul Young's drinking whiskey," says LBJ approvingly. The subordinate who isn't immediately available when the President phones is sure to hear about it from him. Budget Director Kermit Gordon made the mistake, for instance, of attending

POST OFFICE DEPARTMENT

May 10, 1966

MEMORANDUM TO THE PRESIDENT

SUBJECT: Principal Decisions, Projects and Developments

Report #283

1. UNSEALED LETTER OF JACK ANDERSON

Columnist Jack Anderson reported on April 23 that a letter he had sent to Hartford, Connecticut, arrived with a notation: "Received unsealed at Washington, D. C." The large envelope contained matters pertaining to Senator Dodd, Anderson said. An investigation by Postal Inspectors revealed that the letter had apparently been poorly sealed, although Anderson's secretary denied this. After the investigation, Anderson said he believed the FBI opened his mail. Anderson thinks the letter was taken from a collection sack by FBI agents after it was deposited by his secretary in the lobby of the office building at 1612 K Street, N. W.

5. MAIL SERVICE TO VIET NAM (See Reports #243, 244, 245, 246, 247, 251, 253, 259, 260, 261, 264, 266 & 273)

In April there were 61 complaints of delays in delivery of mail to servicemen in Viet Nam, compared with 125 last January. There has been a steady decline in complaints each month. Improvement is attributed to airlifting of first-class letter mail and increases in number of APO's in Viet Nam.

7. 789 UNIFORM ALLOWANCE INFRACTIONS (See Report #259)

A total of 789 instances involving employee infractions in the uniform allowance reimbursement program were reported to the Senate Post Office and Civil Service Committee in response to a request from Senator Milward L. Simpson. The majority of cases involved purchase of "dualiners" for jackets and non-uniform shoes. Disciplinary actions to date have ranged from letters of reprimand to suspensions, ranging from 2 to 30 days. Some actions are still pending.

Lawrence F. O'Brien

Lawrence F. O'Brien
Postmaster General

Extracts from a memo to President Johnson from the Postmaster General. The President insists on getting details of this sort; he feels he has to know about everything going on throughout the government.

a concert one evening when the President tried to reach him. Next morning, LBJ greeted Gordon with a sarcastic: "Well, playboy, did you have a good time last night?"

Lyndon Johnson is a man of enormous vitality. He puts in longer hours, gives more dogged service than anyone in government. But he is inclined to forget that his subordinates are normal men who begin to flag after their energy is spent, who don't have servants to mow their lawns, and walk their dogs, who often work late into the night to keep up with their demanding boss. They speak privately of a "deep gap." Undersecretary of State Ball, after a series of exhausting conferences in Europe, arrived back in Washington barely in time to keep a speaking date at the Federal City Club. "What this country needs," he told his audience wearily, "is a good night's sleep." When he finally reached home and prepared to take his own advice, he was summoned to the White House to report to the President on the European conferences. Not until 3 a.m. was he allowed mercifully to go to bed. Four hours later, he was up again getting ready to testify before Congress at 9 a.m.

The President likes to deal with his aides separately, has held few staff meetings since he became President. Under his alternate lash and caress, the staff turns out a prodigious amount of work. They sift and digest the bulky reports that come in from government agencies, then summarize them in short, punchy, no-words-wasted memos. At the bottom, they usually write "Approved" and "Disapproved" with a space opposite each word for him to check his verdict. But he insists on having on his desk not only the summary but the whole report. He manages to plow through most material, scribbling instructions in the margins. He also scrawls notes to himself as he talks on the telephone.

Curiously, those closest to the President take the most abuse from him. "It's a mark of intimacy to be cussed out by him," explains an aide. By this index, assistants Marvin Watson and Jake Jacobsen are on the closest terms with the President.

While the rumpled George Reedy was press secretary, he was fried on the LBJ pan daily. The President seemed to blame him personally for every unfavorable reference that slipped into the newspapers. After Reedy's daily press briefings, LBJ would read the transcript with hot eyes, then berate Reedy for the slightest slip. His angriest outbursts were often over the most trivial matters. Once he was expecting to read a message before the television cameras. For technical reasons, the White House television room couldn't be used that day, so Reedy arranged the filming in the cabinet room. When the President was told about the switch, he never gave Reedy a chance to explain. "You stupid . . . ! ! !" exploded Johnson. "Why do we spend money on a television room if we're not going to use it?" Ferociously, he ordered Reedy to rearrange the session in the television room. Not until he ran out of steam and Reedy had departed wordlessly did the President learn that the television room equipment was out of order. Without apology, he stomped off to the cabinet room.

George Reedy's highly capable successor, Bill Moyers, receives somewhat gentler treatment. The placid personality of this ordained Baptist preacher seems to have had a subduing effect on the President. Moyers consoles other aides by reminding them softly: "The President has great faults, but he also has great virtues." The bland Moyers manages also to placate the press by keeping his words soft and sweet ("because I never know when I'll have to eat them") and by refusing to take himself too seriously. "Not since Moses scribbled on a slab of granite while the Almighty dictated," Moyers once said of his job, "has the role of amanuensis been accorded so exalted a position in the society of men."

Dapper and diminutive Jack Valenti, Johnson's favorite whipping boy until he became the head of the Motion Picture Association at $150,000 a year, never quite knew when he might step into a sudden presidential windstorm. Once he was roundly berated over a malfunctioning door knob. Another time the President barged into Valenti's office and found him on the phone. *"For Chrissake," belowed the President, "do you spend all day on the phone?"* Again, when Valenti took three minutes to respond to a presidential summons, Johnson shouted in front of visitors: "Where the hell've you been?" Valenti said that he had stepped out a moment for coffee. "How many times have I got to tell you," thundered the President, "not to leave your office without telling me where you're going?"

LBJ's humor can be as scathing as his wrath. Once Valenti slipped into a cabinet meeting to whisper a message to the President, who elaborately halted the meeting, turned toward Valenti, and, in front of the entire cabinet, proclaimed jovially: *"You look like a man who had just cheated on his wife."* The flustered aide retreated in embarrassed confusion. Yet more often, the President treated Valenti with all the warmth and affection a father might show for a son. He frequently invited Valenti and his wife, Mary Margaret, to the White House for intimate family dinners. Occasionally he still drops by their home to romp with their four-year-old daughter, Courtney.

The President is more reserved with aides who are not close to him personally. There is mutual respect but little love, for example, between Johnson and the few Kennedy holdovers still around. All the while he was Vice President, they could never seem to get on the same wave length. He felt as if they looked upon him with disdain, as if they viewed him through invisible monocles. More than once, he complained that they were running him down in what they told newsmen. They, in turn, never quite forgot how Johnson had referred to Kennedy condescendingly as "young Jack" and had tried to make an issue of his health during

Office of the White House Press Secretary

Presidents and Recessions Since 1837

Administration	Term	Recession began	Months of recession during term
Buchanan	3/57 - 3/61	6/57 10/60	23
Lincoln I	3/61 - 3/65	--	3
Lincoln II Johnson	3/65 - 3/69	4/65	32
Grant I	3/69 - 3/73	6/69	18
Grant II	3/73 - 3/77	10/73	41
Hayes	3/77 - 3/81	--	24
Garfield Arthur	3/81 - 3/85	3/82	36
Cleveland I	3/85 - 3/89	3/87	15
Harrison	3/89 - 3/93	7/90 1/93	12
Cleveland II	3/93 - 3/97	12/95	30
McKinley I	3/97 - 3/01	6/99	21
McKinley II Roosevelt I	3/01 - 3/05	9/02	23
Roosevelt II	3/05 - 3/09	5/07	13
Taft	3/09 - 3/13	1/10 1/13	26
Wilson I	3/13 - 3/17	--	21
Wilson II	3/17 - 3/21	8/18 1/20	21
Harding Coolidge I	3/21 - 3/25	5/23	18
Coolidge II	3/25 - 3/29	10/26	13
Hoover	3/29 - 3/33	8/29	43
Roosevelt I	3/33 - 3/37	--	--
Roosevelt II	3/37 - 1/41	5/37	13
Roosevelt III	1/41 - 1/45	--	--
Roosevelt IV Truman I	1/45 - 1/49	2/45 11/48	10
Truman II	1/49 - 1/53	--	9
Eisenhower I	1/53 - 1/57	7/53	13
Eisenhower II	1/57 - 1/61	7/57 5/60	17
Kennedy Johnson	1/61 - 1/65	--	1

Propaganda by comparison — an unusual White House press release playing up President Johnson as the only chief executive whose administration hasn't had a recession. It may turn out to be somewhat premature.

the rivalry for the Democratic presidential nomination in 1960.

When Johnson and Kennedy teamed up, they regarded one another with cold political eyes. Both confessed private doubts about the partnership. *Certainly, of all political marriages solemnized before the altar of expediency, none seemed less likely to succeed.* For eight years Johnson had been Kennedy's Senate leader; Kennedy had been a mere back-bench Senator. Even more pronounced was the difference in personality. *It would have been hard to find two men more opposite: the Irish Catholic intellectual, laconic, crisp, ruled by New England reserve; the Southern Protestant politician, loquacious, homespun, filled with Texan flamboyance.* Washington sophisticates wondered how Johnson, who for so long had generaled the Democratic ranks, would work under one of his spear carriers. Some were convinced that Johnson's chemistry simply wouldn't allow him to sit still while another led.

At first the new Vice President brooded quite a bit over his subordinate spot on the totem pole. He generally withheld his advice at policy meetings, speaking only when spoken to. Kennedy expected Johnson to be headstrong, found him humble and respectful instead. This took considerable effort on the part of the vain and vibrant Johnson who nevertheless managed to walk not only with but a step behind Kennedy. However, a bond developed between these two disparate men that never extended to the Kennedy staff, most of them made in his image.

Once in the White House, Johnson tried to thaw this New England chill by inviting them, as he put it, "to break bread" with him. They were asked separately, along with their wives, to join him for what most remember as a remarkably intimate tete-a-tete. Of all the Kennedy holdovers, the President became closest to Larry O'Brien, the present Postmaster-General. Once LBJ scolded him gently for waiting until the next morn-

DEMOCRATIC NATIONAL COMMITTEE
1730 K STREET, N.W.
WASHINGTON, D. C. 20006

TELEPHONE
FEDERAL 3-8750

Oct. 26, 1964

MEMORANDUM

To: Speech Writers

From: Jerry Werksman

As you are well aware the recent major international developements call for special care in speeches and informal remarks.

It is important, in connection with the Soviet Union, that we not inadvertently signal anything which might prejudice our future relationships with the new Soviet leaders or lead them to assume foreign policy moves we are not ready to undertake.

The detonation of the nuclear device in Communist China will naturally come up in speeches and in informal remarks on foreign policy and the world situation in general. We should be careful not to prejudice any future moves we might wish to take with respect to China.

To guard against both these dangers it has been suggested that speech writers adhere closely to the line laid down in the President's speech pn Sunday, October 18. A copy of that speech is herein enclosed.

Note that speech writers are pressed to adhere to LBJ line.

ing to phone in the results of a backroom legislative knockdown that lasted most of the night. *"Next time wake me up," said the President. "I want to bleed with you."*

Most of the Kennedy crowd has never warmed up to LBJ; he has treated them, in turn, with more coolness and courtesy than he accords his intimates. This hasn't stopped him from snapping at them, however, when he felt they were out of line. The crisp MacGeorge Bundy, accustomed to barging in on President Kennedy, was quickly broken of the habit by President Johnson. Once Bundy had an urgent cable to show the President and poked his head in the oval office while Johnson was conferring with Ambassador Henry Cabot Lodge. *"Goddamit, Bundy," sizzled the President, "I've told you that when I want you, I'll call you."*

Johnson always defends his subordinates in public, heaping on the praise in Texas hyperbole. *But he often cuts them up in the privacy of his White House office.* Only Defense Secretary Robert McNamara and State Secetary Dean Rusk, the two cabinet members he admires most, seem to have been spared the sharp slash of his tongue. He has made belittling remarks about all the others, often in colorful language. *"John Connor," he once said of his Commerce Secretary, "couldn't find his ass with both hands."* Even Vice President Hubert Humphrey has come in for his share of presidential digs. Unfortunately, the snide remarks have a habit of getting back to the victims, which doesn't endear him to them.

Though he may stab them in the back with his tongue, he also doesn't hesitate to bawl them out to their faces when his dander is up. He is more considerate of the girls in his office only in the choice of the language he uses to rebuke them. He has driven them to tears more than once, but he has also treated them with rare thoughtfulness. He understood, for example, how thrilled his secretaries would be to meet Britain's Princess Margaret. So he invited them to the White House dinner in her honor, the most glittering social event of the year. Let anyone on his staff get sick, and he not only sends flowers but takes out time from world affairs to place a solicitous phone call. Other times, he may impulsively invite a staff member in, pull out a drawer full of gifts, and invite him to help himself.

One aide describes the President as "multi-phrenic," a man of many personalities crowded into one complex being. *He can be domineering, demanding, callous, cantankerous, impatient, vain, and shortsighted. He can also be demeaning, compassionate, sensitive, humble, thoughtful, and foresighted.* Above all, he is unpredictable, a man of many moods. Restless, he often changes his schedule abruptly. With tongue in cheek, Moyers once told newsmen that the President had telephoned him about plans for a trip to Honolulu. "Fine, Mr. President, I'll come over and talk to you about it," said Moyers. "Where are you?" Replied the President: "Over Los Angeles."

LBJ primps and preens before appearing in public and tries always to turn his best side toward the cameras. The money he saves on electricity is spent many times over on presidential photography. Three full-time photographers take turns traipsing after him, camera at the ready, to record every presidential move. White House files are crammed with tens of thousands of glossy photographs of LBJ in every possible pose. He mails out copies, appropriately inscribed, to everyone who wanders near enough to appear in the same camera finder with him.

The President keeps telling cameramen to feature his left profile; the right side of his face, like the hidden side of the moon, is seldom seen. He can get exasperated easily with press photographers who sneak up on his right side or explode flash bulbs while he is delivering a speech. The photographers didn't follow his directions, for example, while he was giving an informal talk in the White House garden to the State Department's Foreign Service graduates. LBJ was so aggravated that he walked off, after his remarks, waving his arms wildly in a show of hopeless frustration.

For his television appearances, President Johnson has experimented fussily with lighting, prompting devices, facial make-up, and contact lenses. (He finally settled on conventional eyeglasses with transparent plastic rims, carefully chosen for their TV appeal). Early in 1966 he also abandoned the transparent prompters which flashed his text on one-way mirrors to his left and right. At the suggestion of Robert Kintner, former president of the National Broadcasting Company who came to work for him, LBJ began reading his speeches from manuscripts typed in large letters. Kintner convinced him it made him appear more relaxed and natural.

From time to time, the President has sought to refurbish his image by brazenly seducing the press. He has passed out presents to correspondents, invited the favored to White House extravaganzas, taken others on high-speed joyrides in his Lincoln Continental and gay parties aboard the presidential launch. One joyride with some lovely ladies of the press wound up on the front pages; the stories told how LBJ had wheeled his Continental around the Texas range at 90 miles per hour with one hand, sipping beer with the other. Mourned Johnson afterward: "Everybody is going to walk at the LBJ ranch from now on, and I am going to do what Lady Bird tells me, and we are going to make everybody drink nothing but pure rain water or Pepsi-Cola."

Nothing nettles the President more than stories comparing him unfavorably with the late John F. Kennedy. During one White House huddle with a group of Senators, Johnson blurted bitterly: "They say Jack Kennedy had style, but I'm the one who gets the bills passed." Another time, he summoned the government's top press agents to the White House and berated them for failing to build him up to hero dimensions. "You're not getting my picture on the front page the way you did Kennedy's," he grumped.

The government even uses the comics to peddle its propaganda, as illustrated by this extract from a comic book entitled "Superman's Mission for President Kennedy." According to the publisher, this comic book was originally "prepared in close cooperation" with President Kennedy and issued because "President Johnson wanted it published."

Lyndon Johnson's massive ego is easily bruised. Criticism is hard enough for him to take, but ridicule he can't stand. He saw nothing at all funny, for example, in a parody prepared by Robert Stapp, assistant to Congressman Roy McVicker (D-Colo.), for the private amusement of freshmen Congressmen. Rising solemnly at a gathering of their 89th Club (named for the 89th Congress), Stapp read from *St. Lyndon's Epistle to the 89th Congress:*

"Then the voters were herded into the polling places to be counted. And, lo, 61.3 percent bore the brand of Elby Jay.

"Then the faithful Democrats rejoiced. And they swarmed into the headquarters holding aloft their precinct tabulations and crying out in a loud voice, 'See how I delivered my district. There is no President but Elby Jay, and my cousin Herman is his postmaster.'

"Then, when the results were confirmed, and the computers had ceased to compute, and David had said goodnight to Chet, the politicians started forth on their pilgrimage to the Perdenales — to receive the blessings of the chief politician and to pluck the sacred fruit from the tree of patronage.

"But when they were ushered into the presence of Elby Jay, they found him sitting disconsolately on a mound of morning papers. And the music was stilled. And no Bird sang. And the mournful howl of the beagle was heard in the land.

"Then the politicians drew near and questioned him, saying: 'Wherefore art thou sad? Thou has overwhelmed thine enemies — yea, even unto the 61 point 3 percentile.'

"But Elby Jay answered them, saying: 'But what of the 38 point 7? Who among you having lost a sheep from his flock, does not leave the 99 and go in search of the one that is lost?'

"Then Elby Jay spoke in a voice of thunder, saying: 'I shall build a Great Society in which there will be no percentages, no poverty, no razor burn. Where the humblest will have the same opportunities as Bobby Baker.'

"But the politicians murmured against him, for they feared that if all partook, the pork barrel would soon be empty.

"Then Elby Jay, knowing their thoughts, spoke to them through his Council of Economic Advisers, saying: 'Oh ye of little faith, did he not cause the NAM to lie down with the CIO-AFL? Did he not resurrect medicare after the physicians had pronounced it dead? All these miracles has he performed. Yet still you doubt.'

"Come let us reason together. Or else . . ."

President Johnson enjoys hugely the powers and privileges of his office. He keeps his aides, servants and bodyguards scrambling to satisfy his wants and whims. He demands an oversized bed, suitable for containing his six-foot-four-inch frame, wherever he alights for the night. He also insists upon keeping plenty of Scotch whiskey handy for liquid emergencies. As Vice President, he once sent a Navy plane all the way from Taipei to Hong Kong for a case of Scotch.

The President puts in about two working days every 24 hours. The first starts at 6:30 a.m., the second at 5:30 p.m., with an hour's nap in between. *He sometimes takes 100 phone calls a day on instruments strategically scattered wherever he may light — in the bathrooms, at poolside, near his hammock outside the LBJ ranchhouse.* He holds animated discussions throughout the day with visitors who stream through his oval officc, stroll with him on the White House green, swim in the nude with him in his private pool. More than once he has arranged for Vice President Humphrey to join him for a haircut, so they could make the most of the time it took for them to get trimmed and pomaded. *The President is on the go not merely from dawn to dark but, in times of crisis, from dawn til dawn.* He works at such a terrific pace that Lady Bird sometimes pins a warning note on his pillow.

Before he dozes off at night, he plunges through a pile of

papers, boning up on problems, scribbling instructions to subordinates, making decisions that affect the lives of all Americans. He calls this his "night reading"—weighty bedtime stories which a White House aide has estimated at more than 100,000 words a week.

For that matter, the President's day reading is enough to make most men dizzy. He begins with the *Washington Post* and *Baltimore Sun,* picking out stories that interest him, pausing over the editorials, checking what columnists have to say. He scans other papers—including the *New York Times, Philadelphia Inquirer, Christian Science Monitor,* and *Washington Star* — less thoroughly. Frequently during the day he strides the 10 feet from his desk to the two white cabinets which contain the AP and UPI news tickers, their clattering muted by rubber matting. He also reads dozens of urgent documents, intelligence reports, and staff memos that demand his immediate attention.

There can be no eight-hour day for the President, no laying aside the awesome responsibilities, no setting down the overwhelming burdens. Only he can unsheath our nuclear missiles. A chance remark from him could start an economic down-slide. He sits at the center of government with a thousand hands, pulling strings, controlling movements, touching everything. He directs the preparation of figures he is expected to understand in detail. He conducts the Vietnam war, sets foreign policy, guides legislation, makes domestic decision, controls the government news output, plans political strategy.

Archaic laws and traditions also impose upon him a thousand and one minor chores, many of them requiring his personal signature. He is supposed to be the nation's chief greeter, civic pitchman, and father-confessor. This man with the finger on the nuclear button is also expected to press the button that lights the national Christmas tree. He is supposed to take time out from any but the most pressing crises to toss

CONFIDENTIAL
DEPARTMENT OF THE AIR FORCE
WASHINGTON

NOTED BY THE SECRETARY OF THE AIR FORCE

OFFICE OF THE SECRETARY

24 JAN 1964

MEMORANDUM FOR THE SECRETARY OF THE AIR FORCE

I feel you should be aware of some of the circumstances surrounding the military service of former Major Don B. Reynolds, who testified before the Senate Rules Committee in the Bobby Baker case day before yesterday. According to Reynolds' testimony, he bought an expensive Hi-Fi set and had it shipped to then Senator Lyndon B. Johnson, at Baker's request, shortly after $100,000 of insurance on Mr. Johnson's life was purchased through his agency in 1957. During a press conference yesterday, the President considered it sufficiently important to speak about the gift of a "stereo" set which he said had been given to him and his wife by an employee -- Mr. Baker.

The testimony showed that Reynolds, a former intelligence officer in the Air Force, had received an honorable discharge but that he was not fully aware of all the circumstances involved. He admitted he had had the assistance of former Senator McCarran and stated he thought his problem started because of his appearance before a Senate committee in 1953 concerning security matters in the State and Defense Departments, where it was felt he had given classified information to a Senatorial committee. He said his case was similar to that of Otto Otepka, who was fired from the State Department last November after he was accused of passing information to a Senate committee.

According to available Air Force records, Reynolds was dropped by the U.S. Military Academy in 1938 and again in 1940 because of academic deficiencies. He was commissioned in the U.S. Army Reserve in 1941. Later, while on duty with the Air Force in the Directorate of Intelligence in 1952, he made a false report to the FBI which resulted in an extensive and expensive investigation. The investigation backfired on him and disclosed that while serving as an official of the State Department during 1946-1949 in Germany and Austria, he had committed adultery, promiscuously, and used his official position to obtain intimate relations with attractive visa applicants. He reportedly had engaged in "black market" sales of various scarce items with many individuals, including Russian military officers. Additional derogatory information was disclosed, including his falsification of official Air Force documents and his threat of deportation to two German immigrants, after his return to the United States, because of their failure to respond to his personal requests.

This confidential memorandum about Don B. Reynolds, who figured prominently in the Bobby Baker case, sought to undermine the credibility of his charges about private transactions by Lyndon B. Johnson

CONFIDENTIAL

Charges were initiated under the Air Force security regulation, AFR 35-62, in July 1953, and they were subsequently approved but not issued. Drew Pearson reported in July 1953 that Air Force Major Don Reynolds, a former State Department official, had been a key witness before the Senate Judiciary Committee and that he had made charges that the State Department staff which screened immigrants overseas was loaded with communists, sex deviates and jews. Another newspaper account stated that in order to avoid official complications with the Air Force, Senator McCarran had requested the issuance of a subpoena to require the appearance of Major Reynolds before the Senate Judiciary Committee.

In the meantime, Major Reynolds gained admittance to Walter Reed Hospital with a complaint of kidney trouble and hypertension. A Physical Evaluation Board found that he had a 30% disability and recommended his retirement. Subsequently, the Physical Review Council found Major Reynolds physically fit and recommended his return to duty. Former Senator McCarran and other Congressional leaders interceded directly with top Air Force officials, including Secretary Talbott and General Thomas White, on Reynolds' behalf. The Secretary approved the Board's findings. According to the records, Major Reynolds then exerted intense political pressure. At the time, Major Reynolds was eligible normally for separation under the then current RIF policy, as an excess officer.

Finally, following an inquiry from a Congressman to then Assistant Secretary White concerning the willingness of the Air Force to accept an unqualified resignation, Major Reynolds voluntarily submitted his request for separation under AFR 36-12, on November 19, 1953, with the understanding that, if accepted, his resignation would be under honorable conditions. On recommendation of the Air Force Personnel Board, the Secretary of the Air Force accepted the "unqualified resignation" submitted by Major Reynolds and he was discharged effective November 20, 1953.

BWF

BENJAMIN W. FRIDGE
Special Assistant for Manpower
Personnel & Reserve Forces

Continuation of the Air Force memo about Don B. Reynolds.

out the first baseball of the season and to attend the annual Army-Navy football game. He has to serve as host at banquets for kings, queens, and potentates. And he must also greet pickle queens, poster girls, and Boy Scout delegations. Nobody knows how many hands a President shakes in a year, but LBJ's hands often get as tender from handshaking as his huge left ear must ache from telephoning.

The President's grueling schedule raises an urgent question: *has the world's biggest job become too big for any single person to handle?* Not only is he expected to comprehend the full significance of the thousands of words and figures that pour across his desk each day; not only must he decide immediate issues and cope with each new crisis; but he must also give constant thought to the future and chart a reliable course for the ship of state to follow.

When does the man in the White House find the time to ponder? Vice President Humphrey recently told me he was "staggered by the sheer magnitude of the presidency." *Its physical strain is almost more than one man can endure; the range of responsibilities, some political scientists believe, go beyond one man's power to make decisions.*

George Washington started out with nine executive agencies, employing a grand total of 1,000 federal workers. From this small bureaucratic beginning, the federal government has spread and swollen into a crazy quilt of nearly 2,000 agencies with four million employees (not counting the armed forces. *If the President gave each agency an hour of his time, it would take him three months, going without sleep and neglecting all other duties.*

As late as the turn of the century, Grover Cleveland was able to answer most of his mail in his own longhand. Now the President's mail is delivered by the truckload. LBJ can't even keep up with his Congressional mail, which must be answered chiefly by his staff. Each month the White House also receives more than 3,000 requests, almost all from important people, to see the President. Of these, he takes the time to see about 90.

How does the President bear up under his heavy load of burdens? He has an extraordinary energy that exhausts ordinary men who try to keep up with him. He has also learned to pace himself, to save his mind and strength for crises. "He has the ability of a great athlete to relax — like Joe DiMaggio on the bench between turns at bat," explains an intimate. He has given up trying to solve insolvable problems, and he no longer lets everything ruffle him. When he does fly into a fury, it is usually over a petty annoyance, never a great crisis.

The LBJ technique is to commit to memory the key facts and figures he needs to understand a problem. These become guideposts, which he uses in his discussions with subordinates. More than once he has flabbergasted them by remembering some detail — a guidepost he had picked out of the fine print — that they had forgotten. But if an intelligence dispatch brings news of a sudden crisis, he clears the deck at once for action. He has a unique ability to put first things first, to brush aside the trivia when crucial decisions are needed.

The President manages to thrive on less than five hours of sleep each night. Even this is often interrupted, sometimes by urgent messages, sometimes by his own troubled mind. "I have watched the President a hundred times," an aide told me, "when he is deep in thought, and I have wanted to reach out to help him. But there is that final moment, when all the aides and officers, all the information and intelligence, have done all they can — and the President is alone with his decisions. These are the time when the phrase 'the President's burdens' becomes real, and you wonder if we are asking too much of any mortal man to carry so much so far for so long."

After a tense day, he will shed the pressures by talking with close friends. Sometimes he will chat on the phone for 30 minutes or more about whatever is on his mind. Other times, he will spin yarns about the past. He can tell a story surpassingly well with a rare talent for mimickry. LBJ also finds it relaxing to mix with his visitors. It is the delegations, that call upon him for special favors, which annoy him the most.

Despite the superhuman energy and effort Lyndon Johnson puts into the presidency, he simply doesn't have time to do all that is expected of him. Since he has to spend about 75 percent of his time on foreign affairs, he has too few hours for domestic affairs, legislative planning, guiding political strategy, and taking care of all the other presidential chores.

A cabinet officer confessed to me that he seldom is able to consult with the President. In theory, he can get through to the President any time he feels the need, but in practice, he is expected to clear with White House aides. Rarely do they consider his problems important enough to take up the President's time.

If the presidency is too much even for the likes of Lyndon Johnson, how can future Presidents with normal exhaustion points be expected to hold down the job? The lesser post of Defense Secretary drove James Forrestal to suicide. On May 22, 1949, he plunged to his death from the 16th floor of the Bethesda Naval Hospital where he had been sent for psychiatric treatment. Many observers believe exhaustion and illness adversely affected the decisions of Woodrow Wilson and Franklin D. Roosevelt during their last years in the White House. The conclusion is inescapable. The presidency is too overpowering for any one human being. The most modern country in the world is at the same time one of the most archaic in its political structure. The presidency should be streamlined.

Some have suggested the Vice President should be given a greater share of the load. But he is strictly a stand-in; there are statutory limits to what he can do. "I have no authority," Humphrey told me. "I preside over the Senate, but I can't vote except in the rare case of a tie. I attend White House meetings, but I am like the sixth teat on a cow. The Constitution provides for only one President, and he can delegate only a limited amount of his authority. It will take a Constitutional amendment to make a change."

If President Johnson spends most of his time on foreign problems, he is also most criticized for his handling of them. In reaching decisions, he is still guided by some homely precepts he learned from his father. "A man's judgment is no better than his information," old Sam Johnson used to say. His son now soaks up information, seeking details from many sources.

From early in the morning until after midnight, the President relentlessly pursues facts. He solicits advice from just about everyone — invites them to his office for eyeball-to-eyeball talks, draws them aside at White House receptions, takes constant surveys, scribbling the findings on slips of paper and stuffing them into his pockets. "The President sounds out everyone," says a White House aide. "Then after his list has been exhausted, he comes up with someone else." Sam Johnson also used to counsel his son to seek out specialists. "You don't send a shoemaker to cut the calf's hide," he would say. Ever heedful, the President consults the best specialists he can find.

LBJ also takes pains to seek out the opinions of opponents. He sprang his voting-rights proposal, for example, on a group of Southerners during a weekend at the LBJ Ranch. For three hours he explained his arguments and listened carefully to their objections. Included in the group were Georgia's Governor Carl Sanders and Senator Richard Russell. After hearing them out, the President phoned the White House and ordered his aides to start work on a voting-rights bill.

After the last adviser has been consulted and the last opinion has been noted, the President customarily takes up the final decision with the cabinet, National Security Council or Joint Chiefs of Staff. He will ask each person for his opinion, then bore in with searching questions. "The President conducts the most intensified interrogations I have ever heard," Vice President Humphrey told me.

All the study and staff work, all the advice and arguments are merely the preparation. Then the President must draw upon the ultimate loneliness. In the last hours, few people are around him — the First Lady, the Vice President, his spiritual advisers. The President regards his faith in God as his surest shield against mistakes. "I pray several times a day," he once told me, "but it is difficult to know God's will." He seeks spiritual guidance from his pastor, the Reverend Dr. George Davis of the National City Christian Church, and from evangelist Billy Graham. Both have prayed with him. But after the comfort and the prayers are over, the decision still has to be made by the President alone.

Lyndon Johnson's most difficult decision was the order to bomb North Vietnam. Not only did it involve the risk of a more terrible war with 650 million Chinese but also the knowledge that he was ordering men in the flower of their lives on missions that must inevitably end in death for some.

Long before the President faced this grim choice, he and his advisers prepared for the possibility that North Vietnam might have to be bombed. First the world's most exhaustive intelligence network had gathered information from every available source — from agents with their ears to the keyhole, from high-flying reconnaisance planes, from voluminous Communist economic and military reports, from captured documents and monitored broadcasts. Meanwhile, the Defense Department prepared detailed contingency plans for striking every possible target in North Vietnam, and in every possible way.

All these were ready when, on Feb. 7, 1965, the Viet Cong struck in the dark of the night at the American base and barracks at Pleiku. Opening fire on the silent installation with mortars, the guerrillas killed eight Americans and wounded more than 100 others. Moments after the first word of the attack was flashed to the Pentagon, Defense officials put through an urgent phone call to the President. It was shortly before 2 p.m., Washington time. "What are the details?" Johnson asked tersely. He was told the first reports were sketchy. "Keep me informed," he ordered. When more details came in, they were phoned at once to the President. Simultaneously, U.S. forces in the war zone were alerted.

At the White House, the President cleared his desk for action. He summoned Under Secretary of State George Ball, Deputy Secretary of Defense Cyrus Vance and General Earle Wheeler, chairman of the Joint Chiefs of Staff, to his office for a 4 p.m. meeting. (Secretary of State Dean Rusk was out of town, and Secretary of Defense Robert McNamara had viral pneumonia.) In Saigon, Ambassador General Maxwell Taylor and his deputy, U. Alexis Johnson, were waiting in the American embassy. With them was the President's national security adviser, McGeorge Bundy, who by coincidence was in South Vietnam for an on-the-spot look.

Instantaneous communications were opened, first by coded messages flashed on screens half a world apart, then by wiretap-proof telephone. The President, in contrast to his usual practice, let others handle the phone. With great urgency, he fired questions, listened grimly to the answers. He had the telephoners ask Taylor and his aides for their recommendations. *They replied without hesitation — strike North Vietnam.*

General Taylor and Deputy Ambassador Johnson suggested limited attacks on guerilla staging areas above the 17th parallel, which divides North and South Vietnam. The President ordered General Wheeler to gear up the war machine and hold it in readiness, but still did not commit himself to a course of action. Back to the Pentagon hurried the

General. Picking up a direct line to the war room at Pearl Harbor, he relayed the President's command to Admiral U. S. Sharp, Jr., Supreme Commander in the Pacific.

The National Security Council was summoned into session at 8 p.m. for the final decision. On the long mahogany table in the cabinet room were spread intelligence estimates, contingency plans, and position papers. As the President reviewed the day's dramatic events, a bronze bust of John F. Kennedy watched over his shoulder. For weeks he had rejected appeals from the Joint Chiefs to take the war to North Vietnam. Now he declared with quiet fury, *"I've had enough of this."*

A gaunt and gray McNamara, who had risen from his sickbed to attend the meeting, recited the cold military logic for bombing the North. Not a dissent was heard. Only a question of timing was raised by Ball, who pointed out that Soviet Premier Aleksei Kosygin was visiting Hanoi and asked whether it might be wiser to wait until he got out of town. The President dismissed the idea. He wanted the Communists to have no doubt about the consequences of any more Pleiku-type attacks. Grimly, the President declared, *"I want three things: I want a joint American-Vietnamese attack. I want it to be prompt. I want it to be appropriate."* The room went totally silent, and the atmosphere was electric with tension. Finally, McNamara asked if he could take two minutes to explain a technical detail. "I'd hug you if you would," sighed the President, and the tension was broken.

In the weeks that followed, a tired and troubled Lyndon Johnson rarely settled into bed before 1 a.m. Half the world away, squadrons of American planes roared off for new raids on North Vietnam. The President was advised they would probably be back in two hours. Precisely at 3 a.m., he awoke without prompting from an alarm clock. He reached for his bedside phone, asked for the Situation Room, and, in a voice blurred by fatigue, mumbled: "How're my boys?" When he was told that planes were missing, it was difficult for him to get more sleep. Often the morning sun was glinting through his bedroom window before he would get the final report.

President Johnson, a man who lives by the telephone, confessed to me once that his greatest dread is the urgent ring which rouses him in the dark of his bedroom. Beside him, he said, the First Lady would stir and murmur "Oh, no!" Then both would wait in anguish to learn what new crisis or emergency has arisen. A chief executive is seldom wakened to hear good news.

When the tall Texan became President at a time of national tragedy, he found himself faced with a series of decisions as soul-wracking as any ever to confront a President. It's no secret that leaders around the world were more than a little apprehensive about how he would handle the crisis situations. To old-style diplomats, schooled in the niceties of protocol and the delicacies of double-talk, Johnson seemed almost a caricature of a wheeling-dealing American politician. His folksiness, shoulder hugging, hand wringing, and homely speech lacked the finesse they admire. After the polished performance of John F. Kennedy, they viewed the Texan with polite dismay.

Many a diplomat shuddered at recollection of Johnson, as Vice President, uttering a cowboy yell and bussing Lady Bird at India's Taj Mahal, where kissing is forbidden. His invitation to a Pakistani camel driver to visit his Texas ranch and "see how we slaughter hogs" offended some Moslems with a horror of hogs. And during a European visit, he riled the touchy Dutch by handing out ball-point pens which they spurned as "gifts to the natives."

The polished Arthur Schlesinger, Jr., blubbering in his martinis after Lyndon Johnson moved into the White House, sobbed that he simply couldn't bear to hear American foreign policy being proclaimed in a Texas twang. His misgivings were shared by some State Department diplomats who were worried about how the Johnson "treatment," so effective in the smoke-filled backrooms of American politics, would go down with sophisticated world leaders. Washington wits made cracks about Johnson's "Stetson statesmanship." Stubbornly refusing to change his style, he soon confounded the skeptics by pushing his Stetson right up there with the high hats.

He began his ruler-to-ruler diplomacy at the Kennedy funeral, where he met some 200 presidents, premiers, monarchs and ministers. He made a point of giving them all a big hello and a hearty handshake. Although he was cautioned not to single out any for private meetings, he went into huddles with 17 of those he considered most important. He invited many to come back for formal visits; hence the persistent cavalcade of foreign dignitaries through the White House.

With each world leader President Johnson strives to strike up a personal relationship. His technique depends upon the individual. For most Latin American leaders, the *abrazo,* or embrace. For the others, an earnest handclasp which varies in intensity with how well he knows the leader and how anxious he is to win him over. LBJ favors the two-handed shake, a vigorous pumping action with the right hand while the left hand grasps the other fellow's wrist, elbow or shoulder. This is what the President calls "pressing the flesh."

He likes to entertain his foreign guests in folksy, Texas fashion. He prefers barbecues to ballets; once he arranged a hootenanny for Italy's opera-loving President Antonio Segni. When aides suggested he was laying on the Texas sauce a bit thick for West Germany's Ludwig Erhard, President Johnson replied: "When I go to Germany, I, too, want to be treated as a guest and friend."

During the diplomatic give-and-take, he hears out his foreign visitors with what one White House aide calls "150 percent attention." Needless to say, he's no pushover for their pleadings. "We have our problems, too," he usually rejoins. Then he makes his points, one at a time. "Let's get our ducks in a row," he will say. He is usually persuasive, often overpowering. He speaks the blunt language of the politician rather than the delicate language of the diplomat. He likes to address potentates "as one politician to another." Indeed, he believes there are few differences that can't be talked out. When a phone call to President Roberto Chiari failed to settle a Panama problem, for instance, Johnson told aides that if he and Chiari had been able to meet face to face, a lot of misunderstanding could have been avoided.

Almost every statesman who has conferred with Johnson has come away talking about his "grasp." And they don't mean his handshake. Until the deep causes of world tension are reduced, he has told them, one crisis will follow another. But he doesn't intend to "send in the Marines" every time there's a blowout. He keeps his eye focused on the Big Picture — world peace, backed by American strength. "The United States is the most powerful nation in the world," he affirms. "We can afford to be patient."

Yet in foreign affairs Johnson probably has had a tougher time than his predecessors. Our allies, restored by American aid and now hitting peaks of prosperity, are growing more independent daily. After the Soviet backdown over Cuba, which brought the world to the brink of nuclear war but also did much to remove the threat of an ultimate holocaust, other nations have felt freer to seek their own destinies in their own way.

Of all the allied leaders, the most difficult has been Charles de Gaulle. In seeking to move into the vacuum in world leadership caused by the murder of President Kennedy, the French President has repeatedly snubbed Johnson. At the Kennedy funeral, the towering Frenchman dwarfed Johnson with a display of diplomatic upstaging. He managed to make himself the center of every gathering of the world leaders, even arriving last at Johnson's reception, as if it were his own command performance. When he departed for Paris, he gave the impression he had accepted Johnson's invitation to pay a state visit to Washington, but he haughtily canceled out.

Not long afterwards, De Gaulle announced his decision to recognize Red China, which he knew would be anathema to Johnson. About the same time it was learned that the French leader had instructed his U.N. delegation to watch how the U.S. voted on certain issues, then cast France's vote with the opposition. Johnson's aides were furious, but the President, though angry, refused to be rattled. "Calm down," he told them. "We aren't going to solve our problems by being disagreeable." As for the rejected invitation and De Gaulle's intimation that Johnson would have to come to Paris for any confab, LBJ wasn't particularly put out. "If something useful can be accomplished, I won't let protocol stand in my way," he told aides.

American Presidents and British Prime Ministers have always got along well—or have at least managed to put a good face on their differences. This was evident at the White House state dinner for Prime Minister Harold Wilson. Johnson was so relaxed he loosened his stiff collar — and protocol manners. At one point, as he introduced several distinguished guests, the former Ambassador to Britain, Lewis Douglas, began to sit down. "Now, Lew," admonished the President. "You stand up a little longer. There are some girls down here who didn't get to see you."

Commenting on how his talks with Wilson were going, Johnson recalled the time Mark Twain asked directions to a friend's farm in New Hampshire. "How far is it to Henderson's place," Mark Twain inquired. The farmer said it was "about a mile and a half." Twain continued along the road until he met another, again asked the distance to the Henderson farm. "About a mile and a half," replied the second farmer. Still farther down the road, Twain asked another passing farmer the distance and was told, "about a mile and a half." Mark Twain replied: "Thank God, I am holding my own." The President noted that he wasn't so sure whether he was holding his own with Wilson.

When the British Prime Minister invited Johnson to dinner at Buckingham Palace, he warned frankly that the Scots Guards or Gordon Highlanders might suddenly start "parading around and playing the bagpipes in your ears as you try to eat. And you thought," he added, reverting to the language of weaponry, "that you had the great deterrent." Johnson roared.

The President keeps in closer touch with Harold Wilson than with any other ruler. A direct circuit links the White House and No. 10 Downing Street. Inside the White House, it is called the "Mac-Jack" line, a nickname that has stuck since Harold McMillan was Prime Minister and Jack Kennedy was President. Daily messages pass over this "hot line" between the British and American leaders. The President also has direct lines to De Gaulle and Ludwig Erhard, West Germany's Chancellor, but these go into the French and German Foreign Ministries, respectively.

Johnson uses the telephone to reach most other rulers, particularly Canada's Lester Pearson. Indeed, they talk on the phone like old friends. When Johnson called Pearson to urge that Canadian troops be rushed to help keep the peace in Cyprus, he recalled that the Canadian Prime Minister had asked a favor during their last conversation. "Now you have to pay for our last phone call," quipped the President.

During Erhard's first visit, Johnson almost smothered the West German Chancellor with hospitality at the LBJ Ranch. Then during a deer-spotting jaunt, Johnson laid it on the line. He said he didn't want to hear any more lectures, Adenauer-style, on the dangers of communism. Johnson fully understood those dangers, but the American people were tired of bearing most of the burden. The President expected West Germany not only to share the load but also to take a more realistic attitude toward the Berlin problem. "Ja!" agreed the West German leader gravely.

The President likes to mix pleasure with protocol. After talks with Erhard at the White House came dinner and dancing. LBJ swirled Mrs. Heinrich Knappstein, wife of the German Ambassador, around the floor. Then he grabbed the most beautiful girl within reach, singer Roberta Peters, and monopolized her most of the evening. For a while they disappeared together, presumably for a private midnight tour of the White House. Chancellor Erhard, heavy of foot, kept off the dance floor and stood briefly in a corridor, puffing on one of his long cigars, not the least intimidated by an earlier Johnson crack that West Germany's air pollution program had been set back by the Chancellor's cigars.

Most important to the world, of course, is the relationship between Johnson and the Kremlin. From the moment Johnson was sworn in, he has been fully aware that the Soviets are studying his every move and getting elaborate reports on his strengths and weaknesses.

For the first real look at Johnson, the Kremlin sent shrewd Anastas Mikoyan to the Kennedy funeral. The new President spoke softly but with impact of America's strength, sought to give the appearance of a reasonable man but one who was not going to be pushed around. On his way home to Moscow, Mikoyan informed the British that he had been "impressed." Johnson at once began exchanging messages with the Kremlin. Some have been published, but most have been private. The style of Johnson's letters is markedly different from Kennedy's. The latter tended to be literary; he might start with a description about the sea at Hyannis Port to make a point. Johnson's letters are short, clear and to the point. The State Department usually offers him a draft, but in the end he prefers his own direct prose.

Johnson gets "the word" to the Kremlin in many forms. It may be delivered orally by an intermediary; a birthday greeting may be worded to carry another meaning; or a public statement may contain a pointed, special message for the Kremlin. Even an off-the-cuff statement may be carefully phrased for the Russians' benefit. Similar messages, both written and oral, arrive at the White House from Moscow. Intermediaries who come from the Kremlin are asked to repeat word-of-mouth messages carefully, and they are taken down verbatim. All are studied intensively for meanings between the lines.

Stetson statesmanship, hootenannies, barbecues down on the LBJ range, visits to cousin Oriole and Zephyr's red-hot chili may not suit every taste. But Secretary of State Rusk, whose ever patient, never pressuring diplomatic style is diametrically opposite from that of the President, has told me that Johnson's rural background gives him an advantage in dealing with the people of the world. "He knows about plain people because he came from plain people," said Rusk. "When the President talks about poverty or hunger or disease, he knows what he is talking about. This is something which people around the world will appreciate. One cannot look at the little house in which he was born without realizing that the Johnson story is the story of America, the classless society, the society of opportunity."

Rusk's birthplace on a small farm in Cherokee County, Georgia, was even more modest than Johnson's. At the local high school near the LBJ Ranch, Rusk once glanced around the gymnasium. "Yes," he said with satisfaction, "it could be Cherokee County, Georgia." This kinship makes it easier for the impeccable Dean Rusk to administer LBJ's down-to-earth diplomacy.

The President appreciates subordinates like Rusk, quiet, capable, who don't intrude into the spotlight. *He expects his subordinates to submerge their ambitions, swallow their egos, and maintain strict anonymity.* He delights in telling them how Franklin D. Roosevelt once called him down for getting his name in the newspapers. Even the ebullient Hubert Humphrey has learned to behave like the monkey with hand over mouth, speaking only when spoken to, holding his tongue in the presence of reporters, saying nothing that might displease the President. ***On those seldom and secretive occasions that aides dare to talk about the President, they agree that Lyndon B. Johnson is the most difficult, the most demanding, but the most devoted boss in America.***

7

THE TRUTH ABOUT OUR FIRST LADIES

This is the story of four women of different generations, vastly different tastes and backgrounds, who are linked by a bond no other women in the world can share. Though their lives are now far apart, all know what it is like to be the First Lady of the United States, to share the drama of the White House, to live at the heights of political power and social prestige. Two of the four are grandmothers: Bess Truman, in her 80s, and Mamie Eisenhower, approaching 70. Lady Bird Johnson, in her 50s, with two grown daughters, could become a grandmother before she leaves the White House.

The fourth, Jacqueline Kennedy, is still in her 30s with two small children. Yet this young woman has suffered the ultimate experience that every First Lady dreads — the blow against her husband from some fanatic lurking in the shadows. There remains about her the look of a serene but vaguely sad storybook princess. Something about her gently pensive manner, the touch of whimsy flicking about her lips, keeps reminding the world of her great tragedy. But those who know the woman behind the beauty, charm, and Sorbonne polish believe she has deliberately created the aura of aloofness and remoteness about herself. She is a great performer, strong willed, playing her role flawlessly.

Of the four, Bess Truman was the first to know the danger of the White House. Two Puerto Rican nationalists tried to shoot their way into her husband's office in 1950. Mamie Eisenhower also worried about threats against the life of her husband, although she had come to terms with this dread earlier as an Army wife.

Lady Bird Johnson was riding with her husband in the

fateful Dallas motorcade that carried President Kennedy under the assassin's sixth-floor window on November 22, 1963. She saw her husband, then Vice President, flung to the floor of their car by Secret Service bodyguard Rufus Youngblood. A few hours later, she dictated into a scratchy tape recorder that, after their car had lurched to a stop in front of the hospital, she "cast a last look over my shoulder and saw a bundle of pink just like a drift of blossoms lying on the back seat [of the President's car]. I think it was Mrs. Kennedy lying over the President's body. (She was wearing a pink suit.)"

Inside the hospital, Mrs. Johnson asked to be taken to Mrs. Kennedy: "Suddenly I found myself face to face with Jackie in a small hall. I think it was outside the operating room. You always think of her as being insulated, protected — she was quite alone. *I don't think I ever saw anyone so much alone in my life.* I went up to her, put my arms around her and said something to her. I'm sure it was something like 'God help us all,' because my feelings for her were too tumultuous to put into words."

On the return flight to Washington with the martyred President's body, the new First Lady had a dramatic encounter with the former First Lady. "Although," dictated Lady Bird, "it was a very hard thing to do, she made it as easy as possible. She said things like, 'Oh, Lady Bird, it's good that we've always liked you two so much.' She said, 'Oh, what if I had not been there! I'm so glad I was there.' I looked at her. Mrs. Kennedy's dress was stained with blood. One leg was almost entirely covered with it, and her right glove was caked — that immaculate woman — it was caked with blood, her husband's blood. She always wore gloves like she was used to them. I never could. Somehow that was one of the most poignant sights — exquisitely dressed and caked in blood. I asked her if I could get someone in to help her change, and she said, 'Oh, no, perhaps I'll ask Mary Gallagher. But not right now.' And then with something — if you can say a person that gentle, that dignified, you can say had an element of fierceness — she said, 'I want them to see what they have done to Jack.' I wanted to help her, but there was nothing I could do to help her."

This stirring moment of history offers a glimpse into the characters of both women, revealing the compassion of the one and the inner strength of the other. *For beneath the delicate softness, the Dresden-doll appearance of Jacqueline Kennedy is a character of steel.*

The four First Ladies are little alike. Bess Truman is a shy homebody, Mamie Eisenhower a bubbly Army wife, Lady Bird Johnson an astute politician, Jackie Kennedy an exquisite aristocrat. They exchange Christmas cards and polite messages on special occasions. Otherwise, they keep in touch hardly at all. Lady Bird has invited her predecesors back for a White House visit, but only Mrs. Eisenhower has found it convenient to accept. Yet there can be no doubt about the bond between these women.

There is one special trait they have in common. They are devoted to their celebrated husbands, though their devotion is not entirely uncritical. Bess Truman is an artist at the tug-on-the-coat-sleeve and the under-the-table-kick when Harry is feeling explosive. She has never liked some of his saltier expressions and lets him know about it. Lady Bird Johnson also tries to protect her man from himself. "Over adulation or the acid bath of criticism," she says, "isn't healthy for anyone." She has become his balance wheel. Jacqueline Kennedy, who had the same quiet influence upon her husband while he was alive, is now devoted to honoring his memory.

The three older women constantly fret over their husbands' health. In her gentle way, Lady Bird coaxes the President to take naps, conspires with the cook to hold down his calories. She has mounted a meaningful little sign in the White House kitchen: "*Please don't offer the President second help-*

ings unless he asks for them." Bess Truman tries to soothe Harry when he gets his dander up, and Mamie Eisenhower tries to calm down Ike when he becomes excited. He got carried away, for example, while watching a football game between Gettysburg College and Bucknell University. Alarmed, Mamie whispered to Mrs. C. A. Hanson, wife of Gettysburg's president: "I think Ike is getting too involved in the game." She turned to Ike: "Are you all right?" "Yes," he said. "Are you ready to leave?" she asked in a tone that suggested they should. "I can't hear you," said Ike.

As Gettysburg started to lose, Ike grew more agitated. Again Mamie asked whether they should leave. "I can't hear you," Ike repeated. They stayed until Gettysburg's defeat was final.

Though the Johnsons, Eisenhowers and Trumans have been married from three to five decades, all three wives like to pretty up for their husbands. When Lady Bird moved into Bethesda Naval Hospital following the President's gall bladder operation, she bought a gay new robe and made sure her make-up was packed. She was often seen, before going into the President's room, carefully applying lipstick and combing her hair. Mamie also tries to stay young for Ike, whom she calls "my boy friend" or "my beau." She dolls up in bright dresses, wears her hair in bangs, and keeps it reddish blonde by discreet rinsing. Mamie's gay dresses, which might look bizarre on most other women her age, tastefully compliment her cheerful personality. When occasionally she wears a gray suit, she brightens it up with a colorful scarf and hat. Bess Truman, though past 80, likes to crown her gray curls with a fussy, flowery hat when she steps out with Harry.

First Lady is not an elected office and draws no salary. But it is a full-time job that goes with being married to the President. After the Kennedy assassination, an alarmed Congress authorized government protection for all the former

First Families. The Trumans put up with Secret Service agents less than a week, then sent them packing. Bess explained to friends that they were "nice boys" but that she could take care of Harry and drive the family Chrysler herself. The Eisenhowers welcomed the Secret Service men, and Mamie happily told how one gallant bodyguard had thrown his raincoat over her when she was caught in a sudden squall. Jackie Kennedy also found the agents useful in keeping an eye on her two active youngsters.

Harry Truman, that master of common sense, declares: "Presidents need many many things. But brains, ability, and a loyal following mean nothing unless — by his side — there is an intelligent and understanding wife." Here is a glimpse into the private lives of the four living ladies, who have held this unique position:

Lady Bird Johnson, known for her soft Southern charm, has rare character and courage beneath all the magnolia blossoms. When White House aide Walter Jenkins was arrested on a morals charge in the middle of the 1964 campaign, for instance, everyone else around the President panicked. Even LBJ's own first impulse was to disclaim and disown Jenkins, thus sacrificing him on the altar of political expediency. But Lady Bird wouldn't permit it. Disregarding all the political advisers, she came quietly to Jenkins' support. "My heart is aching today," she said in a public statement, "for someone who has reached the point of exhaustion in dedicated service to his country. I know our family and all of his friends pray for his recovery."

It wasn't the first time that Lady Bird, with gentle firmness, had bucked up the President. Hers is a quiet courage, much admired by her intimates. She never speaks, for example, about her five miscarriages. *Her sweet talk also conceals a sharp political sense.* Before a White House party, she carefully bones up on her guests. Customarily, she takes notes on the guests with her to the beauty parlor. (It saves $5, she says, to go out to get her hair done.) It is not uncommon for her to phone a secretary from under the hair dryer to ask for more details. At the party, she has something personal to say to each guest.

She has shown the same attention to her campaign to beautify America. Once, she impulsively took off one afternoon to see for herself how Washington schools might be beautified. When she returned to the White House, she remembered the exact number of windows that had been broken at one school and pointed out that attractive schools, in which the children could take pride, had no broken windows.

Lady Bird is affectionate and demonstrative, not in the least inhibited about telling her family how much she loves them. She has a habit of ending phone talks with her daughters with some tender remark like "You are loved," or "I have faith in you." To keep up with them, she began skin diving and water skiing at 52.

Though Lady Bird would deny it, intimates say she has been privately hurt by Jacqueline Kennedy's aloofness. Lady Bird wanted to name the new White House garden, for example, after the lovely Jackie. Advisers pleaded it shouldn't be identified with any individual but should be named the First Lady's Garden in honor of all First Ladies. But Lady Bird insisted upon calling it the Jacqueline Kennedy Garden. Jackie not only failed to show up for the dedication, but she has virtually ignored the honor. President and Mrs. Johnson sent her a beautiful color photograph, warmly inscribed, of the garden. Yet those who have visited Jackie's New York office noticed it had been laid aside among books and letters on a ledge. If Lady Bird is offended, she gives no inkling of it. She understands completely, she says, how painful it is for Mrs. Kennedy to be reminded of her life in the White House.

Of all the four surviving First Ladies, Jacqueline is the most complex character. Young and beautiful, she has found herself cast in the role of an American queen. The more she has seemed to avoid the role, the closer the regal robes are placed round her slender shoulders. *Yet for all her pursuit of privacy, intimates insist, she is never so aloof as to be unaware of the effect she is creating.* Former playmates recall that she always liked to play the part of the queen in their girlish games. "It is fantastic," says one, "how Jackie's dream world materialized for her." Certainly she has all the grace and poise of a queen. And her regal manner must be obvious to some intimates, including her sisters-in-law, who sometimes teasingly refer to her as "the queen."

Quite aware of her position as the capital's social leader while she was First Lady, *Jackie once punished her stepsister by banishing her from the White House in the manner of an 18th century monarch.* The victim: Mrs. Nina Steers, who shares the same stepfather, Hugh Auchinloss, with Jackie (he was married to Nina's mother before marrying Jackie's mother). Nina's offense was supporting Richard Nixon for President in 1960. Such disloyalty from a member of the family circle was an unpardonable sin among the Kennedys. Jackie, embarrased and offended, kept her silence throughout the campaign. But after the election, she phoned Nina and, speaking sharply, let her know that the Steers would not be welcome at the White House. As Nina described the call to a friend: "Jackie really let me have it. She almost bashed my face in." The ban was dropped only once. When Jackie invited her classmates from the exclusive Miss Porter's School to the White House, Nina was asked to come with the rest and received a friendly kiss from the First Lady.

Certainly it cannot be said that Jacqueline Kennedy puts on offensive airs or is at all spoiled. As her mother, Mrs. Hugh Auchinloss, expressed it: "I wonder in the middle of the night occasionally how Jackie can cope with it all. She's essentially a very nice person." Unlike the intense young men and women of her late husband's New Frontier, Jackie was usually relaxed and unperturbed. She has a sense of humor that pricks without wounding, and her laughter is the most lighthearted sound around. Nina Steers remembers a girlhood incident that is typical. Jackie's sister, Lee, was entertaining three boy friends in the drawing room one afternoon. At Jackie's instigation, she and Nina pulled blankets over their heads and dashed through the drawing room screaming hideously, disappeared into the sun parlor and quietly circled back upstairs. Later, Jackie came tripping lightly down the stairs, poised and dead-pan. "Oh, pardon me," she said sweetly, "have you seen my two crazy aunts?"

For all her gentle humor and exquisite softness, Jackie is no helpless, sweet young thing. She has a quiet courage, *sangfroid,* the French call it, or coolness under stress. She has had it since her youngest days. Once, when she and Nina were horseback riding, Nina took a nasty spill. Jackie remained calm, rigged a sling for Nina, ran to the nearest gas station for help, then took off after the fugitive horse. Years later, she happened to be alone with her sister, Lee, when Lee gave birth to a premature two and one-half pound baby. *With both mother and baby in critical condition, Jackie calmly took charge, phoned the doctor, called for an ambulance and kept everything under control.*

Throughout her own history of miscarriages and Caesarian operations, Jackie has always quietly put her babies' lives ahead of her own. Not even the overpowering Kennedy clan has been able to smother her independence or individuality. Jackie's mother is not unaware of the stubborn streak in her. After the election, Mrs. Auchinloss didn't care for her daughter's hair-do and tried to persuade her to change it. Failing, Mrs. Auchinloss went to the hairdresser both of them use and asked him to urge the change upon Jackie. But the new First Lady's mind, and hair-do, were set.

Though she never liked politics, she worked hard to be a First Lady of whom President Kennedy could be proud. She protected her children from the glare of the spotlight, still loves and protects them fiercely. Indeed, if anything can crack Jackie's composure, it is her feeling for her children. Any suggestion that the children might be sad or hurt can bring her to the verge of tears. Unlike many mothers in her wealthy circle, Jackie has not turned the children over to nurses and governesses to rear. She plays with them, studies with them, tells them stories, takes them on frequent outings. "The children are the biggest thing in her life," confides a friend. "She has a natural delight in youngsters. She often pretends not to be looking, but sees them out of the corner of her eye and chuckles to herself."

She makes no attempt to shield the children from the past. There are no awkward attempts to steer the conversation away from White House happenings. John, Jr., still talks of helicopters, airplanes, and cars that he remembers from the White House. Jackie bears it all in silence. On occasion, close friends have seen how it will bring her momentary pain. Once, for example, little John asked a visiting friend: "Are you a daddy?" The man acknowledged that he was. "Then throw me up in the air," begged John. Her little boy's words caused a flicker of pain to pass over Jackie's face.

She has become closer to the Kennedy clan than she ever was while Jack Kennedy was alive. In part, this has been for the children's sake. She has been anxious to keep their world as intact as possible, to maintain the familiar relationships with their cousins, and to provide in Uncles Bob and Ted Kennedy a father figure. The Kennedy clan, in turn, has moved closer around her to protect her and the children.

Now that Jackie has emerged from the trauma that followed the assassination, she has become part of a young, sophisticated New York set, perhaps a dozen or so couples, who are interested in the arts but also discuss politics. She has been escorted to parties, more to preserve the balance of men and ladies, than out of any romantic interest. She entertains at small dinners in her apartment and dines out at the fashionable restaurants. She spends the summer at tennis and swimming at Cape Cod and Newport, returns to New York City for the winter concerts, ballets, and plays.

Her intimate friends believe it unlikely she will ever remarry. "How could she ever find anyone to fill Jack Kennedy's shoes?" asks one friend. She is deeply conscious of her role as the widow of a beloved President who is rapidly becoming a legend. She is afraid, suggest friends, that she might tarnish his memory if she became Mrs. Anybody Else. She has also become so close to the Kennedys that it would be difficult to step out of their circle into another man's life. There is the political impact to consider, too, on the careers of the ambitious Kennedy brothers. She has become imbued, say intimates, with the fierce family loyalty she once resisted.

She is committed, say intimates who should know, to installing Robert Kennedy in her late husband's place in the White House. To this end, she has gone so far as to try to copyright history. She selected William Manchester to write the story of President Kennedy's martyrdom, shutting off information to other writers. Jackie even tried to persuade Jim Bishop to abandon his book, "The Day Kennedy Was Shot," and Robert Kennedy tried to persuade Random House not to publish it. Explained Jackie in a handwritten note to Bishop: "I hired William Manchester—to protect President Kennedy and the truth. He was to interrogate everyone who had any connection with those days—and if I decide the book should never be published—then Mr. Manchester will be reimbursed for his time. Or if I decide it should be known —I will decide when it should be published."

Bishop protested politely: "I knew all along that many books would be written about that tragic day in Dallas. They will be written whether you stand in the doorway of history or not. They will be written whether I die this day or not . . . If you want to deny me any personal assistance, I will respect your wishes, but I ask, in fairness, that you reopen the doors to the other parts of the story. In return, I shall permit anyone you designate to study my manuscript for errors of fact or good taste before publication." But he did not reckon with the iron will of Jacqueline Kennedy. She wrote back: "I would like to reiterate that I meant exactly what I wrote you earlier. None of the people connected with November 22 will speak to anyone but Mr. Manchester. That is my wish, and it is theirs also. . . . I will not discuss those events with anyone else—nor will I 'reopen the doors to other parts of the story.' "

For all her inner strength, distant manner, and carefully concealed stubbornness, Mrs. Kennedy is more relaxed, less posed, more warm than she appears in public. But she never lets her hair down so far that she loses her grace and charm. Those who have been watching her agree that history will not soon forget Jacqueline Kennedy, the former Cleopatra of the Potomac, who still conducts herself like an American queen.

Mamie Eisenhower and Bess Truman never really liked the White House. They were proud that their husbands made it to the top, but they tried to avoid the spotlight and are happy to be out of it. Mamie, now grayer and more gregarious, seems to have aged not at all since leaving Washington. Her blue eyes are bright and snappy; her personality can light up a dismal day. But friends say her health is delicate. "Where my health is concerned," she confided to one of them, "nothing is trivial."

After a lifetime of moving from one Army post to another, Mamie has found her real home at the Eisenhower farm in Gettysburg. Her grandchildren aren't far away at

Valley Forge. Unless Ike is going away for more than a week, Mamie prefers to remain in Gettysburg. She frequently slips into town to do her own shopping. She squeezes the tomatoes, thumps the watermelons, and inspects the vegetables with a practiced eye. But she takes along Sergeant J. R. Brechbill to drive the car and push the grocery cart.

Her friends are delighted with her cute mannerisms. Typical was her wry little pout recently after she squeezed some fragrance out of a perfume bottle and a bee suddenly appeared. "Oh," she said, "that bee is attracted by my perfume. I hope it keeps going." But most of all, they appreciate her thoughtfulness. She always makes a point, for example, of wearing her own Girl Scout pin when she greets a Girl Scout delegation. And she has placed a standing order with a local florist to send flowers daily to the sickest person in Gettysburg's only hospital.

Unassuming Bess Truman, who was always ill at ease in the White House, loves the quiet life of Independence, Missouri. She runs her own errands and does all her own shopping, always waiting her turn in the check-out lines. She attends Trinity Episcopal Church faithfully, usually dragging along a grudging Harry Truman. She is still active in the ladies' guild and takes her turn shining the communion silver. Their large white frame house is much the kind of house you would expect grandpa and grandma to live in. But once inside, you begin to live with history, particularly in the great library with its books and pictures of the Truman era.

Both Grandpa and Grandma Truman keep up with the times. Almost any evening, they can be seen reading the eastern newspapers in their library. Bess, who also likes to keep up with local happenings, complained when the Independence Examiner wasn't delivered on time. Characteristically, she phoned a friend on the paper and made sure her complaint wouldn't get the paper boy in trouble.

She does much of her own housework with the help of a family maid and a girl who comes in to assist with the evening meal. But Bess fixes breakfast and lunch for her husband who usually comes home at noon from his office in the Truman Library. When she asked what he liked for lunch, he suggested a glass of milk and a roast beef sandwich. Afterward, she fussed to a friend: "He talks as if I have roast beef in the refrigerator all the time." She seldom touches lunch herself. A relative told me she suffers from a stomach disorder; others claim she merely watches her weight. Except for occasional complaints about arthritis in her hand, she appears to be fitter than Harry who has lost his old bounce since his illness in mid 1966.

The city provides a police sergeant to drive the former President to his office now that the morning walk has become too taxing. But Bess often picks him up in the great Chrysler and drives him around town. She is a baseball fan, loyal to the Kansas City Athletics, and enjoys fishing. Not long ago, she showed up with a bored Harry Truman in tow to try an indoor trout pool. Her greatest interest, second only to Harry, is her four grandchildren. When President Johnson came to Independence to sign the medicare bill and handed out pens, Bess boasted triumphantly to a friend: "I got a pen for each of my grandchildren."

She avoids publicity like the plague and flatly refuses to be interviewed. When a friend tried to persuade her to see a reporter, she said firmly: "I'm not going to be tricked into seeing these people." When the press gathered to see the Trumans off for New York City recently, Bess didn't show up until the train whistled. She timed her arrival until the last minute so she could avoid talking to reporters.

The nation remembers Bess Truman, Mamie Eisenhower, and Jacqueline Kennedy with a quiet nostalgia. And they look fondly upon Lady Bird Johnson, carrying the burden of the day.

8

WASHINGTON'S CURIOUS CASTE SYSTEM

Periodically, a new device is tried out in Washington to shoo the starlings from the eaves of government buildings. The startled birds rise fluttering and twittering, then settle back after the alarm has past. Much the same effect is produced on the bureaucrats, bigwigs, and brass hats every time a new President moves into the White House. He may barge about his new domain, switching off the lights, moving around the furniture, and otherwise creating the impression that changes will be made. Customarily, he sounds a solemn warning to the vast federal bureaucracy that he expects renewed vigor from them. But like the starlings, the officials flap and flutter a little, then invariably return to roost among their status symbols.

Such symbols are held sacred by the stuffed shirts who, as evidence perhaps that hot air rises, often ascend to high office. *Their* VIP *standing is determined in exacting detail by their office acreage, rug plushness, furniture array, and limousine service.* They are known, too, by their dining, parking, washroom, and elevator privileges. Whether they sip water from a silver decanter, brown plastic jug, or water fountain in the corridor is another sign of their status. The protocol extends even to dog tags, the lower numbers going to the pooches of the prominent.

A bureaucrat's immediate domain, his office, provides the real clues to his importance. Is it large enough, say, for football scrimmage? Is there a trim of woodwork around the walls? What color is the rug, and how deep do you sink in it? Does the office contain a kingsize desk? a flag stand? a sofa suitable for taking naps? These are the things to watch for. For sheer size and splendor, few grand ballrooms can compare with a cabinet member's office. Secretary of State Dean Rusk's sumptuous suite, for instance, not only could accommodate a United Nations session; it could provide the delegates with built-in television, meals from an electric range, and washroom-shower facilities. Many a sub-cabinet officer, too, has room on his rug for a public event.

The biggest status scramble in each department is for office space near the Secretary's suite. It's who's up front that counts. This sometimes can be expensive for the taxpayers. During the construction of the new, $35 million State Department building, for instance, the builders were obliged to keep juggling the plans to satisfy everyone. Final formula: the Secretary and Undersecretaries got 684 square feet apiece, Assistant Secretaries 450 square feet, Deputy Assistants 350 square feet, office directors 270 square feet. Not only do the officials with the biggest worries have the most floor space, but Secretary Rusk and his two Undersecretaries stride back and forth on beige carpets of luxurious thickness. Deputy Undersecretaries pace on brown and black rugs. Assistant Secretaries have green rugs, their deputies common grey. It takes at least an Assistant Secretary to rate foam rubber padding underneath.

In all government bureaus, of course, the plushest furniture goes to the biggest bosses. Most coveted item: a sofa. To get one, a bureaucrat must be at least in the top three civil service grades. But only presidential appointees are allowed to display the American and departmental flags in their offices. Then there is the protocol of the water jugs. Presidential appointees are entitled to chromium-plated jugs which are kept filled by messenger boys. Lesser government bosses get plain plastic jugs, usually brown, and are obliged to send their secretaries out for water.

In the Pentagon, status works outward from the interior

"A" ring of the five-sided colossus. An individual's advancement is measured by his progress toward the outer "E" ring which the top brass inhabit. The civilian chiefs (Assistant Secretaries and above) are entitled to a fresh paint job and new, wall-to-wall carpeting when they move in. *But the real yardstick is a three-foot trim of woodwork around the walls.* Enter a Pentagon office with this executive paneling, and you are dealing with a man of consequence. Also, only the highest ranks ride the Pentagon elevators; all others must use the stairs or escalators. In the downtown departments, across the Potomac, elevator privileges are also a measure of a man's importance. Most cabinet officers have private elevators, running in some cases from office to limousine. In figuring status at the State Department, possession of a key to the Secretary's elevator is akin to being able to unlock the Pearly Gates.

Who's who in our bureaucracy can also be calculated by the sleekness of their limousines. *The Cadillacs, Lincolns and Chrysler Imperials carry the top brass; the Chevrolets, Fords and Plymouths transport the lesser officials.* The line-up of glossy government cars at any big Washington function is enough to take a taxpayer's breath away. Cabinet officers are permitted to use their glory wagons for private as well as business purposes, and their wives often are driven to the supermarket in sumptuous style. This is a sore point with Senators and Supreme Court Justices who have no standing at the government motor pool. Only the Chief Justice and Senate-House leaders are entitled to limousine service. The others, though they outrank the chauffeur-driven Assistant Secretaries, pilot their own cars and console themselves by displaying low-number license plates.

Next to a limousine, a parking sticker is the most prized badge of distinction. The State Department provides only one parking space for every eight employees. The situation is even worse surrounding other government buildings. The

Commerce Department, for example, has 140 parking spaces for more than 3,000 employees.

The worst sticklers for protocol, as might be suspected, are the brass hats. There is a constant stir, for example, over who should be allowed to embellish their hats with scrambled-egg designs. It used to be that no one below Navy captain or Army-Air Force colonel could wear this golden scroll. Then the Navy opened the privilege to commanders, and the Army responded by authorizing scrambled-egg hats for majors. Now the status seekers in the Air Force are demanding equal hat privileges.

But the most coveted symbol of Army status is tenancy in one of the cavernous, barn-like houses along "Brass Row" at Fort Myer, Virginia. Senior Admirals are scattered around town in Navy homes, but they have had their status troubles, too. When Arthur Radford became the first Admiral to head the Joint Chiefs, there arose the prickliest of protocol problems. The Navy chief traditionally lives in a rambling old house at the Naval Observatory. Admiral and Mrs. Robert Carney were ensconced there. But since Radford outranked Carney, the question was: could the Carneys be evicted? This became a battle of the wives. Mrs. Carney egged her husband into getting a ruling from the Navy's legal department that the Observatory house was the official residence of the Navy chief. Thus she outmaneuvered Mrs. Radford who threatened to pull her husband's rank but ended up in a three-story, eight-bedroom house formerly occupied by a mere Rear Admiral.

Despite the urgent manpower needs in Viet Nam, the brass hats always seem able to spare enough men from the war to wait on tables, mow their lawns, and perform other menial chores. When some heretic suggested that the Generals should adopt the communist practice of taking occasional turns at KP duty in order to maintain "comradeship" between officers and men, the idea was regarded with horror.

The Pentagon's civilian chiefs, once initiated to the privileges of rank, sometimes become even more protocol-minded than the brass hats. When Assistant Secretary Arthur Sylvester learned that he was entitled to fly a five-star flag on his auto fender, he not only insisted upon displaying the flag at one base but stopped the car to unfurl it when it became wrapped around the staff.

The top man on the protocol pole, of course, is the President. Lyndon Johnson has too much Texan in him to be impressed with striped-pants formality. Yet he clearly enjoys the accouterments of office, takes satisfaction from the scurry of subordinates. His favorite song is "Hail to the Chief." When he was a mere Vice President, he delighted in lunching at a table that rose like a giant lily out of his swimming pool. Barefoot servants with pantlegs rolled high splashed in and out of the pool to wait on him. LBJ still likes to be pampered.

Vice President Hubert Humphrey hasn't yet been spoiled. He discouraged efforts to uproot him from his modest, eight-room suburban home and ensconce him in an official mansion. He settled finally for a fashionable downtown apartment that reportedly cost about $85,000. He hasn't forgotten his college days when he and his bride lived in an attic. In case of fire, their fire escape was a rope which they kept handy to heave out the window. His wife Muriel still sews her own clothes, though she splurged and bought an expensive blue gown for the 1965 Inauguration. "I hope you wear it every day," said the Vice President when he saw the bill. "It's the only way we'll get our money's worth out of it."

Congress has its own peculiar protocol. *On Capitol Hill seniority is sacred. It is worked out to the last decimal point.* If two Senators, say, are sworn in the same day, the one whose state was admitted first to the Union has the seniority edge. But suppose both states were admitted at the same time; then the advantage goes to the Senator whose state comes first in the alphabet. Seniority governs everything from committee assignments to office space. This produces a biennial game of "musical offices" after each election takes its toll of senior solons. Those who gain in seniority move to better offices, causing a chain reaction down the line. A Senator at the bottom of the seniority ladder, if he is too brash to suit his elders (as Senator Robert Kennedy was), may find his office space scattered between three floors and two buildings (as Senator Robert Kennedy did).

In the matter of washrooms, sex triumphed over seniority on at least one memorable occasion. The Founding Fathers, for all their foresight, believed a woman's place was in the home—certainly not in the Senate. Thus, the Senate facilities simply weren't designed for ladies. Adjoining the august Senate chamber is only one restroom—for men. The first lady to be concerned with this problem was Hattie Caraway, erstwhile Senator from Arkansas. A patient woman, she bided her time until she gained a committee chairmanship. This gave her the necessary seniority for an office with washroom facilities near the chamber.

Not so patient was Senator Margaret Chase Smith (R-Me.), who, lacking seniority, invoked her femininity instead and demanded equal washroom facilities. Senate Rules Chairman Carl Hayden (D-Ariz.), the gentlest of men and painfully shy where ladies are concerned, was quite unnerved. Blushing furiously, he called Mrs. Smith three times to explain the Caraway precedent and to stammer out his excuse for turning down her request. The situation so preyed on his mind, however, that at last he could stand it no longer. He quietly waived seniority rules and assigned Mrs. Smith an office near the chamber—one with no washroom as it turned out. This was quickly remedied at some small expense to the taxpayers.

Senators, regardless of their seniority, are Olympian. They

can command any Senate elevator by ringing three times. Every operator understands this summons. With a hasty slamming of doors, the elevator swoops up or down—with complete disregard for all other passengers—to answer the call. Once a tourist was trapped for 20 minutes as an elevator dashed up and down during a Senate roll call. He merely wanted to go to the second floor. After the opening of the new Senate Office Building, there was a brief crisis because the builder had installed elevator buttons which lit up. One ring would light the button, the other two didn't register. Thus the hapless operators could never tell whether the call came from a Senator or some lesser human, like a taxpayer. The problem was solved by reserving extra elevators for the exclusive use of the Senators. Subway cars, which run between the Senate office buildings and the Capitol, are also subject to preemptory senatorial summons. By ringing a special bell, a Senator can bring the car to a screeching halt. Once the Senator is seated, he is whisked off to his destination—no matter how many stranded passengers may be left behind.

More serious than the matter of the luminous elevator buttons, a temporary and unforeseen crisis developed over another Senate tradition following the retirement of Felton "Skeeter" Johnston in 1965 as Secretary of the Senate. Skeeter kept a private stock of liquor in his office, just off the Senate floor, for legislators who needed a small pick-up during the rigors of debate. His office had become a favorite gathering place for Senators on slow afternoons when they sought more stimulation than they could get from their colleague's speeches. Even non-bourbon drinkers such as Senator Frank Lausche (D-Ohio) would drop in for a glass of beer and some friendly conversation. To the dismay of many Senators, Johnston's successor, straight-laced Frank Valeo, wasn't the convivial sort. But Sergeant-at-Arms Joseph Duke, whose job it was to enforce Senate regulations (including one against serving liquor in the Capitol building), found them a new hideaway with an adequate liquor cabinet.

Political protocol is always puzzling. Of all the rare creatures inhabiting the political woods, none is more mystifying than Homo Candidatus—the candidate, who hibernates between elections then backs out into the sunlight, loudly protesting every step of the way that he has no designs on higher office. His cry is a piercing "No! No!" which almost invariably means "Yes! Yes!" For his habits and ruses are so well known that only the most guileless are really deceived. Political ambition is honorable enough, the heritage of every red-blooded American boy. Yet most politicians would rather lose their pants in public than allow their hats to be blown prematurely into the ring. *For an aspirant to get caught with his ambition showing is considered indecent exposure.*

There is a certain strategy behind these peculiar folkways. The first candidate who pokes his head above the mob, for instance, risks having it knocked off by his opponents who will probably gang up on him. The front runner invites a "Stop Him" campaign, since the object of each hopeful is to stop everyone but himself. Says Vice President Humphrey pithily: "It's like shooting pheasants out of season." In his view, the wise candidate should wait until there are other birds in the air to attract the attention of the guns.

It's the diplomatic set that takes protocol the most seriously. Some 115 Ambassadors and Ministers suffer ordeal by cocktail because protocol requires them to call on each other and to attend the parties they must give on national holidays. For the seat of diplomatic society has long since moved from Europe's royal courts and Victorian settings to Washington's tree-shaded Massachusetts Avenue, otherwise known as Embassy Row. Here the pomp and protocol of bygone days, when diplomats wore beards and string ensembles played Viennese waltzes, are still in flower. The diplomats may be better shaved, and they may dance the frug, the jerk, and the Watusi. But none of the glamor has been lost. Awed tourists can watch chauffeured limousines sweep up to the grey embassies and discharge passengers, resplendent in white ties and tails, evening dresses with trains. There are more sables than at a Fifth Avenue fashion show, more gaudy uniforms than at a doorman's convention.

Yet along Embassy Row, parties are serious business. The tinkling glasses, sparkling wines, and sophisticated chatter are merely trappings for high diplomatic drama. *A smile, say, could signal a change in East-West relations; a whispered word might reverberate around the world like thunder; an innocent faux pas could cause an international incident.* At one function, for instance, the Soviet Ambassador passed pleasantries with a Western diplomat. Suddenly, the Russian shifted vocal gears and spoke intently for a few moments, nervously pressing his fingertips together. His listener nodded, hurried over to a State Department official, and whispered urgently in his ear: Russia might share more nuclear secrets for peaceful purposes.

Most diplomatic parties are quiet, courtly affairs. The cocktail party is the least formal. Ambassadors come and go in quick order, usually stopping only to shake their host's hand and gobble a canape. The young diplomats, social climbers, newsmen, and gate crashers last longer, a few hanging around until the portable bars are put away. The dinner party is more de rigueur. The program, down to the last detail, is dictated by social tradition: the guests eat at 8 o'clock, leave the table at 9:30, dance until 11. But the ultimate in formality is the diplomatic "white tie" dinner which Perle Mesta, Washington's famous "hostess with the mostest," has described as the only social function where "everything is perfect."

Washington's society queens are quick to spot the slightest imperfections. The silverware, for instance, tells a lot about a party. "If the silver has a very glossy shine and there aren't any finger marks," a dowager confided, "it means the servants handled it with gloves and used a proper rouge." Or you can judge a party, if you're in the social know, by noticing the butler and doorman. "If you see Dominick in the house and Cowler in the driveway," she advised knowingly, "you know it's going to be a good party."

Parties for Presidents, Prime Ministers and royalty almost always call for white tie and tails. Protocol demands that President Johnson or Secretary of State Rusk give a super-formal dinner for each visiting head of state. At formal dinners, the guests are seated by rank from the head to the foot of the table, downward through Cabinet officers, Ambassadors, Senators, Congressmen, lesser officials and finally—when they are invited—representatives of the three news services. Often a prominent guest, outranked protocol wise, finds himself seated below the salt. At a dinner for Japan's ex-Prime Minister Shegeru Yoshida, a noted but non-official guest, John D. Rockefeller III, wound up at the newsmen's end of the table.

One famous hostess has found how to get around protocol and keep unwanted guests from her parties. She waits until the last day, then personally phones the person—an ambassador, say, whose country is in disfavor or a Senator in political eclipse, or perhaps an official under security investigation. "I want you to come to my party tonight, but I know how busy you are," she coos. "You are more than welcome if you can possibly make it." He usually can't.

The guest list is more flexible, of course, at private parties than embassy affairs. But the hostess at any Washington social event "simply must know who's who," says one who does. "The European diplomats are more chic than the South American corps, except for Peru and Brazil. Peru is very smart right now," she says. As for domestic celebrities: "I always invite Senators to my parties, but I seldom play around with the lower House." This hostess builds her parties around one "attractive couple," then starts adding other couples "who blend in." If, as she puts it, "you have enough pretty women and clever men at your party, then you can afford to invite a homely cabinet officer and his wife."

After a diplomatic dinner, the caterer promptly counts the silverware. *Over* 600 *teaspoons* (*not to mention assorted plates, knives, forks, glasses, etc.*) *annually disappear from Embassy Row.* Examples: A Czechoslovakian Embassy party ended up minus 1 dinner plate, 1 silver fork, 3 teaspoons and 6 glasses; an Argentine Embassy dinner was short 6 teaspoons and 4 glasses. Occasionally the losses run to serious proportions. Once the Dominican Republic tossed a major reception for its nationals from the Washington-Philadelphia-New York area. Cab drivers mingled with ambassadors for a few magic hours. Later inventory showed 157 teaspoons missing.

Worst headaches are the Soviet Embassy parties; the silver service disappears almost as fast as the food. Souvenir hunters who swipe spoons from the Russian Embassy might do well to take a look at the back. They are stamped with the caterer's initials, not the embassy's. Most popular "souvenirs" are bottles of whiskey. These have a remarkable proclivity for disappearing from under a bartender's busy hands. Full cases have been known to vanish without so much as an "abra cadabra." Worst place to keep liquor stocks safe during a party, caterers agree, is the Pan American Union. The distance is too great between the banquet hall and the nearest room with a lock.

Although correspondents have no official status in the Washington social order, they enjoy all the trappings. They consult and consort with the mighty, receive special privileges accorded to no other citizens, and rate invitations to Washington's best soirees. Though they like to decry government subsidies, they have special facilities set aside for them in all major public buildings. The government provides telephones and typewriters for their use, hires clerks to attend to their wants, and sometimes furnishes them with free airplane transportation. A reporter desiring to cover Washington need bring only his own pencil.

The Washington press corps also has a definite pecking order. At the top are the Pashas of the press—the columnists and commentators, bureau chiefs and interpretive byliners—who remain largely above the clatter of the teletype machines and the crassness of hourly deadlines. They survey the Washington scene from serene heights, often passing down more profundities than facts. They scarcely deign to grub around for news. At this lofty level, they indulge more in weighty judgments than in journalistic hustling. They would rather propound than pry, interpret facts than dig them up. Their specialty is deep thinking; for them news is merely a commodity to be transformed into a rare essence by their cerebral converters.

Some radio-television news celebrities aren't even required to think. They owe their success to the thrust of their jaw and the boom of their baritone. When the ABC network debated whether to hire a new telecaster, one executive wanted to know: "Does he have his own hair?" Indeed, ABC's own Jim Hagerty, a former White House press secretary, once remarked: *"There are some radio and television voices in Washington, who to my personal knowledge, never attended a presidential news conference in the eight years I was in the White House. There are also individuals who have never been to Capitol Hill to cover the Congress or to the State Department or to any other departments and agencies."* He was referring to performers, not reporters, men who wouldn't recognize a news story unless they saw it on a teleprompter.

The press Pashas, having persuaded themselves that Washington is constantly shaken by the rumble of their typewriters,

U.S. Propaganda Odd Jobs Pay Reporters $175,000

Covers 5-Year Fees to Stringers; Practice Questioned on The Hill

By Fred Bertram

America's propaganda arm has built a nation-wide backstop of newspaper reporters and other free-lance writers to supplement its own full-time force.

The United States Information Agency's 1962 budget hearings showed $30,239 paid out to free-lance writers in the year under review. Over a 5-year period, some $175,000 went to the USIA's "propaganda reservists."

The USIA's "stable," as the budget probers have referred to it, has been reported as running around 300 members from year to year. Some reporters pick up under $100 a year. Others have earned $1,000 and $2,000 and more a year.

Washington Mill

From free-lance typewriters across the country, the propaganda material funnels into the USIA's Washington editorial mill at 1776 Pennsylvania Avenue. From there it is filtered abroad to United States Information Service offices in close to 100 countries around the world. There translated into local languages, the Hometown-U.S.A. products reappear in foreign newspapers, form the basis for local radio broadcasts or are used in USIS publications abroad.

These free-lance word-pictures of the American scene feed into the nation's propaganda mill in three main forms. There is what the USIA calls its "General Current Events Coverage." For example, From Russell L. Faist of the *Cleveland News*, 500 words on a crippled Negro nominated for the Carnegie medal for rescuing a drowning white man from Lake Erie, for which Mr. Faist received $20; from Robert Breen of the *Baltimore Sun*, 800 words on dedication of a new Leprosy Research Laboratory at Johns Hopkins, $25.

Particularly important for propaganda purposes, the USIA has indicated, is its "Visitor Coverage." Stories of foreign visitors to the U.S. are relayed back to their home countries. For example, from Don Ashbaugh of the *Las Vegas Review Journal*, 800 words on the King of Nepal's visit to Las Vegas and vicinity, $25; from Allan Hoschar of the *Des Moines Register*, 700 words on visit of the Polish Minister of Agriculture, $25.

"Special Articles," make up the third and smallest classification of free-lance production. Examples: From Managing Editor Robert J. Landry, of *Variety*, an article on "Television—Live — Filmed — Tape," $75; from Charles A. Clay of the *Raleigh* (N. C.) *News & Observer*, a story on textile education in the United States, with emphasis on the Textile School at North Carolina State University, $60.

One Editor's View

Not all managing editors approve of their reporters working or filing for the U.S. Information Agency on the side. Publicity received by a few reporters at budget hearings on The Hill is said to have disturbed some publishers.

A House Appropriations Subcommittee heard from a USIA spokesman of one managing editor who had even spoken in public against the practice, complaining that a newspaper reporter could not be entirely objective if he was "making little commissions of $20 and $25 in his spare time for the USIA."

The USIA spokesman said that while this editor's opinion was not the majority view, the Agency fully respected his views. The same editor's newspaper had supplied considerable material to the Agency free of charge, it was added.

Criticism of the USIA's habit of hiring outside reporters crops up from time to time during the yearly budget hearings on Capitol Hill. The Agency indicated that it would be much more expensive to try to cover nationally-scattered events by sending its own reporters around the country.

When the subject came up again at this year's 1962 budget hearings, Subcommittee Member Frank T. Bow (Rep. Ohio) wanted to know why the USIA's three full-time New York reporters couldn't cover the New York stories. More than $4500 had been paid out during the year for more than 300 New York stories.

This colloquy took place:

MR. HUTCHISON. (John N. Hutchison, Director, Press and Publications Service, USIA.) One of the people in New York covers the United Nations full time. Two of them cover general news in New York full time. But there are frequent occasions when it is more economical to buy material from a writer for a given purpose than to send and maintain another staff person in New York.

MR. BOW. You have one at the UN and the other two are general reporters.

MR. HUTCHISON. Yes sir.

MR. BOW. Why can they not cover these stories?

MR. HUTCHISON. They do not have the time to do it, sir. They are engaged full time as it is.

MR. BOW. In doing what?

MR. HUTCHISON. In writing stories.

* * *

MR. BOW. Harold A. Klein has written a number of stories in New York. Why could not your local people have handled the stories Mr. Klein has written.

MR. CANNON. (Thomas L. Cannon, Deputy Director, Editorial) A great many of these stories, sir, are evening and weekend events and also occur during the day when both of our reporters are assigned to other stories.

* * *

Use of Wire Services

Mr. Bow then called for the workload of two of the New York reporters for nine specific days, broken down according to "what they did on those days, what they were writing and where they were."

As a subscriber to the wire services, the USIA has been asked at budget hearings why wire service coverage couldn't be used in place of the free-lance network.

"We have found from experience," a USIA spokesman replied, "that the wire services writing for domestic clients either ignore the angle we would be interested in or the story is written for a domestic audience so it is not too useful for us. Where we can use the wire services we do."

At this year's 1962 budget hearings, Subcommittee Chairman John J. Rooney, (Dem. New York), got into the record that in the fiscal year 1961, the Associated Press had been paid $50,837, Reuters $32,100 and UPI $42,104, a total of some $125,000 for the year.

For 'Voice' Use

From Reuters, the USIA said the general news service was purchased essentially for use by the Voice of America. From UPI the trunk service was purchased for $37,377 and the Washington City news service for $4800.

The AP wire services are bought only for information and may not be used, the USIA said. AP services are purchased for information in Washington, in the Near East and South Asia and in West Europe.

The subcommittee learned that the terms of agreement under which USIS posts in Western Europe subscribe to the AP service preclude use by USIS of AP news material. "The service is subscribed to for information and to assure that posts' press output does not duplicate material transmitted by the U.S. wire services."

•

Harry Brooks Elected To Montana Shrine

GLACIER PARK, Mont.

Montana State Press Association elected the late Harry B. Brooks to the Montana Newspaper Hall of Fame

Mr. Brooks, who died of a heart attack in 1944, was nominated by Dan Whetstone, publisher of the *Cut Bank Pioneer Press*.

A native of Minnesota, who graduated from the University of Minnesota at the age of 18, Mr. Brooks began his Montana newspaper career in 1905 as manager of the *Chinook Bulletin*. He purchased the Chinook Opinion in 1906 and published it until 1928. He was editor of the *Havre Daily News* from 1928 to 1934 when he joined the *Great Falls Tribune* as an editorial writer.

The hall of fame is at the Montana State University Journalism School in Missoula.

Fred J. Martin, publisher of the *Park County News* of Livingston, was elected president of the Montana State Press Association for 1961-62.

EDITOR & PUBLISHER for September 2, 1961 15

Newsmen still supplement their salaries by moonlighting for the United States Information Agency along the lines described in this Editor & Publisher article.

are inclined to be condescending toward government officials. Columnist Joseph Alsop, whose face seems to be drawn in a perpetual half-sneer, once told an Atomic Energy Commissioner: "You have just wasted half an hour of my time." Even society sleuth Betty Beale, when Lyndon Johnson was a mere Vice President, turned down an invitation to fly to the LBJ Ranch to write an exclusive story. "I bet there's ragweed down there," she said suspiciously. "I'm allergic to ragweed." Without so much as a ragweed count, she chose not to go.

Members of the "think" corps, whose speculations don't always keep pace with the amount of space they are expected to fill, practice journalistic incest. They interview one another on great developments, feed off each other's material, and trade tidbits. Some correspondents, who may happen to serve clients at opposite ends of the land, merely exchange "black sheets" as carbon copies of their stories are called in the trade. *Even the New York Times' esteemed James Reston, who would never be expected to traffic with the Chicago Tribune, has slipped items to the Tribune's Walter Trohan that the Times would not consider fit to print.*

The initiative of Washington correspondents, *outnumbered two to one by government press agents,* is also blunted by official handouts. It takes much less effort to rewrite an official announcement than to pursue the facts. When presidential press secretary Bill Moyers issues bulky releases he is often asked to identify key passages so that reporters won't have to waste their time searching for important facts. *Indeed, some correspondents become so imbued with official lore that they take on the attitudes, even the personalities, of the bureaucrats they cover.* "The State Department reporter," as columnist Russell Baker has pointed out, "quickly learns to talk like a fuddy-duddy and to look grave, important, and inscrutable. The Capitol reporter eschews the raucous spirit of the Congress and effects the hooded expression of the man privy to many important deals. Like the politicians he covers, he tends to garrulity, coarse jokes, and bourbon, and learns to hate reform. The Pentagon man always seems to have just come in off maneuvers."

If one Pasha can be said to tower over the others, it is the aging Walter Lippmann, still recognized as Washington's foremost political philosopher. Most of his work is done in the book-lined study of his ivy-covered stucco home where, in an atmosphere of detachment and serenity, he scrawls his column in longhand. Yet he is no recluse. A friendly, witty cosmopolite, he can often be seen in earnest discussion with high officials over lunch at the exclusive Metropolitan Club. Lippmann cares nothing about the scramble for scoops, uses the information he collects merely to broaden his outlook.

Another old timer, still hunched over his typewriter, is stodgy David Lawrence, aging prophet of the far right, who writes sourly about the changing world. His style is only slightly less cumbersome and conservative than that of Arthur Krock, the fusty dean of Washington correspondents and a fixture in the Capital since the days of William Howard Taft. A kindly uncle figure, the venerable Krock launched the journalistic careers of a mop-haired Harvard graduate and a shy young debutante who later met, married and settled down in the White House. But once the John F. Kennedys moved into the presidential mansion, Krock, true to his conservative credentials, wrote caustic, critical columns about them.

For sheer star status, the TV commentators easily out-dazzle their cohorts of the pencil and pad. One of the most popular is David Brinkley who, unlike most others, writes all of his own copy. To people who know him only from the elbows up, Brinkley appears to be a small man. In fact, he is a gangling, six-feet-two inches and wears size 11 shoes. On the screen, he is never ruffled; in real life, he is shy and will flee in mild panic from a backslapper or a cocktail party.

But there is no suppressing his quiet sense of humor. A few years ago, when he lived in an apartment building with a sun deck on the roof, he became impatient with a tenant who folded his deck chair after each use and locked it securely with a chain and padlock. Brinkley quietly added two more padlocks to the deck chair and threw the keys away. In time, he moved to a fashionable Washington suburb and selected the color for his new home from a small swath sample. In full bloom, however, the house turned out to be a nauseating yellow, an eyesore, an affront to gracious living. Brinkley hastily mounted a sign on his front lawn: "Please be patient, this is NOT the final color. It's just a horrible mistake."

Washington also has its news hens who soar above the clucking flock of society reporters and compete with the men in chronicling great national events. Perhaps the best known, before her recent retirement, was May Craig, an arsenic-and-old-lace character who wielded one of the sharpest hat pins along the Potomac. Few escaped her jabs who dared tangle with her at press conferences. One exception: President Johnson who once, as she gestured to make a point, grabbed her hand and held it tenderly. The President flirts unashamedly with many of the lady reporters. He calls them "sweetheart," plants affectionate kisses on their cheeks, and inscribes pictures to them "with love."

The best read lady columnist is Doris Fleeson, who looks deceptively grandmotherly but oils her typewriter with a special acid. Mrs. Johnson once gushed over a new dress Miss Fleeson was wearing at a dinner party. Cooed the First Lady: "It makes you look like a sweet old-fashioned girl." Listening nearby, Mrs. Stuart Symington, wife of the Missouri Senator, cooed: "Yes, a sweet old-fashioned girl with a shiv in her hand." Miss Fleeson works her feminine wiles to sweet-talk news out of doting Senators, but she can also blow dragon flames upon anyone who displeases her.

THE SECRETARY OF STATE
WASHINGTON

April 3, 1963

Dear Mr. [redacted]

The Department of State will hold the next National Foreign Policy Conference for Editors and Broadcasters on Monday and Tuesday, April 22 and 23. President Kennedy and principal policy-making officers of the Department of State and other major Government agencies will again join us in this two-day conference on foreign policy for the information media.

We hope that you will be able to attend, or to designate an appropriate member of your staff to attend in your place.

We have had many requests to conduct the conference sessions on the record, instead of on a background (no attribution) basis as previously. A number of the presentations at the April conference will be on the record.

Further details concerning the conference will be mailed to you shortly.

I would appreciate your replying by means of the enclosed card to Mr. Daniel W. Montenegro, Director, Office of Public Services, Department of State, Washington 25, D. C.

Sincerely yours,

Dean Rusk

Dean Rusk

At the type of "briefings" referred to in this letter, editors and broadcasters are usually told what the government would like to publicize without being identified as the source.

It is a curious paradox of the nation's capital, where the clash of opinion is a way of life, that controversial correspondents are sometimes treated like outcasts. Those who depart from the beaten news paths, who ignore the "no trespass" signs, who pry behind the scenes, are regarded with distrust. There are belittling remarks about their inaccuracies and unorthodoxies, their unwillingness to play the game by traditional rules.

The rise to the National Press Club presidency was as automatic as an escalator ride for those elected to the board until the Cowles papers' Clark Mollenhoff reached the top. He had alienated The Clique by digging for stories upon forbidden ground and unearthing news that occasionally embarrassed them with their editors back home. So the New York Times' more acceptable William Blair challenged and defeated Mollenhoff.

It is also fashionable at the press tables to underestimate columnist Drew Pearson. Since he contributes substantially to my income, any views of mine on him may not be wholly objective. Yet for the better part of this century, he has rocked Washington with his stories. His columns have led to the convictions of at least 18 scoundrels, including four Congressmen, in the 20 years I have been associated with him. All I know about investigative reporting, he has taught me. Together we have tried to expose wrongdoing in high places from the indiscretions of White House aide Sherman Adams to the misconduct of Senator Thomas Dodd (D-Conn.). Though the Sherman Adams affairs was voted unanimously as the top story of 1958, the journalistic prizes went to reporters who had uncovered some junkyard and mental-hospital scandals. Early in January, 1951, Drew revealed the highlights of the secret Wake Island conference between President Harry Truman and General Douglas MacArthur. The following April, the New York Times published the same

Certificate of Notable Achievement

Beyond the Normal Call of the Fourth Estate

Land and People Tour

Know ye that

____

Having displayed high personal courage on The Land and People Tour with The First Lady, Mrs. Lyndon B. Johnson, and The Secretary of the Interior, Stewart L. Udall, and having exhibited outstanding ability to chronicle the events of that arduous safari through the States of Montana, Wyoming and Utah -- knowing full well that they would never be the same again after exposure to the wondrous beauties of Grand Teton National Park and the spectacular Flaming Gorge Dam and National Recreation Area -- and having bravely volunteered to float down the Snake River after a venture into Indian territory, protected only by their sharp wit and keen appetite for fried rainbow trout and barbecued buffalo --

Now therefore, the above individual is entitled to this Certificate of Notable Achievement.

Montana, Wyoming, Utah
August 14-17, 1964.

Gimmicks of this sort are sometimes given to reporters who cover President and Mrs. Johnson during their "non-political" trips. The above, handsomely printed for framing, was issued at public expense.

U.S. DEPARTMENT OF COMMERCE
BUREAU OF THE CENSUS
WASHINGTON, D.C. 20233.

FOR RELEASE UPON RECEIPT

THIS LOCAL NEWS ITEM WAS PREPARED BY A CENSUS BUREAU ELECTRONIC COMPUTER AND TYPED AT 10 LINES PER SECOND ESPECIALLY FOR ------

EDITOR 003
ENTERPRISE
POCATELLO IDAHO

U.S. CENSUS BUREAU REPORTS COUNTY'S '63 RETAIL TRADE

BANNOCK COUNTY'S 893 RETAIL ESTABLISHMENTS HAD $ 73.0 MILLION IN SALES IN 1963, AN INCREASE OF 21 PERCENT FROM 1958. THE U.S. BUREAU OF THE CENSUS HAS JUST REPORTED AFTER TABULATING DATA GATHERED FROM ALL FIRMS IN THE 1963 CENSUS OF BUSINESS. THE LAST PREVIOUS BUSINESS CENSUS CONDUCTED BY THE CENSUS BUREAU, AN

A Commerce Department press release devised by a computer.

story with less detail and no quotes. The Times was awarded the Pulitzer Prize for it.

Next to heaven, Washington correspondents can aspire to nothing higher than an invitation to join the exclusive Gridiron Club. Active membership is limited to 50 Pashas of the press who, with a single blackball, can bar undesirables as vacancies occur. This group throws an annual banquet, sort of a posh Saints and Sinners frolic, at which the high and mighty are roasted figuratively over the gridiron.

Less exclusive is the National Press Club whose chief attraction is a $30,000 bar. "The bars, lounges and dining tables of the National Press Club," observes the New York Times' Cabell Phillips, "have been a kind of alchemists's retort in which thousands of Washington stories have been distilled, synthesized, or even induced out of the thin but susceptible air." Members still talk about the query the late Ed Jamieson got from one of his editors demanding: "Understand something catastrophic is about to happen in the financial world. Please confirm." Jamieson puzzled over it a bit, then checked it out at the Press Club bar. After ordering an extra round to stimulate their memories, the habitues agreed they knew of nothing catastrophic, financial or otherwise. Satisfied, he returned later to his office and wired the paper: "Nothing to it."

Press Club membership can be granted to anyone who is a "newsworthy source," a phrase that excludes practically no one except women. This exclusion has long angered lady reporters, who are permitted in the sacred confines only to cover the appearances of notables from a small balcony where they fret and fume.

In 1959 a precedent was set by Soviet Premier Nikita Khrushchev when he insisted that his Press Club appearance be open to all accredited reporters. First in line for the great equalitarian event was the National Jewish Post's attractive Lillian Levy, followed by May Craig. Third was columnist Joe Alsop who, rising to the occasion, bussed Mrs. Craig and made an appropriate remark about peaceful coexistence. The Washington Post's Molly Thayer, tracking down some jovial noises, ended up in the men's bar, blissfully unaware of its sanctity. She was promptly, and not too politely, ejected. In the crush at the gate, Elsa Sturm, a Swedish correspondent, fainted. "Is anyone doing anything for her?" cried another female. Growled a male: "Yes, they're trying to get her ticket."

After this debacle, the men refused to let the ladies come down from the balcony in 1962 to hear Konrad Adenauer, then West Germany's Chancellor. The dears, pouting and petulant, stormed the White House. Taking no chances with the women's vote, President Kennedy agreed cautiously that "all working reporters" should be permitted to hear Adenauer. This brought howls of outrage from the men. William Lawrence, ABC's commentator, was heard to plead for a place where "men may retire from the shrill argumentative voices of the lady reporters." After LBJ moved into the White House, the militant suffragettes of the typewriter pressured him, too. Only result: The State Department's protocol office has passed the word discreetly that the President would prefer to have visiting dignitaries deliver their speeches to audiences not segregated by sex.

During the tenure of Joe Dear of the Dear Publications as president of the Press Club, a time honored tradition went into limbo. It had been the custom for each new board member to provide a bottle of Scotch and a bottle of bourbon at each board meeting. Determined to reduce the dragging out of board meetings, Dear instituted prohibition at the conferences.

Clearly, the easy course for correspondents is to become a pundit, accept the plaudits, fall into a social trap, and avoid digging into stories that will embarrass their important friends. Yet it must be conceded that the Capital's correspondents manage to keep the world well informed of what goes on in Washington. In this age of complexity and anxiety, newspapers are sending better educated, better paid and more specialized reporters to Washington. Some of them know more about economics, science, space, agriculture, etc., than the bureaucrats they cover. But there is a tendency for bureaucrats and correspondents alike, secure among their status symbols, to regard themselves as judges of what the public should or should not be told.

9

HOW THE INSIDERS WORK

Dexter Warren, as sly a predatory animal as ever stalked a client in the Washington jungle, had every reason to be pleased with himself. His bank statement, which had arrived that morning by special messenger, had never been more satisfying. In the previous week alone he had increased it by $25,000, the amount he had charged Bonanza Aviation, Inc., for making one telephone call to the Pentagon. The call had lasted precisely three minutes by his expensive precision wristwatch. An involuntary chuckle bubbled out, like a merry hiccup, as he recalled how Bonanza's president had pleaded with him to intercede with the Air Force over a contract dispute. Dexter had learned from his phone call that a satisfactory settlement already had been decided upon; he merely had passed on the good news.

Scrupulously, he had not claimed to have influenced the settlement. But the president of Bonanza knew that influence was Dexter Warren's business. If he chose to assume that influence had been used, Dexter saw no reason to disillusion him. The company's Washington counsel had whistled when Dexter had blandly named his fee. "I know you think $25,000 is too much, and the client will think it is too much," Dexter had said. "But when he goes down to the steam room in the Fountainbleau, he will boast to his friends that Dexter Warren charged him $25,000 for making a phone call, and it will be worth $25,000 to him as a conversation piece."

If you have never heard of Dexter Warren, it is because this isn't his name. *He is not even one person but half a dozen. He is a composite of an exclusive breed—the Insiders —who whisper into the ears of the mighty, influence gov-*

ernment policy, but never answer to the public. Every incident of Dexter's story actually happened. Only the names are changed. I know the actual names, and I have verified the events. But the Insiders are so powerful, my sources so fearful, that this story has to be written as though it's fiction.

Dexter Warren is king of beasts in the Washington jungle—that tangle of red tape and bureaucratic underbrush, a political jungle prowled by sophisticated beasts of prey. Compared with him, the lesser wanglers, fixers, and five percenters are but jackals, slinking around waiting to snap up the scraps. It is difficult to fix a label on Dexter. He is not a registered lobbyist, though he has direct telephone lines to two of the Senate's most important members. He holds no official status, though he sometimes has given orders in the President's name to the highest officials in government. He is one of the most prosperous attorneys in town, though he rarely performs any legal service.

He might best be described as a fixer without portfolio, who has handled White House assignments too delicate to be performed by anyone in official position. He also advises the President on speeches, appointments, and politics. His phone calls are put through promptly to cabinet officers, commissioners, members of Congress, and special contacts in the FBI and CIA. His quiet counsel is whispered into the most important ears in Washington. For all this, Dexter collects not a penny of pay. However, this is a sacrifice that does no injury to his Dun and Bradstreet rating. He makes up for his patriotism by charging his clients all the market can bear—and his market value suffers not at all from his access to the high and mighty. He has charged a South American coffee combine $250,000 for bringing his influence to bear on coffee legislation. He expects to collect $100,000 from a financial house whose investment practices have been under government scrutiny.

No one—his clients perhaps least of all—can describe

NEWS RELEASE
OFFICE OF ASSISTANT SECRETARY OF DEFENSE (PUBLIC AFFAIRS)
WASHINGTON, D.C. - 20301
PLEASE NOTE DATE

IMMEDIATE RELEASE | January 17, 1964 | NO. 59-64
OXford 53201 (Info.)
OXford 73189 (Copies)

DOD TO CONDUCT CLASSIFIED BRIEFINGS FOR INDUSTRY
ON ITS LONG-RANGE BUYING & DEVELOPMENT PLANS

A series of classified briefings for American industry on what the Department of Defense will be shopping for over the next five years was ordered today by Deputy Secretary of Defense Roswell L. Gilpatric. The briefings will relate to long-range development and procurement plans of the Department of Defense and will be organized along industry lines rather than Department of Defense missions.

The Gilpatric Memorandum was addressed to the Military Departments and to the Heads of Defense Agencies engaged in development activities. Six briefings are scheduled for the first half of 1964. The industries to be invited to briefings are: Aircraft, Arms and Ammunition, Chemicals and Biologicals, Electronics, Missiles, and Nuclear Products. Each of the three Military Departments will serve as host for two of the briefings.

An additional six briefings are scheduled for the second half of 1964. Industries to be invited will include: Clothing, Internal Combustion Power, Mechanical Products, Research, Shipbuilding, and Ground Transportation.

The intent of the briefings is to provide industrial leadership with a DOD-wide picture of long-range development and procurement needs. Emphasis will be placed on projected shifts in development and procurement plans to meet the changing requirements of the United States military program. The briefings will be classified to permit a full and frank discussion of the major factors influencing military goals. Emphasis will be on trends rather than technical details.

An important feature of the new series of advanced planning briefings for industry is the participation in a single briefing by all three Military Departments and the Office of the Director of Defense Research and Engineering. Heretofore, military briefings have been conducted for industry by the individual services.

Department of Defense briefings have been one of the subjects of special interest to the Defense Industry Advisory Council (DIAC). At its meeting last May, the Council gave strong endorsement to changes in the briefing procedures which were later incorporated in a Department of Defense Instruction. The Council will be informed of the program for the new series of briefings at its meeting next month.

Owing to the high-level approach being taken in this new series of briefings, invitations to industrial firms will permit attendance of no more than three persons from among the top corporate offices engaged in top management research and planning. Participation by individual industrial

Secret defense information is disclosed to carefully selected groups of businessmen, as this not-so-secret Defense Department press release reveals.

precisely what Dexter does for them. His operations are largely extra-legal; the more left to the client's imagination, the higher the fee. A leonine toss of his iron grey mane, a steady stare of the cold blue eyes, and a brisk handshake is usually enough to impress the most skeptical client that, in Dexter Warren, he is dealing with no ordinary man.

Indeed, Dexter is more remarkable than his clients could suspect. In leaner days, before his party came to power, he maneuvered his way into the confidence of three leading presidential candidates. He sat solemnly on the strategy councils of all three, advising each how to wrest the nomination from the other two. The three were veteran politicians, not easily conned and not unaware of his divided friendship. But each believed only he possessed the true loyalty in Dexter's political shell game.

The two weaker candidates agreed to help one another take on the front runner, each in the presidential primary of the state where he felt strongest. But Dexter persuaded them separately that they had no hope of overtaking the leader in any state and that a primary loss might spoil their chances later at the convention. His advice happened to coincide with the strategy of the front runner, who hoped to keep his bandwagon rolling through the primaries, ever gathering momentum, until it couldn't be stopped. Each of the rivals continued to believe in Dexter's loyalty. But the two outsiders might have felt a flicker of doubt if they had kept more up to date on his law practice. For the front runner had reinforced his faith in Dexter's friendship with a quiet financial gesture. Two family business associates had suddenly become clients of Dexter's firm.

Dexter was still chortling over the Bonanza Aviation deal when his unlisted phone rang. It was Craig from his office. "Dex," said Craig, "I think we're in trouble, real trouble. You know about this House investigation into lobbying. I've got an idea they're going to get tough about unregistered lobbyists." As a hedge against such an embarrassment, Dexter had carefully required his two legislative assistants to register as lobbyists. "You and Willoughby are properly registered," he said. "We have nothing to worry about. Our clients are eminently satisfied."

"But what about you?" Craig reminded him. "You're not registered." Dexter, of course, considered himself above such petty requirements. He preferred to let Craig and Willoughby operate as his front men. Both were valuable men, personable, convincing, thoroughly grounded in the nuances of politics and the intricate workings of Congress. He didn't have a reputation for overpaying; their salaries were only $12,000 apiece. But they got their expenses and could bask in his prestige.

"Keep me informed," Dexter ordered curtly. While he didn't fully share Craig's concern, he was too astute to dismiss it. You could never tell where an investigation of this kind might lead. He couldn't afford any bad publicity, not while he was negotiating the biggest deal of his life. He had been offered a cool $1 million—$100,000 a year for 10 years—to engineer a tax break for Allied Motors.

Two weeks later, the subpoena arrived. Dexter accepted it with the incredulity of a police chief receiving a traffic summons. Dexter Warren, treated like a common lobbyist! After he got over his disbelief, his reaction was scarlet fury. Fiercely, he tore open his Congressional Directory to check on the membership of the offending House committee. Just as he had thought, he had arranged campaign contributions for many of them. He had wined them, dined them, listened to their vainglorious talk, and been gracious to their tedious, dowdy wives. Now they would repay him by putting him under the kleig lights.

For long, raging minutes Dexter stared fiercely at the private telephones on his desk. Then he slowly relaxed, breathed gently on his manicured nails, polished them on his lapel, and picked up the direct line to Senator Wilbur Clarke's office. His voice was deep and silky: "Ah, good morning, Bill, glad to find you in. I know you're going to be busy on the floor, so I'll be brief. Congressman Glass needs your support to get his Rivers and Harbors bill through the Senate, I believe. He is running this House lobbying investigation, you know. Now. . . ."

Dexter mentioned the subpoena as if it were a petty nuisance. It might embarrass him with his clients, he said, if he were compelled to answer questions in public.

Later, Dexter phoned a White House aide and a member of the investigating committee. That evening he was as urbane and witty as ever at a dinner party. But there was an urgent 20 minutes with his host and some other VIP's in the study. If outwardly Dexter was calm and confident, panic was forming like a lump of ice in his stomach. It was bad enough to have his name dragged into an investigation, but to testify was out of the question. He would have to admit, in the end, that he had sought to influence Congressional action in behalf of his clients. By his failure to register, he could be accused of violating the law.

The first call back came from Senator Clarke. "Dex," he said, "I've had a few words with Congressman Glass. Why don't you drop in to see him this afternoon? He'll be expecting you." Without a trace of anxiety in his voice, Dexter thanked the Senator. "I'll be happy to do that," he said.

Gavin Glass was waiting, fingering a pencil nervously, when Dexter was ushered into his office. Dexter knew the symptoms of a man under pressure, but he allowed no glint of triumph to appear in his eyes.

"Congressman," he said almost humbly, "we are both men of honor. You have my word that I have done nothing improper or illegal. But if this matter is pursued, the publicity might well cost me a retainer of $100,000 a year. I believe I can prove to your satisfaction that my relationship with my clients is that of a lawyer and not of a lobbyist. I will be happy to open my files to you, but I hope there will be no need to make a public spectacle of my private business."

"No, no, of course not," said Glass. "Your word is enough. You may consider the subpoena answered, and you are excused from testifying."

Dexter Warren nodded gravely. "Thank you, Congressman," he said. "Thank you."

The next several minutes were spent in dignified banter and a discussion of the Rivers and Harbors bill. Then solemnly, Dexter excused himself. As he stepped out of the Sam Rayburn Building, he breathed deeply of the balmy air and savored the sunshine. The tension drained away. It was a good day, he decided, for walking. By the time he reached his apartment, he was completely at ease. He was also completely convinced that what was good for Dexter Warren really *was* good for the United States.

To protect my sources, I cannot identify the real-life Insiders from whom I have drawn the portrait of Dexter Warren. But there are many engaged in the quiet practice of influence whose operations need not be masked by fiction.

A familiar figure around the White House, for example, is soft-spoken Dale Miller, a low-pressure lobbyist of gray-haired southern dignity, who is on such intimate terms with Lyndon B. Johnson that he ran the 1964 inaugural for the President. *Miller represents such blue-chip Texas clients as Texas Gulf Sulphur, Intracoastal Canal Association, Dallas Chamber of Commerce, and Port of Corpus Christie.* President Johnson took time out from preparing his 1965 State of the Union Address to greet Miller's Dallas clients, take them on a stroll of the White House grounds, and discuss their dream of a new federal office building in downtown Dallas. With the President's blessing, the desired $22 million was quickly appropriated. Back in Texas there is at least one span that bears the proud name, "Dale Miller Bridge," in honor of the lobbyist who pushed through the $603,565 appropriation to build it. At this writing, Miller is seeking $900 million to deepen the Trinity River for 370 miles—far enough upstream to make a seaport of landlocked Dallas. *The betting is that he'll get it,* perhaps with an extra million or so to build a Dale Miller Wharf.

Another close to the President is curly-haired Clark Clifford, who forsook Harry Truman's White House to practice law. He was happily at home in Jack Kennedy's White House, now has the run of Lyndon Johnson's White House. Clifford has made no bones about his preference for fat legal fees over a government salary. This once led the late President Kennedy to crack: *"Clark is a wonderful fellow. In a day when men are seeking rewards for what they contributed for the return of the Democrats to the White House, you don't hear Clark clamoring. All he asked was that we advertise his law firm on the backs of one dollar bills."* Clark hardly needs to advertise to get big-money clients. One client, the giant FMC corporation, hired him over the phone. Paul Davies, the board chairman, simply put through a long-distance call, introduced himself over the phone, and asked Clifford to persuade the Justice Department to approve the purchase of the American Viscose Company for $115 million.

Clifford didn't need to ask why Davies had picked him out of the hundreds of attorneys who practice law in Washington. Though he has indignantly denied going to the President or any other high official with a client's problem, Clifford hardly conceals that he helped make the White House ready for the late President Kenedy and is now on close personal terms with President Johnson. *Few know precisely how Clifford works his miracles in Washington, but he has a remarkable record for shaping government policies to suit his clients.* At the same time, he has performed many a quiet service for Uncle Sam. He heads the President's Foreign

Intelligence Advisory Board which is supposed to keep vigil over the operations of the Central Intelligence Agency.

The Washington influence market has an impressive clientele—great corporations, labor unions, farm organizations, veterans groups, trade associations—indeed, every special interest and pressure group that has a stake in the multimillion-dollar decisions coming out of Washington. For, if the Capitol is ruled by power and politics, it is also swayed by the less visible forces of pressure and persuasion constantly applied by lawyers and lobbyists, manufacturers' representatives and public relations men, fixers and expediters, who are dedicated to the proposition that the national interest is identical with their particular interest. *These paid persuaders use every method from subtle suggestion to political threat. They usually prefer cocktails and caviar, buttonholing and backslapping. But if charm should fail, they can generate political heat with money, propaganda, and voter-pressure.*

The subtle principles of modern lobbying, as practiced by the skilled operator, include the knowledge (1) that a call from a constituent is worth a dozen contacts by a professional lobbyist; (2) that the best way to a Congressman's vote is through his ego; (3) that a big-name witness will draw more committee members to hear testimony on behalf of a given interest; (4) that an expert witness, such as a college professor, adds class to a case.

When pocketbook issues are involved, contending lobbyists will jockey for position on the witness stand more furiously than housewives at a bargain counter. They prefer the first to the second day of a hearing, mornings to afternoons; they have found that the lawmakers are much less bored at the outset. The hectic hearings on tax cuts produced such a scramble that Leo Irwin, chief counsel of the tax-writing House Ways and Means Committee, sent a private and plaintive memo to the members entitled: "Funny Things Happen to the Staff on the Way to a Hearing." Philosophized Irwin: "Mr. X does not care when he is scheduled, just so it is before Mr. Y and he is given five more minutes than Mr. Y."

Behind the solemn deliberations, the influence boys have easier-to-take ways of impressing their arguments upon lawmakers. *Many big corporations keep full-time suites in plush Washington hotels where Congressmen can come to imbibe. Others prefer to lavish their liquor on lawmakers at private parties.* Few entertain more royally than Albert E. Wilkinson, the courtly, white-haired lobbyist for Anaconda Copper, who usually goes about his lobbying in a chauffeured Cadillac. He once lured the entire House Ways and Means Committee to an exclusive stag dinner by disguising the invitations. These men, the most courted of Congressmen, showed up in full force because they thought the dinner was given by three fellow members: Representatives Hale Boggs (D-La.), Syd Herlong (D-Fla.), and Howard Baker (R-Tenn.). Not until they arrived did they discover that their host was really the gruffly affable Wilkinson, who not only issued invitations in the names of the three committee members but also used committee aides to make telephone calls arranging the party.

The practitioners of pressure also use the birthdays of the mighty as excuses for tossing celebrations that would make Louis XIV feel at home. For years, the two most glittering affairs in town were the birthday balls of the late Speaker Sam Rayburn (D-Tex.), and Senate GOP leader Everett Dirksen (R-Ill.). Lobbyist Dale Miller and his dynamic, dark-haired wife, "Scooter," laid out the champagne and cake for Rayburn. This whoopla every January 6th became an opening-of-Congress ritual, attended by everyone who was anyone, until Rayburn's passing in 1961. Then the Millers switched their Big Party to the August 27th birthday of an even more celebrated Texan—Lyndon B. Johnson. Nationwide Food Services, Inc., which operates the Senate restaurant, throws the annual birthday ball for Senator Dirksen. It, too, has become a gala affair, attended by Washington's brightest celebrities. Dirksen, in turn, always goes to bat for the company at appropriations time. He has managed to increase subsidy authorizations so it can continue to sell food to Senators at bargain prices.

On more than one occasion, the shipping lobby has broken out enough champagne to launch a thousand ships at parties honoring John Rooney (D-N.Y.), *who can always be counted upon to battle for the maritime industry against all reforms.* The shipping crowd proclaimed February 18, 1965, for example, as "John Rooney Night" and rented the grand ballroom of Washington's Mayflower Hotel for a suitable celebration. To make sure no one missed the point, the invitations that went to the shipping companies contained a picture of U.S. currency opposite the U.S. Capitol. For the bantam from Brooklyn is chairman of the House Appropriations subcommittee which decides how much subsidies the steamship companies will get. Beneath the picture of the greenbacks was the statement: *"This is a very important occasion, so please order your tickets now."*

When in the company of Congressmen, the hail fellows of the special interests must never appear cheap. *They must be faster on the draw than Wyatt Earp in reaching for luncheon checks or night club tabs. They are also expected to load up the largess in the matter of campaign contributions, Christmas gifts, and other good-will remembrances.* I have been told of at least one running poker game at which shipping lobbyists sit down once or twice a week with Congressmen and maritime officials. The lobbyists almost always manage to lose.

The most effective lobbyists are those who stay in the shadows and, in fact, pretend they are not really lobbyists at all. They have long since learned to be subtle about the influence they possess and the favors they dispense. They watch the Washington scene closely for their clients and report the first sign of smoke. But they seldom put out the fire themselves, preferring to send in friends, constituents, or contributors to deal with Congressmen. A typical bulletin was sent out to advertising agencies by their association headquarters. The bulletin inquired confidentially:

"Have you a political candidate as a client? Have you recently handled the campaign of a Senator or Congressman? Do you or your key people have any personal connection with Members of Congress or political leaders? Your political acquaintances might be of help to advertising, and we would like to know about them. . . . We have in the agency business a good deal of latent political power. It should be used sparingly. But we shall have to be prepared on occasion to present our case as forthrightly as possible and as high in our government as we can reach."

Of course, not all influence peddlers are as subtle as the real professionals. Every lion in the federal jungle is hounded by jackals who follow at his heels and feed upon his kills. They are the phonies who pretend to know their way around, drop names with abandon, and trade on influence they don't possess. They are the smiling strangers who pop out in front of VIPs and introduce potential clients, counting upon the VIPs' uncertain memory of face to help them get away with it. With the big bluff, they land occasional retainers from unsuspecting businessmen in search of the "fix." These fixers and five percenters, who are the most careless and easiest to catch off base, taint the Washington air.

But in all fairness it should be stated that the pressure brigade indulges in comparatively little bribery, and the percentage of impropriety per billion dollars of federal spending is remarkably small.

ACT NOW

WARNING!

DO IT TODAY

YOUR EARNINGS FROM SAVINGS AND INVESTMENTS MAY BE TAXED 20% IN ADVANCE . . . .

UNLESS YOU DO SOMETHING ABOUT IT NOW!

This Message Is Of Vital Importance To Anyone Who Has Savings In A . . .

- SAVINGS AND LOAN ASSOCIATION
- OR A BANK

Or Who Owns

- U.S. SAVINGS BONDS
- STOCKS OR BONDS
- LIFE INSURANCE
- MUTUAL FUND SHARES

YOUR INTEREST OR DIVIDENDS WILL BE SUBJECT TO WITHHOLDING TAXES OF 20% BY THE FEDERAL GOVERNMENT UNDER BILLS NOW PROPOSED BY CONGRESS –

This means that churches, synagogues, orphanages, union trust funds, hospitals, all charitable organizations, widows, pensioners and even little children must file complicated tax forms to obtain refunds. Can you imagine the red tape involved in getting a fifty cent tax refund for a two-year-old child!

Who gains when funds rightfully belonging to United Appeals, local hospital building fund, or Red Cross are delayed by the tax collector?

The aged, blind or indigent earning less than necessary to pay income tax will have to wait months or perhaps a year to get refunds. Meanwhile who buys the groceries while the government keeps their dividend money . . . at NO interest?

THE COST OF SUCH A MOUNTAIN OF PAPER WORK COULD VERY EASILY BE MORE THAN THE ADDED REVENUE TO OUR GOVERNMENT!

REMEMBER – *THIS INSIDIOUS BILL IS NOT YET PASSED, BUT HEARINGS TO DECIDE THE OUTCOME ARE BEING HELD NOW IN WASHINGTON*

ACT NOW BEFORE IT'S TOO LATE!!

If you feel this withholding tax against your savings is unfair, now is the time for protest . . not after the bill is passed.

WRITE OR WIRE YOUR SENATORS AND CONGRESSMAN TODAY

OHIO SENATORS

FRANK J. LAUSCHE
ROOM 1327
NEW SENATE OFFICE BUILDING
WASHINGTON, D.C.

STEPHEN M. YOUNG
ROOM 485
NEW SENATE OFFICE BUILDING
WASHINGTON, D.C.

THIS MESSAGE SPONSORED IN THE PUBLIC INTEREST BY THE FOLLOWING LOCAL FINANCIAL INSTITUTIONS

THE METROPOLITAN BANK of LIMA
CENTRAL SAVINGS ASSOCIATION
FIRST NATIONAL BANK and TRUST COMPANY
SOUTH SIDE BUILDING and LOAN
CITY LOAN and SAVINGS COMPANY
FIRST FEDERAL SAVINGS and LOAN ASSOCIATION
The CITIZENS LOAN and BUILDING COMPANY

Washington lobbyists encourage propaganda of this sort to prevent passage of legislation they oppose. The above appeared in a Lima, Ohio, newspaper.

Big Business and Big Labor apply pressure to government with scientific efficiency. The lobbyists of labor—such men as the AFL-CIO's portly, articulate Andrew Biemiller, the Hod Carriers' affable Robert Connerton, and the Retail Clerks' youthful Charles Lipsen—furnish research, write speeches, and raise campaign funds for friendly lawmakers.

Even that pariah of labor, Teamsters boss Jimmy Hoffa, can crack the political whip and make Congressmen of both parties jump through the hoop. His chief lobbyist, shrewd, chunky Sid Zagari, easily rounded up a dozen congressmen to defend Hoffa on the House floor. On few other subjects has California's James Roosevelt, a liberal Democrat who gave up his House seat to accept an appointment to the United Nations, found support from such Republicans as Indiana's Ross Adair and William Bray, Iowa's Fred Schwengel, Minnesota's Clark MacGregor, Missouri's Thomas Curtis, Washington's Thomas Pelly, West Virginia's Arch Moore, and Wisconsin's Alvin O'Konski. All agreed solemnly that Hoffa's basic rights as a citizen may have been trampled by the Justice Department.

The corporate lobbyists, if less obvious, are no less efficient. The archly conservative National Association of Manufacturers is able to bring powerful pressure upon Congressmen from the country's businessmen. Its lobbying brigade is commanded by bespectacled, balding Ted Compton, who looks like the Yale economics professor he once was. Despite LBJ's flirtation with businessmen, the NAM staff cannot quite bring itself to embrace a Democratic President. Even as the romance blossomed, the NAM planted editorials around the country attacking his anti-poverty program as a boondoggle that "will gobble up a hundred billion dollars in a decade." These editorials, passed out free to any newspapers that would publish them, declared starchily: "It will take a prodigious amount of planning even to squander that much money, let alone use it wisely." NAM's publicists tried to conceal the

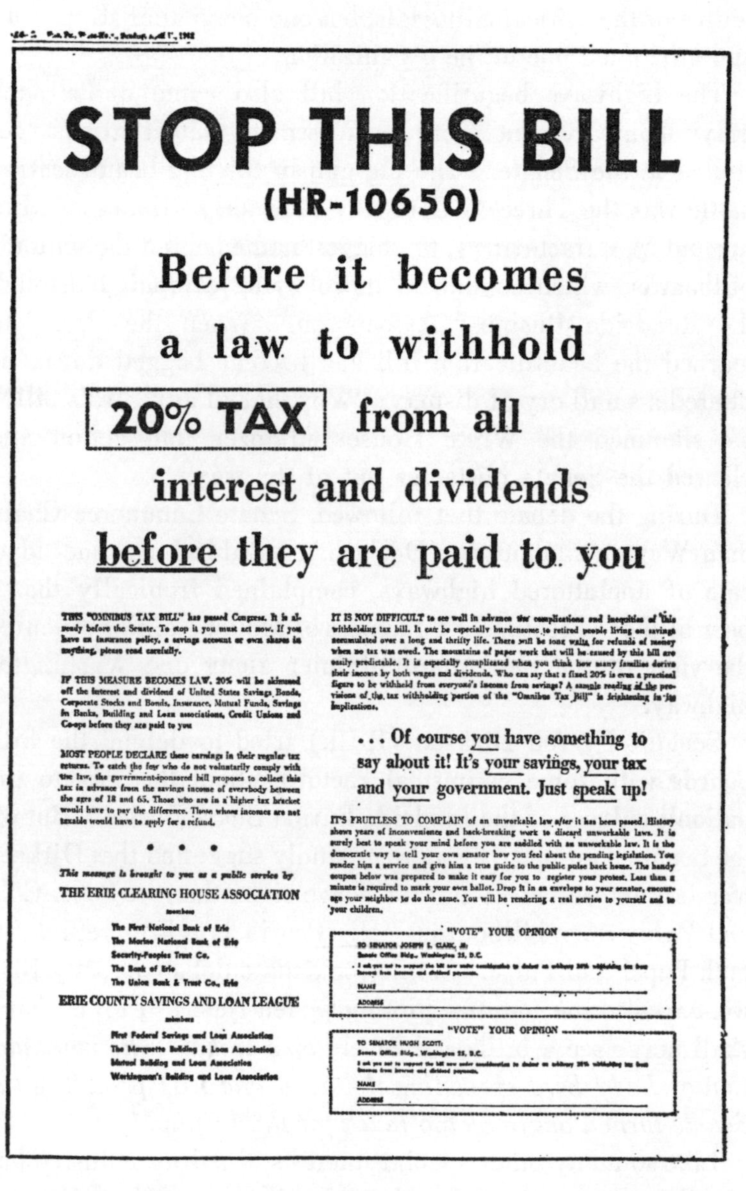

STOP THIS BILL

(HR-10650)

Before it becomes a law to withhold 20% TAX from all interest and dividends before they are paid to you

THIS "OMNIBUS TAX BILL" has passed Congress. It is already before the Senate. To stop it you must act now. If you have an insurance policy, a savings account or own shares in anything, please read carefully.

IF THIS MEASURE BECOMES LAW, 20% will be skimmed off the interest and dividend of United States Savings Bonds, Corporate Stocks and Bonds, Insurance, Mutual Funds, Savings in Banks, Building and Loan associations, Credit Unions and Co-ops before they are paid to you

MOST PEOPLE DECLARE these earnings in their regular tax returns. To catch the few who do not voluntarily comply with the law, the government-sponsored bill proposes to collect this tax in advance from the savings income of everybody between the ages of 18 and 65. Those who are in a higher tax bracket would have to pay the difference. Those whose incomes are not taxable would have to apply for a refund.

• • •

This message is brought to you as a public service by

THE ERIE CLEARING HOUSE ASSOCIATION

members

The First National Bank of Erie
The Marine National Bank of Erie
Security-Peoples Trust Co.
The Bank of Erie
The Union Bank & Trust Co., Erie

ERIE COUNTY SAVINGS AND LOAN LEAGUE

members

First Federal Savings and Loan Association
The Marquette Building & Loan Association
Mutual Building and Loan Association
Workingman's Building and Loan Association

IT IS NOT DIFFICULT to see well in advance the complications and inequities of this withholding tax bill. It can be especially burdensome to retired people living on savings accumulated over a long and thrifty life. There will be long waits for refunds of money when no tax was owed. The mountains of paper work that will be caused by this bill are easily predictable. It is especially complicated when you think how many families derive their income by both wages and dividends. Who can say that a fixed 20% is even a practical figure to be withheld from *everyone's* income from savings? A sample reading of the provisions of the tax withholding portion of the "Omnibus Tax Bill" is frightening in its implications.

. . . Of course you have something to say about it! It's your savings, your tax and your government. Just speak up!

IT'S FRUITLESS TO COMPLAIN of an unworkable law *after* it has been passed. History shows years of inconvenience and back-breaking work to discard unworkable laws. It is surely best to speak your mind before you are saddled with an unworkable law. It is the democratic way to tell your own senator how you feel about the pending legislation. You render him a service and give him a true guide to the public pulse back home. The handy coupon below was prepared to make it easy for you to register your protest. Less than a minute is required to mark your own ballot. Drop it in an envelope to your senator, encourage your neighbor to do the same. You will be rendering a real service to yourself and to your children.

"VOTE" YOUR OPINION

TO SENATOR JOSEPH S. CLARK, JR.
Senate Office Bldg., Washington 25, D.C.
[illegible]
NAME
ADDRESS

"VOTE" YOUR OPINION

TO SENATOR HUGH SCOTT:
Senate Office Bldg., Washington 25, D.C.
[illegible]
NAME
ADDRESS

Another example of pressure generated by Washington lobbyists. The above appeared in the Erie, Pa., Times-News.

source of the critical editorials, but one newspaper slipped up and attributed one to the organization.

The highways beautification bill also came under such heavy bombardment from businessmen that it almost got stalled in the Senate. The big gun in the anti-beautification battle was the Three M Company (formerly Minnesota Mining and Manufacturing), the biggest name behind the nation's billboards, which conducted its lobbying campaign through the Roadside Business Association. When the President learned the beautification bill had become bogged down, he uttered a small cry of dismay: "Why that's Lady Bird's bill!" He slammed the White House bulldozer into action and cleared the Senate obstacles out of the way.

During the debate that followed, Senate Commerce Chairman Warren Magnuson (D-Wash.), voluble long-time advocate of uncluttered highways, complained ironically that a beer billboard featuring a likeness of Mount Rainier obscured the view of the real Mount Rainier along one Washington highway.

Senator Everett Dirksen (R-Ill.) tried to defend the billboards with some whimsical rhetoric about the loss to the nation's culture of the roadside Burma Shave ditties. But off the Senate floor one colleague unkindly suggested that Dirksen was less interested in Burma Shave signs than in Pepsi-Cola and Pabst Beer billboards. His Peoria law firm represents both Pepsi and Pabst. While the Senate debated, Lady Bird went around the country quoting Ogden Nash: "I think that I shall never see a billboard lovely as a tree." *The combination of Lady Bird spreading the word and LBJ prodding the Senate turned out to be too much for the Triple M.*

Like so many other special interests, the drug industry has also found an anti-reform champion in the meliflous Senator Dirksen. *The industry's attorneys not only operated right out of his office but, on at least one occasion, used his credentials to infiltrate a secret Senate session.* The two industry lawyers, Lloyd Cutler and Marshal Hornblower, acting right at home as if they represented Dirksen instead of the drug companies, offered 12 amendments which would have gutted reforms. Hornblower, who on more subdued occasions is called simply "Whistle," did most of the hornblowing at the secret meeting. But it was all in vain. The world-wide scandal over thalidamide, which caused deformed babies, resulted in such a public uproar that the reforms were saved. Even Dirksen, his hands folded and his eyes cast heavenward, kept silent during the final debate.

Probably no lobby is more determined than the American Medical Association, that staunch defender of the status quo. Its Washington lobbyists—headed by dignified Dr. Roy Lester and respected ex-Associated Press chief Cecil Dixon—wage an unceasing battle against anything likely to alter in any way the doctor-patient relationship. *Anything that might bring about any change, no matter how slight, is diagnosed darkly as "socialized medicine"—the worst ailment the* AMA *can imagine.* The AMA stimulates doctors all over the country to bring political pressure on their Congressmen, an effective technique since the legislators look upon doctors and ministers as pillars of society and, therefore, leaders of thought in their communities.

Under the law, the AMA cannot engage openly in politics and still retain its tax-exempt status. The doctors got around that by forming a political arm, called the American Political Action Committee, *which they took pains to disguise as an independent body.* Yet the AMA not only formed the new organization but selected the doctor-directors who run it. At first, AMA picked five doctors, all Republicans; then it hastily added five conservative Democrats to give its political step-child a bipartisan appearance. When the records of Congressional candidates are reviewed to determine who should get the doctors' support, AMA and AMPAC participate together in the screening process. First call upon AMPAC's treasury usually goes to the

House Ways and Means members, who battled faithfully against medicare. But anyone who will stand four-square against "socialized medicine" can count upon a donation from the doctors.

During the 1962 Congressional campaign, AMPAC sent funds from its national treasury to four Senatorial candidates—Senators Wallace Bennett (R-Utah) and Peter Dominick (R-Colo.), who won; candidates Joe Bottum (R-S.D.) and Horace Seely-Brown (R-Conn.), who lost, and to 80 Congressional candidates. The doctors also contributed to several other races through their local AMPAC chapters. In California, a doctors' delegation, headed by Dr. Malcolm Todd of Long Beach, called upon Senator Thomas Kuchel (R-Calif.) to ask whether he would modify his pro-medicare stand in return for their support. When he turned them down cold, the delegation put the same proposition to Democratic candidate Richard Richards, who also refused to compromise on health care. As a result California was one of the few states where the doctors had no candidate for the Senate. *The doctors dumped an estimated $3 million into the political kitty in 1962, though the exact amount can only be estimated.* It is known, for instance, that Alabama's 2,240 doctors donated $33,000 to the national fund though not a cent of this was spent in Alabama. They kicked in far more money to their own local candidates.

Because of my stories about AMPAC's activities in 1962, the doctors took extra pains to conceal whom they supported and how much they spent in the 1964 and 1966 campaigns. It is evident, however, that they passed out even more money in their last great stand against medicare. Ignoring such issues as the Vietnam war and the extremist threat, the doctors crowded aboard Barry Goldwater's bandwagon and kept on beating the medicare drum as they went down gloriously to defeat. They mounted an organized letter-writing campaign against other pro-medicare candidates, calling these unenlight-

CODE OF ETHICS FOR GOVERNMENT SERVICE

Any Person In Government Service Should:

Put loyalty to the highest moral principles and to country above loyalty to persons, party, or Government department.

Uphold **the Constitution, laws, and legal regulations of the United States and all governments therein and never be a party to their evasion.**

Give **a full day's labor for a full day's pay; giving to the performance of his duties his earnest effort and best thought.**

Seek **to find and employ more efficient and economical ways of getting tasks accomplished.**

Never **discriminate unfairly by the dispensing of special favors or privileges to anyone, whether for remuneration or not; and never accept, for himself or his family, favors or benefits under circumstances which might be construed by reasonable persons as influencing the performance of his governmental duties.**

Make **no private promises of any kind binding upon the duties of office, since a Government employee has no private word which can be binding on public duty.**

Engage **in no business with the Government, either directly or indirectly, which is inconsistent with the conscientious performance of his governmental duties.**

Never **use any information coming to him confidentially in the performance of governmental duties as a means for making private profit.**

Expose **corruption wherever discovered.**

Uphold **these principles, ever conscious that public office is a public trust.**

Despite the above Congressional resolution, many federal officials and legislators put their personal interests above those they have sworn to defend and protect.

ened souls "enemies of private enterprise" and "advocates of socialism." An instruction sheet to Ohio doctors cautioned: "*Secretaries and doctors should address their envelopes and sign the letters now and hold them for mailing until the week before election . . . Add a* P.S. *in ink to make the letter more personal.*"

The doctors were so obsessed over medicare that they entered into a weird lobbying alliance with the cigarette makers. Anticipating the Surgeon General's report on smoking and health, the tobacco men sought to counteract it. They offered to finance a new AMA study of the smoking hazard, thus hoping to give the impression that the government report wasn't conclusive and that smokers need not kick the habit until the AMA results came in at some indefinite date. In return, the tobacco lobbyists promised to use their influence in Congress to block the medicare bill. The doctors were more concerned about medicare, which they fancied to be a threat to their fees, than about the threat to the nation's lungs. *So it happened that those who cause and those who cure illness lay down together in millennial bliss.*

After canceling an earlier tobacco study on the grounds that the Surgeon General's investigation would make it unnecessary, the AMA suddenly approved a brand new study December 4, 1963, on the eve of the great struggle over medicare. To finance the study, the AMA accepted a $10 million grant for tobacco research from six cigarette companies on February 7, 1964. Three weeks later, the AMA astounded government doctors (and not a few of their own members) by agreeing blandly with the tobacco industry that cigarettes should not be labeled as a health hazard. The AMA's letter to the Federal Trade Commission sounded almost as if it had been written by tobacco men instead of medical men.

"More than 90 million persons in the United States use tobacco in some form," argued the AMA, "and, of these, 72 million use cigarettes . . . The economic lives of tobacco growers, processors, and merchants are entwined in the industry; and local, state, and federal governments are the recipients of and dependent upon many millions of dollars of tax revenue." *Thus by official declaration of the* AMA, *the doctors put the economic welfare of the tobacco industry ahead of the health of the American people.* On March 19, 1964, Representative Frank Thompson, Jr. (D-N.J.) charged that the AMA's curious attitude toward cigarettes was part of a deal to get tobacco-state Congressmen to vote against medicare. Though the AMA issued a formal denial, the doctors' lobby and cigarette lobby continued to work in tandem on Capitol Hill.

The tobacco growers also are able to blow smoke rings inside the government. At the same time that the Surgeon-General is spending the taxpayers' money to warn against the tobacco menace, the Secretary of Agriculture is spending the taxpayers' money to subsidize tobacco production.

Indeed, the farmers once operated the most powerful lobby on Capitol Hill. *Though the farm organizations now squabble among themselves over farm policy, they still pack a political wallop.* Most farm-state legislators wear the brand of one of the three major farm groups. Senator Karl Mundt (R-S.D.), for example, frequently takes to the soapbox to cry for economy in government, but no one hollers louder if the budget cutters take him so seriously that they start economizing on agriculture. When the Agriculture Department tried to reduce expenses by insisting that all available government storage space be utilized before storage contracts were granted to private warehouses, Mundt came out four-square against economy. Once he sent a confidential letter to M. W. Thatcher, general manager of the Warehousemen's Association, in which he claimed credit for killing the economy measure. "*I hope and believe,*" *he added,* "*you can get whoever prepares your daily radio round-up to give us a little credit for pulling this one out of the fire, since I am sure this is not only good for the storage industry, but the farm people generally. It would seem to me that it might deserve a little mention in one of your nightly broadcasts."*

Washington's most potent lobby operates not on Capitol Hill, but in the cocktail lounges and hospitality suites of Sixteenth Street and Connecticut Avenue where personable people from the defense industries seek to ingratiate themselves with the Pentagon brass. The corporate scramble for defense dollars is so intense that companies pay big salaries to affable gentlemen who know the right people in Washington. From the manufacturers' point of view, the fine art of gaining contracts depends as much on political influence as professional competence. *All too many multi-million-dollar contracts are awarded because of a bouillabaisse of cocktail parties, old Army ties, political pressure, geographical appeal, and greed.*

One company with inside influence is Brown and Root, the Texas construction company which has been able to flout the labor laws yet still snap up fat government contracts. George and Herman Brown, partners in the company, own an estate in the Virginia horse country, where government officials are their week-end guests. It was at the Brown estate that Lyndon B. Johnson, then the Senate Democratic leader, had his celebrated heart attack in 1955. When Johnson was an upcoming Congressman, he pulled strings inside the White House to settle a criminal tax case against Brown and Root. Internal Revenue agents, who worked on the case, told me they recommended prosecution but were overruled after LBJ's intervention. For the Brown brothers, listed among the 100 wealthiest men in America, influence is still paying dividends. Their company was dealt in for a generous share of the multi-million-dollar construction work in South Vietnam shortly after Lyndon Johnson moved into the White House.

In the executive suites of almost every airplane company, electronics company, and oil company are three or four retired Admirals and Generals who are on a first-name basis with the Pentagon's top brass. *"In business circles,"* comments Business Week, *"the word has gone out: get yourself a general. What branch of the government spends the most money? The military. Who, even more than a five-percenter, is an expert on red-tape? A general or an admiral. So make him chairman of the board."* The last time someone bothered to count them, there were more than 1400 military officers on company payrolls. These companies—at least most of them—do lots of business with the Pentagon.

Many a defense contract has been nourished by a joyful mixture of booze, blondes, and business. Commenting on all the partying at military-industry conventions, Missiles and Rockets, the trade magazine, suggested: "Their explanations to their wives probably would make far more interesting reading than many of the technical papers presented at the meetings . . . Industry prestige at [one meeting] was enhanced by at least one fist fight and the drunken antics of several Air Force generals, corporate presidents and vice presidents."

When George Bunker took over the management of the Martin Company, he made it a policy to provide fun in the sun for the big brass in the Bahamas. One year he picked up an $18,000 tab at the Cotton Club on Eleuthera Island and tried to deduct it as a "necessary business expense." Congressman F. Edward Hébert (D-La.), after an investigation, suggested that Bunker's lavishness had paid off. "I can only say," said Hébert, "that when Dr. Bunker became president of the Martin Company, it was on the verge of bankruptcy. *Today the Martin Company not only is high on the defense contract list, but it does not do a dime's worth of work for private business. Every nickel comes from the government in subsidies."*

If the defense industries have their pipelines into the Pentagon, they also have their contacts in Congress. A cancelled defense contract will bring the lobbyists swarming into Washington like high school seniors at cherry-blossom time.

They prowl the Capitol corridors, spreading dark warnings about how federal economies in their plants will undermine the nation's defense. In consequence, Congressmen who inveigh volubly against the waste of paper clips sometimes defend the most impractical of weapons. The test is not whether the weapon is worth the cost but whether its production will benefit the Congressman's constituency. Though everyone on Capitol Hill is, of course, for God, country and economy, the average legislator favors economies in someone else's district. When North American Aviation lost a missile contract, the outcry from California Congressmen was so shrill that Senator Thomas Kuchel (R-Calif.) sent the Air Force an apology.

Legislators even began investigating their own watchdog, the General Accounting Office, when it became too critical of military spending. The GAO apparently looked too closely into the profits of the big missile makers. For the Aerospace Industries Association, which represents 60 of the leading missile-space contractors, set up a yowl. Its chief Washington lobbyist, Lloyd Kuhn, complained to Congressman Chet Holifield (D-Calif.), whose subcommittee is supposed to investigate Pentagon purchase practices. The audit work is done by the GAO, which submits its reports to the Holifield committee. *But Holifield began investigating the GAO instead of the contractors it had caught padding their profits.*

Not only domestic interests but foreign countries hire lobbyists to polish the Washington apple. *Since the end of World War II, the capital has been besieged by foreign agents representing just about every cause and country under the sun.* Far from being cloak and dagger men, most agents are highly respectable American citizens who are required by law to register with the Justice Department. They range from two-time presidential candidate Tom Dewey, who as a Turkish agent arranged to send a special government mission to Turkey, to Manhattan attorney John Maurice Kessing, who is pressing the claim of Prince Raymond Mouton Seagham Donough VI to the Irish throne.

Most foreign agents operate in the open. They give legal advice, seek capital, promote tourism, offer business opportunities, arrange cultural exchanges and publicize their client countries. But a few work under cover to undermine official U.S. policy. *An inside source has confided, for example, that emissaries from a Far Eastern country met a prominent Senator in a New England farm house and handed him a cool $500,000 to distribute as "campaign contributions" to candidates of his choice.* The Senator was left free, of course, to decide what his own rake-off would be. Since the country was virtually bankrupt, the huge bribe had come indirectly from U.S. foreign aid funds. Its purpose was, of course, to win sympathy in the Senate for the country's request for more foreign aid.

Not long ago, two urbane, well-dressed men met briefly in a San Francisco hotel room. Their conversation was so guarded as to be meaningless to anyone else. Then one held out a roll of bills. The other took the money, grinned sheepishly and said: "My fingers are sticky." This scene, described to me by the one with the wad of money, concluded another deal to influence U.S. policy.

The money which changed hands was a $5,000 "campaign contribution" to a prominent, widely respected politician from an agent for a Latin American dictator. It, too, probably came from the American taxpayers via foreign aid. Prosecution would be almost impossible in this case, since the only two witnesses would never incriminate themselves.

When Castro's seizure of American property in Cuba forced the United States to suspend the Cuban sugar quota, the agents for other sugar-producing countries came swarming in like flies. For a few weeks' work, some collected fees of more than $100,000 for getting their clients' quotas increased. *There are reports that some of these agents actually are con-*

spiring to keep Castro in power, so their clients can go on collecting increased sugar benefits.

It has become an open scandal how House Agriculture Chairman Harold Cooley (D-N.C.), the greatest sugar daddy of them all, let the sugar lobbyists virtually dictate how much sugar their foreign clients should be permitted to sell the United States. Cooley first tried to persuade the Agriculture Department to let him, rather than the sugar experts, decide how much the quotas should be. He phoned the Department repeatedly, sometimes threatening, sometimes cajoling, to urge it to give his favorite lobbyists what they wanted. When Agriculture officials resisted his pressure, he ignored their recommendations and drafted a bill to suit the lobbyists.

At the hearings in late 1965, Cooley bedeviled government witnesses and beatified the lobbyists. He singled out Arthur Quinn, mouthpiece for sugar clients in Ecuador, Panama, British Honduras, and the British West Indies, for special words of honey. *At one point, Cooley actually admitted two lobbyists behind closed doors to help his committee draft the bill.* The public and press were barred from the room, but the sugar lobbyists were allowed inside. Thus, Irvin Hoff of the Cane Sugar Refiners and Phil Jones of the Beet Sugar Association were permitted to sit around the drafting table with the Congressmen, quietly suggesting what should go into the bill and what should be left out.

The committee benevolently included in the bill, for example, a 10,000-ton sugar quota for the Bahama Islands, which had never produced sugar in the past. Since there was already a sugar surplus in the world, the committee should have been encouraging less, not more, production. It turned out that the entire windfall was to go to the Owens-Illinois Company, which was famous for its glass, paper, and plastics but had never produced a pound of sugar in its corporate history. Yet the entire Bahamas quota, which would cost the taxpayers $1 million a year above the market price, was earmarked for this one company. The quota request came not from the

Bahama Islands, which didn't even put in a bid, but from Owens-Illinois, which sent its vice-president, Hugh Laughlin, around to see committee members.

Few foreign agents ever worked against U.S. policy more openly than Michael Struelens, the Belgian-born $100,000-a-year agent for the Congo's go-it-alone Katanga Province. He bombarded Congress and the press with anti-U.S. propaganda, stamped passports with Katanga visas though he had no diplomatic status, and indulged in other less-open activities. *Among the latter was an alleged attempt to buy official recognition for Katanga from Costa Rica by offering fat bribes to Costa Rican diplomats at the United Nations.* A State Department source told me that the bribe was made through a New York society dentist.

The Hamilton Wright Organization, long the major voice of Chiang Kai-shek in the United States, found itself torn between cash and conscience when asked to drum up "editorial support" for the Gimo's desire to invade Red China. To his credit, Hamilton Wright, Sr., checked with the State Department, found that an invasion was against policy, and declined to renew the $127,000 contract with the Formosa government.

Not so scrupulous was Martin Camacho, a Portuguese-born Boston lawyer, who formed the Portuguese-American Committee on Foreign Affairs in 1961. He led a delegation to Washington to influence Senators, Congressmen, the White House and State Department officials against American policy toward the Portuguese colonies in Africa. *But he neglected to mention that, at the time, he was collecting $400 a week from a firm which Portugal had hired to promote its case.*

Washington attorney Charles Patrick Clark, who combines Brooklyn pugnaciousness with Irish blarney, collects $87,500 a year for representing Franco Spain. When he took over the job in 1948, Spain received no U.S. aid, had no diplomatic relations with Washington, was excluded from the United

Nations. Now it has an embassy here, is a UN member, draws millions in military aid from the U.S.

Though Clark may not deserve credit for Spain's improved fortunes, he is a man who knows everybody worth knowing. Once he hosted a lavish party attended by the late President John F. Kennedy, then-Vice President Lyndon B. Johnson, ex-President Harry S. Truman, Chief Justice Earl Warren, and the late Speaker Sam Rayburn. In his campaign to get more American aid for Spain, Clark has a curious and constant need for pretty new secretaries. He interviews them at the rate of about a dozen a month, inevitably takes the prettiest ones out to lunch, and presents each with a red rosebud as if it were the first time he had ever so flattered a pretty girl.

Chicago press agent Julius Klein, who until recently received over $150,000 a year for representing West German interests, traded on his Jewish credentials at a time when the Bonn government was eager to wipe out its anti-Semitic past. Often his activities and advice ran contrary to the efforts of the West German embassy. Lately his operations have been hampered somewhat, particularly since Drew Pearson and I revealed how the Caesar-nosed *Senator Thomas Dodd* (D-Conn.) *delivered speeches, signed letters, and entertained clients for Klein.*

In 1964 Senator Dodd even flew to Germany to help save fees Klein was in danger of losing. *The trip was financed by the Senate Internal Security Subcommittee, but Dodd carried in his briefcase secret instructions from Klein.* These directed the Senator to call upon West German leaders and explain that a Senate committee's investigation of Klein's operations had been misunderstood and that Klein was really respected by the U.S. Senate. Dodd, as a member of the Senate Foreign Relations Committee, which was doing the investigating, was in a position to be convincing. The Senator, defending himself before the Senate Ethics Committee, denied he had done Klein's bidding—except for a fleeting mention of Klein's problem to former Chancellor Konrad Adenauer.

As evidence that Dodd had carried out the mission to Klein's satisfaction, however, the West German agent wrote Dodd a jubilant letter: *"I had a very nice letter from former Chancellor Adenauer and am very pleased. I heard many fine things about your recent mission to Germany . . . I presume, Tom, you will write the various people you saw over there and if you do, I would appreciate it if you would add a* PS: *'I was indeed glad to discuss with you also the fine work of our mutual good friend, General Klein.'"* To make sure Dodd worded his letters just right, Klein drafted at least two of them for the Senator.

Klein asked Dodd to congratulate Dr. Ludger Westrick on his promotion to the West German cabinet and to add a couple of paragraphs of praise for Klein. "To save you time," wrote Klein helpfully, "I am enclosing herewith a rough draft. Maybe you want to paraphrase it and add a little bit about the President's stand on Vietnam." Klein took the precaution of scrawling across the bottom of his letter to Dodd: "Please destroy this letter. I made *no* copy." The obliging Dodd didn't even bother to paraphrase the message Klein had asked him to write to Westrick but sent it under his own signature almost word for word as Klein had dictated.

"I saw General Klein recently who, as you know, works hand in hand with all of us," wrote Dodd in Klein's own words to Westrick. *"He has the confidence of my Democratic and Republican colleagues and is especially close to our leaders. It is for this reason that we all regretted the distortions in the German press and the slander which originated in the press behind the Iron Curtain as General Klein has been rendering a great service not only to our nation but also to your country. His advice has always been most valuable to us Democrats as it was and is to his Republican friends."*

Westrick, unaware that Klein had prepared his own plug for the Senator's signature, was impressed. "I was extremely interested," Westrick wrote back to Dodd, "in hearing your opinion on General Julius Klein."

The law governing foreign agents—requiring them to disclose their duties, doings and finances—was passed in 1938 in an effort to curb Nazi propaganda. The whole emphasis is on the word "disclose," which has the widest of legal interpretations. At the Justice Department there are only half a dozen lawyers to keep track of the activities of more than 400 foreign agents. Result: The registrants disclose less and less on the theory of why should Macy's tell Gimbels? Agents are supposed to label their propaganda material, but they have developed the fine art of planting it in the words of others. For example, they pay authors to write and publishers to issue flattering books about client countries and their leaders, and they offer free films to television stations and newsreel companies. *Little of this vast flood of material is ever labeled as the propaganda it is.*

Perhaps the biggest scandal resulted in the conviction of Alexander L. Guterma, former president of the Mutual Broadcasting System. *For $750,000 in cash, handed over to him in a cotton bag, he agreed to broadcast a steady flow of news favorable to the late Dominican dictator Trujillo.* The deal was arranged through international playboy Porfirio Rubirosa, who numbered Trujillo's daughter among his wives and once served as a Dominican diplomat. According to Guterma, Rubirosa's rake-off was $25,000. Guterma was in a powerful position to influence American opinion. Desperate because of stock ventures, he tried to peddle this power. He was sent to prison for stock frauds.

A few years ago, American Mercury editor John Clements and his Washington editor, Patrick McMahon, hired out as agents for Guatemala for $8,000 a month. They promptly began loading their magazine with articles on Guatemala. McMahon, while still on Guatemala's payroll, also acted as consultant to a House committee which praised the Guatemalan government. Another who went on the Guatemalan payroll, while he was briefly out of Congress, was Senator Dodd. After his election to the Senate, he resigned as a paid Guatemalan agent, then led the Senate battle for more American aid for Guatemala.

Of course most Communist countries have registered agents here, though they are closely policed. Chief among them is the Four Continent Book Corporation in New York, the U.S. outlet for the great Russian book combine and propaganda factory, Meshdounarodnaja Kniga. Best known of the combine's agents is Edwin S. Smith, who dispenses news and photos from behind the Iron Curtain for a $20,000 a year salary. Often investigated for Communist ties, he insists that he is strictly a commercial agent and does "nothing sneaky."

The most strident hate-America propaganda comes into the country from Red China and is distributed chiefly by Imported Publications and Products of New York. World Books, another New York firm, also puts out the bound works of Mao Tse-tung, politically slanted novels, ghost stories and songs.

Fidel Castro's Movimiento 26 de Julio (July 26th Movement) has a branch office in New York which distributes his fulminations. Another Cuban propaganda outlet, Prensa Latina Agencia, was indicted along with its New York correspondent, Francisco Portela, for failing to register as an agent. Castro's New York attorneys, Victor Rabinowitz and Leonard Boudin, were also ordered to register.

Though it is distasteful to Americans, there are good reasons for allowing Communist literature into this country. It is one way of watching the ever-shifting Communist line. But more important, American propaganda is allowed to pass behind the Iron Curtain in exchange. It's a chance worth taking that the truth will somehow win the most converts in the end.

What's most troubling about all this is the amount of hidden persuasion, the extravagant use of foreign aid funds, and the evidence of corruption in high places. Clearly, new laws to control foreign agents are required—not so much to prevent a country from stating its case, but to make sure its propaganda is labeled. *There should be restrictions, too, on foreign aid expenditures to insure that it doesn't go to buy influence in the U.S.*

Meanwhile, lobbyists and agents, both registered and unregistered, continue to throng and thrive in Washington, squandering money on cocktail parties and, occasionally, greasing the palms of politicians.

10

LUBRICATING THE GOVERNMENT MACHINERY

Oregon's fiery Democrat, Senator Wayne Morse, his voice crackling with anger, his bushy eyebrows bristling, seized the Senate floor to deliver a lecture his colleagues didn't want to hear. "Great courage is required," he roared, "to stand against the powerful oil and gas combine of this country, which exercises such a powerful influence in the halls of Congress that it is able to steal from the American people. The industry is supported by members of Congress who do not represent the people of this country, but who really represent the gas and oil interests. I say, too, that the oil and gas interests are exercising an undue influence upon the foreign policy of this Republic."

Some Senators squirmed a little, as if Morse's open mouth were causing an uncomfortable draft. But most of them put on an act of massive indifference. If his rebuke stung any ears, if his barbs pricked a few consciences, they showed no evidence of it but merely sat listening in studied nonchalance. For all the attention they paid to Morse, he might have been reading aloud from a report on the Seed Quarantine Amendment. *Yet the speech the Senators pretended not to hear happens to be the shocking truth.*

No group in America collects more benefits from Uncle Sam and passes out more favors to politicians than the recklessly greedy, unbelievably wealthy oil barons. They keep the taxpayers' money circulating in dizzy circles, perhaps the closest thing to perpetual motion in corruption ever achieved. The more the patricians of petroleum drain from the government through tax loopholes, the more they slip to politicians to make the loopholes in the tax laws still bigger. And each time the corruption goes full circle, the pockets of the oil men are a little fuller. Few men who administer or vote on oil matters have not been tempted. For their favors, the oil barons offer them campaign contributions, law fees, even cash under the table.

This is a pattern that has kept the oil gushing around the world, spraying the profits far and wide. Governments may rise and fall; wars may shake the world. But the dividends keep pouring in, remarkably unaffected by international boundaries and politics. During secret Senate questioning Secretary of State Rusk divulged, for example, the startling information that American oil companies have been paying protection money to the Viet Cong, thus contributing to the communist war effort in South Vietnam. The question was put to him by Senator George Aiken (R-Vt.), who had heard that petroleum firms were paying the Viet Cong not to molest their trucks and facilities. *Rusk whispered with Foreign Aid Chief David Bell at his side; they admitted cautiously that oilmen were known to be paying "tolls" for access rights through communist-controlled territory.*

Intelligence sources tell me that the oil payments are "substantial" and that, as a result, oil trucks are allowed to travel unhindered anywhere in South Vietnam. "The only danger," said one source, "is that they might run over a road mine intended for a military vehicle." Service stations throughout South Vietnam have been largely untouched. The great oil depot at Nhabe 20 miles from Saigon has never been attacked, though it is located in a "secured area." Of course, there have been some oil losses. The Viet Cong, striking the Marine base at Danang on August 5, 1965, damaged the Esso bulk plant and destroyed about $120,000 worth of oil. An observer suggested that the Marines might have saved the oil by pulling off their guards and mounting huge Esso signs around the plant.

Three oil companies — Esso, Caltex, and Shell — do business in South Vietnam. In denying that they pay protection money, Esso officials mournfully informed Senator Aiken that the Viet Cong destroy 40 percent of their Vietnam shipments. The Senator pursued this point with Secretary of Defense Robert McNamara behind closed doors of the Senate Foreign Relations Committee. How much oil, asked Aiken, had been lost in South Vietnam? Before McNamara could reply, General Earle Wheeler, the Joint Chiefs chairman, broke in. "Only a fraction of one percent," he said.

The protection money is used by the Viet Cong to buy arms, ammunition, and other war needs right in South Vietnam, thus saving the long wait for supplies to be smuggled over the tortuous Ho Chi Minh trail. Cement purchases, for instance, have been traced to the Viet Cong, who bought it on the Saigon market and used it to fortify their underground bunkers. The communists also paid in American greenbacks for machine tools, disguised as watch parts, which were smuggled from Switzerland past South Vietnamese customs. The cash for such transactions comes, at least in part, from oil pay-offs.

From the Cuban underground have come other stories of the strange sanctity of oil property. *Cuban commandos have told me that the Central Intelligence Agency has ordered them not to attack Havana's three oil refineries, which supply the fuel for Dictator Castro's military machine.* Destruction of the Esso, Texaco, and Shell refineries would bring Castro's tanks, trucks, and planes to a grinding halt. Such is the power of the great oil companies, however, that the CIA seems more concerned about protecting their property than crippling Castro. An aide to Cuban exile leader Manuel Artime lamely explained to me: "We don't want to damage foreign property."

The awesome influence of the oil barons was felt early in the Cuban struggle. During the Bay of Pigs fiasco, a freedom fighter plane, loaded with bombs, radioed that it was over the Esso refinery in Havana and asked permission to bomb it. *But the* CIA *command post actually ordered the plane to ignore the refinery and look for gun emplacements to bomb.* Also, Mike McLaney, an American gambler who had continued to run his casino in Havana for 18 months after Castro's take-over, sent the CIA a detailed plan for knocking out the three refineries. But instead of getting his plan approved, McLaney got an urgent phone call warning him not to attempt such an attack under any circumstances.

Even more astonishing, as Senator Morse charged in his speech, the State Department has often taken its policies right out of the executive suites of the oil companies. When Big Oil can't get what it wants in foreign countries, the State Department tries to get it for them. In many countries, the American Embassies function virtually as branch offices for the oil combine. Of course, the State Department is supposed to protect American interests abroad, but it isn't supposed to favor the big companies against others. And the small, independent companies have been getting the hairy end of the lollipop. The State Department quietly cooperated with the big oil companies, for example, to persuade Libya to boost oil taxes retroactively. This was a naked attempt to force the independent companies, which couldn't afford the huge increase, out of Libya.

The State Department can be found almost always on the side of the "seven sisters," as the oil giants are known inside the industry: Standard Oil of New Jersey, Standard of California, Socony, Gulf, Texas, Shell and British Petroleum. *It seems to make no difference that the latter two are foreign-owned.* Through the foreign aid program, for example, the State Department guaranteed the entire investment for a new refinery in Thailand, a joint venture of British Shell and Standard of New Jersey. This was discovered by Congressman Tom Steed (D-Okla.), who conducted a one-man investigation of the Agency for International Development.

Representative Steed concluded that AID's policy "not only

OIL, GAS, AND MINERAL DEPLETION is computed by two methods: (1) cost depletion and (2) percentage depletion. You should always compute your depletion each year by both methods and use the method which results in the greater deduction.

Cost depletion, in general, is figured by dividing the total number of recoverable units (tons, barrels, etc., deter-

The above illustration in the Treasury's Income Tax Guide was dropped after the Independent Petroleum Association complained it was "grossly inappropriate for the [government] to engage in this type of propaganda" relating swimming pools and bikinis to oil and gas wells. The drawing appeared in the section of the guide advising oilmen on how to make the most of the depletion allowances that the law affords. Contending that it was unfair to imply "that the affluent life, with private swimming pools, is made possible apparently exclusively by the depletion provision in the tax laws," the Petroleum Association denounced the illustration as an innuendo that is "neither subtle nor veiled: it is propaganda that appeals to the emotions of the 'average taxpayer' . . . It reflects on the judgment of Congress, which for 38 years has maintained these tax provisions as both necessary and proper."

can guarantee an investment by the world's largest oil company but also insure the investment of its foreign partner." He added sourly: "If this does not stifle competition and promote monopoly, then I do not know the meaning of the words!" The Congressman also charged that the oil giants "have no real interest in the economy or security of the United States but, like the huge munitions manufacturers, are in fact internationalists, concerned only with making billions of dollars, however and wherever they can."

The full story of Big Oil's influence on foreign policy is buried in the State Department's secret files, but I have been able to dig out part of the record. When the Congolese cabinet granted a license to an Italian oil company to build a refinery in the Congo, for example, the State Department intervened. Then-Undersecretary George Ball, whose former law firm has oil ties, fired off several cables to our Embassy in Leopoldville, bluntly instructing our diplomats to help Standard of New Jersey get the license. The Congo capitulated.

In Haiti, an independent operator wangled a permit to build a refinery. Alarmed, Standard of New Jersey sent its local manager to protest to the American Embassy that the proposed refinery, of all things, would create a monopoly. Apparently, Standard is opposed to any oil monopoly that it doesn't dominate. The Ambassador passed on the complaint to Undersecretary Ball who directed him to oppose the independent's permit and try to get it cancelled.

In the Far East, oilmen used their influence to get the U.S. government to punish tiny Ceylon for daring to nationalize service stations owned by Standard of New Jersey and Texaco. The nationalization was ordered out of pique, because the two oil giants had stalled for 12 years over construction of a refinery which Ceylon needed badly. The companies sought to invoke a foreign aid clause, which, if activated, can shut off all foreign aid to any country that seizes American-owned property and fails to pay for it within six months. Ceylon offered to reimburse the oil companies, but both firms delayed furnishing the necessary financial figures for six months. It had all the earmarks of a deliberate stall so the amendment could take effect. One oilman gleefully remarked: "This will teach the Ceylonese a lesson." Instead, Ceylon stood her ground and turned to Russia for petroleum products. The Ceylonese also invited Russia to bid on the new refinery. Thus, for the sake of teaching Ceylon "a lesson," our oil-oriented diplomats gave Ceylon a firm push in the direction of Moscow and injured American-Ceylonese relations perhaps for years to come.

It is upon Washington that the oil giants concentrate the most pressure. Their lobbyists are the smoothest, most skilled, most elite of all Washington pressure people. Well-tailored and turned-out, they are skilled at the "soft sell," seldom are found engaged in blatant lobbying. They belong to the hush-hush, plush-plush Carlton Club on the second floor of Washington's Sheraton-Carlton Hotel. Here, in an atmosphere of elegant dignity, they entertain Congressmen and government officials. There are afternoon poker and gin games, subdued bull sessions, lots of liquor. When their oil privileges are threatened, however, these backroom boys can drop their dignity and lobby at any level it takes to win. They can retain a Senator's law firm or deliver cash in a paper sack to those who prefer that sort of gross transaction.

Such a sack, filled with $2,500 in $100 bills, was offered to the late Senator Francis Case (R-S.D.). The receptacle made it obvious that he could have pocketed the money without reporting it. Instead, he strode onto the Senate floor and denounced the bribery attempt in a voice shrill with outrage. If he had taken the money, of course, he would have been "hooked" for the rest of his career. *Question: how many politicians have been hooked in this manner? The answer, if it were known, might shake the very foundations of our Republic.*

Many a candidate for Congress, down to his last campaign dollar, has been promised funds in return for his pledge to vote "right" on oil. Sometimes the contribution is channeled through campaign committees, which permits a candidate to report it without advertising that it came from the oil interests. Sometimes oilmen choose an intermediary to distribute their largess. When Bobby Baker was operating in the back rooms of the Senate, he once called aside Senator Thomas McIntyre (D-N.H.), and hinted meaningfully that he could get rid of a $10,000 campaign deficit if he would simply vote for the oil depletion allowance. (McIntyre said thanks but no thanks.) If a candidate refuses to sell his vote, as Senator Frank Moss (D-Utah) also did in turning down a $5,000 oil offer routed through the Democratic Senatorial Campaign Committee, the money is merely shunted to someone less scrupulous.

Another payoff pattern is suggested by the number of politicians whose law firms have been retained by the oil industry. Politically, they run a wide gamut from Thomas E. Dewey, the two-time presidential candidate, to Senator John McClellan (D-Ark.), the grim investigator; from the late John Foster Dulles and Christian Herter, both Republican Secretaries of State, to "Tommy the Cork" Corcoran and Clark Clifford, braintrusters for Democratic Presidents.

As a measure of their boldness, three oil millionaires contributed to the upkeep of former President Eisenhower's Gettysburg farm during his eight-year term. *This certainly should be recorded as the most incredible scandal in White House history.* Harried tax agents, trying to find a category for the money the oil entrepreneurs shelled out to the President, finally were obliged to list it as a gift. Thus by an official Internal Revenue ruling, the oil interests gave Ike more than $500,000 during the same period that he was mounting the executive rostrum to advocate still more privileges for the industry.

Those who cannot be bought are investigated. During a gas bill fight, the *New York Times* reported that "the gas bill lobby ran a complete genealogy on Senators," quoted an unnamed Senator as saying he had received letters from almost-forgotten relatives asking him to support the bill. One Senator was buttonholed by the son of his mother's classmate; another was pressured by one of his wife's former suitors. Commented Senator George Aiken: "They have checked on who you have ever been associated with, who are your friends, who has supported you in the past, anybody who has ever worked for you or with you. And they get them to contact you."

The giant among the giants is Standard Oil of New Jersey, which also does the most subtle job of disguising its power. It maintains only a modest office in Washington and handles government relations from New York, thus attracting less attention. The quiet, suave squads of Standard Oil men, who commute regularly between Manhattan and Washington, are directed discreetly by Luke W. Finlay, who works closely with Humble Oil (a name that belies its resources). Humble's Washington office is headed by Charles Keeble; Gulf Oil's Washington office is run by Claud Wild, Jr.; Socony uses Z. W. Ross; and Texaco has Jim Pipkin, a roly-poly Texas politician-type.

These men pull powerful strings inside the federal government; indeed their representatives are scattered strategically throughout the government. Not the least of them was former Assistant Interior Secretary John M. Kelly, a New Mexico oil man, who guided the department's oil policies. Usually, he didn't even bother to check petroleum problems with his chief, Secretary Stewart Udall. A memo of a secret Interior Department policy meeting quotes Kelly as speaking scornfully of public-minded officials as "red-hot bureaucrats."

Then he recommended Governors John Connally of Texas and Jack Campbell of New Mexico to serve on an oil study group, "they both being primarily from the oil industry."

From the Teapot Dome scandal which rocked the Harding Administration to the Gettysburg farm scandal which scarcely ruffled the Eisenhower Administration, the oil boys have followed the principle that oil and politics definitely do mix. *They have escaped investigation by practicing bi-partisan corruption, thus neither party dares blow the whistle.* Only a few lawmakers like the late Senator Thomas Hennings (D-Mo.) have dared to speak out. Shortly before his death, Hennings warned Americans that "gas and oil money not only talks but votes." But Hennings' voice, like that of Senator Morse, was lost in a wilderness of silence.

Special oil privileges have spawned the lusty Texas tycoon who flashes $1,000 bills, drapes his women in mink, and turns in his Cadillacs when they get dirty. Oil fortunes have built towns and cities; Dallas, for one, has been described as "a monument to the 27½ percent oil depletion allowance." Lately, the ever-widening oil tax loopholes have lured movie stars and other holders of the long green to invest in oil wells as a tax dodge. Stars of such magnitude as Jack Benny, Danny Kaye, George Burns and George Jessel were overheard singing the praises of oil tax loopholes at the luxurious Hillcrest Country Club in Los Angeles. *Among them, they held more than a million dollars worth of oil shares, but paid only a fraction of the taxes which the law would ordinarily require of people in their tax brackets.*

An insider has described the year-end scene in a certain Washington office where big oil deals are made. During the last week of December, the accountants spread lists of wells out on tables. The place hummed with activity, telephones jangling and messengers arriving with telegrams and checks (pre-dated checks because a well must be held six months to qualify for a tax write-off). All the commotion merely marked the year-end exchange of gushers and dry holes, as each oil syndicate member worked out the combination which would give him the best possible break on taxes. Many ended up paying no taxes at all.

The most glaring tax loophole is the 27½ percent depletion allowance, which gives oilmen a tax rebate on the cost of every barrel taken from the ground. The argument is that the owner should be permitted to write off the declining value of his well. The hooker: he can go on taking the deduction long after he has recovered his investment. *The figures show that, for the average oil well, the owner deducts from his taxes 19 times the original cost.* Other "golden gimmicks" have been less advertised. George E. Allen, the oil-rich pal of Presidents, once confided that the intangible drilling and development allowances were even more lucrative than the depletion allowances. He said, chuckling: "*Almost no one outside the industry knows about the intangible allowances.*"

While other corporations are socked the full 52 percent corporate tax rate, oil companies end up paying only a token tax. Even the smallest businesses and the lowest wage earners pay 20 percent of their income in federal taxes. Yet the 22 largest oil companies paid only about 4% of their income to the U.S. treasury in 1964, the latest year for which I could dig out the figures. Though the oil companies do their best to suppress information about their tax payments, I was able to determine that five big oil companies — Atlantic, Marathon, Richfield, Sinclair, and Sunray — paid no federal taxes at all in 1964. And Pure Oil paid only $600,000 on earnings of $32,282,000, which amounts to a tax rate of one-hundredth of 1 percent.

Even the giant of the oil industry, Standard of New Jersey, paid only a 1.7 percent rate. Uncle Sam took a mere $29,-000,000 cut out of Standard's whopping $1,628,555,000 gross. Texaco, the number two oil company, did even better. Its $5,500,000 tax payment on a $660,761,000 income was only eight-tenths of 1 percent. Standard of California paid $8,300,000 on a $393,188,000 income — a 2.1 percent tax rate. Standard of Indiana took in $204,817,000, but paid only $8,486,000 in federal taxes. This was a cheap 4.1 percent rate. Shell was taxed only 1.3 percent—$2,800,000 on a $213,575,000 income. Moreover, this negligible tax rate for the top 22 oil companies has been constant. It was 4 percent in 1962, rose to 5 percent in 1963, then dropped back down to 4 percent in 1964. Indeed, President Johnson didn't need to raise taxes to finance the Vietnam war; he could have met the extra expense merely by closing the oil loopholes and compelling the oil companies to pay their fair share of the tax load. For it shouldn't be overlooked that every cent the oil companies get out of paying must be made up by the less privileged taxpayers.

Thus, drilling for oil has become a "heads I win, tails you lose" proposition. If an oilman strikes it rich, he keeps the lion's share of the profit. If he hits a dry hole, Uncle Sam stands most of the loss. Result: too many wells are sunk, because too many greedy people are lured by the tax benefits. Thousands of wells are drilled not primarily to strike oil but to qualify for tax privileges. The ritual is becoming self-defeating. For the bigger the benefits, the more money is invested in oil and the greater the over-supply.

The oil tycoons have made themselves at home not only on Capitol Hill but at the White House. President Johnson has been a staunch oil ally as far back as 1938 when, as just another young Congressman from Texas, he hired a room in the rear of Washington's Munsey Building and passed out $100,000 in cash to Democratic candidates. The money, of course, came from the oil-gas interests that had backed him for Congress. In those days, Johnson worked in tandem with the late Speaker Sam Rayburn who saw to it that no Congressman was appointed to the tax-writing Ways and Means

Committee who couldn't give the right answer to one question: "Do you favor the oil depletion allowance?"

During the 1960 campaign, Johnson said again and again: "There are no loopholes in oil." He criss-crossed gas and oil producing regions, sometimes with Rayburn in tow, promising great things for oil if the Democratic ticket won. They also raked in the green from oilmen, most of whom hedged their bets by giving to both sides. Rayburn told one audience of dollar-laden donors that he and Congressman Frank Ikard (D-Tex.) had "held the line" against bills to reduce the depletion allowance. Later Ikard was rewarded with a $100,000-a-year job as head of the American Petroleum Institute. But Rayburn was furious about this and lectured his oil buddies that Ikard was far more valuable to them on the Ways and Means Committee.

The oil crowd, of course, pitched in to build the Sam Rayburn Memorial Library near Bonham, Texas. *Life's* story about the dedication showed a photograph of Johnson with a wide grin on his face and a big arm around the late oil czar, Sidney Richardson. *Life* described the assembly as an "impressive gathering of Texas millionaires." A reporter who covered the affair later added: "I walked in and forgot for a moment whether it was supposed to be a Republican or a Democratic gathering. I see the same men at Republican affairs."

Once Johnson moved into the White House, he became more circumspect about his oil associations. The oilmen who called upon him came by the back rather than the front door, and he no longer delivered speeches defending oil loopholes. But neither did he plug up the oil drains, though the tax savings would go a long way toward financing the Great Society. *If Washington needed any reminding of the oil in Johnson's past, it was splashed upon the pages of the Bobby Baker transcripts.* The irrepressible Bobby, while he was Johnson's protege, partied and parleyed with oil millionaires constantly. It is worth recording that one of them, Clint Murchison, Jr., who made millions from oil loopholes created by a benevolent Congress, turned in a voucher to Congress for $420.26 to pay his expenses to testify at the Bobby Baker hearings.

For a refreshing moment in history, the late John F. Kennedy spoke out against oil tax privileges and called for a reduction in the depletion allowance. *But not even Kennedy could stand up against the great oil tide.* While he was preparing his tax reforms in late 1962, he felt he should make at least a token recommendation to cut the oil depletion allowance. But this small straw in the wind got no further than the Oklahoma ranch of the late Senator Robert Kerr (D-Okla.), a big, bluff oil millionaire who had become a power in the Senate, trading public works projects for oil votes.

Kerr started burning up the telephone wires to Washington. "I have been double-crossed," he bellowed like one of his prize Black Angus bulls. To placate the angry Oklahoman, President Kennedy sent two ambassadors, Secretary of the Treasury Douglas Dillon and House Ways and Means Chairman Wilbur Mills, winging westward. In the privacy of Kerr's 350-foot ranch house, gazing over his 50,000 acres where his 4,500 Black Angus grazed, Dillon assured the Senator that the oil reform was just so much window dressing. Mills added the assurance that the reform would be safely sidetracked by his committee.

Two great oil champions were lost when Kerr and Rayburn died. But the oil tycoons, wasting no time mourning, moved right in on President Kennedy — not with offers of personal gain but by helping the Democrats raise desperately needed campaign cash. It was oil millionaire Clint Murchison's associate, Bedford Wynn, who offered to stage a $1,000-a-plate Democratic dinner in January, 1963. *The dinner raised* $500,000, *largely from oil men, to pay off the whopping* 1960 *Democratic debt.* Shortly after the dinner, Clint Murchison's son, John, paid a private 90-minute call on the President. His arrival was never announced and no one overheard their conversation. Murchison emerged, smiling, and assured fellow oil men they had nothing to worry about. Later, President Kennedy introduced a series of complicated accounting changes in the method of computing percentage depletion, claiming this would have the effect of reducing the oil depletion write-off, but it took IBM machines to figure it out. And once again, the word was passed that it was just window dressing.

Nothing illustrates the influence of Big Oil so graphically as the story of how the oil crowd virtually captured the White House in 1953. The tale might begin with George Allen, the oil operator, non-practicing attorney and bon vivant, who served as court jester for three Presidents and made the White House his second home for more than a quarter century. Since he wangled his first rent-free suite in Washington's fashionable Wardman Park Hotel in 1929, Allen has been neck-deep in complex deals revolving around government power, personal influence and private gain. In his book, "Presidents Who Have Known Me," he declares that "politics runs on juice — on the kind of influence by which the proper man can get a ticket fixed." Probably no one in modern history has been more adept at generating "political juice" than Allen. The dexterity by which he switched loyalties from President Truman to President Eisenhower, two men who would scarcely speak to one another, is positively astounding. His finesse might be illustrated more specifically by his golf games with Ike; Allen always managed to achieve a score just above Eisenhower's.

As Truman neared the end of his term, Allen looked about for a replacement and decided on Ike, then NATO Commander. Allen was a close crony and business partner of oil millionaire Sid Richardson, considered the nation's third richest man and ruler of a 20-company empire with an estimated worth over $1 billion. Together, Allen and Richardson flew off to Paris to persuade the General to be the Democratic candidate for President. Unfortunately, while they were enroute, Eisenhower announced as a Republican. This failed to daunt Allen who pledged his support anyway and accompanied Ike to the London funeral of King George VI. Soon the oil millionaires were all pitching in to persuade Ike to run. They financed a Tex McCrary-staged Madison Square Garden rally; oil money gushed freely into the Eisenhower campaign coffers; and there were many Texas accents heard in the official reviewing stands during Eisenhower's 1953 inauguration.

Yet even before the first flag was unfurled in the inaugural parade, the new President entered into a fantastic secret agreement with three oilmen to take over his Gettysburg farm. Allen, who arranged the deal, chastely explained: "When Ike became President, he decided it wouldn't be proper to be in partnership with anybody. He's supersensitive about doing the proper thing, so I bought him out — wrote him a check for his share of the farming operation and now I lease the entire estate." Ike, himself, explained the relationship to a farm group, saying that he didn't have "any interest in the income and the debts of my farm — that is something that properly belongs to the fellows leasing it."

Allen brought two partners into the Gettysburg farm deal, Texas oil millionaire B. G. "Billie" Byars and the late W. Alton Jones of Cities Service. Among them, the trio represented a substantial segment of Big Oil. Allen and Byars promptly opened an account in the Gettysburg National Bank and began paying Ike's farm bills. Although they later told tax agents they were running the farm as a business, they made no serious effort to produce a profit. But they did transform the Pennsylvania Dutch country farm into a luxurious Presidential retreat by adding such extravagant improvements as a $30,000 show barn, three smaller barns worth

$22,000, and landscaping that cost another $6,000.

Little was told the public about the farm lease, nothing mentioned of Allen's other partners. Jones, in fact, was such a silent partner that he didn't sign any checks but was dunned privately for his share. His role in the Gettysburg farm was revealed only after Drew Pearson got hold of a letter from the farm manager, retired Gen. Arthur Nevins, to Allen and Byars with a copy marked for Jones. The letter read:

"Dear George and Billie. The funds for the farm operations are getting low, so would each of you also let me have your check in the usual amount of $2500. A similar amount will also be transferred to the partnership account from Alton Jones' account. I bought an exceptionally fine cow, a daughter of Eva's Bandolier Lad, Karama family, at the Thomasville sale, but I can handle purchase price from our normal operating funds . . . With warm regards to all of you."

With three oilmen pumping thousands of dollars into it, the farm still lost money every year. Yet by Allen's own admission, Ike received a check "for his share of the farming operation." Using the President's name, the trio also arranged an elaborate aerial survey of the farm by Soil Conservation experts at the expense of the taxpayers. Later, the three financial angels decided the raising of pure-blooded Angus show cattle would do more for Ike's status, although officials of the Maryland Aberdeen Angus Breeding Association describe Angus ranching as an "avocation" — in other words, a rich man's hobby, not a commercial operation.

With fiscal abandon, the oilmen didn't confine their favors to the Eisenhowers but also helped establish Mamie's brother-in-law, Col. Gordon Moore, on a lush 550-acre estate in the picturesque horse country of northern Virginia. Before Ike's nomination, Moore lived modestly as a hired hand for a group of small airlines at the unprincely salary of $8,500 a year. When Ike began climbing the peaks, Mamie's brother-in-law started up the foothills. Once Ike moved into the White

House, Col. Moore's fortunes suddenly soared with help, as an investigation disclosed, from some of the same oil men who were subsidizing the Eisenhower farm. To pay the upkeep of Moore's Holiday Hill estate, a syndicate of Texas oil millionaires — using the name Murcain-Byars, derived from Clinton Murchison, Wofford Cain and "Billie" Byars — maintained a fabulous stable of race horses on the place. Moore supervised the raising and training of horseflesh worth an estimated $250,000. In 1958, Moore was a middle-man in the purchase of the Charles Town, West Virginia, race track by a Texas group headed by Murchison and Byars. Later, Moore found another purchaser, and the oilmen sold their track. Both sales brought Moore fat commissions.

Meanwhile, back at the White House, Ike with a loud clanking of the crusader's armor was busy slaying the Dragon Corruption. Behind the piety and the preaching, the oil industry was quietly making its own killing. *The Eisenhower Administration, during its first term, issued 60 oil leases in government reserves.* This contrasted with only 16 leases issued during the entire 55-year history of the National Wild Life Refuge program. *Yet it was only birdseed compared to the valuable tidelands which Ike also handed over to the oil interests.*

In 1954 the new President appointed a Cabinet Committee on Energy Supplies and Resources Policy to determine federal policy toward the oil industry. The group was run by Secretary of the Treasury George Humphrey who simply called in the oil industry to write the recommendations. Those who came to the White House to work on the project were: Cecil Brill, chief economist, Standard Oil of New Jersey; Richard Gettell, chief foreign economist, Texaco; Richard Gonzales, treasurer, Humble Oil; Robert Hardwicke, Fort Worth oil attorney; Serge Jurenev, assistant to the chairman, Continental Oil; Edmundson Parkes, vice president, United Gas Pipeline; and C. Pratt Rather, president, Southern Natural Gas. These men received no government pay but remained on company payrolls while drafting policy for the White House.

Their recommendations, which not surprisingly would have freed the industry to charge higher gas rates, were accepted by Eisenhower without change. Only the ill-timed attempt to bribe Senator Case prevented them from becoming the law of the land. Case raised such a ruckus on the Senate floor that Ike, sadly, had to veto the bill. Yet, he remained unreformed, announcing that he was vetoing the measure with "regret" because of the "arrogant" lobbying. He hastened to add: "I am in accord with [the bill's] basic objectives."

True to the last, Ike signed an executive order changing the regulations for importing residual fuel oil just three days before leaving the White House. His Secretary of the Interior, Fred Seaton, barely had time to issue procedural instructions. The order benefitted mostly Gulf Oil, which had sued for a larger share of imports but had lost the suit. Ike's action simply increased their daily quota by ten times without benefit of legal action. Cities Service, which had had no residual quota, was also granted 3,000 barrels a day. Its head, of course, was W. Alton Jones, the friendly financier of Ike's farm. A few weeks after hunting quail with Eisenhower in Georgia, Jones was killed in a plane crash en route to California to fish with Ike. On the oilman's body was found about $61,000, mostly in cash.

Men like Senator Morse and Congressman Steed, who have dared to call the turn on Big Oil, are but small voices in the wilderness. Not until enough voices reach a roar of indignation will the curtain be pulled aside to reveal the living-in-sin arrangement between government and oil, and the amoral offspring the relationship has spawned.

11

THE CRUDE ART OF INTIMIDATION

To protect themselves from the dishonest and the disloyal, the American people may have created a Frankenstein's monster which is turning on the citizens it is supposed to serve. This is the relentless and rapacious federal enforcement complex, which has produced a new and frightening trend toward government by investigation. The federal bureaucracy is literally crawling with investigators who, if they are to earn their salaries, must investigate *someone.* Today, this could be almost anyone who deals with the government or makes out a tax return.

It has become an all too frequent practice, in conflicts between private citizens and federal agencies, for the government to try to settle disputes by investigating the disputants. *The power of investigation, which is supposed to be used for the good of the citizens, is often used instead to intimidate, coerce, and strike back at persons who challenge the rulings or oppose the policies of the government.*

The contractor who won't accept the government's terms, the taxpayer who contests a ruling, even the associate of someone else under investigation may find himself hounded by gumshoes. Of course, the government has no power to prosecute innocent men. So an ambitious federal agency, seeking to extend its authority, must create new criminals. This is done by passing new laws or reinterpreting the old ones, thus producing guilt where none had previously existed. Then out swarm the investigators, those faceless men in blue serge suits, to look for violators. No one can say exactly how many investigators are on the government payroll, for they are often camouflaged as attorneys, accountants, and consultants. A top General Services Administration official has admitted: "We used to have a large staff of engineers and a few lawyers and investigators. Now we have a large staff of lawyers and investigators and a few engineers."

The government has spun such a web of regulations, each new agency adding to the tangle, that it is almost impossible for a citizen to go about his business without committing violations. *More than 50 permanent agencies, employing 2.5 million people, oversee every phase of life from teaching birth control or baby care to prescribing burial methods. The federal government has make-or-break power over more than 40 percent of the nation's businesses.* The regulatory agencies, for example, can all but destroy any transportation, telephone, electric, or radio-television company simply by giving the thumbscrews an extra twist.

These regulatory agencies, if they are to justify the expansion dear to the hearts of all bureaucrats, must constantly find more people to investigate. Since June 30, 1961, the Securities and Exchange Commission, for instance, has almost doubled its payroll. Each new employee has brought a corresponding boost in investigative zeal. Comments Barron's, the national financial weekly: "The SEC and its friends are seeking new worlds to conquer. They are questioning the propriety of financial public relations. They are moving in on corporate accounting practices. They are whittling away at management's right to buy and sell." Claiming jurisdiction over the intrastate securities market on the grounds that the brokers use interstate telephone lines, the SEC sent a team of investigators into Indiana in late 1964. They stayed on and on, questioning hundreds of businessmen and brokers, collecting thousands of documents, and generally disrupting the market. Of some 800 salesmen who had dealt actively in Indiana securities, one insider estimates, no more than a dozen remain. Many business enterprises have been hurt and hundreds of investors have lost substantial amounts of money.

Of course, some of the targets of investigation are Reds, racketeers, and others not wholly deserving of sympathy. And in theory, an innocent person has nothing to fear from investigators. But once the gumshoes have come around questioning a citizen's neighbors and associates, a cloud of suspicion is raised that may never be dispelled. His reputation may be ruined even though he is innocent of any wrongdoing. I have talked to several attorneys who have defended clients in federal cases. All but one complained of the government's tactics. The most outspoken was Urbana, Illinois, attorney Joseph M. Williams, who declared: *"The government is the most unfair and corrupt opponent that you will have in a courtroom. Federal agencies have conducted investigations of my clients that were unbelievably improper."*

Although most federal officials try to be fair and most agencies do not condone coercive investigations, the bureaucratic system tends to uphold the abuses of those few entrenched office holders who regard themselves as the masters rather than the servants of the people. They usually are able to summon the massive weight of the U.S. government behind their rulings and recommendations. For most agency heads, unfamiliar with the details of a case, are inclined to accept the judgment of their subordinates. Investigators in particular are held sacrosanct in many federal bureaus. Once they start blood-hounding a case, only the boldest bureaucrat would dare to intervene. "It isn't safe to stick your nose into an investigation," an official has admitted to me. "What if the guy turns out to be guilty? The next thing you know, the inspectors wil be trying to link *you* to the case."

When the SEC rejected an investigator's recommendation that a Connecticut company be indicted for fraud, the agent bounced back his recommendation in even stronger words. The SEC commissioners, nervous that they might be ac-

UNITED STATES DEPARTMENT OF AGRICULTURE
Agricultural Stabilization and Conservation Service
Office of the Administrator
Washington 25, D. C.

To: State Executive Directors APR 12 1963
State Committeemen

From: Deputy Administrator, State and County Operations

Subject: Public Service Time on Radio and Television for Wheat Program Information

The purpose of this memorandum is to encourage you to make full use of radio and television public service time in getting to farmers the facts they need to have before voting in the National Wheat Referendum on May 21. Radio and television have special advantages in communicating to farmers because of their timeliness and their broad availability to rural people wherever they live.

An additional advantage is that broadcasting stations have a special obligation to the public which does not exist in the case of publications.

Stations have an obligation to provide free time for the presentation of public service information -- especially in the field of agriculture. This is spelled out in the laws governing the licensing of stations by the Federal Communications Commission. These stations must renew their operating licenses every three years, and they want to make a good record in public service programming because this is a factor in renewal.

Radio and television stations, in applying for licensing and renewal, make this promise (of public service programming) in return for two special favors granted by the government: (1) The exclusive use (in an area or in the Nation) of a frequency within a broadcast band which is the property of the government and the American people, and (2) The policy of the Government not to establish Federally-operated stations in competition with stations being operated commercially. (Federal stations are the rule in many other countries.)

This does not, of course, make the stations subject to dictation.

A given station does not have to devote any specific share of its broadcast time to public service programming. Nor is it required to give attention to any particular government program or any particular government agency.

Nevertheless, a station does have the general obligation to provide its listeners with information on public programs of importance to them. This has been particularly emphasized in the case of farm listeners, which have been a special concern of the Congress. (Service to agriculture is a special function of the Clear Channel Broadcasting Stations, under their establishing legislation. Also, power to serve areas outside a city implies an obligation to meet the needs of rural areas.)

Although the Agriculture Department insisted it didn't try to influence how farmers voted in the 1963 wheat referendum, the above memo, sent to field officials, indicates otherwise.

cused of a whitewash, decided to pass the buck to the Justice Department. The case went to a U.S. attorney who later admitted there was insufficient evidence for an indictment. But he didn't want to take the responsibility for overruling the agency. Playing it safe, he submitted the matter to a grand jury which in turn felt he wouldn't have presented the case if an indictment weren't justified. *Result: company officials were duly indicted, though no one except the original investigator thought they deserved to be.* The trial jury, of course, found them innocent—after two years of mental anguish, federal harassment, and legal expense.

How many individuals can stand up against the awesome power of the federal government? No private bank account can match the bottomless vaults of the U.S. Treasury. No private staff can marshall the manpower available to the government. Once caught in the federal vise, a private citizen must rely upon the restraint and fairness of the authorities if he is to get an even break. They are supposed to seek justice for everyone, and it is heartening how many do. Others, however, don't seem to understand the difference between "prosecute" and "persecute". Some citizens contend that the government should offer no quarter to those crooks and communists who will twist every comma in the Constitution to thwart justice. But others warn that any tactics the government is permitted to use against them could be turned against anyone.

Many attorneys who would like to see Teamsters' boss Jimmy Hoffa behind bars, for example, believe the government has gone too far with its campaign to put him there. His every move has been shadowed, his every transaction scrutinized, his every associate investigated. Even two Congressmen, who spoke up in behalf of Hoffa on the House floor, suddenly had their taxes audited. After indicting some of his business associates, the Justice Department offered to drop prosecution if they would testify against him. A Miami banker, who had never been accused of anything worse than a traffic offense until he got involved in a business deal with Hoffa, was hauled before a grand jury on tax evasion charges. When the evidence wouldn't support a tax indictment, the grand jury indicted him for perjury instead. Even this charge was later dropped. Meanwhile the banker was so discredited that he was forced to sell his banking interests at a sacrifice.

A Baltimore insurance man, who did business with Hoffa, was so harrassed that he told me bitterly: "Five years ago, I would have been willing to die for my country. Now I hate my country for what it has done to me." (Other businessmen who have had dealings with Hoffa, contend the government has been perfectly proper in its prying.) According to sworn testimony, disputed by the Justice Department, agents have even used voodoo in an effort to persuade Thomas Ewing Parks, an uncle of a Teamsters official, to testify against Hoffa. A Nashville voodoo doctor, Bishop St. Psalm, allegedly was retained to perform the mystic rites. Reportedly he lit two candles on a portable altar, then placed upon the altar an article of Parks' clothing borrowed from a dry cleaning shop. Though a believer, the superstitious Parks apparently didn't respond to the voodoo spell.

A favorite harassment is to toss difficult cases, no matter how unrelated they may be to taxes, to the Internal Revenue Service. "A lot of agencies like to use us," Commissioner Sheldon Cohen has acknowledged. "We try to discourage this, but these disputes often have tax overtones." When the government moved to take over private housing on military bases, owners who resisted were suddenly besieged by tax agents. The Justice Department's Land Acquisition Section brought tax pressure, for example, on Nashville builder Edward Carmack, who was unwilling to sell 600 homes at Sewart Air Force Base, Tennessee, at the government's price. Ralph Luttrell, then section chief, admitted to me that he had drafted an official letter to Internal Revenue, pointing out "the possibility of tax evasion" in the Carmack case. The builder was subjected to an intensive investigation, which ended in dismissal of fraud charges against him. One high official even used the Internal Revenue Service to get revenge against a driver whose car bumped his Cadillac at the Washington National Airport. The official copied the license number of the other car, traced the owner's identity, then secured an investigation into his taxes.

Though the rich often benefit by tax adjustments during litigation proceedings, the poor fare worse. When comedian Charlie Chaplin quit the United States he left behind a bad joke: $700,000 in unpaid taxes. After a long legal hassle, Uncle Sam settled for $425,000. Negro singer Paul Robeson, whose devotion to Russia is well known, also seemed the object of strange benevolence. After a five-year fight, Internal Revenue agreed that his $25,000 Stalin prize should be tax free. Yet at the same time the government was relentlessly pursuing a host of small tax debtors, poor but loyal Americans, many of whom were in debt for reasons beyond their control. Uncle Sam garnisheed their wages, seized their property, confiscated their bank accounts, and deprived them of their jobs, stripping them of almost everything they possessed except the mere clothes on their backs.

Why are tax enforcers more lenient with people like Chaplin and Robeson? Is the color of their money more persuasive than the color of their politics? "The more taxes you owe, the better deal you can get," is a common lament.

More than one hard-pressed taxpayer has found himself in trouble because of a trivial or unintentional error in an old return, the failure of an employer to withhold the correct tax, or a personal tragedy which cleaned him out of the money he set aside for Uncle Sam. The files at Internal Revenue are stuffed with complaints from taxpayers who say they have been hounded, bullied, and browbeaten by collectors whose methods would put a loan shark to shame. Many a widow's last mite has been snatched from her. Men have been stripped of their livelihood and, along with it, their only means of paying the government. "The Internal Revenue Service can be tyrannical, arbitrary, and undemocratic", according to a Denver attorney who has handled many tax cases.

Uncle Sam's aim is to be firm but fair with *all* taxpayers. Rich and poor are supposed to be equal in the sharp eye of Internal Revenue, which tries to administer the tax laws without regard for social standing or political pull. Yet policy and practice don't always coincide. Often tax settlements are reached by a process about as equitable as a medieval trial by fire and water. The rich man has recourse to lawyers and experts who can find loopholes in the law or stall a case in the courts. Since Uncle Sam loses almost half the cases that are tried, he sometimes settles for what the court would likely award. This saves legal costs which whittle away the money Internal Revenue is trying to collect. In the Chaplin case, the irascible Charlie stashed away most of his funds out of Uncle Sam's reach in those Swiss banks that have become a haven for the world's runaway money. Internal Revenue probably squeezed every dime out of Chaplin its collectors figured they could get. Robeson's lawyers claimed his Stalin Prize money was a gift, not payment for services. They found enough legal tape to truss up the government until it could no longer move. While the rich may have the advantage of expert advice, Internal Revenue insists they get no special privileges. "We seize mink coats and yachts, too," a top official points out. To thousands of small taxpayers, struggling against arrears, this may seem cold comfort.

Many a big defaulter has been able to slip off the hook by learning the tax tricks. Consider these examples taken at random from Treasury's settlement file: A New York City printer settled a $211,552 tax bill for only $7,500.; a New Jersey button manufacturer arranged to satisfy a $1,791,378 claim for $130,000; a Flushing, New York, belt maker owed

$127,879 but got off for $11,000; an Indianapolis beer distributor paid only $262,094 of a $1,242,013 tax debt. Against such leniency is the harshness which many small taxpayers have encountered. Consider these cases:

• A man, so hopelessly paralyzed that rehabilitation officials refused to give him vocational training, studied watchmaking on his own, devised a work bench with a sliding chair and set up his own small shop in the nation's capital. He eked out a bare living for his wife, small son, and himself. Sometimes he had trouble meeting his bills, including Uncle Sam's annual bite of his tiny income. He arranged a $200 bank loan to cover his 1956 tax but couldn't raise enough to pay $68 still owed from the previous year. Revenue men tried to attach his bank account until they found it contained only $20. When they threatened to take away his car, the cripple pleaded that his wife could not get him to work without it. His family would become a total charge on the community, he pointed out, if he were put out of business. No one knows what might have happened if a friend hadn't written out a check for the $68 tax bill.

• A Negro laborer, bewildered by the complex tax forms, hired an "expert" who promised to reduce his taxes — and did so simply by underpaying the government. Agents showed up at the Negro's home, demanding $400 more on his tax. Because he had no way of raising that sum, three successive pay checks were garnisheed, leaving the man nothing to live on. He had to go to a Mount Rainer, Maryland, loan company for rent and food money.

• A Gonzales, California, vegetable grower mortgaged his home to the hilt and borrowed on his life insurance to pay off back taxes. When the government slapped liens on his land, he went to tax court. The examiner didn't take long to arrive at the obvious: the man could hardly pay up if Uncle Sam wouldn't let him grow vegetables. The court ordered the liens lifted.

• A Washington free-lance writer has been hounded to despair for $571 back taxes. He claims federal agents have called on him dozens of times, questioned business and personal friends about his finances, notified neighbors he is evading taxes, and asked his mailman to report any envelopes that might contain checks. The writer pleaded that his fixed expenses, including the care of an invalid mother, exceeded his income. "What do you want me to do," he asked, "move into a tent?" He quotes the agents as replying: "We don't give a . . . what you do, just so you pay the bill."

• A Huntington, West Virginia, businessman, plagued by alimony troubles, was forced into involuntary bankruptcy by government liens on his drugstore. His brother borrowed $3,000 so the man could meet a tax payment. Reported a tax court examiner later: "The creditors seized all his assets. He lives alone in a small apartment . . . His only assets are a few pieces of furniture . . . His net worth is almost nil . . . He cannot get any credit . . .The taxpayer appears to be a good businessman and if the liens were lifted so as to obtain credit, he could again go into business and earn a better income."

• The day after a Miami television station criticized the Internal Revenue Service, agents came around to ask ominous questions about the station's taxes. Thoroughly intimidated, the station refused to air a TV tape from its Washington correspondent about IRS abuses.

• Tax agents dropped in on Lew M. Warden, Jr., Oakland attorney, and asked to see his books. To protect his clients, he refused permission unless they would specify what they were looking for. He was slapped with a subpoena but managed to get it vacated in federal court. Next, all the expenses he reported in his tax returns were arbitrarily disallowed, and he was ordered to pay up $20,000 in back taxes. Then his bank account and sailboat were attached. Through all this, he was told that the actions would be dropped if he opened his books to investigators. However, Warden fought back, and in the end, as the case was about to go to court, the government capitulated and agreed to a "settlement" that said he owed them nothing.

One of the most insidious federal weapons is the jeopardy assessment, which is supposed to be used to tie up the funds of a taxpayer who might try to skip the country. Agents have used this power indiscriminately in order to force settlements out of reluctant taxpayers. A Tulane, California, high school counselor wrote to me: "I am a respected, responsible citizen, no arrest record, a veteran of World War II with a family of five children. On February 1, 1966, I was sent into a state of shock when the business office politely informed me that Internal Revenue had confiscated my entire paycheck. I am in debt, have no collateral; several checks were outstanding in anticipation of the deposit . . . The [Treasury's] trick was to satisfy a back tax assessment which we have proof we do not owe. I don't know how to cope with power this extensive."

Noel Smith, a Taylor, Missouri, farmer, had all his funds tied up for four years after he refused to pay a $570,000 tax claim. He was obliged to live off the proceeds of a business deal in Canada. The government finally offered to settle the claim for less than 10 cents on the dollar. Though he stoutly insisted he didn't owe anything, he coughed up $54,000 in order to get access to his own bank account again. He complained that the four-year ordeal had ruined his reputation, broken his health, and cost him $1 million in lost profits. "If I had it to do over again," he said, "it would be easier to go to jail."

Chairman Wilbur Mills of the House Ways and Means Committee, which writes the nation's tax laws, appointed a panel of 22 prominent tax attorneys and accountants to investigate how the laws are being administered. The group found many acts of "overzealousness" which had infringed "the vital rights and dignities" of individuals. Treasury's claim that these acts were outside official policy was disingenuous. Agents have been known to bring fraud charges against a taxpayer simply to lengthen the time to investigate his returns. The statute of limitations runs out in three years on delinquent taxes, but extends to six years for fraud. The panel declared: "*We are aware of situations in which agents have made reckless and inexpert overstatements of a taxpayer's liability in order to justify fraud charges and prevent the running of the statute of limitations.*"

The power to levy assessments and liens, residing in the hands of Treasury's field agents, has been used as a club to force a taxpayer to give in without a fight for his rights. The panel also complained of "a tendency to punish a suspected taxpayer by adverse publicity. Sometimes agents do not take adequate steps to avoid unnecessary injury to the reputation of the person under investigation." Another practice, found in some local offices, is the "quota system" to stimulate collections. Agents are in effect threatened with dismissal if they don't get results in enough cases. Some go after unpaid taxes as if it's their lone mission to collect enough revenue for President Johnson to reduce his budget.

Most states won't permit a creditor to garnishee more than 10 percent of a person's wage. Uncle Sam isn't bound by such legal niceties; a tough collector sometimes demands whole pay checks. The favorite target is the taxpayer's car, which can be seized without notice. One collector confided to me: "Nothing brings a delinquent to heel quicker than taking his car. He'll let everything else go to pay for it. Once the car is confiscated, he'll beg borrow or steal to pay up back taxes." A tax debtor can be put through a third degree, which requires him to bare his finances right down to the last dime in the family sugar bowl. He can be asked such unnerving questions as: "What would your assets bring at a forced sale?" and "Do you carry life insurance?" Taxpayers have been told to borrow on their insurance. If they should die, leaving a tax debt, revenue agents try to get the insurance money ahead of the beneficiaries. Some courts have permitted this; others have not.

Harassed debtors sometimes threaten to commit suicide, but the Treasury's revenue men are seldom moved. When an hysterical taxpayer talked about drowning himself, he was advised to wait until spring when the water would be warmer. Most suicide talk obviously is intended to gain sympathy. Yet homicide officers claim a majority who take their own lives are driven to it by money troubles. Whether Internal Revenue has helped push any of these unfortunates over the brink can only be surmised.

Revenue agents naturally defend themselves against charges of wholesale callousness. They point out that, since Biblical times, the tax collector has always been the most disliked of officials. It is their duty, they point out, to rake in money on which national security and domestic services depend. Every defaulting dollar means a dollar that some other citizen must pay. Officials cite the strict code laid down for Internal Revenue dealings with the public. "Every taxpayer is entitled to careful and courteous attention," collectors are instructed. "Employees should remember that their duty requires them to pay the same heed to the taxpayer's interest as to the government's." Says a Treasury spokesman: "We're not insensitive to human problems We'll take into account hardship cases, if not always the convenience of the taxpayers, in collecting back taxes."

When one of Uncle Sam's relentless collectors recently called on a delinquent payer and found him out of work, his seven children hungry, the agent dipped into his own inadequate means to buy food for the family. Another agent stopped at a laundry to ask a $32-a-week laundress about her back taxes. He was so touched by her weeping that he found her a job at another laundry for $67-a-week—and collected the taxes out of her increased pay packet. Internal Revenue would like its agents to be loved. To this end, it tries eagerly to make more friendly contact with the public. Originally called Internal Revenue Bureau, it dropped the "Bureau" for "Service" because the agency chiefs felt the former word had too harsh a ring. They wanted to emphasize that their job was to help the taxpayer, not merely pluck him. The 6,000 collectors have been designated "revenue officers" to get away from the old stigma of their calling. The word "warrant" has been eliminated from final tax notices because of its unduly frightening connotation. A special committee has examined all form letters to make sure they contain no implied threats or disagreeable language.

But, as in any large organization, petty tyrants do exist. Even an occasional misfit turns up. A Washington attorney was given such a rough time over his taxes that he started checking on the agent's background. It turned out that the revenue man was an escapee from Baltimore's Shepherd Pratt insane asylum. A paranoid type, he believed himself to be the illegitimate son of ex-President Woodrow Wilson and the Duchess of Kent. This is, of course, a unique case. The great majority of Internal Revenue employees are decent, hardworking people doing their best in a difficult, unpopular job to serve both the government and the public. Yet hardships and inequalities, perhaps inevitable when a great bureaucratic machine begins to grind, do exist. Tax disputes more than any other have given many harassed citizens a glimpse of the other face of Uncle Sam when he scowls.

The multiplication of Federal agencies has resulted in a corresponding proliferation of paper work. Several government contractors have complained to me that they have become so entangled in red tape they can hardly avoid tripping over it. They must spend so much time filling out forms, auditing books, contending with attorneys, and warding off investigators that they cannot possibly give full attention to their government projects. In part, this is the fault of profiteers who have bilked the taxpayers in the past and have compelled the government to tighten controls. But some agencies have now become obsessed with audits and investigations. They have seized upon technical violations and treated respectable businessmen like criminals. In a case that has become all too typical, the Court of Claims recently lectured a federal contracting officer for his arrogance and arbitrariness. "He merely took a shillelagh and struck [the contractor] down," declared the court.

For many contractors, government profits no longer are worth the harassment. Some have served notice they will never bid on government contracts again. A top General Services Administration official admits he doesn't blame them. "We are fighting with every contractor we do business with," he said wearily. Sometimes Uncle Sam holds up payment until the contractor, desperate for money to meet his bills, settles for less than he is supposed to get. One contractor, in order to rush work on the Bomarc missile, lived for four months in a trailer and worked around the clock at the missile site. But the government was in no such rush to pay him. Eight years after the contract was completed, he was still trying to collect what was owed him.

Worse, Uncle Sam doesn't hesitate to use criminal charges to coerce an obstinate contractor into accepting a civil settlement. Fraud investigations follow civil disputes with surprising, even automatic, frequency.

S. Harvey Klein a Philadelphia electronics manufacturer, got into a legal hassle with the government over the termination of a contract. After rejecting the government's settlement offer, he suddenly found himself under investigation for allegedly filing a false claim.

The Renegotiation Board, after reviewing a Brussel Sewing Machine contract, concluded that the company's profit had not been excessive. Once the case was closed, however, an "informer" charged that the company had misstated its estimated cost. Investigators immediately swarmed all over the company, and the Justice Department filed a false-claim charge. Unimpressed with the government's arguments, the court concluded that it wasn't "the intention of the statute to make dealing with the government hazardous should someone later conceive the notion that the government had paid too much."

John A. Maxwell, a Michigan manufacturer, was fined $30,000 and sentenced to a three-year prison term because he followed the government's own suggestion and filed estimated instead of exact cost figures. It had been agreed that the exact cost could be calculated later. Though the government had been a party to his act, it brought criminal charges against him for submitting estimated, hence false figures. The Appeals Court found the government's position so outrageous that it set aside a guilty verdict.

Increasingly, the government seems tempted to use its investigative powers to intimidate its critics. Many a newsman after writing a critical article, has suddenly become aware of watchdogs sniffing his trail. Some citizens who wrote to President Johnson, opposing his Vietnam policies and expressing sympathy with the peace demonstrators, received replies from the Justice Department's Internal Security Division. A spokesman blandly denied this was an attempt to intimidate anyone. In another incident, Jack Ferriss, Jr., of Chattanooga exercised his inalienable American right to call the President "tyrannical, dictatorial and domineering"; he was promptly visited by Secret Service agents.

Dr. Carlton Fredericks has felt the hot breath of the federal government on his neck ever since he started feuding with the Food and Drug Administration 17 years ago. The agency has called him "a crackpot, culturist, food faddist, and dispenser of nutritional nonsense." *Yet amazingly, it has never taken him into court to prove the charges but has tried his case instead in the newspapers.* The record against him consists almost entirely of press releases. More than once, agents have raided food-supplement producers that had absolutely nothing to do with Fredericks; yet the press releases, announcing the raids, have been devoted primarily to attacks on him. Food and Drug officials have warned newspaper and radio stations against him, have enlisted the help of the Federal Communications Commission to drive him off the air, and, of course, have inspired an investigation into his taxes. "Food faddists," Fredericks contends, "have a right to their beliefs. They have a right to buy the foods they want. They should not be made half criminals."

In their zeal to investigate, some bureaucrats become so obsessed with the letter of the law that they will spend $1,000 to save $10. Since Red Chinese imports are barred from the United States, for example, the intrepid bureaucrats of the Foreign Assets Control Office confiscated a $150 panel screen from University of California Professor Maynard Amerine on the suspicion it may have come from behind the Bamboo Curtain.

Dismayed, Prof. Amerine set about to prove that he had not been dealing with the Chinese communists. After considerable trouble, he produced a certificate of origin from the Ashai Art Company, Tokyo, certifying that the screen had been made in Japan by a safely anti-communist artist. But Director Margaret Schwartz, determined to protect the nation from this screen, demanded more proof that it was free from communist taint. Dr. Amerine engaged a Tokyo law firm which painstakingly traced the screen to its creator, a Japanese artist named Genjiro Machida, who began work on it 80 years ago—long before there were any Chinese communists around to inflict their subversive influence on Oriental art. Still unimpressed, Mrs. Schwartz refused to let Dr. Amerine reposses his screen.

Similarly, Foreign Assets controllers saved the nation in the nick of time from a giant panda that was on its way from Red China to the Chicago Zoo. Thanks to the vigilance of these bureaucrats, Americans also were spared the peril of contamination from duck eggs which, though laid in British Hong Kong, might just possibly have come from ducks hatched inside China. And while State Department officials minimized the extent to which free world ships have been providing Peking and Hanoi with valuable supplies, the Foreign Assets controllers have done their part by triumphantly negotiating an agreement with eight countries not to export to the United States wigs made of Chinese communist hair.

It is not the nitpicking but the harassing, however, that troubles most Americans. After Parade magazine published an article of mine on intimidation-by-investigation, mail poured into my office from hundreds of citizens who wrote about their own experience with federal snoops. Several declared bitterly that their faith in their country had been shaken. One said he had been driven almost to the point of suicide by the government's hounding. Another swore he was ready to renounce his citizenship, another that he was pulling up stakes to move to Canada. Though a few were cranks, the majority wrote sober, sensible letters. Some included documentary evidence to back up their stories. "To win their way," wrote an Indianapolis man, "the bureaucrats use intimidation, threats and blackmail. There is small limit to their power, and they use it to the utmost."

What can be done? A Miami housewife, who wrote about her humiliating experience over a false accusation, urged: "The motives of the accuser should be scrutinized before the government puts its weight behind an investigation." A Detroit doctor, who said he had been hounded for daring to question a decision of the Food and Drug Administration, suggested legislation to make government officials accountable collectively and individually for destroying reputations. But perhaps the most practical proposal came from a Denver citizen who refused to knuckle under to the demands of Internal Revenue and was hounded by its agents. "I do not belong to any vocal, marching and picketing pressure group," he wrote. "My case is no grist for anybody's political or pecuniary mill. But if [the Treasury's] sort of dispensation of justice is in harmony with the Bill of Rights, then the latter may be meaningless." He called for creation of a post similar to that of the Swedish "ombudsman" who has the power to investigate complaints made by private citizens and to prosecute officials found dealing unfairly with the public.

Most Americans look upon Uncle Sam as a benevolent big brother, which he tries to be. But there has been developing in our federal uncle an alarming vindictive streak.

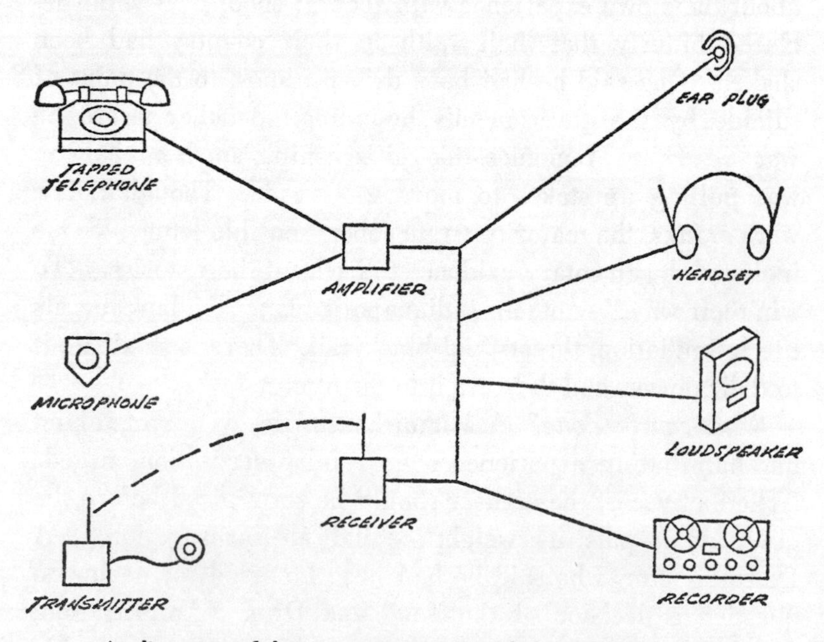

A diagram of basic equipment used for eavesdropping.

12

GOVERNMENT AT THE KEYHOLE

The realization that he had been blackmailed came to Senator Thorne Patch as a sickening shock. But it was only after he had shelved his investigation of Project Quantam, the price demanded, that he learned how cynically and ruthlessly the plot against him had been carried out. The plotters, failing to find any blemish on his political career or private life, had not hesitated to strike at him through his son. Though an innocent, the boy he loved must now live his life under a cloud. For a youthful folly, he had become a hostage to his father's enemies.

Thorne Patch, known in real life by quite another name, is the central figure in a sordid Senate story. Though the identities are veiled in these pages, it is a shockingly true story of political blackmail and espionage. Every incident actually occurred; only the names have been changed and some details have been fictionalized. This is necessary, as the disclaimers say, to protect the innocent.

Senator Patch, brooding alone is his private hideaway in the Old Senate Office Building, felt as drowning men are believed to feel; suddenly his whole life was passing before his eyes. Once a young midwestern lawyer, he had gone into politics as a reformer battling a corrupt city hall. Then he had run for Congress and had gone in triumph to Washington. From the House, he had moved up to the Senate. Now entering on his third term, he had acquired the seniority to make him a power on Capitol Hill.

He was deeply conscious of the honor of serving in the Senate. He loved its dignity and its disorder; he was jealous of its prerogatives and its traditions. Though some of the rules were quaint, even slightly absurd, there was reason behind all of them. Until this morning he had always felt a thrill when, driving to the Hill from his home in Georgetown, he came within sight of the Capitol dome.

No man, Thorne Patch reflected, is without vanity—a politician least of all. With his big, raw-boned frame, rugged, broken-nosed face and bluntness of speech, he had never considered himself a "character." Yet he had become a national character. He had secretly enjoyed the nickname which the press had pinned on him and which his colleagues and constituents had accepted with glee—"Old Briar" Patch.

Once convinced of the rightness of an issue, he proved a hard man to get past. He was not an obstructionist but a man who liked to shred out the truth. He could also leave scars on those who crossed him. In the smoke-filled back rooms, where the political deals are made, he had traded votes with the best. But he had no reason to be ashamed; he had always sought to advance the causes in which he believed. He had resisted the financial lures—the stock market tips, investment opportunities, law fees—available to Senators for the plucking. He had accepted campaign contributions, true, but he had spent every last nickel for the purpose intended. Indeed, he had put in long extra hours of lecturing and writing to help pay his campaign debts.

Thorne Patch smiled wryly to himself. Though he had voted against it, he had looked forward to the new Congressional pay raise. But now he felt that he had lost all right to his salary. Faced with the most crucial choice of his political career, he had surrendered. That he had done so to protect his son and spare his wife did not absolve him, not in his own eyes. He thought of the Japanese who commit *hari-kiri* rather than face disgrace; perhaps there was some justice in this.

It had started with Project Quantam, a billion-dollar construction program undertaken by the Federal Development Agency. The Senate sub-committee, which Thorne headed, was supposed to oversee it. Aside from the smell of the pork barrel, there was nothing extraordinary about the project. Thorne had no very high opinion of Duncan Sloan, the FDA director, who was a fair administrator but one of those infuriating bureaucrats who never make a statement without an escape clause in every sentence. Suave and pompous, Sloan had a gift for saying nothing in a most impressive manner—a trait that had always exasperated Patch. Before making a decision, Sloan would also process it through endless committees, not from necessity, but to provide plenty of scapegoats should the decision backfire.

Out of the routine staff inquiries came a whisper—a most disturbing whisper—that deep in the excavations of Project Quantam was a financial link between Duncan Sloan and a subcontractor. Old Briar Patch gave the order to track down the facts.

Duncan Sloan, that pillar of executive rectitude, had surrounded himself with a grapevine, sensitive to the faintest rumor affecting his bureaucratic domain. He quickly learned that he was being investigated. To protect himself, he decided to strike back with a discreet counter-investigation of his own. He might need some dirt on Senator Patch for trading purposes. Sloan could not, of course, afford to be caught investigating a U.S. Senator. Nor could he ever hope to get budget approval for extra-curricular eavesdropping. But there are many ways for a bureaucrat to camouflage a cat. He had authority to order an "efficiency" study, which could be financed from the agency's contingency fund. To direct the survey, he retained a Washington attorney, a trusted friend, with experience in handling discreet investigations.

"This is a sensitive matter, a most sensitive matter," Sloan emphasized. The lawyer understood. He assigned to the case private detectives, carefully chosen for their quiet methods and buttoned lips. Though indirectly paid by the government, they had no government credentials. Even if they had been disposed to talk, they knew only that they had been hired by the attorney who, even under oath, could not be compelled to divulge the client's name.

Senator Patch, alone in his office, now knew the facts—in outline if not in full detail. First, the gumshoes had gone completely into his background, grasping at rumors to whet the client's appetite but finding nothing to substantiate the gossip. They had gone so far as to count the empty liquor bottles in his garbage cans and to check the waste baskets in his office for indiscreet scribblings. They had also acquired, second-hand, a green telephone company truck and had driven it up to his home. Quite openly, they had installed a tap on his telephone line. No one had guessed that they were other than telephone crewmen. One private eye, posing as a repair man, had actually borrowed a screw driver from Mrs. Patch.

Monitoring the Senator's office calls was a bit more tricky. To accomplish this, Duncan Sloan was obliged to take a much greater risk than he found comfortable. He instructed the liaison office which his agency maintained on Capitol Hill to make a room available to researchers. His lawyer's private detectives moved into the room unobtrusively. Pretending to be members of Patch's staff, they persuaded the Senate switchboard to connect the phone in their secret room with those in the Senator's office. Every time Patch or an aide picked up a phone, a button would light up on the detectives' instrument. They used a transmitter cutoff gadget, known in the trade as a "snooper button," to shut off the background noises while they listened in.

But Old Priar Patch, aside from some salty sallies, stubbornly would not incriminate himself. Trying another approach, the gumshoes installed a special operative in a hotel near Capitol Hill. He presented himself as Jerry Lester, a West Coast businessman, a hail-fellow-well-met who in minutes could make new acquaintances feel like old friends. First, Lester cultivated staff members, then Senators on

Patch's subcommittee. In his suite there was always plenty to drink and long-legged girls decorating the couches. Sometimes he invited a few Senators over for a stag party of beer and pretzels while they watched a football game on television. Thorne came along from time to time.

Patch was more amused than suspicious at the antics of this gregarious man with the seemingly bottomless pocket. For Lester never asked for a favor; he seemed merely to enjoy being around important people. Sometimes he would draw out his guests in conversation, but it was in character for the talkative Lester. Once or twice Thorne let down his hair with Lester, but he said nothing that could not be repeated in public if it was necessary to do so. Still, it came as a shock to him later to learn that the innocent looking pack of filter cigarettes in Lester's shirt pocket had concealed a tiny transistor transmitter powerful enough to relay every word to a tape recorder in a bedroom closet.

But the tape recorder and the wiretaps had picked up nothing at all titillating, certainly nothing that would force Old Briar Patch to call off his investigation of Project Quantam. Then, from a most remote and unlikely source, came the tip that Duncan Sloan had been looking for. An anonymous crank, reading of the investigation, had written to Sloan that Senator Patch ought to clean his own house before he investigated others. The letter alleged that his son, Thorne Jr., had been involved in a homosexual act in the Army.

It was not true, it turned out, not true at all. But there was sufficient substance to make it stick. Unlike his father, Thorne Jr., was not a rugged type. At 18, when he was drafted into the Army, he had made a barrack-room friend of an older, more sophisticated man who turned out to be a homosexual. The man invited Thorne Jr. to a party. He went along and found himself with deviates. Before the shy boy could extricate himself from the mess, there was a raid by military police. Thorne Jr. was picked up.

The officer in charge of the raid became convinced of the boy's innocence and, incidentally, discovered his father's identity. From compassion and perhaps a little cowardice—what Army Captain wants to tangle with a U.S. Senator?—he hushed up the matter. It probably would have stayed hushed up, Senator Patch had to admit, if he had not become involved with Project Quantam. For Duncan Sloan had not been long in finding an ally in the Army, a General who owed him a favor. The General accommodatingly passed on to Sloan the facts about the raid.

The first hint came to Senator Thorne from an old school friend who had been deliberately tipped off by an acquaintance on Sloan's staff. Next, a well-planted whisper reached Mrs. Patch. Shocked, the parents gently questioned Thorne Jr., who blurted out the story. Though he was not guilty, he became deeply morose. The mother, fearful that the ugly publicity would destroy the boy, became almost hysterical.

None of this would have happened, Thorne told himself, if he had not gone into politics. He knew he should fight on and expose the blackmailers. But no political battle was worth ruining his son's life and bringing untold grief to his wife. Suddenly he was tired, very tired. To save his wife and son, he abandoned the principles upon which he had built his political career. He called off his investigation of Project Quantam; he surrendered to a despicable bureaucrat. For a lesser man, this might have been a small compromise. But for the proud and principled Patch, there was no place in the Senate for a man who betrays his convictions.

In real life, Thorne Patch was not one but two Senators whose stories I have merged. The one who compromised his principles to save his son from a public smear sobbed out his story to me. Eyes afloat, he bit his lips and choked on his words—a painful performance for a man whose outer crust at least had been tempered in the political furnace. He was afraid, he said, that his wife might do something desperate.

POLYGRAPH EXAMINATION
STATEMENT OF CONSENT
(AR 195-10 and AR 381-131)

PLACE	DATE	TIME

STATEMENT OF CONSENT OF *(Name, Grade, & Service No.)*.	PLACE OF BIRTH
	DATE OF BIRTH

In the presence of the witness(es) whose signature(s) appear(s) below, Article 31 of the Uniform Code of Military Justice (and the Fifth Amendment to the Constitution of the United States) *(Strike out only if person completing Statement of Consent IS a Member of the Armed Forces)* (has) (have) been read to me by who informed me that he is a polygraph examiner of the United States Army. He has informed me that this statement is being completed in connection with

of which I am (accused) (suspected) *(Strike out if inapplicable)*. He explained to me the nature of the polygraph examination and told me that I cannot be required to submit to such examination without my consent. He explained to me that I do not have to make any statement whatsoever but that any statement I do make may be used as evidence against me in a trial by court-martial or in any other military or judicial proceedings. Understanding my unqualified right to refuse, I, , do hereby, this date, voluntarily and without duress, coercion, unlawful inducement, or promise of reward, submit to a polygraph examination.

WITNESSES	SIGNATURE OF PERSON TO BE TESTED
SIGNATURE, GRADE, AND SERVICE NUMBER	
ORGANIZATION AND/OR ADDRESS	ORGANIZATION AND/OR ADDRESS
SIGNATURE, GRADE, AND SERVICE NUMBER	SIGNATURE OF EXAMINER
ORGANIZATION AND/OR ADDRESS	
	TYPED NAME AND ORGANIZATION
EXHIBIT NUMBER	

DA FORM 1 JAN 64 2801 REPLACES DA FORM 19-65, 1 OCT 61, WHICH IS OBSOLETE. GPO 872-421

If a government worker wants to hold his job, he has no choice but to consent "voluntarily" to taking a lie detector test. Above is a form that has been used by the armed services.

I never guessed, even as I watched his cheeks grow wet, that he would commit the desperate act. One morning, he smuggled a .22 rifle under his coat into his Senate office and, there, ended his torment with a bullet.

One other time, a prominent member of Congress broke down as he told me how he, too, had become a blackmail victim. After an excruciating operation, he had taken dope to relieve the pain. The day came that he could not get along without the pain killer. His addiction became so bad that a confidential assistant had to inject the drug frequently with a hypodermic needle. *The Congressman rose in seniority to become a powerful committee chairman, privy to some of the nation's most guarded secrets. Yet he was a security risk, subject to blackmail, which indeed was attempted by one of his former aides.* This important chairman could not give up dope; so he gave up his House seat, resigning at the peak of his power.

One of the principals in the Bobby Baker investigation also fought back with some enterprising blackmail. He hired a private detective who laid a silken trap for unwary Senators. He arranged with a lady of the night, who had a clandestine acquaintance on Capitol Hill, to wire her boudoir for sound. She obligingly lured into her web a few romantic Senators. *The recording equipment picked up some senatorial conversations the like of which has never been heard on "Meet the Press."*

Still another racy recording was circulated in the back rooms of Washington during the Bobby Baker hullabaloo. *A confessed call girl, who goes by the name of Ruth Spitini, dictated a titillating account of her relations with high officials from the White House on down, including at least two Senators then investigating Baker.* She later claimed the lurid, two-hour recording had been doctored by Richard Bast, a fast-talking private eye, who first tried to peddle it to newsmen, then offered it to Senator Hugh Scott (R-Pa.). The Senator lost all interest in it, however, after learning the lady of questionable virtue had been bipartisan in her accusations. Confronted by the FBI, she tried to brazen it out until agents asked whether Senator Carl Hayden (D-Ariz.) had been one of her customers. She blithely added him to her list, boasting of some unlikely high jinks with the Senate dean, then 86 years old.

The ease with which recorded conversations can be altered to change their meaning was effectively demonstrated by Robert Coar when he was director of the Joint House-Senate Radio Facilities. Following a speech by Sir Winston Churchill before Congress, reporters who failed to catch some of the Prime Minister's words asked to hear the tape recording. Coar's office, as proof of what can be done to recorded statements, changed one paragraph. Sir Winston had said: "I come not to ask you for money. I come to ask you for military aid. We English are putting out all we can toward this effort." *What the reporters heard was this: "I come here to ask you for money. The English do as they please. What we do with your money is our business."* The reporters, who had just heard the original speech and were familiar with Sir Winston's voice, were completely duped. They kept right on taking notes until Coar called a halt and explained the joke.

The story of how Thorne Patch was artfully spied upon won't come altogether as a surprise to some Senators. During a recent investigation into government eavesdropping, Senator Edward Long (D-Mo.) asked the Federal Communications Commission to check various senatorial suites for electronic taps. Listening devices were discovered in the offices of two Senators.

Long's investigations have turned up some astonishing facts about government snooping. *Federal agents have planted secret microphones in everything from picture frames and desk sets to lamps and telephones. Listening devices have even been slipped into pillows for eavesdroppers who like pillow talk.* But perhaps the most remarkable is a set of low-frequency coat buttons which can be fitted to a victim's coat in a matter of minutes. The top button is a microphone, the second a transmitter, and the third a miniature battery unit. These will turn the wearer into a walking radio station whose every word is broadcast to snoopers.

Real-life James Bonds can instantly tune in on almost anyone with devices from a catalog that includes: wiretaps which not only can pick up phone conversations but can listen in on everything said in your home; electronic or radio-wave bugs smaller than a match book; two-way, peek-aboo mirrors; automatic movie cameras that can snap periodic pictures from an undetectable spot (including the bedroom clock); "sniperscopes" capable of scanning a house perfectly from 100 *yards in total darkness.*

The government also uses less sensational but equally offensive prying techniques such as mail covers, trash inspections and credit checks. *Most government agencies traffic in information about the sexual habits, financial affairs, personal friendships, political and religious beliefs of their employees.* Some agencies have required job applicants to take lie detector tests and submit to psychological examinations that probe into their sex and family life.

There is a prevailing attitude that government snooping is a matter for TV spy spoofs or cocktail party jokes about bugged martini olives. But the laugh may be upon unsuspecting citizens who are closer to George Orwell's concept of 1984 than they may think. Orwell described an advanced police state whose citizens couldn't make a move without Big Brother knowing it. For some time, our federal uncle has been developing a Big Brother complex. He may not be watching everyone at the moment, but he can concentrate an infinite variety of eyes and ears—electronic, mechanical and human—on anyone who stirs his suspicions.

In the not-too-distant future, both the spying devices and intrusive interrogations may be brought together in eternal union. That day, which could extinguish forever the right of privacy, may come if the government approves existing studies for a national data center. The idea, still vague in its specifics, is to set up a computerized master file on all Americans. *All-knowing, never-forgetting electronic machines, crammed with all the information ever divulged by or pried from private citizens, could produce at the press of a button a person's life record from cradle to grave.*

Advocates of this idea claim that a master file could provide the government with speedy and accurate information needed to solve national problems. They say the data would be used for statistical reference, not personal prying. Yet the very existence of such a computer file would encourage fact-finders to introduce ever more revealing questionnaires. Dr. Edgar S. Dunn Jr., Harvard-educated economist who sketched out the data center plan for the government, acknowledges: "It is conceivable for any kind of information about anybody or anything to be programmed into any kind of a system."

Comments Congressman Cornelius Gallagher (D-N.J.), who is deeply concerned over the invasion of privacy: "It is certainly conceivable that a potential Big Brother might make excellent use of a big button on a dosier bank for his own purposes and for the sake of increasing his own power."

The Defense Department alone has accumulated more than fourteen million life histories in the course of its security investigations. These are loaded with derogatory comments—true statements, deliberate lies, idle gossip—whispered into the ears of eager gumshoes. The Civil Service Commission keeps in its secret files another eight million dossiers on people who have applied for federal jobs. These files hold the darkest secrets of many persons who may have at some time in their past committed improper or questionable acts.

Even the Federal Housing Administration receives confidential reports on the marital stability of prospective home buyers. The purpose is to spot couples who are likely to get divorced and may no longer keep up their house payments. For reasons that have never been explained, the State Department's Passport Office keeps a special record of passport applicants who have been married more than twice. The General Services Administration maintains a blacklist of businessmen who are considered poor business risks.

Of course, the FBI is constantly checking into the backgrounds of people for one purpose or another. *It has on file an astounding 175 million sets of fingerprints, not to mention dossiers on tens of thousands of suspected communists, security risks, and crooks.* It is no secret that the FBI also keeps files on controversial figures suspected of nothing more incriminating than speaking their own mind. The FBI often conducts private investigations for top officials. President Johnson, for instance, was able to get an FBI report on the sexual indiscretions of a Senator.

The dirt that government gumshoes pick up on people is swept into dossiers which are freely exchanged between federal offices. When the State Department is asked to watch the movements of an overseas traveler, for instance, the raw charges against him are distributed to at least four offices. The traffic in unproved allegations is so promiscuous that a postal inspector familiar with it told me he quit his job in disgust. *Not only are the dossiers widely circulated, but most of them carry a low security classification. This gives an alarming number of government employees access to derogatory information about fellow citizens.* If the subject happens to be a prominent person, the gossip from his file travels quickly in titillating whispers. At least one blackmailer has been uncovered at the General Services Administration; infor-

INTERNATIONAL SECURITY SERVICES, INC.

August 10, 1966

Dear Congressman:

International Security Services, Inc., is providing to Members of Congress a special monthly security check to help protect your privacy and maintain the security of your confidential matters.

International Security Services will electronically "sweep" your offices, and check your telephones to assure your privacy, and to discover any attempts at penetration, and will personally consult with you on any special security problems you may have, on a regular monthly basis for a fee of twenty-five dollars ($25.00).

This preventative program will provide you with the most modern defensive measures, techniques and equipment for the preservation of your privacy and security.

Be assured this matter will be handled in the strictest confidence and I will be pleased to work directly with you.

Appointments will be arranged at your convenience by telephoning me. Service to begin prior to your return to Washington in December.

Respectfully yours,

Albert P. Senteio
President

Capitalizing on widespread fear of electronic snooping, firms like International Security Services Inc. offer counter-protection on a regular monthly basis.

mation obtained from FBI dossiers was his chief stock in trade.

Private employers seem to have no trouble getting hold of government security reports. For $1.50 to cover the handling charges, mortgage lenders can obtain confidential FHA reports on applicants for housing loans. Information from the files of the House Un-American Activitives Committee, most of it unverified and unreliable, is shipped all over Washington.

Even individual tax returns, thought to be inviolate, are often made available to investigators for frivolous reasons. With a minimum of ceremony, snoopers from a long list of federal, state, and local agencies can pry into almost anyone's financial secrets at the nearest Internal Revenue office. The authorized list runs from A (Agriculture Department) to V (Veterans Administration). Outside agencies not only have access to Internal Revenue files, according to Senator Warren Magnuson (D-Wash.), but sometimes assign employees to work right inside IRS. In some cases, individual and corporate returns are taken back to the agencies for further study. The only rule seems to be that the sleuths should be careful not to tip off the taxpayer. The IRS has issued strict written instructions that "the taxpayer should be given no indication that the national office or other Federal agency is interested in this matter." The tax returns of more than one candidate for high office has been peddled to newsmen by his political opponent.

Apparently, not even the mails are inviolate. Almost any agency can ask the Post Office for a mail check to find out who's writing to whom. Patent adviser H. Lawrence Blasius, whose registration was revoked when he ignored new regulations against advertising, recently laid before a Senate subcommittee evidence that his mail had been intercepted—and even answered—by the U.S. Patent Office. A Michigan man who mailed Blasius a retainer got his check back and a terse reply, not from Blasius, but from the Patent Office. *"You would be well advised," wrote the Patent Office, "to obtain a registered patent attorney or agent."*

Federal snoops have even been caught poking into people's garbage. A Washington woman, glancing out of her window, happened to notice that her trash was segregated and hauled away in a burlap bag. After it had happened twice, she made inquiries that led to an investigation. It turned out that the garbage collectors of the District of Columbia had a list of some 50 persons whose trash was set aside and delivered in burlap bags to a special room in a government building. Here unidentified men would come in the night to spirit away the bags for scrutiny.

How widespread the garbage game is nobody knows. When Congressman Gallagher demanded an explanation from the Sanitation Department, Commissioner C. M. Duke responded that the trash was segregated "to determine from typical household units the characteristics of refuse for statistical and design purposes." He didn't explain why the trash for this solemn study should be collected only from people about whom some official agencies had a special curiosity.

The government's keyhole practices, the availability of space-age snooping devices and the glorification of the gumshoe has created a pressing need for clear and enforceable laws on how far federal agents should be permitted to carry their investigations and how much personal privacy should be surrendered for the sake of police efficiency.

Take the case of Bernard McGarry, a Boston liquor dealer, whose sort of business seems to intrigue Treasury tax agents. There was no evidence, mind you, that he was a tax evader or any other kind of criminal. Nor was he convicted of anything as a result of the investigation. Yet the Internal Revenue Service blatently invaded his privacy, harassed his attorney and accountant, broke into his house, stole his records, evaded a court order to return them, and threw at McGarry just about every slick snooping device in the catalog.

The T-men established a "confidential relationship" with his neighbor and set up an "observation post" in a barn less than 100 yards from McGarry's home in Milton, Massachusetts. Some agents watched the house at night through the sniperscope, waiting for a chance to break in. They copied down the license numbers of his visitors and investigated them, too, though they may have had only passing associations with a man who himself was merely a suspect. The agents maintained radio contact with unmarked cars covering the other side of McGarry's property that couldn't be seen from the "observation post." They tapped his telephone, of course, and traced his mail. One agent was dispatched to Philadelphia to probe the finances of a college-student son to whom McGarry had written. They also pulled the tax returns of McGarry's attorney for six straight years, though he admittedly was not suspected of evasion.

The climax of the case came, according to one of the agents involved, when all check points reported the McGarry house empty. An agent, directed by walkie talkie, advanced through an open back door. The T-men had expected to find a cache of cash in the basement, because a stolen floor plan seemed to show a vault. But the "vault" turned out to be an unlocked cedar closet stuffed with clothes. The disappointed housebreaker, loath to draw a total blank, jotted down the company labels on a sports jacket and a fur coat, then called upon the New York City clothing stores that had sold them.

Is the McGarry case far removed from the average citizen? Not at all. "Easy, cheap electronic espionage has changed everything," says a Washington specialist. "In and out of government, it's an everyday matter affecting you and me and Harry Smith at his corner newsstand."

You don't have to be James Bond or Napoleon Solo to own this "008" Wireless Transmitter

FROM CALLING U.N.C.L.E. HEADQUARTERS TO TAKING INVENTORY IN YOUR PLANT . . . THIS AMAZING DEVICE DOES THE JOB!

A Transistorized FM Transmitter With Built-In Jewel Mike

$150.00

NO BIGGER THAN A PACK OF CIGARETTES! NO WIRES !

From calling U N C L E headquarters to taking inventory in your plant... this amazing device does the job!

HERE'S HOW IT WORKS: Place the small transmitter any place on your person (pocket or purse)... that's all. No restraining wire to get tangled. All voices and sounds will be picked up on any FM receiver. Just tune to a blank spot between 88-108 mcs. Reception is loud and clear - perfect static-free fidelity - no background noises.

THE USES ARE UNLIMITED:
. Wherever a concealed transmitter is needed
. Public address system . Musical and theatrical productions . With tape recorder for surveillance. Taking inventory in a large plant area. Excellent burglar detector . For waiters to call orders to kitchen . With tape recorder during important meetings . Keep in touch with associates in crowded places - stock exchange, stadiums.

SPECIFICATIONS
- All metal case (all transistor circuit)
- Tunable between 88-108 mcs
- Built-in jewel mike (picks up voices up to 50 feet away)
- External mike input
- Size: Smaller than a package of cigarettes
- Weight: 5-1/2 Oz.
- Powered by standard 9V battery (intermittent use)

An ad about a snooping device no bigger than a pack of cigarettes.

Federal enforcement agencies keep lists of likely criminals who get the full bugging-tailing treatment. Ex-FBI agent William W. Turner, writing in a magazine about his former role in Los Angeles, confessed: "I found that agents had installed wiretaps and electronic bugs on hoodlums and foraged through their refuse for clues." Secondary lists are also compiled of people associated with those on the prime lists. Indeed, there are even further-removed lists which, like the others, are distributed to investigators around the country. Internal Revenue agents trace every cancelled check and credit transaction, for example, of most people on the lists. All the information that is picked up is cross-indexed, computerized, and coordinated.

The ease of eavesdropping seems to foster an indifference to privacy. One tax agent dropped by to audit the books of a businessman out West. "Make yourself at home," the businessman said. He hardly intended, however, that the agent should read his mail, verifax a letter from a lady friend on his own office machine and take it to his wife, seeking her cooperation to "get something" on her husband.

Wiretapping already is a federal crime if the conversation overheard is divulged "to any person." The Attorney General has chosen to interpret "any person" as anyone outside the Justice Department. On this flimsy pretext, he has authorized J. Edgar Hoover to use his own judgment in placing wiretaps "in the national interest." Needless to say, the eminent FBI chief has taken full advantage of this loose authority.

Most official agencies have engaged in electronic snooping with no authority whatsoever. Government gumshoes conceal recorders in ordinary brief cases or, more in fashion with today's spy movies, in "minifones" tucked under the arm. Tie-clip devices are a little dated but still in use. A Coast Guard conference room had wall sockets that were really microphones. Indeed, Senator Edward Long (D-Mo.), re-

This fountain pen picks up voices while its user is making notes.

ports: "I was shocked to discover that we were even giving bugging and wiretapping devices to foreign countries as part of foreign aid, then sending experts to teach them how to use the devices. In one instance, we sent more than $30,000 worth of equipment."

The government has set the style for private investigators. One former private eye estimates that businessmen place tens of thousands of bugs in competitors' showrooms, insurance offices, lawyers' offices, hotel rooms and elsewhere.

Wiretapping has virtually become kids' stuff. For as little as $100, anyone can purchase his own bug, which will convert vibrations to radio waves then reconvert them to sound at a remote receiver. One neat package, sold to the suspicious husband or wife for only $400, is designed for a domestic snooping program called "The Ten Day Blitz." Before departing on a business trip, the suspicious spouse can quietly bug his wife's room, telephone, and car and can set up a tiny automatic camera focused on her bed. One suggested adaptation is to place the camera in a shaving kit behind a two-way mirror.

A government investigator told me frankly that modern science has made snooping "the fastest growing, but dirtiest, small business in the world."

Can the snoopers be stopped? Congressional champions of privacy are not optimistic. They have repeatedly confronted investigative agencies with evidence of illegal snooping; but the agencies usually deny it, always get away with it, and don't seem to care about the legal questions. Since the wiretaps are intended to pick up leads rather than evidence, they don't care whether the information isn't legally admissable in court.

Indignant Congressmen have pressured the Defense Department into giving fewer lie detector tests, but many are still given. Some agencies now make psychological tests "voluntary," but they remain intrusive. The Post Office

LIMITED OFFICIAL USE

POST OFFICE DEPARTMENT
REQUEST FOR INFORMATION CONCERNING MAIL MATTER

IN REPLY REFER TO

FROM

DATE

For a period of ________ days, please furnish me daily on Form 2009, copies enclosed, information concerning ________ class mail received for delivery to the person(s) or address(es) listed below. If no mail is received, please so advise at end of period specified.

Under no circumstances should the addressee or any unauthorized person be permitted to become aware of this action. Do not delay delivery of mail to obtain this information. Destroy this form at end of period specified. Do not retain any copies of Form 2009.

(Signature)

TO:

POD Form 2008
Nov. 1963

LIMITED OFFICIAL USE

POD, WASH., D. C.

Government agencies can arrange for surveillance of your mail by filling out the above Post Office form. The phrasing of the second paragraph is particularly interesting: "Under no circumstances should the addressee or any unauthorized person be permitted to become aware of this action . . . Destroy this form at end of period specified. Do not retain any copies of Form 2009." The latter is a record of addressee, sender, return address, and date of postmarks.

☐ SEALED ARTICLE REQUIRES EXAMINATION BUT IS NOT ENDORSED THAT IT MAY BE OPENED FOR INSPECTION.
(Complete the following "Authorization To Open" and bring the notice to the post office or return it in an envelope, postage prepaid, addressed to the Postmaster)

AUTHORIZATION TO OPEN

I hereby authorize the opening of the sealed article in the presence of a representative of the Postmaster.

(Date) *(Signature)*

☐ DUTIABLE PACKAGE BEARS CHARGES TOTALING .... $________

YOU MAY
BRING this notice and get the package.
PHONE and request delivery.
SEND notice with person you name below to receive the package. *(Identification required.)*

INSTRUCTIONS TO POSTMASTER:

DELIVER TO

INSURED | REGISTERED | NO.

ENTRY NO.

SENDER

ORIGIN *(City and country)*

THE MAIL IS HELD AT *(Postmark)*

(Signature of addressee or agent)

★ GPO : 1958 O—476655

You may receive the above notice from the Post Office Department if your foreign mail looks suspicious.

claims it has stopped peering through peepholes at its employees, but it still runs thousands of mail covers annually.

The federal government's 2.6 million employees feel the presence of Big Brother most keenly. Fortunately, they have a champion in Senator Sam Ervin (D-N.C.), who declares: "Psychological testing, psychiatric interviews, race questionnaires, lie detectors, loyalty oaths, probing personal forms and background investigations, restrictions on communicating with Congress, pressure to support political parties financially yet restrictions on all other political activity, coercion to buy savings bonds, extensive limitations on outside activities, rules for speaking and writing and even thinking, forms for revealing personal data about finances, creditors, property and other interests—all of these increasingly shrink the realm of personal liberty and violate individual privacy."

The 18-year-old daughter of an Army colonel applied for a summer job with the State Department. She had interim secret clearance because she had worked for the department the previous summer. Nevertheless, she was subjected to a four-hour grilling. The personal probe got around to the subject of a boy she had dated. Then her interrogators fired these questions at her: "Did he abuse you? Did he do anything unnatural with you? There's kissing, petting, and intercourse. After that, did he force you to do anything to him, or did he do anything to you?" A top official later admitted the cross-examination was part of a "uniform policy."

A 28-year-old State Department secretary, who spoke four languages and had an outstanding record, decided she wanted to transfer from South America to Europe. Because she had been living in a city high in the mountains and the air was heavy with pollen, she complained of a mild asthmatic reaction. State Department personnel officers decided she should take psychological tests before going to Europe. She refused to answer questions about her religious, family and sex life.

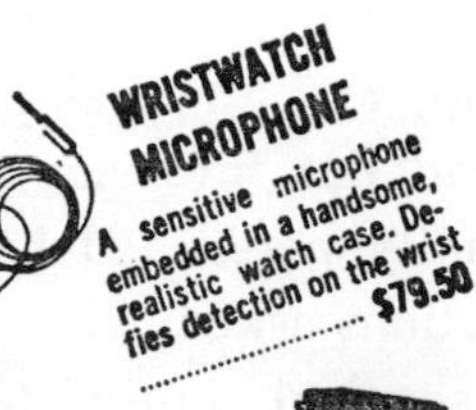

WRISTWATCH MICROPHONE

A sensitive microphone embedded in a handsome, realistic watch case. Defies detection on the wrist $79.50

TIE MICROPHONE

Jewel-like subminiature microphone designed to be used as a tie clip. Perfect for recording in cars or whenever hands are not free $24.95

SHOT GUN MICROPHONE

This very unique microphone in the shape of a rifle is constructed with the maximum in sensitivity, fidelity, and reliability for long distance pick up. Shot Gun Mike is actually able to pick out a group of voices in a crowded area up to several hundred feet away. Comes with two different size shot gun barrels with built-in wind screens for outdoor use. Self-powered transistorized amplifier allows monitoring thru cushioned aircraft type headphones while in use. Three output impedences. A must for the professional investigator $425.00

SUGAR CUBE MICROPHONE

A compact highly sensitive, precision engineered microphone. The 'ultimate' in the subminiature field.......... $39.95

FOUNTAIN PEN MICROPHONE

Ultra sensitive miniature microphone concealed in a dummy pen case. Impossible to tell it's a microphone even when visible $24.95

BUTTON-HOLE MICROPHONE

A highly sensitive microphone designed to operate deceptively behind a tie in shirt button hole, replace a cufflink or use as a lapel pin.......... $24.95

PAPER CLIP MICROPHONE

'Small' and 'concealable' are hardly the words for this sensitive microphone! $24.95

THROAT MICROPHONE

Subminiature microphone with special adjustable, comfortable neck loop. Designed to be concealed under collar for deceptive recording $24.95

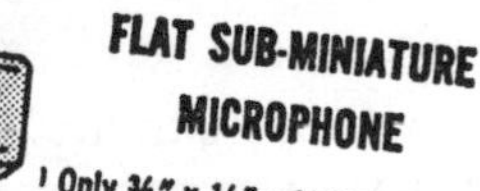

FLAT SUB-MINIATURE MICROPHONE

Only ¾" x ½" x ¼" highly sensitive ideal concealable microphone for most situations $24.95

PIN HOLE / KEYHOLE MICROPHONE

A truly unique microphone containing an extended acoustical tube which fits into the smallest places and defies detection. It can be poked thru a door, crack, over a wall and, even unreels like a fishing line out the window $119.50

Various devices used in connection with electronic snooping.

Result: her transfer was held up, and she indignantly resigned. A high official, who read her file and recognized her value to the government, finally persuaded her to take the European post—no more questions asked. Here are some typical true-false questions that she had refused to answer:

"I am very seldom troubled by constipation."

"Evil spirits possess me at times."

"I have never been in trouble because of my sex behavior."

"Everything is turning out just like the prophets of the Bible said it would."

"I have had no difficulty in starting or holding my bowel movement."

"I have never indulged in any unusual sex practices."

"There is very little love and companionship in my family, as compared to other homes."

Hundreds of wide-ranging complaints pour into Senator Ervin's office every day. Many denounce a new "Minority Group Status Questionnaire," which asks employees to check whether they are American, Indian, Negro, Oriental, Spanish American or "none of these." Providing answers is supposed to be voluntary, but angry follow-ups have hounded those who chose not to fill the questionnaire. Some complaints charge that employees in the South are compelled to listen to records extolling racial integration.

One veteran civil servant, angry about a financial-disclosure form, summed up the feelings of those who believe tough new laws are needed to protect individual rights. He complained that the government seemed all too eager for "information that can be of no practical value to anyone except some bureaucrat determined to establish a 'Big Brother' complex. In many seemingly innocuous but prying little ways, the government is compiling data on each one of us which can lead to a highly regimented society reminiscent of Stalin's Russia, Hitler's Germany, and Mussolini's Italy, to name a few."

Occasionally, Washington's electronic eavesdroppers trip over each other. A few years ago, lobbyist John Monroe actually had so many taps on his line that his phone went out of order. There is also the case of a certain Army officer, whose security clearance had been questioned. Unknown to him, a security agency had planted a microphone in his home. He found the gadget, darkly concluded it had been planted by subversives, and tipped off the Pentagon. A new squad of gumshoes, not knowing the officer was under investigation, started trailing the "spies." Result: a bewildering ring-around-a-rosy.

For the tapper, the trick is to locate a suitable listening post. One security squad thought they had solved the problem when an unmarried woman agreed, as a patriotic service, to allow her apartment to be used by the men. She hadn't counted, however, on the scandal her male "visitors" would cause. Other arrangements had to be made. One Pentagon wire-tapper operated for months from the Washington Zoo. Unknown to the Zoo's director, the tapper monitored the conversations of several officers living in a nearby apartment.

Tap-conscious Washingtonians have developed many tricks to fool the tappers. Some try to speak in cryptic language, intended to be unintelligible to eavesdroppers. Often it is just as unintelligible to the guy at the other end. Some speak in a code worked out in advance. Like their employees, government agencies are also tap-shy. Top-secret lines are checked regularly by electronic engineers. Several years ago the government even laid gas-filled lines on the theory that tappers would puncture the lines and let out the gas. But these lines turned out not to be tap-proof at all; sensitive induction coils could pick up the conversations without plugging into the line.

Apparently, no one is safe from the eavesdroppers. A former Army Intelligence agent, Willis Adams, has admitted that he monitored private conversations of the late Eleanor Roosevelt while she was First Lady. Even President Johnson is worried about the privacy of his office. He evidently fears that one of his own agencies might attempt an inside bugging job in a misguided effort to keep tabs on him. Perhaps with this in mind, he has gone on record against indiscriminate government eavesdropping. In a memo to agency heads, he recently declared:

"In my view, the invasion of privacy of communications is a highly offensive practice which should be engaged in only where the national security is at stake. To avoid any misunderstanding on this subject in the federal government, I am establishing the following basic guidelines to be followed by all government agencies:

"1. No federal personnel is to intercept telephone conversations within the United States by any mechanical or electronic devices without the consent of the parties involved (except in connection with investigations relating to the national security).

"2. No interceptions shall be undertaken or continued without first obtaining the approval of the Attorney General.

"3. All federal agencies shall immediately conform their practices and procedures to the provisions of this order.

"Utilization of mechanical or electronic devices to overhear non-telephone conversations is an even more difficult problem, which raises substantial and unresolved questions of Constitutional interpretation. I desire that each agency conducting such investigations consult the Attorney General to ascertain whether the agency's practices are fully in accord with the law and with a decent regard for the rights of others."

Yet not even the President of the U.S. is certain his orders are being obeyed. Warns Robert M. Hutchins: "Electronic devices make it possible to keep an individual under constant surveillance all his life. The computer makes it possible to record everything he does. It will all go into the infinite memory bank. Who will have access to it?"

Bill Sims
OCI/WA/IA/SB

Richard K. Betters
OCI/WA/IA/SB/Action

Wiretapping

11 Jan. 1965

Bill:

Re our conversation on illegal interstate wiretapping on 5 January in the CIA cafeteria at tea break, I thought that you and possibly some of your friends would be interested in the attached pamphlet that I picked up over the weekend.

Indeed it might be wise for you to give it more than a casual glance since this problem, according to the pamphlet, is coming to a head.

It seems to me that the American Civil Liberties Union is convinced that this vicious threat to americans in their own country has at times been viciously applied by persons who could be described as almost Stalin-like in their viciousness.

Of Course many other dirty and vicious invasions of privacy also occur. One particular form of viciousness according to the pamphlet, sometimes reveals to hidden punks, gumshoes, tinhorns, and assorted goons, the most private and intimate of man and wife utterances often deliberately confined to ones home.

But then we limited ourselves only to wiretapping in our conversation, as I recall.

Dick

A memo on wiretapping written by a C.I.A. official.

13

ALICE IN WASTELAND

With vacuum-cleaner intake, the federal government consumes cash at the rate of $220,000 a minute. Every disappearing dollar is painfully extracted from the long-suffering taxpayers who don't begrudge money for the nation's needs but hate to see it wasted. Yet, for all the lights that are switched off in the White House, appalling sums of the taxpayers' money continue to be squandered. *Misspent millions have gone down the Pentagon drain like so much green cabbage. More millions have disappeared into the pockets of foreign potentates from Afghanistan to Zanzibar.* Countless government greenbacks have been burned, buried, blown to the winds, and blasted into space with there's-more-where-that-came-from abandon.

Millionaires have been subsidized, and the poor have been pampered by a benevolent and beneficent Uncle Sam. In the scramble for a place at the federal trough, the rich have juggled their books while others have resorted to less sophisticated duplicity. It's not at all unusual for women on relief, for example, to live with employable men. This has led to many a bizarre game of hide-and-seek. Government investigators have found it prudent to work in pairs, one covering the back exit to catch a paramour on his way out. One team, after waiting two hours for the woman to dress, found her lover hanging from a rod in a closet, covered by her clothes. In another case, a man was found under a bed but above the floor. With rare enterprise, he had hidden his shoes and socks and was hanging to the bedsprings with his fingers and toes.

No higher tribute can be paid a salesman than to say he

could sell a refrigerator to an Eskimo. But our foreign-aid spenders have topped even this. Senator Herman Talmadge (D-Ga.) *tells of refrigerators being given to Eskimoes. In Iran, Uncle Sam built a $500,000 sawmill that has never been used; the only available lumber is teak, too hard to be cut by the mill. Another time, Uncle Sam presented astonished Cambodians with 150,000 tubes of toothpaste. There was one small oversight; Cambodia happens to be a nation without toothbrushes.*

Careless waste of taxpayers' money by overseas agencies especially haunts American businessmen. Surplus property, sold to foreign buyers at prices as low as four percent of the acquisition cost, often turns up on bargain counters back in the United States. More than a dozen major American industries have recently filed formal protests against foreign competition indirectly financed by American taxpayers in various ways.

Nor is waste found only abroad. At home, the Air Force wound 136 miles of plastic cable around Cape Kennedy, Florida, as "nerves" for the missile firing center. Florida's dampness soon seeped through the insulation, causing a bewildering rash of short circuits. The whole tangled mess had to be replaced by technicians who could have saved the taxpayers over $600,000 by consulting any local electrician.

Procurement officers have a traditionally cavalier attitude toward government funds. Enough is never sufficient; with Oliver Twist-like tenacity, they must have more. The Army once stockpiled 100,000 bottles of embalming fluid, enough to preserve a couple of divisions for eternity. At the same time, the Air Force and Veterans Administration were buying embalming supplies from private firms at a high market price. To prevent Uncle Sam from buying with his right hand what he already holds in his left hand, government purchasing agencies have tried to standardize common-use items and improve inventory control.

Waste has reached its most alarming peak in the military field. The squabble for dollars sometimes seems to occupy the brass hats more than the strategy for defense. They spy on one another, pour out propaganda against each other's weapons, court key Congressmen with every blandishment in the books. *Men have died in South Vietnam on the altar of service jealousy merely to win an advantage over a sister service.* Staggering amounts have been lavished on armaments that should have been scrapped or never built in the first place. Sometimes weapons have been chosen more for expediency than for effectiveness against the enemy.

From military generals to carrier admirals, the brass hats have clamored for pet weapons which have turned out to be impractical or obsolete. In some instances their greatest value has been to give some military chief an excuse to demand more money, more men, more gold braid. Occasionally the Defense Department has rushed ahead with new weapons before they have been proven. Its storerooms hold billions worth of spare parts for cancelled and antiquated weapons. *"This stuff is about as useful to us as so much junk," Secretary of Defense McNamara has admitted.*

Moreover, science has put weapons out of service faster than the advocates have been able to adjust their military thinking. *Thus the generals and admirals sometimes have become obsolete along with the weapons they have commanded.* On the other hand, the armed forces have produced their share of Billy Mitchells—career officers who have looked ahead to the weapons of the future. Understandably, the advocates of dubious weapons usually fight for them in all sincerity, genuinely believing them to be in the best interests of the country. And some officers argue that it is sometimes necessary to gamble in order not to get left behind in the technological race. However, new weapons have been developed faster than they can be assimilated. Missiles have been sprouting, electronic gadgets blossoming like mushrooms in our technological hothouses. *Result: widespread duplication and disorganization.*

No one is more aware of this than McNamara, who invited me to his office for a disarmingly frank discussion of the problem. Drawing rapidly with his left hand, he sketched a diagram of how the dollars can disappear. He showed how fatal flaws were discovered in Project Advent, a military space communications system, after $30 million had been spent on research. He had no choice but to cancel the project. Parts and fixtures ordered prematurely cost an extra, and wholly unnecessary, $140 million. *When McNamara came to the Pentagon he found 24,000 people working on a nuclear-powered plane that would never fly.* They had spent about $1 billion, mostly on air-frame and combat design, radiation-resistant tires and oils, and other items that could not be used until the power plant was perfected. Unfortunately, suitable nuclear engines couldn't be devised.

Perhaps the most grotesque monument to poor planning is the Navy's F3H1 experimental plane. The designers kept adding to the frame until it became too big for the engine. The first planes were so cumbersome they couldn't be flown and had to be carried down the Mississippi on barges. Another costly boo-boo, the "Big Dish" radio telescope, depended upon a mammoth precision bearing which the scientists found almost impossible to design. Still the Navy plugged blithely on, submitting optimistic reports. Then a trade magazine smelled trouble and reported that the problem of the bearing appeared to be insurmountable. "Who's right about the progress of this project?" a McNamara aide asked the responsible admiral. Sheepishly, the admiral answered: "Send my last report back, and we'll do it over." *That was the end of the Big Dish. Money down the drain: $70 million.*

The Air Force designed the Goose decoy missile, a pilotless aircraft, to fly at the speed of a B-52 and appear on enemy radar screens as a manned bomber. But a major general, with a model of Goose on his desk, was stumped when he was asked: "How will you synchronize the decoy launchings with the bomber take-offs? In case of a false alarm, you can call back the bombers; can you bring back the decoys? If not, wouldn't a flight of decoys alert the Russian defenses and probably bring retaliation?" The general flushed. Nobody had thought of all that. *Goose was dropped—along with $80 million of the taxpayers' hard cash.*

Defense tries to save money by stopping the multiple development and duplication of weapons. McNamara believes that jet engineering, for example, has reached a stage where the development of new engines is less profitable than the improvement of proven engines. He sees no purpose, either, in developing separate fighter planes for the Air Force and Navy when one plane, with some adjustment, can serve both and cut costs.

McNamara chose the Navy's F4B and dropped the Air Force's F105 because they were much alike and the Navy aircraft had a better performance record. There was bitter resistance by Air Force generals and politicians in the area where the F105 was manufactured. McNamara stuck to his decision. Some time later he was forced down by bad weather at Langley Air Force Base, Virginia, headquarters of the Tactical Air Command. He paid an unscheduled call on Lt. Gen. Gabriel Disosway, who had been using the Navy plane. Crowed the Air Force general: "It's the finest fighter in the world today." McNamara was less successful, however, with the controversial TFX fighter. The Air Force model came out all right, but the Navy could not adapt it for carrier operations without running up the costs.

For all his famed toughness, McNamara has not been able to stop the three services from feuding over weapons and missions. The Army, for instance, has tried desperately to get back into the air. In 1962 General Hamilton Howze, a dashing officer given to wearing jump boots and neck scarves, convened a 100-officer Army board which in 90 days came up with recommendations for a full-fledged Army Air Force. The goal: 11,000 aircraft and 20,500 pilots by 1968, 30,000 aircraft and 56,000 pilots by 1975. The Howze board recommendations, officially secret but discreetly "leaked," charged that Air Force giant bombers and supersonic fighters don't meet the Army's battlefield needs. The board called for front-line planes and helicopters to support ground troops. The Air Force answered angrily that Howze was asking for planes too low and slow to survive in jet-infested skies.

Even the head-butting McNamara, who is frequently subject to political pressures, couldn't prevent the Army from going ahead with its aircraft procurement. He ordered maneuvers to test Army vs. Air Force tactical planes; but Army generals, impatient to grow wings, began testing their planes and helicopters not in mock war, but in real war in South Vietnam. *They virtually ignored the Joint Operations Center, established expressly to coordinate all air strikes.*

While General Paul Harkins commanded U.S. forces in South Vietnam, he was careful not to send vulnerable Army helicopters into major operations without fighter support. But under pressure from Army advocates, he relaxed his orders once and gave field commanders the option of using their own judgment in special circumstances. Here was a loophole for impatient men. A strike was planned against the communist-held village of Ap Bac. Five armed helicopters were sent as escort for 10 banana-shaped troop carriers. They lumbered into deadly machine-gun fire. The Joint Operations Center wasn't even informed of the strike. The first it heard was two hours later when a panic call came for fighters. *By that time four of the carriers and one armed chopper had been shot down; the others, bullet-riddled, had been driven off. Haunting question: was it right to risk men's lives for the sake of interservice spite?* Finally, in early 1966, McNamara ruled that the Army should continue operating its helicopters but that most of its fixed-wing planes should be turned over to the Air Force.

Before McNamara's reign, when the Air Force was assigned responsibility for strategic bombing, the Navy tried to cut in on the role. The admirals dreamed up the idea of a jet-powered flying boat, armed with nuclear bombs, which could take off and land wherever there was water. *When the Air Force howled "foul," the admirals smoothly presented an 18-page paper for the same aircraft disguised as a mine layer.* They spent $450 million on the project—$200 million of it prematurely on the production contract—before it was scrapped in 1959. By that time the development of the Polaris had given the Navy a strategic mission. The admirals were content, the taxpayers poorer.

Top Pentagon officials are currently taking a hard look at that most sacred of sea cows, the aircraft carrier. *A secret defense study claims that sea-based planes, taking into account the cost of their support, cost four times as much as land-based planes.* McNamara recently told me he still favors aircraft carriers because they can transfer air power about the world wherever trouble may flare. Yet the Marines have developed a prefabricated airfield that can be flown into an area and set up within three days. Uncle Sam can buy 100 of these prefab fields for the price of a single carrier.

Defense officials have a highly developed proclivity for treating their mistakes as the most sensitive of secrets. They have hidden under the security label most of the evidence of misspending and mismanagement in the Pentagon and far-flung outposts. Take the military assistance program in Thailand, for instance. It must be less trouble for spies to steal military information than for taxpayers to find out how their money has been squandered in this faraway land.

Thailand is a strategic jungle kingdom that obstructs the Chinese push to the south. It has been publicly proclaimed next on Red China's list of countries to be "liberated." Shortly after Thai Communists formed a "liberation" front in Peking, Red guerrillas began infiltrating from Laos. The U.S. has responded with the usual outpouring of military aid. And with each new threat to the Asian country, it has poured in more shipments.

It hasn't mattered that the tough but small Thai armed forces have been unable to utilize all the equipment. American officials seem firm in the conviction that more aid is the answer to every crisis. Planes and helicopters have been left in crates for months, waiting to be assembled. Others have been grounded for lack of spare parts or too many of the wrong parts. Thai air crews can't be trained fast enough to man all the aircraft that an eager Uncle Sam has pushed upon them.

Unneeded supplies, including a staggering accumulation of repair parts urgently needed elsewhere, have been dumped on the Royal Thai Army. Military roads were hacked through jungle-choked mountain passes in such haste that landslides and cave-ins have become commonplace. *Enemy saboteurs couldn't have been more effective than our own engineers.* Furthermore, the new and often unused highways are still strewn with costly road-building equipment that never got repaired.

American planes have been thrust upon the Royal Thai Air Force so fast and prematurely that less than half are operational. The rest need parts, overhaul or pilots. All-weather fighters that should have flown 2295 hours during one nine-month period actually were in the air only 252 hours. In one squadron inspectors found only two of 18 planes functioning. In another squadron only nine of 22 F-86 fighters were able to fly. And four of the nine had no radar gun sights, hence would have been useless in combat. Half of the T-33A jets in another squadron had no guns at all. Though a 17-plane helicopter squadron made only the most limited use of the craft it had, seven more were shipped in to accumulate rust.

Of 34 light planes turned over to the Thai army for artillery spotting, inspectors found that only two had been delivered to artillery units. Most were being used to chauffeur brass hats around Thailand. At least six were discovered still in crates months after their arrival. *Yet despite complaints in Washington that these planes weren't being used as intended, more were promptly delivered for the same purpose.*

A 1964 inventory showed that if the Thai army could get all its motor vehicles running there would be a massive traffic jam on the nation's few roads. Replacements were purchased for several hundred World War II vehicles; then the Army was authorized to keep the old vehicles as well as the replacements. The Thai army now has an estimated $5 million worth of excess vehicles on its hands, not to mention $5 million worth of surplus parts. This equipment could be used by other Far Eastern allies who are desperately short of parts.

A U.S. audit also uncovered unneeded signal equipment, worth $1.1 million, rotting in Thai warehouses. Requests for ammunition had been overstated to the tune of $1.8 million. The supply records seem hopelessly snarled. A review of 666 requisitions revealed that 180 items weren't needed because they were already on hand. The Defense Department, spurning competitive bids, also sent Thailand ten locomotives. These developed so much trouble that only one could ever be put in service; officials simply scrapped the ten engines and ordered ten more, again not bothering to take bids.

The biggest boondoggle has been in highway construction. All that was needed for military purposes were some narrow roads with timber bridges, costing about $5.5 million. But the Thai government insisted on wider roads with concrete bridges suitable for civilian traffic. The bickering got so heated that Prime Minister Thanom Kittikachorn called in the U.S. Ambassador for a tongue-lashing. Kittikachorn complained about changes and delays in the construction program, grumbled that the U.S. was giving Thailand obsolete handouts and demanded that the U.S. "make up its mind" whether she intended to provide assistance or not. In the end the ambassador agreed to construction of the wider roads, which will probably cost the American taxpayers close to $12 million when finished.

One of the key roads, now completed, has been plagued with trouble. An engineer who inspected it counted 20 landslides. One stretch was so bad that it was blamed for accidents in which 20 persons died. Another stretch was open only to one-way traffic. *When the landslides and cave-ins continued, engineers finally were ordered to undertake a soil survey they hadn't bothered to make before the road was built.*

Not only Thailand, but just about every other nation in real or apparent need, has received substantial aid from the U.S. Whether the need has been for weapons or wheat, the American people have displayed a generosity unequaled by any other people in history. Since World War II, they have been concerned neither with revenge nor with spoils. Their concern has been to get the world going again. All too often, however, Uncle Sam has offered handouts to hands that were only too quick to pick his pockets.

Most of the nations we have helped go through the motions (but not much more) of paying Uncle Sam for his bounty. Payment is made in local currencies which our government has agreed not to take out of the issuing countries. As a result Uncle Sam has accumulated a mammoth foreign currency collection, literally billions which he owns but can't spend. These huge mountains of money, a virtual Himalayan range encircling the earth, consist of strange, multicolored currencies called counterpart funds. Stockpiled in 83 different countries, they range from $3 billion worth of Indian rupees to $1 million in Laotian kips. *Our captive currencies are* *found even behind the Iron Curtain, where Uncle Sam is stuck with a staggering $440 million in Polish zlotys and $275 million in Yugoslav dinars.*

Though up to his whiskers in foreign tender, Uncle Sam permitted American firms to buy another $2 billion worth of these currencies through commercial channels during fiscal year 1963. In alarm, Congressman John Moss (D-Calif.) pushed through a law authorizing U.S. corporations, volunteer agencies and religious organizations abroad to draw on our surplus currencies. They are supposed to turn in their dollars for counterpart funds, thus reducing our great hoard of foreign money. But at this writing the Treasury Department has failed to issue the necessary regulations to implement the law. The State Department has ignored still another law directing the government to use surplus currencies for foreign aid purchases abroad.

Of course, it isn't entirely accurate to say these funds can't be spent. Congressmen and bureaucrats have been known to plunge joyfully into our surplus currencies like boys into an accumulation of autumn leaves. All this money waiting to be squandered has become a temptation for those permitted to draw upon it.

Actually, the rules governing the accumulation and use of counterpart funds seem simple enough. Most of the money comes from the sale of U.S. surplus food. The surplus is paid for in local currency, which then must be spent within the buying country. The U.S. gives back much of the money in the form of loans or grants, uses some for such things as embassy operations, buildings and other necessities. It also can be used for the entertainment and expenses of legislators, bureaucrats, and certain businessmen.

For instance, the Foreign Agriculture Service, an arm of the Agriculture Department, sends both government men and businessmen abroad to promote the sale of U.S. farm products. The mission of these men, who represent trade groups

ADMINISTRATIVELY CONFIDENTIAL

Subject:

Dinners, cocktail parties and luncheons - U.S. Feed Grains Council. (Sup. Report - p 24).

The Findings:

The practice of using dinners, luncheons and cocktail parties as a means of market promotion is criticized in general. Specifically cited is the request by the European Director of the U.S. Feed Grains Council to attaches in Switzerland and Denmark to "arrange luncheon, dinner, or reception cocktail party for officials and representatives of feed mills, dealers in mixed feeds, etc.." The Committee staff indicates that these functions are used in market development instead of personal visits. It is also indicated that almost anyone will come to a free dinner.

Date:

July and November 1963.

Comment:

Such functions serve a very useful purpose in getting together representatives of the trade for informal discussions relating to the feed industry and its problems. Much useful information and many useful contacts are obtained at such functions. In most instances local visits with selected trade representatives are made in addition to the dinner functions, but it is virtually impossible to schedule individual visits to all plants or offices of the trade. In the case of very short visits, functions as are here criticized are practically the only means of keeping in contact with people in the trade, especially in countries such as Denmark and Switzerland in which the cooperator does not maintain an office.

Luncheon and dinner meetings of this kind can hardly be put into the "free dinner" class. The people who are invited are far too busy and too important in trade circles to be interested in "free loading."

Such functions also serve a very useful public relations function in advertising the Council and its program.

Conclusion:

Dinners, cocktail parties and luncheons serve a very useful purpose where they are used as a supplement to a program of personal visits. In some instances this is practically the only feasible means of maintaining contact with a wide sector of the trade.

Dinners and cocktail parties, paid for out of public funds, are approved in this Agriculture Department document.

but technically are employees of the government, is to stimulate overseas purchase of American commodities. Because their efforts are supposed to benefit the entire American economy, they are entitled to spend government money instead of their own. Unfortunately, these men often match our wasteful lawmakers tab for tab.

In all fairness, it must be said that some of our touring promoters have been remarkably successful in boosting foreign sales of ripe Virginia tobacco leaf, surplus Kansas wheat and other American-grown products. But it is interesting how many promoters prefer to spread the gospel of trade in such global pleasure spots as Paris, Rome, Tokyo and Hong Kong. *Complains a confidential Agriculture Department report: "The world seems to be full of people who want to see the other side of the mountain and preferably in high style at someone else's expense."*

These traveling pitchmen also seem unable to tout American beans and beef except while sipping French brandy or Italian Chianti. Wherever they go, they throw dinners and luncheons, parties and receptions—all cavalierly charged to the taxpayers. The feed grain promoters, for example, like to hold their world staff conference each year in Rome. All the expenses, of course, are borne by Uncle Sam, who pays each participant ample per diem to provide generously for his daily bread and bed. Yet the U.S. customarily is presented additional bills for dinners and receptions accorded the conferees.

The individual itineraries indicate that many promotional trips are more concerned with tourism than trade. The number of consultants and officials who have gone to Hong Kong, for example, suggest that this tourist town is the world's most promising market for our crops. Records show that at least one grain expert was given a tour of Europe and the Mediterranean as a reward for past services. He collected government per diem all but 14 of the 37 days he and his wife spent abroad. Traveling trade promoters used government cameras and film to take so many personal pictures that the Agriculture Department was obliged to warn recently: "We wish to remind you that project funds may be used only for photographs and photographic supplies that are directly related to the purpose of the project." Some feed grain people spent $595 for photography in Holland alone in a short period.

The Agriculture Department is also trying to find out what the poultry promoters have done with three movie films, costing the taxpayers over $21,000 in Egyptian pounds, which were supposed to encourage the sale of frozen poultry in Egypt. The films have not as yet been shown anywhere. *Counterpart funds have been spent for everything from prizes for a Japanese golf tournament ($54.60 in yen) to 50 boxes of crackers for a German farewell party ($12.87 in deutschmarks).* In the latter instance, the Soybean Council triumphantly proved that the crackers were made of soybean flour and thus had promotional value.

Indeed, no group has been more energetic in promoting new markets, at public expense, than the Soybean Council. President Howard Roach hasn't spared U.S.-owned francs or lire to produce a literally favorable image abroad. *His own image was engraved on emblems on 250 silver key chains handed out by the soybean people as souvenirs.* Cost to the taxpayers: about $3 apiece. Roach's image also is preserved in oils on a wall of the Council's ornate Paris office. The $300 which the painting cost the taxpayers was finally refunded to the Agriculture Department after investigators raised Cain about it. Another painting costing $363 was counted as a legitimate expense, since it contained scenery other than Roach's features. But the Agriculture Department decided the soybean promoters were carrying culture too far when they paid $800 to have a mural, titled Nile Boats, calcimined on the wall of their Copenhagen office. Uncle Sam sternly demanded that $700 of its cost be refunded.

Investigators also found that $2,757 in counterpart funds was spent recently to buy 13 gowns for the "Maid of Cotton." The most expensive creation: a $902 number dreamed up by a famed French designer. "What better way to stimulate cotton sales overseas?" coyly contended a cotton promoter. There were mutterings, however, over $31,775 spent in one go-for-broke week in the Philippines to promote the Maid of Cotton a few years ago. That money went for such incidentals as 8 bottles of whisky (160 pesos) for the Filipino board members, 100 pesos for a Manila radio commentator who talked about the Maid of Cotton on his news shows, and 8,000 pesos for gift radios passed out to models at the Cotton Ball.

In Finland more than $30,000 in counterpart markkaa is spent each year to promote cotton products. At first, U.S. cotton sales to Finland shot up spectacularly. *Lately the Finns have been buying more cotton all right, but it has been Russian cotton.* The more money the U.S. spent on promotion, the less cotton Finland seemed to buy from America and the more from Russia. Evidently our experts persuaded the Finns to buy more cotton, which the Russians happily sold to them.

In Japan the Miso Industry Association is paid U.S.-owned yen to boost American soybean sales. *But a confidential report warns that one of Miso's executives has been trying to increase soybean imports all right—from Red China.*

Most U.S.-owned foreign currencies accrue from the sales of surplus commodities overseas—in effect a swap of surplus food for surplus currency. Of the billions in foreign currencies owned by the American taxpayers, the bulk is held in ten countries: Burma, Ceylon, Guinea, India, Israel, Pakistan, Poland, Tunisia, United Arab Republic and Yugoslavia.

The greatest amount has accumulated in India. There is virtually no hope of ever getting the benefit of our $3 billion worth of Indian rupees, short of building a chain of Taj

ADMINISTRATIVELY CONFIDENTIAL

Subject:

Extravagant and unjustified representation expenditure for dinners and similar activities when Mr. Roach visits foreign offices. (Sup. Report - pp 23 and 24).

The Findings:

Visits to Soybean Council country offices by Mr. Roach are frequently the occasion for expensive receptions. The correspondence cited indicates that Mr. Roach encourages this as a means of "perfecting the image of the Council." This image should be so perfected in view of the long continued activity as to create reasonable doubt as to the necessity for further extensive activities of the type.

Date:

Continuing through the operations period to the present.

Comment:

It is a general principle, widely practiced by U.S. and foreign businessmen, to use a visit of an import organization official as an occasion to bring together key figures among those with whom they are doing business. Under this practice, the foreign employees of the Soybean Council generally use the occasion of a visit from Mr. Roach, and of important officials of the U.S. companies supporting the Soybean Council, to have such a meeting - usually a reception, luncheon or dinner. These are often followed or preceded by sessions devoted to joint program business, either before or after, on an individual or group basis. The FAS encourages this practice by the Cooperator for the purposes stated in keeping with the practice of the foreign business community concerned in each country.

The FAS does not accept unreasonable or lavish and ostentatious use of funds for this purpose, or use of funds not apparently in keeping with this purpose. Whenever more than 20 people will be involved, the Cooperator obtains the prior approval of the FAS as represented by the Agricultural Attache. The reasons for the activity, the number of people, the individuals to be invited, and the amount to be spent are reviewed in each such case.

It is not believed that the perfecting of the Soybean Council image is the sole purpose Mr. Roach has in mind, although it is the only one stated in the excerpts from the correspondence quoted. It is known that many, if not all, of such occasions have been preceded, included, or followed by intensive negotiations and discussions between Mr. Roach and other SBC representatives and the principals attending such events of program activities and arrangements and negotiations for them.

Conclusion:

The finding, to the extent that it indicates the need for care and judgment in connection with such use of project funds, is accepted.

ADMINISTRATIVELY CONFIDENTIAL

Perfecting the image of the Soybean Council, a private trade group, at public expense is sanctioned in this document.

Mahals. Although two-thirds of this hoard has been marked for reinvestment as loans or grants, the remainder is so great it would finance our operations in India for the next 50 years. Our supply of rupees is multiplying even faster than the Indian population. With rupees to burn, we continue to buy more rupees through commercial channels. We also spend good U.S. tender to purchase Indian commodities to ship to other aid-receiving nations.

Before President Sukarno's decline in Indonesia, we owned $21.3 million in rupiahs, yet we shelled out hard cash to buy Indonesian oil for other needy countries. The ungrateful Sukarno merely stepped up his campaign of defiance and defamation against the U.S. Cambodia has haughtily renounced our aid; meanwhile, we're stuck with close to $1 million in Cambodian riels that we can't take out. And in Communist Poland and Yugoslavia, we own more zlotys and dinars than we'll ever be able to use.

In return for our food-for-rupees, etc., we hoped, not unnaturally, that our generosity would be recognized and win us friends. *But all too often, thanks to our own bungling and to cynicism on the part of the governments we have helped, our food-for-peace programs have brought neither food to the hungry nor peace to the world.* As for friendship, it sometimes seems to decline in reverse proportion to the amount of food we dish out.

Nowhere has this been truer than in the Middle East. *No one has been more adept than Egypt's President Nasser in turning Uncle Sam into Uncle Sucker.* Thousands of tons of food have been shipped to Egypt. In fact, its people depend for almost a quarter of their diet on American food shipments. Without those shipments the Egyptian masses might be harder to control; Nasser might even find himself with a revolt on his hands. Yet he continues to thumb his nose at us at every opportunity. Our economic aid helps him buy arms to fulfill his dream of vanquishing Israel. We have to compensate for this by providing the Israelis in turn with arms. In effect, we pay twice for the same machine gun.

In 1965 government auditors completed their investigation of the great Egyptian corn scandal, which cost American taxpayers a whopping $23.7 million. The story began in 1962, when Nasser pleaded for emergency corn shipments to save his country from famine. In response the U.S. rushed 186,000 tons of corn to Egypt. They made only one stipulation—that the corn be distributed free of charge to impoverished Egyptian farmers. U.S. officials apparently made no effort to check the Egyptian claim of crop failure. They accepted the latest Arabian Nights story that floods and insects had devastated both the corn and cotton crops. Even as ships were arriving with American corn, Egyptian farmers were harvesting near-record crops.

What happened to the gift corn? Instead of giving it away to the starving fellaheen, Nasser began selling it to raise more money for arms. When we discovered belatedly what he was doing, he changed his policy—but not before he had sold 80,000 tons of corn. At least four shipments of corn weren't even unloaded for several weeks because Nasser had blacklisted the ships for calling at Israeli ports. If the Egyptians felt the corn had been tainted by its brief exposure to Israel, they found it had also been infested by weevils while waiting in port.

President Nasser and his 40 thieves also worked a fast deal in a most unglamorous substance—tallow. Egypt normally buys its tallow from the United States. The inedible tallow goes into soap, the edible into oleomargarine. Our law stipulates that foreign aid must not interfere with commercial sales, but the Egyptians hated to pay scarce dollars for what they could euchre out of the U.S. They begged for tallow as economic aid, which would permit them to pay for it in local currency. The United States already has $800 million worth of Egyptian pounds—more than can be spent in

Nasserland in 50 years. Since local currency must be expended inside the country, it was evident that any payments in Egyptian pounds would remain unspent—thus making the tallow, in effect, a free gift. The State Department's alibi is that the political bonus was worth the dollar loss. *But if the tallow and the corn deals have modified Nasser's attitude toward the United States, he has yet to show it.*

A secret report, classified in order to hide the embarrassing details, has to do with a Middle East wheat deal. When the Iranian government suddenly ran short of foreign exchange, Uncle Sam cheerfully filled the shah's coffers—ostensibly for political reasons. A cool $39 million of the American taxpayers' money was turned over to him. Later it was discovered that Iran spent $12.5 million of this jackpot for wheat from Australia, though there was plenty of surplus American wheat for sale.

Egypt and Iran are only two countries in which Uncle Sam has proved to be Uncle Sucker. There are many more. *American agriculture surpluses, as a result of giveaways and sales, have declined close to the level this country needs for its own security.* Wheat is only in "modest excess." Another big wheat giveaway could put us below the safety margin. Dairy products, once so abundant, have been so sharply reduced that some giveaways have had to be curtailed.

This is not an argument against generosity. But the American people never meant their bounty to be squandered. How can this monetary merry-go-round be stopped? President Johnson is trying to phase out the foreign-currency agreements by the end of 1971. Meanwhile, Congressman Moss and others have suggested that the proper course is merely to obey the laws now on the books. Foreign purchases, they say, should be made out of surplus currencies; U.S. corporations and institutions operating abroad should be required to turn in their dollars for counterpart funds.

Uncle Sam not only has helped to feed the world's hungry people but has helped the free-world's war-wrecked nations build up their industries. *Now our good deeds are coming back to haunt our own economy. For foreign factories, built at U.S. expense, today are putting American firms out of business and American workers out of work.* One industry after another has been forced by foreign competition to cut back production, thus adding to our millions of unemployed and $900 million annual gold loss. Yet our income-tax payments not only helped to finance the competitors but provided them with more advanced equipment than our own. Then we sent American engineers and businessmen overseas to teach the know-how. *Result: a sudden looming around the world of industrial Frankensteins which are now threatening their benefactor.*

This plight reaches all the way down from such giants as steel and oil to pottery makers and even mushroom growers. Yet Uncle Sam, perhaps out of habit, is still building plants for nations that may take future markets away from us. A leading industrialist told me bitterly: *"Maybe it's time the goose that lays the golden eggs started hatching a few for us here at home."* No one seriously suggests that foreign aid should be cut off. With two-thirds of the world living on the starvation line and easy prey to communism, the United States in the interests of its own security must continue to help the underdeveloped nations to help themselves. But this is small consolation for steelworkers near Houston, Texas, and textile workers in Greer, South Carolina, who were thrown out of work by the influx of cheap foreign steel and cotton goods.

Though the AID agency has been perhaps purposely vague about the number of plants it has built abroad, a reported $2 billion of our tax money has gone to build or expand 179 foreign steel mills. This American generosity has helped to reduce our share of the world's steel market from 17% in 1950 to about 6% today. In 1960 Mexico exported only 65 tons of steel plate to the U.S. Two years later the figure had risen to 12,000; it has been multiplying ever since. "Whose tax money," asks Congressman Bob Casey (D-Tex.), "do you think built the 22 Mexican steel mills under our aid program?"

For the textile industry, the aid-pampered competition has been close to disastrous. No one seems able to say exactly how many rival mills Uncle Sam has built around the world. But one AID official admitted to me: "In our efforts to revitalize Japan as a bulwark against communism, we participated technically, financially and otherwise in creating a Japanese textile industry that today threatens our own with ruin." There are U.S.-financed textile plants in India, Korea, Formosa, and Hong Kong, most of them with looms far finer that most American mills have been able to afford.

The textile men are caught in a triple squeeze. Not only must they compete against mills better equipped and using cheaper labor, but their foreign competitors are able to buy American cotton at a lower price. Uncle Sam pays cotton growers a subsidy to keep up the price at home, but sells cotton abroad at the cheaper world price. Shipping included, a Japanese mill owner can buy U.S. cotton for less than an American mill owner, whose plant may be only a few miles from the fields where it was picked. *Result: Japanese textiles have been undercutting American sales not only abroad but at home.* Millions of cotton spindles have been closed down, and hundreds of mill workers have lost their jobs.

Textile leaders have begged the government for some of the aid that has been given to the Japanese industry. But they have been largely ignored. When a flood of zipper tape from Japan almost put the Sullivan-Southern plant in York, South Carolina, out of business, its boss went around hammering on Washington doors. "I felt," lamented John K. Benfield, Jr., "like an innocent man sitting in the electric chair, waiting for the current to be switched on, and yelling for all I was worth that I hadn't committed murder. But nobody believed me." An ailing factory apparently can't qualify for U.S. aid unless it is located overseas.

In the last few years, foreign aid has built, expanded or modernized: 31 pulp and paper plants, 24 chemical plants, 13 aluminum plants, and 22 rubber processing plants. It has given another 27 loans or grants for studies or construction of petroleum refineries. Besides the steel mills and textile factories, our tax money has also built foreign shipyards, plastic plants, pottery works, engineering labs, and industrial research centers. It has been spent to develop foreign mining, manufacturing, even merchandising. *American industrial leaders are more than worried; they are alarmed.*

Declares Karl Bendetsen, president of Champion Papers: "I am astonished at the number of paper mills that have been constructed overseas with U.S. dollars under the foreign aid program. I knew some had been built, financed by our tax dollars, but I am both amazed and dismayed by the number." Those 31 pulp and paper mills, built in 17 countries at a cost to the U.S. taxpayers of a whopping $84,998,000, include three in Finland. The new paper mills in Finland have saturated that country's traditional markets; now, subsidized by U.S. dollars, she is moving into the U.S. market.

Foreign shipyards built with aid money and cheap foreign steel are pushing our own shipbuilding industry to the wall. Since 1948 more than $600 million in aid has gone to build or modernize foreign yards. Add the assistance given to foreign steel founders, and American shipbuilders are working under a $1 billion handicap.

To pick out another example, *Japanese competition is also breaking the American pottery industry.* By 1954 the U.S. had helped Japan put into operation what is probably the world's most modern pottery industry. It immediately began taking over the retail market in the U.S. Of the 24 firms belonging to the U.S. Potters Association, 16 have been forced to liquidate. Only eight limping firms are still managing to hang on.

American mushroom growers have hired a Washington attorney to seek relief from the competition of the foreign aid-financed mushroom industry in Formosa. Uncle Sam's experts after looking around for some way to help the Formosan economy, decided mushrooms might do the trick. They sent over prize spore and taught the peasants how to cultivate. The new industry literally mushroomed. The first Formosan mushrooms started coming into this country in 1960. Exports doubled the following year, doubled again in 1962. Now Formosan mushrooms account for 25% of American consumption of the edible fungi. So American mushroom growers have joined the businessmen and workers who are being steadily hurt by competition financed by their own tax dollars.

The whole panorama of foreign aid is immensely complex. While such aid is necessary to create world-wide prosperity, shouldn't other countries be required to take more of the free world load? Nations which the U.S. helped on their feet are prospering as never before. It is difficult to disagree with those American businessmen who are plaintively asking a rather deaf Uncle Sam: *"Isn't it time some charity began at home?"*

If not charity, then a little more thrift might be practiced at home. Quite a few dollars could be saved, for example, by cutting down on the luxuries to which government executives have become accustomed. The taxpayers maintain a fleet of limousines for top officials, including the governor of the Old Soldiers' Home in the Washington outskirts. Agency heads and military chiefs, called to testify before Congress, usually arrive with their aides in gleaming Cadillacs and Lincolns. Ex-President Eisenhower once pointed out that in the old days only the Army chief had an automobile; anyone else who went to Capitol Hill was given a streetcar token for traveling expenses.

Top brass of the armed forces have confessed using enlisted men as personal servants and drivers. Complained one disgusted colonel: "When I was asked to take part in a seminar at the Army War College, that institution had about 500 students—mostly colonels—and an approximately equal number of enlisted men. Some of the enlisted men were used as clerks, map makers and security guides, but the majority seemed to be employed as drivers, orderlies and bartenders. This struck me as curious since most of the colonels were perfectly capable of driving their own cars and mixing their own drinks."

Dozens of complaints have been written home, like the one from a chemical laboratory specialist whom the Army utilized as a handyman for two colonels. *"I have not only done housework but have also shined shoes for members of both households," wrote the disgruntled* GI. *"Cleaning toilet bowls for a colonel's wife," he added, "is not a desirable occupation." It would also appear to be a waste of a specialist's skills.*

In non-defense agencies, manpower is wasted in more subtle ways. A civilian-suited army of bureaucrats has grown up behind red tape instead of barbed wire. Trifling departmental decisions are processed by time-wasting, paper-consuming committees. Their frequent objective: to evade issues, shift responsibility, and hand the work to someone else. The more committees and sub-committees there are to share the burden of decision, the less chance there is that any single individual will be blamed.

All too often, the true veteran in government service is the one who has proved his ability to maneuver problems safely "through channels" without making any decisions of his own. *One senior official advises newcomers: "Look important. Act busy. Call conferences, lots of them. But don't make any decisions. If you are forced to do so, make sure they are in someone else's name."* A highly placed Interior Department official has admitted he has a special reason for always calling in others for consultations on policy matters. If, he figures, his ultimate decisions stir up unfavorable criticism, he can disclaim responsibility by saying he acted on the advice of others. "The best technique," confesses another decision dodger, "is the staff conference. Anything produced by a staff conference is bound to be innocuous because so many people participate."

These civil servants are not being deliberately facetious. They are seriously expounding the refinements of buck passing so necessary if controversy is to be avoided and job survival assured. *This system also encourages superiors to build staff empires which will justify promotions and salary increases.* Thus the bureaucrat, like the microbe, multiplies within himself. The process begins when an official complains that the work load is too heavy for him to carry alone. Since he has no intention of dividing the work with a rival who might replace him, he starts accumulating subordinates. He may manage to acquire two subordinates who, in time, gather up more subordinates for themselves. After a decent pause, these last subordinates will also claim the right to be moved up the totem pole and be replaced at the bottom. *The result is what bureaucracy terms "staff build-up."*

All this might be reasonable if the amount of useful work increased by the same ratio. It seldom does. The process of swelling a staff means extra paper work to administer the extra employees; in addition, a great deal of work is now duplicated. When the 12th man takes a document from the in-basket, he will read it and pass it on to the 11th official for his consideration. And so on until it finally reaches the director who rewrites the whole thing and sends it back down the ladder for further revisions. In the old days, the director would have handled the document himself. But now he is head of a section, adequately cushioned by a staff against shocks from higher up. Somewhat typical of bureaucracy's weed-like growth is the Naval Caretaking Detachment which mushroomed in Naples after the war. The original 45 men assigned to the unit began multiplying until they numbered 2,103 military personnel, 534 civilians and 3,166 dependents.

To justify the staff build-ups, problems usually are circulated among as many bureaucrats as can be found. This leads to endless frustrations for those citizens who are waiting for action. Take the case of Leslie Boore, who applied to the Social Security Administration for a disability pension. Since 1950 he had suffered four heart attacks, each one more severe than the last. When he sent his first letter to the agency, he was completely paralyzed and unable to work. For five months he lived without income while his Congressman fought bureaucracy for a decision on what sum could be awarded the stricken man. Eventually the agency triumphantly produced a check for $699.30. Unfortunately, Mr. Boore died a week before the check was issued. The agency had been informed of his death before making out the check, but once set in motion, the unwieldy machinery of government could not be stopped. It had to go through the motions of paying a dead man just to keep the record straight.

The machinery of the federal government is also hopelessly clogged with superfluous committees which operate like wheels within wheels. Nobody knows for sure exactly how many committees there are. One defense group that finally got the axe was the "Usually Travelled Route Committee." Established in 1921 to determine which was the usual military route between two points, it had been blithely holding conferences although it had not recommended a "usually travelled route" since 1947. The Pentagon's Public Affairs Committee, which was ordered abolished, was quietly reconstituted a few days later as the Public Affairs Council. One committee actually was formed to discuss whether or not to set up yet another committee.

No chapter on waste can overlook the federal government's correspondence—over a billion letters a year at an estimated cost of $1 each. This astonishing output of words (an average of 522 letters annually by each government employee) is unbelievable. The letters themselves are masterpieces of abstraction, conforming to the traditional civil service conviction that simplicity is not sufficiently impressive. Therefore they cloak their meaning with long words, longer sentences, infinite and infernal paragraphs, obscure legal expressions and bewildering phrases.

In 1964 the AID agency, threatened by a formidable paper blizzard, began to count the pieces of paper turned out each year by its message center. The total: 20 million. John J. Shurman, the records chief, began systematically clearing desks, waste-baskets, and files, cutting down on the carbon copies that had to be processed. By 1966 he had eliminated 2.4 million pieces of paper a year. This resulted in an annual savings of $15,000 in paper alone. But the real savings, estimated at more than $375,000 a year, was in the smaller number of clerks needed to read and file the papers.

The Veterans Administration, for its part, has tried to prune the gobbledygook from its letters. Thousands of employees, including top officials, have taken a special "plain letters" course. Outgoing mail is spot-checked for simplicity; the authors of the best letters receive recognition. One result—a recipient of a VA letter wrote to its author: "Your letters are so free of federal jargon that I fear for your future with the government."

The federal government also prints or mimeographs 18 billion forms annually seeking all sorts of obscure information; it requires 100,000 internal reports and 25,000 field reports each year, and issues nearly 5,000 regulations to the public. During one of the occasional attempts made to curtail official paper work, the Navy examined one project only and was able to consolidate 3,161 forms into 752. This eliminated 21,000 form sheets and saved $3 million. Following this the Navy made a spot check on 11 directives and cut the number of copies from 138,316 to 9,326—a reduction of 93%.

The cost of handling documents is multiplied by the bureaucrats' obsession with secrecy. *"Only 10 percent of all classified documents actually contain security information," a General recently admitted to me.* Secrecy stamps are, of course, often used to hide waste. Then the waste is compounded by the extra handling costs. To ship top secret documents costs $20 per cubic foot, compared to $3.10 for unclassified matter. Classified papers also cost $2 per cubic foot to store, unclassified only 80 cents.

There is a constant battle inside the government service to reduce waste, but creeping bureaucracy, like a force of nature, is not easy to deter.

A safe conduct certificate dropped on enemy troops in North Korea. Similar passes are scattered over Vietcong areas in Vietnam. The desertion rate increased steadily in 1966.

14

BEHIND THE VIETNAM COMMUNIQUES

The United States, the mightiest military power the world has ever known—supreme on the seas and invincible in the skies—often has been out-maneuvered in South Vietnam by ragtag guerrillas, most of whom are simple peasants. Armed with crude weapons manufactured in makeshift jungle arsenals, they're fighting a war of improvisation. Some of their heaviest weapons are mortars which can be dismantled and carried in three parts. They march on sandals hacked from old truck and airplane tires, sleep in hammocks made from the nylon of our own parachutes. Wicks enclosed in the metal of used cartridges provide just enough light to thread jungle trails at night. And they can survive for days on a packet of rice.

It can't be said, however, that the guerrillas are dedicated to a popular cause. Out of South Vietnam's 14,000,000 population, the Viet Cong has never had more than 300,000 disciplined followers. Perhaps 70,000 could be classed as regulars; another 100,000 to 120,000, ostensibly peaceful peasants by day, are guerrilla fighters by night; others have been used to scout, spy, smuggle, and run messages for the Viet Cong. These hard-core disciples have influenced another estimated 500,000 sympathizers. All told, the communists might claim the support of 6 percent of the population. Their real support has come from North Vietnam, whose Red regime has smuggled troops and supplies over the network of jungle paths known as the Ho Chi Minh trail. This infiltration approached the dimensions of a backdoor invasion after the United States began pouring troops into South Vietnam in 1965.

Although substantially surpassed in manpower and firepower, the Vietcong's crude style of warfare, not unlike that used by our own forefathers to wrest independence from the British, has often confounded those who fought by the book. To make matters worse, the U. S. build-up has played into the hands of the communist propagandists who are able to portray the war as a struggle between the American "imperialists" and Vietnamese "people." Intensive anti-American indoctrination has given point and purpose to the Red jungle fighters. A North Vietnamese sergeant, captured at Plei Me, was asked why his unit had kept fighting despite staggering casualties. "We had been taught," he said, "that our duty was to drive out the Americans, to liberate our fellow countrymen, to fight to the last drop of blood. So, in spite of the casualties, we fought hard."

Not until the Viet Cong abandoned their tested guerrilla tactics, not until they began massing for conventional battles and alienating the populace by conscription and taxation, did they start losing the war. Their battalions, gathered in jungle bivouacs, unable to disperse among the people, were caught by our spoiling attacks. Disaffected peasants also began passing along intelligence that enabled us to beat the guerrillas at their own game and catch them by surprise.

General William Westmoreland, the American commander, is one of the few military men who has fully understood what was happening. Most brass hats simply kept trying to apply old solutions to new situations. They fell back on the kind of jungle fighting that had flushed the Japanese out of the South Pacific but didn't necessarily work against the elusive Viet Cong.

Around the world, the generals and admirals have deployed our forces to fight World War II again. Although it is unlikely that there will ever again be great naval battles in the Atlantic, more than half of our formidable naval strength is concentrated there as this book goes to press. Only a skeleton fleet is patrolling the vast Pacific beyond Hawaii where seapower really counts. Guarding the Atlantic and Mediterranean are 450 ships, manned by 200,000 sailors and Marines. The only action they are likely to see is an order to man the mops after an attack by seagulls.

The Pacific Fleet has 425 ships, but most of them are concentrated between Hawaii and the Pacific Coast, where the sailing is pleasant but there is little likelihood of an enemy attack. Only 125 ships are assigned to the Seventh Fleet, which is charged with patrolling our longest frontier against communism, from Russia's frigid maritime provinces down to South Vietnam's steaming jungles.

The backbone of any modern fleet is its carrier striking force. The Navy has 15 attack carriers—six in the Atlantic, nine in the Pacific. But only four are on actual front-line duty; the rest are churning up angry but futile wakes in peaceful waters. Similarly, the Atlantic Fleet has seven support carriers to watch for Red subs. The Pacific has only four, of which one is assigned to the Seventh Fleet. Yet intelligence reports warn that Red China might use her 28 subs to attempt a sneak attack on the Seventh Fleet.

The Atlantic has about 100 submarines, 12 of them nuclear-armed, missile-firing Polarises. The Pacific has about 55 with only 12 operating in the 30,000,000 square miles beyond Hawaii. Of these, only three are nuclear-powered. And of those work horses of the Navy—the cruisers and destroyers—the Atlantic Fleet has about 170, the Pacific Fleet 160. In the fighting zone there are 30.

While the bulk of our Navy is guarding the beaches from the Riviera to Hawaii, one of the strangest armadas the world has ever seen is assembled off the Vietnam coast to fight the war at sea. The Seventh Fleet's giant carriers, sleek destroyers, and silent submarines are bolstered by U.S. Coast Guard cutters and a conglomerate of ancient gunboats and motorized junks manned by black-pajamaed South Viet-

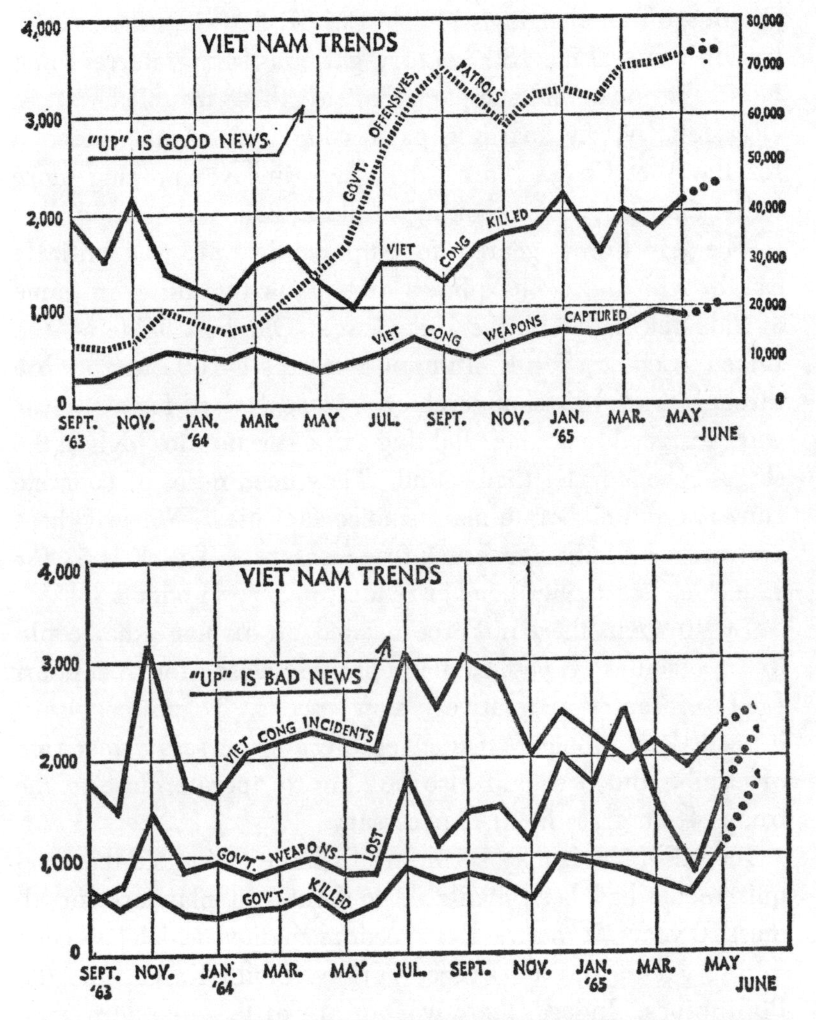

Charts such as these help the Pentagon manage the news about the war in Vietnam. Although U. S. forces were barely holding their own in June, 1965, when these charts were released, Defense Department officials insisted that the war was being won.

namese sailors. The Coast Guard cutters have the job of shutting off another invisible Ho Chi Minh trail: the sea infiltration route. Like 18th century galleons, they intercept and board the junks and sampans that sail those troubled waters. Occasionally, the boarding parties find contraband intended for the Viet Cong. More often, they uncover nothing more lethal than cargoes of choking, stinking fish.

The Air Force, geared for supersonic war, was initially caught with the wrong planes and plans for the grim game of hide-and-seek with the Viet Cong. Our best fighters—the famed "Century Series" running from the F-100 Super Sabre through the F-105 Thunderchief— were devised for a nuclear war, designed to do their fighting some seven miles high in the sky at speeds faster than sound. They need miles of concrete runways and elaborate maintenance facilities. None of these aircraft was built for brush-fire warfare. The F-105, for example, is a fighter-bomber made to carry H-bombs.

In Vietnam, the Air Force needed an airplane that could fly supersonically, yet be able to provide close ground support for the infantry at relatively slow speeds. To protect itself, it needed to be highly maneuverable and possess a fast rate of climb. But it should also be able to operate close to the troops from grass fields if necessary.

Incredible as it may seem, an airplane fitting all these requirements had been available to Pentagon planners for almost 10 years. It was the F-5 Freedom Fighter, which had been sold to such allies as Greece, Turkey, South Korea, and the Philippines. Indeed, there was an arc of these modern combat planes ready for action in Southeast Asia, but they weren't flown by American pilots. The Air Force begged for Freedom Fighters in Vietnam; but a request for 185 of them, comprising two wings, remained stalled in the Pentagon for months.

After five years of evaluating the F-5, Secretary of Defense McNamara finally agreed in late 1965 to send a 12-plane test squadron to Vietnam for "combat evaluation"—though the

Air Force and Navy had flown more than 500 "evaluation flights" with the Freedom Fighter. McNamara asked for still more tests because he was reluctant to spend money for new procurement if he could possibly get along with planes already in the inventory.

Meanwhile, our mighty air armada plastered the Viet Cong with powerful knockout blows. Supersonic fighters streaked over the jungle at twice the speed of sound, so fast the foliage below looked like a green blur. Our great B-52s dumped tons of bombs on guerrilla hideouts, a blockbuster for every guerrilla known to be fighting in the South Vietnam jungle. They were the right planes for the wrong war—at least until the oil depots, industrial plants, and military installations of North Vietnam were added to the target list. Yet not until mid-1966 did McNamara finally get around to ordering the plane the Air Force needed for the Vietnam war.

With the same heavy hand, Uncle Sam dug in with bulldozers and heavy construction equipment on the ground. Permanent installations were thrown up that not only will change the face of South Vietnam but should survive long after the ancient native villages have turned to mold. At Camranh Bay the Navy has constructed a giant, permanent base capable of accommodating the entire Seventh Fleet. The piers, docks, oil tanks, warehouses, repair facilities and airfields make this probably the finest air and seaport in all Asia. All over South Vietnam the Air Force has laid down huge, 10,000-foot runways that would make the chambers of commerce in many American cities envious. Hospitals, barracks, and warehouses have been thrown up. When the war is over and the Americans pull out, South Vietnam should have more housing than it needs and enough hospitals to supply a room for almost every sick citizen.

For the first time in modern warfare, the basic construction work has been turned over to private contractors, who operate a fleet of 550 dump trucks, 306 crawler tractors, 158 air compressors, 142 bulldozers, 125 power shovels, 118 mix trucks, 117 motor graders, 56 wheel tractors, 30 asphalt pavers and 14 pile driver hammers—not to mention 11 asphalt and nine concrete plants. The Army Engineers and Navy Seabees handle only the smaller jobs. It isn't the subordination they mind so much as the fact that they draw an average basic pay of only $100 per month, while their civilian counterparts earn ten times that amount (most of it tax free).

Two construction firms, Raymond International and Morrison-Knudsen, started out in 1962 with a cost-plus-fixed-fee contract to build airfields in South Vietnam. This burgeoned into a construction program that in late 1966 was consuming more than 50,000 tons of cement and 10,000,000 board feet of lumber a month. More than $1,000,000 worth of work was being completed each day.

For the construction industry, this was clearly the biggest windfall that had ever blown their way. In early 1965, two more firms, Brown and Root and J. A. Jones Construction, were cut in for a share. Together they formed RMK-BRJ which, under the name Vietnam Builders, signed contracts to complete the world's largest construction job as a joint venture. It is an interesting coincidence that the Brown and Root firm, whose owners helped finance the political career of Lyndon B. Johnson, was dealt into the contract after Johnson became President.

With its profits guaranteed under the contract, RMK-BRJ hasn't spared the taxpayers' money. It has gone through more than $800,000,000 in government green like a cow through clover. Unless the company somehow manages to rustle up some quick cash from the taxpayers in the near future, it will probably run out of appropriations in early 1967 with barely 60 percent of its projects completed. Saigon's new military port alone cost five times more than the original estimate.

Mountains of lumber, steel, cement and machinery have

piled up faster than the construction crews could use the material. From these dockside mountains, cement foothills, steel cliffs, and lumber slopes have frequently disappeared in the night. Government officials estimate the loss from pilferage close to $75,000,000. In Saigon, alone, according to one report, more than $20,000 worth of U.S. supplies are stolen each week. Occasionally, supplies have been siphoned right off the ships and hauled in junks and sampans up the Mekong River to waiting Viet Cong. More often, black marketeers have sold the stolen supplies right in Saigon to Viet Cong purchasing agents, who paid dollars they had extorted from American oil companies and other firms.

What supplies aren't pilfered often are used to build fancy quarters for company officials and officers' clubs for the brass. More than once, RMK-BRJ has been fleeced by Vietnamese swindlers who would make Billy Sol Estes look like a small-timer. The company, for example, spent $500,000 to develop a training school for its Vietnamese employees in the Saigon suburbs. Not until the land owner had skipped out with $100,000 paid for the lease did company executives discover the land had been zoned for a park. The Vietnamese government closed the costly training school before it could open.

The costly new port facilities at Saigon have been rushed to completion in order to break a gigantic shipping logjam that was holding up vital supplies. After steaming across the Pacific at top speed, naval and merchant ships were obliged to wait interminably in South Vietnam waters to get their cargoes unloaded. Some ships waited at anchor more than 30 days until their food and water ran short. Forced to sail to Manila or Bangkok for fresh stocks, they were compelled upon their return to take up positions at the end of the line and wait another 30 days. All the time these ships lay idle in the war zone, the crews drew extra combat pay. Often the cargoes arrived without bills of lading, and spare parts were piled high on the Saigon wharves for the Army to sort out.

Kosygin has been telling private visitors that he sees no possibility of his country and China reconciling their differences at this time. In several recent interviews off-the-record, Kosygin also said he understands that the United States cannot cease its efforts in Vietnam "by itself", without "the other people doing something reciprocally," and that what is needed is some kind of international meeting. The situation, he went on, is so complicated at the moment that such a meeting is impossible, but that the Soviet Union would do nothing to worsen the situation. He described his country's relations with the U.S. as good and said the USSR intends to continue its policy of no conflict with the US.

That Soviet Russia isn't happy about the war in Vietnam is evident in this secret report to the State Department.

Not only equipment but information is smuggled to the Viet Cong. *One report claims that half the girls in Saigon's night clubs peddle information to the communists.* Others maintain a profitable neutrality by spying impartially for both sides. Small wonder that our security agents have been preaching harder than the chaplains to keep lonely Americans out of the native dives where they might come under the influence of romance or the local joy juices.

The newspapers have, of course, been full of stories about our heroes under fire, but in the heart of the war lies another epic of daily heroism—the epic of men who are in fact fighting against war itself, men who have been trained not to take lives but to save them. To the soldiers battling grimly in the steaming bamboo and the leech-infested rice paddies, the medics are the "Angels of Hell." To one wounded GI, the face of the angel bending over him may be the sweating, grimy face of a medic desperately trying to ease his pain. To another, the angel may appear as a clumsy, hovering helicopter daring a hail of bullets to bring him hope of rescue.

The medic on foot, slogging away with his platoon or

IMMEDIATE RELEASE October 24, 1962

Office of the White House Press Secretary

MEMORANDUM TO EDITORS AND RADIO AND TELEVISION NEWS DIRECTORS:

The following information is considered vital to our national security and therefore will not be released by the Department of Defense. Despite this fact, it is possible that such information may come into the possession of news media. During the current tense international situation, the White House feels that the publication of such information is contrary to the public interest. We ask public information media of all types to exercise caution and discretion in the publication of such information.

1) Any discussion of plans for employment of strategic or tactical forces of the United States including types of equipment and new or planned location of command or control centers or detection systems.

2) Estimates of United States capability of destroying targets, including numbers of weapons required, size and character of forces required, ability of these forces to penetrate defenses, and accuracy or reliability of our forces or weapon systems.

3) Intelligence estimates concerning targets or target systems, such as numbers, types and locations of aiming points in the target system, enemy missile and bomber forces, etc.

4) Intelligence estimates of enemy plans or capabilities, or information which would reveal the level of success of United States intelligence efforts or operations with respect to Cuba or the Communist Bloc.

5) Details as to numbers or movements of United States forces, including naval units and vessels, aircraft, missile forces or ground forces, ammunition, equipment, etc. Announcement may be made of such unit movements after the movement has been completed.

6) Degree of alert of military forces.

7) Location of aircraft or supporting equipment. Presence of aircraft observable in the public domain may be confirmed.

8) Emergency dispersal plans of aircraft and units including dispersal capabilities, times, schedules or logistical support.

9) Official estimates of vulnerability to various forms of enemy action, including sabotage, of United States Armed Forces and installations.

10) New data concerning operational missile distribution, numbers, operational readiness. Estimates of effectiveness of strike capability of missile forces.

11) Details of command and control systems, including new or planned command posts and facilities, estimates of ability to survive enemy attack, security measures, etc., including sea or airborne command posts.

12) Details of airlift or sealift capabilities, including size and nature of forces to be lifted, time limits for such lifts, and supply capabilities, with respect to possible specific areas of operation.

Editors having doubts about information and wanting to establish whether or not it is within the purview of this memorandum should contact the News Desk, Department of Defense, at OXford-5-3201, Washington, D.C. Such advice will be on an advisory basis and not considered finally binding on the editor(s).

Somewhat similar "voluntary" censorship guidelines restrict information about the war in Vietnam.

company, may carry only a first aid kit instead of an ammunition pack. But his courage under fire has proved no less than that of the men with the guns. Time and again, he has administered life-saving aid, often wounded himself, as the bullets have whined around him. Time and again, the unarmed medicopters have gone in where armed copters have feared to follow and have brought out wounded from the thick of the action. Their dedication to healing has not been confined to their own men. Many an enemy guerrilla, left bleeding by his comrades, has reason to be grateful that among the Angels of Hell the quality of mercy is not strained.

Although the end of the struggle in Vietnam is not yet in sight, the war to save lives has produced startling victories. Consider these dramatic facts:

• Of the war wounded who reach hospitals, fewer than two percent are lost. This compares with 2.5% in the Korean War, and 4.5% in World War II.

• Most soldiers felled in battle are rushed to the nearest hospital faster than auto victims back home. More often than not, the wounded are out of the jungle and on to the operating tables within an hour.

• Specialists are available for any kind of emergency operation. In general, GIs can count on better medical treatment on the edge of the jungle than their families at home can expect in the average hospital emergency room.

As in all wars, germs are still more dangerous than bullets. But even the germs are being beaten, slowly but surely. Of every 1,000 men serving in Vietnam, one a day ends up in the hospital. A startling 75% are disease cases; only 11% are wounded. The remaining 14% are non-battle injuries, including snake and scorpion bites.

Malaria has given the most trouble. A new, strong strain of mosquito, the falciparum, has been encountered in the highlands. Its poison resists the usual anti-malarial drugs, though eventually it can be conquered with quinine. The

Department of Defense public affairs crisis planning checklist

	Responsible offices					
	FO	P & P	TFC	DSR	DSA	DNS
1. Recognition (messages, events, etc.) (Examples): (*a*) Preparation for evacuation of officials. (*b*) Movement of military forces. (*c*) Tourists asked to leave. (*d*) Announcement by State, other governments, U.N.	X	X	--------	X	X	X
2. Internal preliminary actions:						
(*a*) Inform PA staff of potential crisis	A	--------	--------	--------	--------	--------
(*b*) Confer with Service Chiefs/Directors of Information	A	X	--------	--------	--------	--------
(*c*) Confer with PA officials of other Government agencies	A	X	--------	--------	--------	--------
(*d*) Check status of media coverage	--------	--------	--------	--------	--------	A
(*e*) Designate special task force chief	A	--------	--------	--------	--------	--------
3. Activate Special Task Force to coordinate DoD actions	A	X	X	--------	--------	X
4. Draft specific PA guidance based on policy from White House, NSC, State, Secretary of Defense, etc., for service information chiefs or directors, JCS, unified and specified commands and other involved Defense activities	--------	A	X	--------	--------	--------
5. Reexamine security rules re release of information and recommend changing or modifying, if necessary; and consider imposition of field press censorship according to situation	--------	X	X	A	--------	X
6. Request Joint Staff and U/SC's to check public information annexes to appropriate plans and update and expand where necessary according to PA guidance	--------	A	--------	--------	--------	--------
7. Arrange for necessary special communications between public affairs offices of departments and agencies at the seat of the Government and with appropriate unified and specified commands involved	A	--------	--------	--------	--------	--------
8. Notification of actions, specifically stating channels of communication:						
(*a*) JCS and unified and specified commands	X	A	X	--------	--------	--------
(*b*) Service information chiefs or directors	A	X	X	--------	--------	--------
(*c*) Department of State	X	A	X	--------	--------	--------
(*d*) USIA	X	A	X	--------	--------	--------
(*e*) White House Press Secretary	A	--------	--------	--------	--------	--------
(*f*) Other DOD:						
1—ISA	--------	A	X	--------	--------	--------
2—DIA	--------	A	X	--------	--------	--------
3—OCD, etc.	--------	A	X	--------	--------	--------
9. Schedule situation briefs for PA staff and service information chiefs and directors	--------	--------	A	--------	--------	X
10. Schedule situation briefs for press	--------	--------	X	--------	--------	A
(*a*) State ground rules	A	--------	X	--------	--------	--------
(*b*) Arrangements for 24-hour coverage	X	--------	X	--------	--------	A
(*c*) Tours to area	A	--------	X	--------	--------	X
11. Maintain chronological record of events and PA actions	--------	--------	A	--------	--------	--------
12. Considering escalation examine and update OASD (PA) portion of defense emergency plan	--------	A	--------	--------	--------	--------
13. Reexamine physical space, clerical and professional assignments making necessary changes required by limited emergency	A	X	X	X	X	X
14. Consider decentralization of authority for release of crisis information at earliest time possible consistent with the national policy	A	--------	X	--------	--------	X
15. Disseminate information concerning crisis through personalized communications media such as national organizations	--------	--------	X	--------	A	X
16. Review participation of Defense personnel and equipment in public events	--------	--------	X	--------	A	--------

NOTES

A—Primary action.
X—Interest or support.

Code for responsible offices:
FO—Front Office.
P&P—Directorate for Plans and Programs.
TFC—Task Force Chief.
DSR—Directorate for Security Review.
DSA—Directorate for Special Activities.
DNS—Directorate for News Services.

Should the war in Vietnam develop into a national crisis, Pentagon information officials are all set to go into action along the lines indicated.

Viet Cong, who have been entrenched in the highlands for years, have slowly acquired immunity. Our men pick up the disease when they come in contact with the enemy dead, wounded, or captured. Thus, the Viet Cong might be said to be waging unintentional bacteriological warfare.

Some suspicious souls, after a mysterious outbreak of black water fever in South Vietnam during the summer of 1965, wondered whether the communists might be experimenting deliberately with germ warfare. It is no secret that a single Viet Cong infiltrator could wipe out or incapacitate an entire Army camp with no more than a spray gun.

To the wary, there was something ominous about the communist propaganda accusing Americans of using germ warfare. It is an old communist trick to accuse their enemies of the precise tactics they may be using themselves. During the Korean War, for example, the communists accused the United States of scattering frozen, disease-laden mosquitoes over North Korea. When the people lit their fires, the mosquitoes supposedly thawed out and with deadly bites started an epidemic. Puzzled American experts wondered how the Reds had conceived such a preposterous idea. Then their research turned up the interesting coincidence that Northern Sibera is infested with a hardy mosquito that comes out of the ice in the spring and bites the natives. Apparently the Russians, taking a lesson from the mosquito, had been experimenting with frozen insects. The use of mosquitoes, ticks, lice and other carriers to spread disease is a weapons system of its own called entomological warfare.

Unfortunately, germ warfare has become such a taboo subject that the public is unaware of the danger. *The blunt truth is that the United States, for all its elaborate and expensive defenses, could be devastated by a few enemy agents smuggling bacteria into the country in suitcases.* A single automobile spraying germs across the country through its tailpipe could cause an epidemic that could destroy crops, kill off livestock, or wipe out hundreds of thousands of people. *One General has estimated that 10 airplanes, each loaded with 10,000 pounds of dry biological warfare material, could scatter enough bacteria over the United States to knock out one-third of the population.*

Moreover, the bacteria can be produced easily and cheaply. Even a tiny country, such as Cuba, would have no difficulty waging secret biological warfare against the United States. Indeed one intelligence report, doubted by Pentagon skeptics, suggests that freebooting scientists may already have been hired by Dictator Fidel Castro to set up a germ warfare ring in Cuba.

While the communists have been experimenting with germ warfare, our own scientists have not been asleep in their laboratories. *They have developed new virus and rickettsia strains against which the world has no immunity.* This has been accomplished by using chemicals, radiation, ultraviolet light and other agents to produce bacteriological freaks or mutants. Some are so deadly that universities in the vicinity of the Army's Pine Bluff, Arkansas, laboratories have been given secret contracts to test the wild life constantly for the slightest sign of escaped virus. Elaborate precautions are taken to confine the bizarre germs to the labs.

A Boston outfit called Physicians for Social Responsibility has circulated a report that "government officials at high policymaking levels are advocating use of biological weapons in Vietnam" and that "a contract has been assigned to a New England concern for a rush program to adapt biological agents for use in Vietnam."

I learned that the alleged contract was supposed to have been granted to Travelers Research, Inc., of Hartford, Connecticut. Pentagon spokesmen told me emphatically, however, that the government had no intention of using biological warfare in Vietnam and had no germ warfare contract with Travelers Research.

I got quite a different story from Dr. Robert Ellis, who is directing germ warfare studies for Travelers Research. He acknowledged that the company had germ warfare contracts with the Air Force's Office of Scientific Research, the Army Materiel Command, and the Army Test Center at Dugway, Utah. He said his company's scientists were studying "the behavior of toxics in the environment." This would include the use of air currents for the possible delivery of toxic clouds over a target. They were also conducting other research too secret to talk about, though he denied that their studies dealt specifically with Vietnam. An Air Force officer, who asked to remain anonymous, contended that biological warfare could be humane. Our laboratories have developed germs, he said, that could incapacitate a whole nation without killing a soul. The population would be too weak to resist an invasion but later would recover without any harmful after-effects.

If germs haven't been spread in Vietnam, sprays and gases have been widely used. Under the code name "Ranch Hand," Air Force planes equipped with sprayers have spewed clouds of chemicals over Viet Cong hiding places. These chemicals have the effect of super-charged fertilizer on vegetation, accelerating its growth to the point that it dies. Two days after spraying, the leaves start turning color. Within a week or two, the sprayed area looks like an autumn scene. It takes six to eight weeks before the leaves fall, then visibility is increased up to 80%. The defoliation operations seem to destroy the vegetation permanently in the brackish mangrove swamps near the sea, but the effect may last no more than a year in the dense jungles.

Carefully controlled, defoliation must be approved by both American and South Vietnamese authorities all the way down to the province level. The clearance process usually takes about three months, though the First Infantry Division, in an emergency, was able to get approval in two weeks to clear the foliage around its perimeter. Common commercial sprays

SECTION B - AMMUNITION

		Total	MAAG Indochina Surplus	To Be Procured From MDAP	Cost
1. .38 Cal.		2,678,000	none	2,678,000	$160,000
2. Carbine Ammo		450,000	available		
3. S.M.G. Cal .45		1,632,000	none	1,632,000	
4. Rifle .30 Cal., MI	(				
5. B.A.R.	(	6,240,000	available		
6. Launcher (Grenade)		32,000	available		
7. Launcher (Rocket-236)		3,200	available		
8. Mortar 60 mm	(Smoke	750	available		
	(H.E.	500	available		
	(Illum.	1,000	available		
9. Rifle 57 mm (recoil-less	(Smoke	750	available		
	(H.E.	1,000	available		
	(Heat	750	available		
10. Riot Gun Ammo		200,000	none	none	20,000
11. Tear Gas Projectiles		4,000	none	none	42,000
12. Grenades Frag, Hand	(Practice	1,000		1,000	
	(Armed	3,500		3,500	
Rifle, M-1 Smoke		1,400		1,400	
Tear Gas		8,000		8,000	48,000*
White Phosphorus		12,000		12,000	
13. .50 Cal.**		72,000	available		
				Total	$270,000

*To be procured from civil sources at once for immediate use.
**For .50 Cal. M.G. mounted on Scout Car and Armored Cars.

A Michigan State University inventory for Central Intelligence Agency operations in Vietnam.

(brands 24D and 24T) are used to defoliate areas adjoining roads, railways, canals, border-crossing points, and sites favorable for Viet Cong ambushes. Thousands of acres of crops have also been destroyed to deny food to the guerrillas.

A non-toxic gas, chlorobenzolmalnotrile, has also been used to flush the Viet Cong out of underground bunkers. Some tunnel systems have been discovered that are too elaborate to be destroyed by high explosives; these are pumped full of gas which makes them uninhabitable for four to six months.

Our use of chemicals have provoked screams of protest from Hanoi. "Thousands of persons were killed, tens of thousands of others affected, domestic animals were killed en masse," screeched a typical broadcast, "by large-scale American use of toxic chemicals and poison gas." One indirect effect of this propaganda has been to scare the Viet Cong who have developed a superstitious dread of sprayed and gassed areas. South Vietnamese forces, on the other hand, have been indoctrinated so they have no fear of entering exposed areas.

Because the use of gas and chemicals gives the communists an effective propaganda weapon, the Defense Department has tried to suppress all public discussion of the issue. This raises the question of whether responsible citizens should criticize our policies in Southeast Asia or hold their fire. As the war has become more ferocious, the debate over Vietnam has become more heated. Does this debate, conducted in the open with all the vigor of a nation that prizes free speech, help or hinder the President? Should his critics, who cannot hope to know all the facts available to him, speak up or shut up? Where, in an emergency, should the line be drawn between patriotism and politics?

By and large, in this country, debate is accepted as a way of life. The protest marches, the picketing of the White House, the arguments in the press, the criticism of President Johnson even by members of his own party—all these are normal here. But they are not normal in Vietnam, North or South. And, the argument goes, signs of American disunity weaken morale in the South and give comfort to the communists in the North. Indeed, the Americans best known in North Vietnam are those Senators who oppose the President's handling of the war. Every critical speech they deliver is repeated throughout that Red-run country.

The President's professed policy is to force the enemy to the truce table—and to go with enough strength to assure an honorable peace. Some of his critics contend he is not fighting the war hard enough. If he doesn't produce a victory, they say, American lives and dollars will have been wasted. Other critics say he is fighting too hard, thus closing out any hope of negotiation.

Some Republicans have complained that Johnson is trying to stifle all opposition, that his endless confidential briefings for Congressional leaders are merely a means of silencing the critics. Among themselves, they refer to briefings as "Operation Smother." Speaking up for his chief, Vice-President Hubert Humphrey has assured me that criticism is welcomed at the briefings. "There aren't only yes-men at these meetings," he says. "The President listens to their arguments. He makes accommodations. He modifies his polices."

But President Johnson also is irritated when Congressmen make their criticisms public. He feels he is following a delicate and dangerous strategy which his critics undermine by sounding off in public. He needs a show of national solidarity, he pleads, to convince the communist leaders that they cannot weaken American determination.

The President contends that those who cry for concession encourage the communists to believe the United States may be bluffing. Such critics only increase the risk, prolong the war they seek to shorten and endanger future peace talks, he believes. In the privacy of his oval office, President Johnson often lashes out angrily at his critics. He is frustrated to the point of anguish over the attacks on his policies from his own party members. "There is a game that goes on in this town, sometimes, of divide," he complains.

One time, he shook a warning finger at members of Congress who had come to the White House for a closed-door briefing. "I know which of you," he declared, "have made statements supporting me and which have made statements critizing me on Vietnam. And when the right time comes, I intend to throw some of these statements from my critics right back in their faces."

It was during such a mood that the President let loose a public blast at an unnamed Republican for supposedly betraying a confidence involving the Vietnam build-up. White House aides helpfully furnished reporters the name he had omitted—that of House GOP leader Gerald Ford. But the ensuing tempest stirred more criticism than it stilled. "The President did this solely to take the spotlight away from the problems he was having with his own people in Congress," charged Senator Thurston Morton (R., Ky). "We had been quiet in our criticism. But not any more. You are going to hear more speaking out from members of Congress."

Senate GOP leader Everett Dirksen, however, discouraged the partisan pot shots by standing so near the President on the Vietnam question that they could not shoot at one without hitting the other. An appeal for unity came, too, from ex-President Eisenhower, who knows what it is like to be responsible for peace-or-war decisions. "When the country is in a crisis," he has said, "there is only one thing for any American to do and that is to support the President."

Then what is the role of the critic in a crisis? Does he serve the country best by confining his statements to closed-door conferences or by delivering them openly? Most critics insist the debate must go on, no matter how much it embarrasses the President. If, they say, we are fighting for the right of

SECRET

(U) **As of 30 June 1966, Air Force's Aerospace Rescue and Recovery Service Had Rescued 357 Personnel from Southeast Asia Combat Areas, Achieving a New Monthly High of 73 "Saves" During June.**

(U) The 73 combat rescues in June included 61 soldiers, 11 airmen, and one Navy flyer. Selected rescue and evacuation missions by the Aerospace Rescue and Recovery Service (ARRS) during June and early July included:

(U) On 29 June, 17 seriously wounded soldiers were evacuated from a combat zone by 2 rescue helicopters dispatched from Bien Hoa Air Base. They were recovered by hoist and litter basket from a dense jungle area of 125-foot trees. Hostile ground fire was encountered, but no additional casualties were sustained. Of the 17 soldiers, 15 survived.

(S) On 29 June, 2 helicopters scrambled from Nakhon Phanom Air Base, Thailand, and intercepted a battle-damaged Air Force A1E which was diverting to that base. After making contact with the helicopters, the A1E pilot ejected when the gaping hole in his plane's wing prevented him from maintaining control of the aircraft. One of the choppers landed and picked up the flyer.

(S) On 30 June, ARRS at Nakhon Phanom was notified that a pilot was preparing to eject from his disabled F-105 about 100 miles northeast of Udorn, Thailand. Two helicopters proceeded to the bailout scene and made contact with the downed officer. He was recovered by hoist pickup and returned uninjured.

(U) On 30 June and 1 July, 7 more wounded soldiers were evacuated from hostile territory in 3 rescue missions.

(S) On 11 July, a rescue helicopter used its hoist and forest penetrator to save an Air Force F-105 pilot shot down over Laos 65 miles west of Thanh Hoa, North Vietnam. The downed flyer was recovered without incident and returned in good condition to Udorn Air Base.

Downgraded At 3 Year Intervals;
Declassified After 12 Years.
DoD Dir. 5200.10

DoD 26 July 1966

SECRET

Though documents of this type do not contain information of use to the enemy, they're kept secret for 12 years. Pentagon files are jam-packed with similar over-classified material.

the Vietnamese to debate their own destiny, we cannot surrender our own right to debate. That would be the negation of all we are fighting for.

The most outspoken critic, Senator Wayne Morse (D., Ore.), points out that Presidents, despite the information on their desks, still make mistakes—as, for instance, John F. Kennedy admittedly did at the Bay of Pigs. Men with grave doubts about the invasion didn't speak up until it was too late. Their silence helped to produce the disaster.

Citing this example, Senator Ernest Gruening (D., Alaska) declares, "I believe the President is misinformed on Southeast Asia. The course which has been followed is the only course which could possibly lead to disaster. I don't want a Bay of Pigs debacle to happen again. I don't want President Johnson to say five years from now that it was too bad we didn't speak out."

Senator Frank Church (D., Ida.) stresses that the Senate has a duty to advise and consent on foreign affairs. "We wouldn't live up to our oath of office and our constitutional responsibility if we remained silent," he says. He believes that the critics who kept urging negotiations succeeded in altering the President's course toward an even greater build-up in Asia. "Our public stand," he contends, "gave the President a wider scope, greater latitude. It permitted him to take a middle role and protected him from the dangerous vise of military pressure."

Senator George McGovern (D., S. Dak.), another critic, agrees that differences should remain in the open. "The only way to exert pressure in our system of government," he says, "is to express our point of view through every medium at our disposal. It would be ironical, indeed, if in the name of defending freedom we suppressed the most worthwhile freedom of them all—the right of dissent."

But Senator John Pastore (D., R.I.), while recognizing the right of critics to speak out, warns it is now too late to oppose the President's course in Vietnam. "The one man," pleads Pastore, "who wants a solution more than any other, the man who has the most at stake, the man who must go to bed at night praying for settlement, is Lyndon Johnson. It is too late to argue whether we should have gone into Vietnam. We are there. Now it is our duty to support the President. We do our cause and our country harm by constantly hacking away at his policies."

Pastore also fears public criticism may damage the morale of the men who are fighting for their country in South Vietnam. "What," he demands, "must the boys who are ducking bullets in Vietnam think of the criticism at home? I don't care how this criticism may impress the rulers of other nations. I don't care how it may impress the armchair militarists. What concerns me is the morale of our fighting men."

House Democratic leader Carl Albert pleads that the "President knows more of the facts than we do. It is his responsibility to make the decisions. If his judgments are wrong, it is a proper issue at election time. Until then, we should all unite behind our national policy."

A Republican, California Congressman Alphonzo Bell, puts it this way: "The President's decisions will continue to be difficult ones. Only he can make them. What is at stake is world freedom and peace. We have a right to ask questions. We should not use that right to harass."

House GOP leader Ford agrees that reckless, unfounded, irresponsible criticism of the President in a time of national emergency could have disastrous results. It could lead the enemy to miscalculate our determination, national strength and unity. But he also contends that "the minority party in Congress has the responsibility to ask questions, raise issues and make suggestions."

"I am concerned," says Senator Jack Miller (R., Iowa), "that the President's critics—some from within his own party—appear to look only at Vietnam without considering the whole picture." Vice-President Humphrey, while stressing the importance of confining his own comments to the inner councils, acknowledges: "Measured words from responsible men can be helpful, but nagging negative criticism only damages the country. The most effective criticism, in my opinion, is offered in private. Yet we cannot expect in a free society to conduct foreign policy without public criticism."

So the debate rages on. Only in Vietnam is the talk drowned out by the thunder of battle. Should the words be muted as the thunder grows louder? The undeclared jungle war has mounted so steadily—a step at a time—that most Americans didn't realize until it was too late for debate that it had reached the scale of the Korean War. If the debate had been more wide open, would the public have understood better the need for the war? Or might more people have opposed it and restrained the President from plunging ahead with a war they didn't want? Or would the public have been better off and more united if there had been no debate at all?

This much is certain. *President Johnson has sought to subdue discussion of the war and to create a war-in-Vietnam-but-peace-at-home atmosphere.* He held off asking Congress for a formal declaration of war, geared the economy to produce both butter and bullets. Until the summer of 1966, however, the Army kept more men lolling in Europe than fighting in Vietnam. There were 10,000 servicemen in Italy, for example, where the only real danger was indigestion from too much pasta.

Some of the most shrill protests have come from servicewomen who complain that though there is a war on, they are still being treated more as ladies than soldiers. One WAC lieutenant, who but for her uniform could have passed for a trim, attractive housewife, fixed me with her bright blue eyes and demanded pertly: "What kind of delicate creatures do the brass think we are? There's a war going on in Vietnam, but you have to be a civilian to get assigned there. Native women are fighting in the jungles with the Viet Cong. Yet we aren't allowed to dirty our dainty hands." She slammed down a picture of a Russian girl in Red Army uniform, squinting over the sights of an automatic rifle. "Look at that," she said indignantly. "The girl can't even hold the thing properly."

Despite the demand for more manpower in Vietnam, the armed forces haven't bothered to recruit their authorized strength of two percent womanpower. The services seem quite content to go along with the present level of one woman for every 100 men. Less than 2,000 servicewomen have been shipped overseas. Most of these chosen few have been sent to safe, snug countries and have been given nothing more dangerous to handle than a typewriter. They are secretaries, clerks and typists, except for a few who have acquired Space Age skills and work with computers and electronics. Though a *few* WAC's are serving in Vietnam, Pentagon officers admit quietly that such service is "discouraged." In fact, Colonel Maribeth Simpson, a WAC personnel officer, has sent a stern note to the Army command in Saigon, insisting that WACs be requested only for "appropriate" jobs.

This points up the fact that our servicewomen, who were regarded as "soldiers in skirts" and treated as such during World War II, are now expected to take a back seat. During basic training the girls spend as much time studying the arts of make-up and good grooming as the military arts. More attention is paid to the rise and fall of hemlines than to the ebb and flow of battle lines. "Sometimes," a WAC officer told me, "we have to speak to girls to make sure their skirts aren't dragging the ground when short skirts are in style."

The prettiest and most poised girls get the best jobs, usually as receptionists for the brass. For the top secretarial posts in the Pentagon, applicants from the women's services are screened almost as carefully as contestants for Miss America. They must not only be lookers but must have charm to soothe tired Generals and Admirals. Before a girl is given a job with any of the service chiefs, she is checked over personally by the top commander in the WACS, WAVES, WAFS or Marines.

The servicewomen in World War II were given "bivouac" training —how to survive in the open, rig pup tents and move noiselessly at night. They also spent time on the firing range and performed all kinds of rugged jobs. But today the tough training has been abandoned for frilly courses on make-up and hair-dos. They are still taught such military subjects as weapons familiarization, but they no longer go into the field to fend for themselves, and the M-1 and M-14 rifles are considered too heavy for a mere slip of a girl to handle. "I know some Girl Scouts who are more rugged than we are," snapped one officer.

The ladies of the armed forces also no longer drive trucks and work as grease monkeys. The official attitude, as expressed by a Pentagon spokesman, is that they "cannot be employed at jobs that are not in conformance with the present cultural pattern of utlizing women's services in this country." The work must be "psychologically and sociologically" suitable.

If the services treat their women like clinging vines, a woman is probably to blame. During the early 1950's rivalry between the WAVES and WAFS became so intense that the Air Force recruited Jacqueline Cochran, glamorous pilot and beauty specialist, to improve WAF standards. The Air Force, Miss Cochran declared, should pay more attention to recruiting women with good looks and attractive figures. She suggested they should be at least 61 inches tall but not more than 72 inches. Taking solemn heed, the Air Force at once set up a four-week grooming course for its recruits. *Now all the women's forces play up femininity and glamor.* This is a program, complain some ladies in uniform, better suited for a sorority than for a military organization. When the nation is in trouble, they contend, women want to respond to the fullest just as men do.

What is the outlook in Vietnam? *Some experts see the war dragging on for 10, 20, even 30 years. At least one Pentagon planning paper anticipates fighting in Vietnam until the year 2000.* Its authors fear the guerrillas may have to be flushed out of the jungle bush by bush. Other experts point out that the Viet Cong have been suffering severe punishment and that their morale has been sagging. Prisoner interrogation reveals war weariness among the jungle fighters; captured documents indicate their leaders realize they can't achieve a military decision as they did over the French at Dien Bien Phu.

If President Johnson hopes to force the North Vietnamese to the truce table, he should remember that the wily and wispy Ho Chi Minh, their venerable leader, is not a man who scares easily. Against what seemed impossible odds at the time, he won victories over the Japanese, then over the French. He has told visitors that he is prepared to evacuate Hanoi, return to the jungle, and carry on the war from one rice paddy and bamboo thicket to another.

It should also be remembered that an integral part of communist strategy is to play for time, to exhaust the patience of the West with the patience of the East. It took two full years to negotiate the Korean truce line before the firing ended. However, the feeling in Washington is that the Kremlin at least would like to see a Vietnam settlement. Soviet leaders apparently have come around to the view that the United States is not going to be backed down from its pledges, not by Hanoi's bravado nor Peking's bluff. The European satellites, though denouncing American "intervention," have also made no secret of their desire for a settlement. Prague Radio has warned that the Vietnamese people "would not be able to agree indefinitely with the Chinese attitude that the struggle must be waged to the victorious end, whatever the price, and that it does not matter how long the war lasts." A Yugoslav newspaper has put it even more bluntly: "China is determined to fight on heroically for 10, 15, even 50 years to the last Vietnamese."

Some advisers in Washington's policymaking councils believe the United States should make whatever concessions are necessary to pull out of Vietnam before American troops become bogged down in a hopeless, endless war. Others believe that a quick victory can be won by unleashing American power to destroy North Vietnam and carrying the war into Red China if the Chinese should interfere. President Johnson has been trying to steer a course between these two poles. To those who seek a quick settlement, he has complained bitterly that all their talk demoralizes South Vietnamese leaders, encourages the communists, and therefore is more likely to prolong the war. To those who call for widening the war, he has warned gravely of the folly of getting locked in mortal combat with 700,000,000 Chinese.

What rankles the President most is that Senators of his own party have taken the lead in calling for negotiation. In a phone call to Senator GOP Leader Everett Dirksen, the President thanked him for his support and grumbled peevishly about getting "kicked around" by Democratic Senators. Dirksen didn't mention that his support was dictated as much by politics as patriotism. At a GOP policy meeting, Republican Senators had decided that their best strategy was to support the increasing military pressure on North Vietnam. However, they figured the pressure for negotiation would force the President to back down from his tough stand, thus leaving the Republicans with a hot political issue. They would be able to claim they had supported the President when he "stood up to the communists" but abandoned him after he "chickened out." When he continued to step up the war, they watched carefully for signs that the public was weary of the war. Then some made self-serving political capital out of portraying LBJ as a wager of war.

President Johnson is aware that, while all wars end at the conference table, it is much harder to secure a peace than it is to win a war. What are the chances of a Vietnam cease-fire? Perhaps not so bleak as some believe. Tough, old Ho Chi Minh is a sick man, pushing 80. His cabinet is divided. Some of his advisers favor Moscow, others Peking. He must know that North Vietnam, even with Chinese support, can never hope to match American naval and air power.

The President, studying a top-secret intelligence summary prepared in news capsule form for his easy reading, recently stroked his chin with satisfaction. The digest reported that the Viet Cong had been hounded out of their hideouts by American search-and-destroy missions and B-52 raids. Left behind in the overrun sanctuaries were literally tons of desperately needed food, arms and medical supplies. The black-pajamaed, bark-helmeted guerrilla fighters, specialists in ambush, were becoming the ambushed. Their morale had been rubbed raw by constant harassment. Their losses both in casualties and defections had been so severe that the Viet Cong had been forced to conscript 15-year-olds from the villages. The President looked up from his reading. *"The war," he told an aide, "should be over in 1967."*

15

THE SECRET WAR AGAINST RED CHINA

The fleeting shadow of a junk slipped through the fog toward the flat, marshy Chinese coast, then scooted up one of the myriad canals that channel the tidewater. At a lonely spot, a huddled figure hopped out. He was an agent of the U.S. infiltrating into Red China. Soon he would melt into the teeming coastal population. His mission: to look for life preservers.

Why risk possible torture and death to check on life preservers? A stockpile of life preservers could be the tip-off to an invasion; the Chinese Communists can't assault the strategic, Nationalist-held islands without them. These islands are protected by reefs that would snag most landing craft 10 to 20 yards offshore. This means invading troops may have to swim ashore. Despite the example of Mao Tse-tung's publicized plunges in the Yangtze, most Chinese are poor swimmers who would need life preservers.

Slipping through the slats in the bamboo curtain is the difficult, dangerous job of a few unsung spies—heroes anonymous—all natives of China, all trained by our intelligence agencies, all risking their necks daily to secure information needed by the U.S. One night, perhaps over a clandestine radio transmitter from inside China, some agent may flash news that would prevent another Pearl Harbor disaster. Until then, less dramatic but equally important information is coming through continuously—about Red troop movements, military construction, defense production and other vital matters.

Our secret operatives usually are smuggled into China along the mudflat, canal-streaked coast between Hangchow and Swatow. We have learned not to put them ashore at Namtau, which is the nearest point from Hongkong but only a few miles from Pao-an, a military garrison swarming with crack Red troops. We don't use Toishan on the southwest bank of the Pearl River either. Since most Chinese-Americans come from Teishan, the Reds expect us to use it as an espionage base and are extra vigilant.

The junks that slip our agents ashore are run by "sleepers" (as our friends inside China are called) or by Chinese pirates who plunder, loot and smuggle along the coast. The pirates work strictly for profit; their motivation is financial, seldom political, although some have enlisted as "deputies" for the Communist shore patrols. But if one of our agents pays enough, they will happily assist him past the Commies. Conversely, if he neglects to pay, the pirates will just as happily cut off his head and deliver him in two parts to their Red employees.

Contrary to published reports, American spies are not dropped into the Chinese interior from airplanes. In China's remote sections, the sight or sound of an airplane is an unusual event, and young Communists are trained to report all unusual events immediately to the local police. A few agents —disguised as merchants, beggars, coolies—pick their way painstakingly over the Himalayas winding along the ancient trade routes from Burma, Bhutan, Nepal and Tibet.

As a correspondent who spent more than two years in China, I developed some contacts in the intelligence field. One recently returned from a secret mission behind the Bamboo Curtain. Let's call him Chen, because it isn't his name.

Disguised in grimy rags that reeked of fish, Chen sneaked aboard a small junk provided by two "sleepers." Under camouflage of night, they pushed off from Hongkong and paddled across the murky Pearl River estuary, gliding noiselessly past the Red island outpost of Lin-tin (Chinese for "lonely neighbor"). Curling around the larger Chung Hsan Island, they joined the junk traffic that flows constantly at the mouth of the Pearl River. They wound among the tiny islands along tributaries leading to Kong-moon ("river gate"), then followed one of the small creeks that reach like muddy, watery fingers into Canton. Among hundreds of other junks, they were inconspicuous.

Chen made his way casually to the home of one of the boat owners, changed into better clothes and came out as a young Communist lawyer—complete with all the necessary forged papers. He had taken the precaution to study the latest Red lawbooks and read up on back newspapers. To complete his background, he now steeped himself in local gossip picked up from his "sleeper" friends. Next Chen answered an ad in a Canton paper; a Communist law firm needed a legal assistant. Thanks to careful coaching, he convinced the firm's head that he had been living and working in Kong-moon.

After two months establishing himself as a bright young Red, Chen wangled an assignment that would take him to Shanghai. This was his destination. His mission: to pick up certain documents and smuggle them out. With the credentials of a Communist attorney in good standing, Chen easily got hold of the documents and stuffed them into a money belt underneath his clothes. He had one close call. Back in Canton, he caught a streetcar to the Marco Polo Temple to meet his two friends. A Red plainclothesman pushed against him, felt the money belt and demanded to know what it contained. Chen's calm explanation that the belt held nothing but personal papers wasn't good enough, but the plea that he couldn't remove the belt on the streetcar struck the Red as reasonable. They departed the streetcar and walked behind the Marco Polo Temple for privacy. Fortunately, the two "sleepers" were waiting; the Red was outnumbered three to one. They were forced to kill him and, after dark, dump his body into the river.

廣東東莞縣萬頃沙地方有一個「華僑集體農場」。共黨把它宣傳爲「歸國華僑的天堂」，但據香港所得到的大陸消息，却將農場的內情完全揭穿了。
原來，這所農場祗是一個集中營，回國的華僑都被迫做了奴工。
現在，該處共有七百四十五人。他們在共幹的淫威下，組織了幾個隊和組，除了整天勞動，充當牛馬以外，這般受騙的華僑，每天晚上還要上兩小時的政治大課，再加兩小時的小組討論，累死和病倒的，日有新聞。

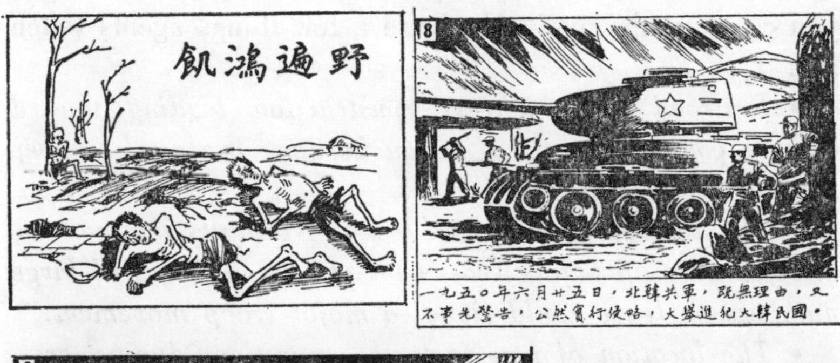

飢鴻遍野
8
一九五0年六月廿五日，北韓共軍，既無理由，又不事先警告，公然實行侵略，大舉進犯大韓民國。

按照英美蘇三國的莫斯科協定……韓國應在一個自由民主的政府下統一……但是蘇俄竟破壞他們的保證，屢次阻撓美國設法實行莫斯科協定的努力。

但是在北韓，蘇俄佔領軍不准此委員會進入他們的佔領區，並剝奪了北韓人民的自由選舉權。

In psychological activities, the Defense Department issues propaganda such as this material about life in Red China and the peaceful intentions of the U.S. Accompanying captions contain phrasing of this sort: "Chinese Forced to be Slave Laborers" and "Today Calamities Sweep the China Mainland."

To get out of China after a mission is often as hazardous as getting in. Usually the agent is assigned a pre-arranged rendezvous point on the coastline, where a friendly junk will ferry him to a waiting patrol boat. One agent found his rendezvous area cordoned off. He finally escaped by pretending to be dead; he had learned earlier that a funeral procession had been given permission to cross into Hongkong. "Sleepers" laid him out in a casket and joined the solemn procession. They gambled, successfully, on the traditional Chinese respect for the dead.

Like Chen, all agents go into China with a specific assignment. As Chen explained to me: "It's like sticking a needle in a fat pig. If you jab at random, you probably will hit nothing but fat. But if you poke the needle in a vital spot, you can hurt the pig." Here are a few things agents watch for:

• *Railroad and highway construction leading toward China's coastline or the Vietnam border. We need to keep track of all likely military routes.*

• *The number of troops on leave. Normally the men are allowed time off before reassignment. So the sight of large numbers on leave could signal a major troop movement.*

• *The location of new factories, munitions dumps, arsenals and other military installations.*

To get the answers, our agents use all the equipment of modern espionage. For example, they transmit messages on microfilm so small it can be sealed under a postage stamp or even hidden under the period made by a typewriter. With tiny tweezers, the infinitesmal film can be moved to an enlarger and blown up into a readable message.

A big problem is sneaking radio transmitters in. The old World War II trick of hiding radio equipment in suitcases won't work; the Chinese don't carry suitcases. A suitcase in China is as conspicuous as a rickshaw on Broadway. The CIA has perfected new tricks, all highly secret and still unknown to the Reds. Even after the radio equipment is set up, transmission is still risky. For best results, agents must send their coded messages at night, preferably from a building top. The Reds have devised a simple but clever trap. When their monitors pick up a secret signal, they systematically cut off electric power in various small sections of the city. The switch that turns off the clandestine transmitter tells them the area in which it is operating. They simply seal off the whole area and conduct a building-to-building search.

To avoid being caught, our agents must also be masters of disguise. They pose as farmhands, beggars, fishermen, merchants, doctors, patients—every conceivable role. And attention must be paid to the smallest details. Some agents disguised as peddlers have been trapped because their feet were too clean. Chinese secret police know the native peddlers, after years of trudging around in clogs, have an impenetrable coat of dirt on their feet, gnarled and cracked toenails and soles hard as shoe leather. One agent was caught because his little toes turned inward. This telltale sign told police that the "peddler" had once worn western-style shoes. Another operative, posing as a farmhand, was picked up because he began plowing a field from north to south. Chinese farmers follow the ancient custom of plowing from east to west, because centuries ago the Mongolian hordes from the north were slowed by furrows running across their path.

If an agent is caught, the penalty is painful torture designed to extract information from him. Death comes very, very slowly. As Chen said grimly: "They never believe they've forced everything out of a captured agent. They'll always keep him alive just a little longer."

Who are these Chinese willing to face death daily working for the Americans? Though often recruited outside China, they must be native Chinese with an ability to speak many dialects and command a keen knowledge of the country. They must not have lived too long in the United States. Somehow, life in America changes their typical Chineseness. Something about their bearing, their behavior gives them away.

It would be suicidal, of course, to send white agents into China. But once in awhile, we get help from Russian "sleepers" who live in colonies in a few Chinese cities. These are former White Russians who fled the Bolshevik revolution, then hastily changed their political coloring from White to Red after Mao Tse-tung's triumph. But, as one whispered to an American agent on a Shanghai waterfront: "Many of us are Radishans. Like the radish, we are Red on the outside but White on the inside."

A few guerrilla groups also are active behind the bamboo curtain. I would like to believe that among them, somewhere on the broad, burdened back of Central China, are Chang Shang-chi's guerrillas. I once marched with Chang's men, and it would please me to know they are still playing their deadly game of hide-and-seek with the communist soldiers. The truth is that I can find no one who knows whether this valiant little band still survives. When I left them shortly after World War II, they were fighting the Communists for control of a stretch of railroad track about 60 miles north of Hankow.

Except for hit-and-run commando raids, the United States supports only scattered guerrilla activity on the Chinese mainland. I have discussed with the highest authorities the feasibility of mounting a major guerrilla operation against the Red Chinese. I believe their vast, ramshackle tyranny can be destroyed more easily from within than from without. Skilled guerrillas could be infiltrated into the Chinese hinterlands where unrest is seething. They should be supplied not only with arms but with stocks of food to win the friendship of the hungry peasants.

Behind the bamboo curtain, large minorities are waiting only for leadership and weapons. Millions of devout Moslems and Buddhists, Mongols and Tibetans are bitterly re-

CENTRAL INTELLIGENCE AGENCY

This material contains information affecting the National Defense of the United States within the meaning of the Espionage Laws, Title 18, U.S.C. Secs. 793 and 794, the transmission or revelation of which in any manner to an unauthorized person is prohibited by law.

C-O-N-F-I-D-E-N-T-I-A-L

NOFORN

COUNTRY	China	REPORT NO.	CS-3/479,154
SUBJECT	Food Robberies and Begging in Kwangtung	DATE DISTR.	29 June 1961
		NO. PAGES	2
		REFERENCES	RD
DATE OF INFO.	May 1961		
PLACE & DATE ACQ.	Cambodia, Phnom Penh	FIELD REPORT NO.	FDP-1199

THIS IS UNEVALUATED INFORMATION. SOURCE GRADINGS ARE DEFINITIVE. APPRAISAL OF CONTENT IS TENTATIVE.

SOURCE: Anti-Communist Chinese educator in Phnom Penh (C); from two overseas Chinese in Phnom Penh who visited Kwangtung in April and May (F). Appraisal of Content: 6.

1. A Chinese woman resident of Phnom Penh who visited the Chinese Mainland in April and May 1961 stated that she was warned by the Chinese Communist customs officials at Shumchun to take extreme care of her baggage, which contained large quantities of foodstuffs that she was taking to people on the Mainland from relatives or friends in Phnom Penh. She was warned not to entrust her baggage to anyone whom she did not know personally, and to be particularly careful of persons claiming to be Government cadres who might offer to help her. She was warned again by the cadres of the Overseas Chinese Hostel in Canton. There she was told that it was much safer to have her baggage shipped to her destination by the Overseas Chinese Travel Service, rather than to try to carry it with her.

2. The woman was told by people in the Swatow area of Kwangtung Province that thievery was becoming more and more frequent. The majority of these thefts are for food. In Swatow, where the majority of the people draw their monthly rice ration to cook and eat at home rather than in the messhalls, there are many cases of theft around the first of each month when the rations are issued. Often, the burglars leave money in the rice containers to show that they are stealing the rice only from necessity. Formerly children were often sent to draw the family rice ration, but so many of them were robbed on their way home that this practice has been largely discontinued. Even adults are often stopped by groups who either beg for some of their rice, try to force them to sell it, or steal it and throw them a wad of Yuan notes in exchange. These groups sometimes include militiamen or low-level Chinese Communist cadres.

3. One day, when this woman was dining in Swatow with friends at a restaurant, a number of young children gathered, begging for just one or two noodles. The restaurant waiters came up, threatening to beat the children, but the children still refused to move. The informant then promised the children that they could have the noodles. The whole group rushed to the table and began grabbing, and the informant and her friends had to stop them and divide the noodles evenly.

5 4 3 2 1

C-O-N-F-I-D-E-N-T-I-A-L

NOFORN

STATE #	X	ARMY #	X	NAVY	X	AIR	X	NSA	X	SECDEF	X	ICA #	X	USIA #	X

CINCPAC# PACFLT# ARPAC# PACAF# MAAG#

Note: Washington distribution indicated by "X"; Field distribution by "#".

A "c-o-n-f-i-d-e-n-t-i-a-l" Central Intelligence Agency report about food robberies and begging in Red China *sentful of the Communist drive to break up their religions and destroy their family life.* They object to the mass movement into their territories of Chinese "settlers," sent by Peking to dilute their population and colonize their land. While the Chinese continue to lead the clamor against racial discrimination in the U.S., they cruelly abuse their own minorities. They have crushed the Kazakhs in Sinkiang, machine-gunned Mongol families trying to flee to the dubious sanctuary of Soviet soil. Little of this record has ever been made public. The worst of Red China's crimes have taken place out of sight of the world—in Tibet, hidden behind the towering Himalayas; in Sinkiang, deep in the center of Asia; on the bleak, windswept plateau of Inner Mongolia. But from the grim accounts of escapees, from films and documents that have been smuggled out, a portrait of the Ugly Chinese is taking form.

The most shocking stories have come out of Tibet, which has become a sepulcher to Peking oppression. For centuries, about four million Tibetans lived in their mountains, 12,000 feet above sea level, cut off from the world, maintaining their independence. Devout Buddhists, they were ruled by their priests. By Asian standards they were prosperous and seldom knew hunger. They asked merely to be left alone.

But Red China wanted Tibet as a base to outflank India and began in 1950 the "liberation" of a people who didn't want to be liberated. A year later, it was all over; Chinese troops were in control. They claimed to have come in peace —"only with our rice bowls and chopsticks." It was a grim joke, for the bowls and chopsticks were almost as deadly as bullets. The Chinese literally ate the Tibetans out of house and home. Within a few months the cost of food rose ten times. Starvation stalked the rugged land.

Then the Chinese began what the International Commission of Jurists has described starkly as "genocide," a monstrous crime the world hoped had died with Hitler. They moved first against the Buddhist priests and their monasteries. Some were shot in cold blood, others horribly tortured, a few even burned at the stake. As celibates, many were forced to marry, humiliated and degraded in every way. Altars and images were desecrated. Priceless sacred books were burned.

At Ba-Jeuba, for example, an old lama was dragged before the people, accused of fornication and ordered to marry a prostitute. Rather than violate his vows, he said he would prefer execution. The Chinese forced him to kneel bare-kneed on broken stones for 15 minutes, then on thorns for an hour, while they pulled his ears and pricked his head with sword points. He died in pain after several beatings.

Three lamas in Rigong, after being put through the bare-knees torture, were thrown into separate pits. Worshipers were forced to urinate on them while the Chinese mockingly called upon the lamas to invoke their holy powers and fly out of the pits. Then the three were chained together around the neck, compelled to carry human dung in baskets, and marched from place to place for public exhibition.

Tibetans who fought against the Chinese were used for target practice, many being shot before the eyes of their wives and children. Some were executed by nails driven through their eyes. One Tibetan leader was asked if he preferred to die standing or lying. Bravely, he said he would stand. He was made to dig a pit and stand in it. The pit was filled with mud and tamped down until the pressure pushed his eyes out of his head. He was left to die in agony.

Children were also encouraged to inform against their parents in the classic Communist pattern. Then Mao began transporting the young to China. In one area, all children below the ages of 15 were taken. No one knows what has happened to these children, whether they ever reached China or were marched off to die.

Declared the Commission of Jurists, a world-wide, non-political organization, in 1960: *"The latest evidence dis-*

closes a continuance of ill treatment of many monks, lamas and other religious figures, resulting in death through excessive torture, beatings, starvation and forced labor and continuance of the forcible transfer of children to China . . . No worship of any kind is permitted, and any sign of worship or prayer is met with severe punishment."

The Chinese claim they have brought "civilization" to Tibet. They boast of building roads, schools and hospitals. Comments Thubeten Nyenjik, ex-governor of Tibet's Gyantse province: "The Chinese have built . . military roads, indispensable for holding down a conquered people and built with the help of forced Tibetan labor. The Chinese have set up schools, but these schools are designed solely for the purpose of the indoctrination of the youth of Tibet with Communist ideas. The Chinese claim to have built many hospitals, but these are, again, like the schools, makeshift affairs established in houses requisitioned from private individuals."

In their hours of torment, the Tibetans got no help from the outside world. Their isolation, on which they had so long relied for their freedom, put them beyond hope of rescue. Yet there are still Tibetan guerrillas fighting for their freedom, and refugees continue to risk death by treking through the high passes to India. In tragic Tibet, the Chinese image is not only ugly but grotesque.

Red China's treatment of the 10 million Moslems within her frontiers has been no prettier. Most are nomadic tribesmen following the grazing of their livestock in Sinkiang, Kansu and Inner Mongolia. Originally, the Chinese promised they would have self-governing republics. But that promise, like so many other Peking pledges, has been cynically violated.

Assiduous in wooing the Moslem peoples of the Middle East, the Chinese have turned the wide lands of their native Moslems into lands of terror. Herds have been slaughtered

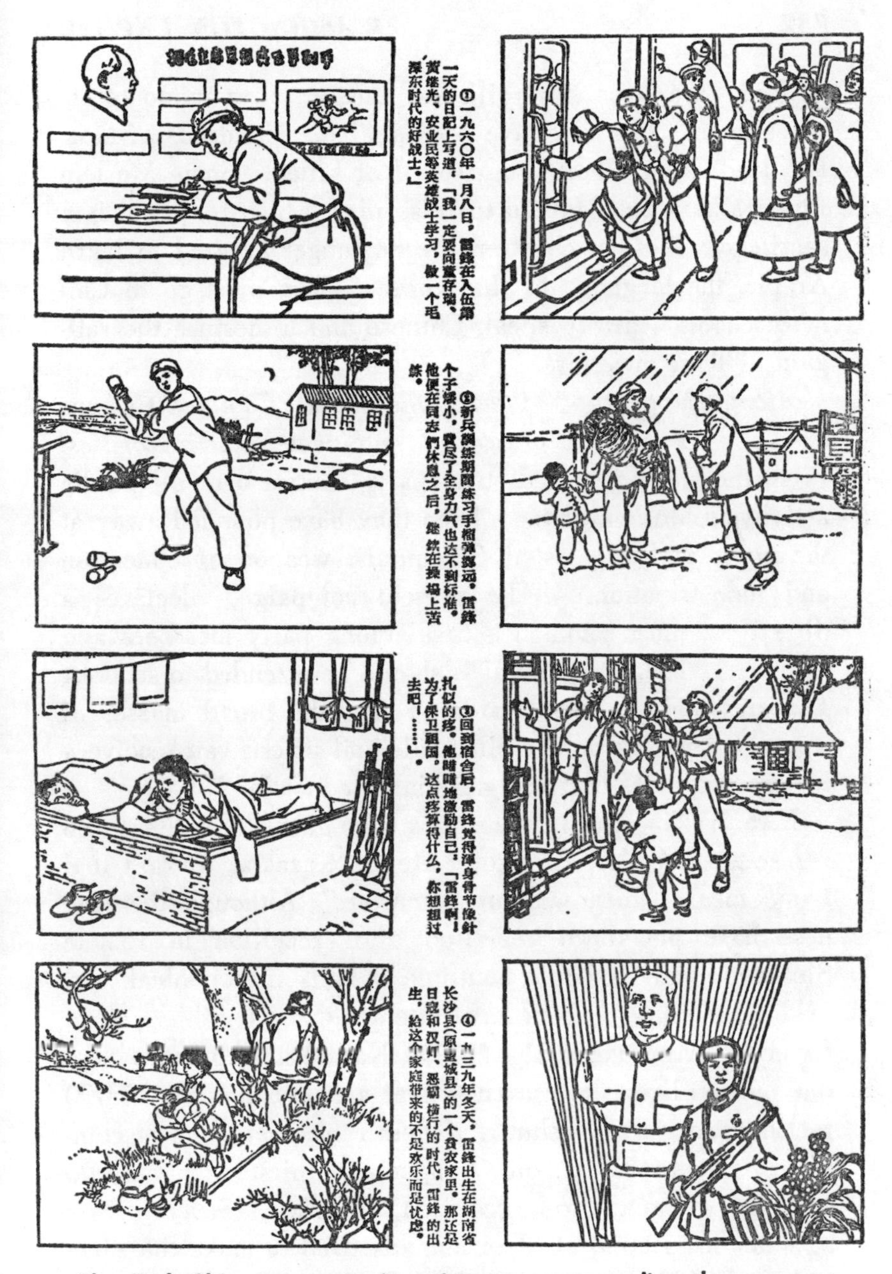

The Red Chinese use comic strips to propagandize the masses. On the left, Lei Feng, the hero, is writing a diary in which he tells of his love of the "New China." On the right, he is shown coming to the assistance of the needy.

to feed China's hungry millions, and no effort made to replace them. Mosques have been defiled. Hundreds of Moslem leaders have been imprisoned or killed. Some Moslem farmers have been forced to raise pigs, which for them is a sacrilege. Moslem children are no longer allowed to learn Arabic, the language of the Koran. They must go to Chinese schools, learn to speak Chinese and to despise the religion of their ancestors.

Along with the prod of terror, the Chinese Communists have used slow, inexorable pressure to subjugate their minorities. First, they have imposed strict party control over all public activity in Moslem areas. Then they have pounded away at the youth with the tested Communist weapon of education and indoctrination. "The present compaign," declares a directive, "must commence first among party members and cadres . . . Then the campaign should be extended to schools, factories and the countryside so that the broad masses of workers, peasants and intellectuals and priests can receive a widespread and penetrating Socialist education."

Like the Tibetans, the Moslems have guerrilla fighters who refuse to surrender. Toughest are the Kazakhs, whose tribal name means "men without a master." Although the Chinese have put down rebellion after rebellion in remote Sinkiang, many Kazakhs continue to fight in their bleak and arid mountains. Others have attempted the terrible trek to freedom. Approximately 45,000 Kazakhs, with more than one million livestock, marched over a frozen plateau 15,000 feet high to get to Kashmir. Their ranks were almost completely decimated by cold, hunger and thirst. Only 3,000 survived, eventually to be resettled in Turkey. Several years ago another 19,000 Moslem nomads tried to make the same trek; only 400 have lived to reach Turkey. No one will ever know the hardships these people have endured to live their own way of life.

From Tibet to Mongolia, the oppressed minorities would,

I believe, support a guerrilla campaign. The Red Chinese, who came to power through guerrilla warfare, should be given a taste of their own tactics. Vice President Hubert Humphrey, with whom I have discussed this idea, is pushing it in Washington's policy councils.

While with Chang Shang-chi's guerrillas, I saw what a few ragged but rugged men could do against the firepower of the Japanese and the treachery of the Communists. I was a witness to a war that began on the day that World War II ended. I was with Nationalist guerrillas as they battled the Communists for control points which the Japanese were abandoning along the Hankow-Peking railroad track. The world took no notice of this warfare; the dispatches I wrote never got through. The feeble cry of our battered, hand-cranked transmitter was drowned out by the joyous news of peace which filled the air waves. But the crackle of our rifles was to explode into the thunder of civil war.

I was strictly a military liability, riding tall in an ornate wooden saddle. Split down the middle, this saddle alternately pinched and stabbed me with splinters. My mount, captured from the Japanese, was still loyal to the Emperor; it dumped me twice in the rice paddies.

Chang straddled a scrawny jackass with comic dignity, but there was nothing comic about him. He was stern, hard, unsmiling. He had only one weakness: as a newly converted Christian, he was apt to burst forth with a strain of "God Be With You 'Til We Meet Again," sung with revival-meeting enthusiasm. His guerrillas marched in sandaled feet, single file, along trails that wound through mountains and rice paddies. The officers wore faded olive-green cotton uniforms, the men rags. The only items that matched were homemade bark helmets, covered with a black, tarlike substance. Their weapons had been taken from the enemy.

The guerrillas patiently steered me away from action that involved the least risk. Every time shots were fired, I was hustled to the rear. It did no good to explain that correspondents were supposed to observe the fighting. Chang & Co. were adamant. I was a guest at their war; they would lose face if anything happened to me. At night I was bundled into a cocoon of thick mosquito netting which also kept out the rats. When I fell sick, a patrol found a cook who had worked for American missionaries. Another patrol was sent 50 miles to Hankow, then controlled and patrolled by Japanese troops, to get food suitable for Americans.

Then came the day in August 1945, when my interpreter, King Junn-shang, came running to tell me that the Japanese had surrendered. Our crackling, wheezing, hand-powered radio brought the news that World War II was over. But the Communists, without pause, were already beginning the conquest of China. We headed up the Hankow-Peking railway for Kung Chu-ling, a mountaintop fortress overlooking a vital stretch of track. Although the fortress was surrounded by Red guerrillas, the Japanese refused to surrender it to them.

Chang's hardy commandos, pushing the Communists back 13 miles, battled their way almost to the edge of the eagle's nest. The Japanese commander consulted his protocol, concluded that our guerrillas—not the Communists—were the proper representatives of the Chinese government and turned his post over to us. Next morning, the Reds ambushed one of our patrols and killed four men. But Chang pushed them off the mountain and brought the track below under the sway of the artillery the Japanese had left behind.

Not long afterward, I was guided back to a grass-camouflaged airstrip to be flown out. We stopped at a village to pick up an American fighter pilot, Maj. Gene Dorr, who had been left there by the Communists. He had been shot down three times. "If I'd been shot down twice more," he told me disgustedly, "I'd have qualified as a Japanese ace."

Chang knew how to use the country, how to melt into the

CLASSIFICATION? OH! MAKE IT SECRET JUST TO BE SAFE
A SECURITY REMINDER
DONT
OVERCLASSIFY
DOCUMENTS!
CONSULT AFR 205-1
FOR GUIDANCE
HQ USAF SECURITY 78291

These conflicting Pentagon posters dramatize the division over what should be classified. Most government officials ignore the top poster, pay more heed to the bottom one.

A SECURITY REMINDER!

IT IS AN HONOR
TO BE TRUSTED WITH
YOUR COUNTRYS
DEFENSE INFORMATION
BE PROUD OF YOUR PART
IN KEEPING IT SECURE
HQ USAF SECURITY 78291

mountains. He had friends everywhere, among the herders on the hillsides and the farmers wading in their rice paddies. His was a rag-tag crew, poorly armed. But brighter and sharper than any man-made sword is the sword of human courage.

China's terrain is made to order for guerrilla fighting. Despite all the manpower Peking commands, the government cannot contain elusive guerrillas. Distances are vast, roads and railways are few, communications are poor. One sharpshooter, perched on some crag, can hold up a battalion. It is also possible to hide airstrips in the most unlikely places, such as the one I used. From the air it looked like a narrow, grassy valley between two jagged mountains. But underneath the grass was good hard core, packed and pounded by local peasants loyal to the guerrillas.

Among Chiang Kai-shek's troops on Formosa are men like those who fought for Chang Shang-chi, men from every part of China, speaking every dialect. They have families on the mainland who will help and hide them. In China also are millions of hurt, hungry, angry people waiting for the chance to fight. It wouldn't be a quick, easy war, but the people of China have patience and endurance. I recall Chang's repeated admonition to his guerrillas: "Harass, harass, harass. Never forget that many little victories can add up to a big victory in the end."

Exactly how ferocious is the great Chinese dragon, that most fearsome creature, which has been breathing fire, emitting terrible roars, and frightening the little nations around its lair? The dragon watchers are beginning to suspect that, for all its size and noise, it more like an overgrown, motheaten lizard. The truth is that Red China, despite its nuclear know-how and nasty talent for trouble-making, is really a second-rate power. *Her economy is foundering; her military machine lacks firepower; her people are disillusioned. Her leaders also have an unenviable record for diplomatic blund-*

ers, economic errors, and military backdowns. Even the 700 million people in the dragon's skin are more a burden than a boon, their appetites ever outstripping their production.

Peking has issued several hundred warnings, threatening all kinds of fearful reprisals, every time an American plane or ship has strayed within sight of the Chinese mainland. But not one of the threats has been carried out. The Chinese have shouted their determination to "liberate" Quemoy, Matsu, and Formosa. Except for an occasional shelling of the two offshore islands, however, the "liberation" has been confined to loudspeaker attacks. The Chinese screamed that they "would not stand idly by" and that Americans would be "repaid in blood" if North Vietnam were attacked. Yet, when the bombs whistled down, the Chinese retaliated with more words and surreptitious support of Hanoi.

Even the 1962 Chinese invasion of India, which caught the unprepared Indian Army by surprise, shifted into reverse when India braced for war. Again in 1965, Peking served a bristling ultimatum on India to dismantle fortifications that didn't exist inside Chinese territory, then lamely pretended India had complied when the bluff didn't succeed. This became a joke among world diplomats, who have now added to their vocabulary the phrase, "as meaningless as a Chinese ultimatum."

Peking still delights in jeering at the United States as a "paper tiger," taking care to step back, of course, when the tiger bares its teeth. The world is gradually getting the idea that Communist China, if not a paper tiger, is a papier-mache dragon. *The Chinese have always been as militarily cautious as they are politically brazen. They ever probe for a weak spot, waging the small battles and avoiding the big battles they might lose, in an endless game of advance and retreat.* Their strategy is to wear down an opponent by a process as remorseless as the notorious Chinese water torture.

The backbone of Chinese military strength is sheer manpower—what Mao Tse-tung likes to call "my human atom bomb." *Red China has a standing army of 2.8 million but could mobilize an additional 10 million men in short order.* The People's Liberation Army, which takes only one in eight men of military age, is a formidable fighting force, highly trained but poorly equipped. It is best in rough terrain, where the endurance of the Chinese soldiers can overcome the mobility of a more modern and mechanized foe. Its 115 divisions are grouped into 30 field armies. "Chinese forces can be moved from area to area," a Pentagon document notes, "but there is no area defense system. The effective defense of any one area would leave many others open to attack. In general, mobility is restricted by a shortage of transport and fuel."

Although China has four armored and two airborne divisions, it lacks the airlift to move more than a couple of battalions at a time. Sums up the Pentagon report: *"The Chinese army still suffers greatly from inadequate logistic support and obsolescent equipment. Indeed, China is probably the only country in the world which is totally deprived of access to the sophisticated equipment and expertise which the world's leading military nations continue to make available to a host of lesser countries."*

Chinese factories supply the infantry with all the small arms, machine guns, grenades, mortars, and recoilless rifles they need. The munitions industry also turns out a limited production of artillery, tanks, and subsonic planes. China has an estimated 3,000 planes which, in numbers at least, makes the Chinese Air Force the world's third largest, but more than half the planes are obsolete. Even the 100 supersonic fighters and 400 supersonic bombers (purchased from Russia before 1960) are often grounded for lack of fuel and spare parts. The average Chinese pilot gets less than 10 hours flying time a month, hardly enough to maintain combat proficiency.

China also manages to keep afloat a Navy of 850 vessels, mostly patrol and gun boats. Her amphibious troop carriers, needed for any invasion of Formosa, are considered "primitive." However, the Chinese Navy reportedly has 28 submarines of which at least a few carry short-range missiles. *Moreover, missiles and nuclear weapons are being feverishly tested on the bleak, remote plateaus of Sinkiang province.* Though Chinese nuclear technology appears to be more advanced than originally thought, she is not likely to be a match for the United States or Soviet Union for years to come. "Without Russian help," an Army general told me, "China can't threaten a major war. The worst she can do is to continue stirring up limited wars on the Asian continent."

Behind their bamboo barricade, China's Red rulers keep the masses in a suffocating embrace. They are smothered with propaganda, which for awhile stirred them but now leaves them numb. The idealism sparked by early Communist oratory has changed to cynicism. Disillusion and disenchantment set in after Mao reneged on his promise of more freedom. "Let 100 flowers bloom," he proclaimed benignly in 1957. But when the flowers sprouted anti-Communist thorns, out came the sickle to hack them down and the hammer to pound them into the earth.

If the Chinese people felt they were in a straitjacket, the thongs were jerked even tighter during the terrible summer of 1966. In the name of culture, teen-age vigilantes, calling themselves Red Guards, were turned loose upon the populace to beat into submission anyone who might have strayed from the communist straight-and-narrow. For a time, it was suspected that the purges were waged behind the back of the aging and ailing Mao by rivals for his power. But most experts finally concluded that old Mao, who had been chafing over China's "bourgeois" drift, sought to rejuvenate his 40-year revolution with a new wave of terror and turmoil.

In conversations reported back to the West, he complained

that communist morale was being sapped away by pleasant dreams of good living. Intelligence reports claimed he personally set loose the Red Guards upon the privileged classes, hoping to impose a new discipline and austerity upon the work-weary, propaganda-drugged Chinese people. It was Mao's idea to leapfrog the present generation, who still have lingering memories of pre-communist times, and entrust the future of his revolution to the younger generation. Beaming blandly down upon the convulsions that wrenched China was the round, serene face of Mao Tse-tung; he emerged more than ever the Red Buddha who sees all, knows all and controls all.

China is still recovering from Mao's "great leap forward," which sent the economy reeling backward. Though the terrible starvation years won't soon be forgotten, there is now enough food in most pantries.

The drab blue work uniforms which most Chinese wear are still shabby for lack of cotton, and the little luxuries once available to consumers are almost nonexistent. Production is picking up slowly. The steel mills, copper smelters, and aluminum plants are obsolete, and the whole textile industry can only be described as antiquated. The Wuhan steel works at Hankow, for example, requires 50,000 workers to produce 3 million tons a year. A comparable American plant can produce 11 million tons with only 10,000 workers. In order to catch up, the Chinese are buying every factory they can lay their hands on from the West and are carefully reproducing them down to the last nail and rivet.

Abroad, Red China has suffered all sorts of setbacks, humiliating reverses from India to Indonesia. The Chinese cannot afford to lose much more of that most precious of Oriental commodities: face. This intangible commodity may, in the final analysis, be the most serious threat to peace in the Far East.

16

SPIES AND SPOOKS

The spies that cavort on our television screens—some performing fabulous feats of derring-do, others bungling through slapstick adventures—are not as satirical as they seem. They have their counterparts in real life; for the James Bond industry is every bit as fantastic as the TV script writers have portrayed it. The cloak-and-dagger crowd get involved in some unbelievable situations, sometimes hilarious, more often deadly grim.

The Central Intelligence Agency, the most lampooned of all spy outfits, deals in operations so secret that its waste paper is classified. Yet it receives more publicity than government agencies that advertize. Even such a routine matter as recruiting a new spy has wound up as an international incident splashed across the world's front pages. The applicant was interviewed in a dingy Singapore hotel by an agent who flew all the way from Tokyo with his trusty lie detector. When he plugged in the machine, unhappily, it blew out all the lights in the hotel.

The indignant authorities caught the CIA agent and an accomplice red-handed. They were dumped unceremoniously in a Singapore clink. The CIA tried to bail them out by offering to increase American aid to Singapore. They were freed only after a formal apology from Secretary of State Dean Rusk. Later, Singapore's Premier Lee Kuan Yew, to prove his anti-Americanism, divulged the whole episode to the press. He had been insulted by a paltry $3.3 million economic bribe, he complained, when he had demanded $33 million.

There is also the case of the CIA's high-soaring camera-carrying U-2 plane which came down in the middle of Russia with an embarrassing crash. All traces of identification had been carefully painted out, but at the controls sat an all-American pilot. This celebrated forced landing has been ascribed to a well-placed Russian rocket burst, but the explanation wasn't sufficiently devious to satisfy the conspiratorial-minded folks at the CIA.

It was solemnly explained to me that Soviet agents had sneaked into the secret U-2 compound at Adana, Turkey, and had planted electronic gadgets on the plane. One device supposedly broadcast the spy plane's progress to Russian tracking stations. The other, more diabolically complex, was an electronic booby-trap that could be triggered from the ground. It was rigged to cause an explosion too small to destroy the plane, so the story goes, but damaging enough to knock it out of commission.

But the blunder of all blunders was the Bay of Pigs invasion. The New York Times quoted the late President Kennedy as declaring afterward that he "wanted to splinter the CIA in a thousand pieces and scatter it to the winds." When he cooled down, Kennedy called in White House adviser Clark Clifford, who had drafted the legislation establishing the CIA. Clifford told me he remembers the late President's words vividly. "I made some bad decisions on the Bay of Pigs," said Kennedy. "I made these bad decisions because I had bad information. My information was bad, because our intelligence was poor. Something is gravely wrong inside the CIA, and I intend to find out what it is. I cannot afford another Bay of Pigs."

Kennedy appointed a civilian advisory board, which Clifford now heads. It has recommended a great many reforms which have been instituted in the past few years. Clifford is now convinced that the CIA is not only an efficient but an essential organization. In the nuclear age, the CIA has become our first line of defense. If some agents have been fools, others have been unsung heroes whose deeds surpass the most valorous in our history yet must remain unrecorded. *Those who have been caught have been subjected to the most skillful type of torture that the human mind has devised. Only after they have been reduced to zombies, more dead than alive, the last fragment of information extracted from them, have they been allowed to die.*

Traditionally, spying has been a warm-blooded business, specializing in torrid boudoir romance, violent death on fog-sheathed waterfronts, low treachery and high courage. To these has been added another, more coldly effective ingredient: science. Both sides have listening devices so sensitive that they can pick up indoor conversations by recording the window vibrations. *Today an expert can transform a building's entire electrical wiring system into a transmitter that will permit eavesdroppers to tune into any conversation in the building.* On a global scale, we have equipment that can monitor the conversation between a pilot and tower in the middle of Russia or intercept a conversation between Moscow and a Soviet sub on the other side of the world. From 100 miles up, our satellites can photograph every Soviet missile whose snout is poked above the ground. The enlargements are so detailed that an expert could locate ex-President Eisenhower's golf ball on the Gettysburg green.

The world's most tangled espionage web has the Kremlin at its center. The Soviet spy system is in effect a dizzy geometric design of spy rings within spy rings. In this country, the Russian network includes imported spies who hide their activities behind diplomatic immunity, home-grown spies who sell out their country for a foreign ideology, refugees who steal information for the sake of relatives behind the Iron Curtain. Anyone is recruited who can be blackmailed or bullied into furnishing information.

Elsewhere, Russia uses the shotgun approach; her agents,

for example, literally riddle Western Europe. They are drawn from every walk of life. The dazzling mademoiselle at an embassy party may be a secret Mata Hari. Just as likely, the garbage collector who carts off the discarded caviar next morning is a Red agent. Some are bribed, some blackmailed, some enticed into service. There are fanatics who carry out their orders with religious dedication, adventurers who simply enjoy intrigue. Others peddle information for profit, often working both sides of the Iron Curtain.

One enterprising undercover man sent simultaneous reports to Soviet intelligence from Bonn and to American intelligence from Budapest. To the amazement of both sides, he was picked up in a raid on a Vienna bordello. He had been culling the facts for his "secret" reports from newspapers which were found stacked in his room.

Except for the elite "class five" agents, Russia's spies are widely recruited, hastily trained, and often easily caught. Typical is the case of Janos Bela Szakacs, who escaped to this country from Hungary. He confessed to the Justice Department that he had spied for the Reds in return for his release from a Hungarian prison. His first assignment was to deliver a sum of money to a mysterious woman, one Madeleine Honig, at a Paris rendezvous. He was promptly arrested by German authorities but managed to destroy incriminating evidence. Later the Russians sent him back to France; he was apprehended again, this time by the American military authorities.

But the Russians, far from dismayed over such arrests, probably planned it that way. Small-fry operatives like Szakacs keep our counter-espionage people so busy that they have less time to go after the real professionals—the "class five" agents who operate so stealthily and so skillfully that they have been known to deceive their own families. *Some are "sleepers" in our midst, who spend years leading ordinary lives, taking no part in suspicious activities, until they have worked their way into a position to help the Kremlin.*

Our pursuing counter-intelligence agents are not unlike blood hounds who know they are supposed to follow a scent but aren't sure what the quarry smells like. The trend in Soviet espionage has been away from known communists. Even the slightest taint of pink is now considered a handicap for a professional spy. One who came over to our side reports he was once reprimanded by his superiors for buying a left-wing magazine at a news stand.

Deep in the Soviet soul is a passion for drama, and nowhere does it find better expression than in the cloak-and-dagger business. The Russians arrange their trysts with all the imagination of a Hollywood director planning a scene for a grade B thriller.

Take the case of Aleksandr Kovalev, an assistant Soviet naval attache who set out to subvert an American officer. The spy chose Lafayette Park, across the street from the White House, as the setting for their meetings. To add to the drama, the American was instructed to carry a copy of "Redbook" magazine under his arm. He stood around looking mysterious until Kovalev strolled up and asked for a match. At this recognition signal, the two moved off together like heavies in a movie and, appropriately, were filmed by FBI cameramen.

But the plot was only the beginning. Kovalev, presumably feeling nervous under the nose of the President, directed the American to drive to New York City and carry out another elaborate rigmarole. The prospective traitor was to park his car in a pre-arranged place and leave microfilms of a Navy manual in a red package visible through the rear window. Kovalev would pick up the package and give a "receipt" by making a code mark on the telephone directory of an uptown restaurant. The conspiratorial Russian continued to star in the FBI's secret films for two years before his usefulness was exhausted and the State Department declared him persona non grata.

Yuri Novikov, another Soviet diplomat, made even more dramatic arrangements for his meeting with an Air Force officer who had been sent to him by Red agents in Vienna. The officer was told to dress in civilian clothes, wear a snap-brim hat low over his eyes, carry a rolled newspaper under his left arm and hold his right glove in his left hand. Place of the rendezvous: the base of the Washington monument. This was followed by nine more melodramatic meetings, all filmed by the FBI, before Novikov was ordered out of the country.

The Soviets, who in real life often follow the script of the James Bond movie "From Russia With Love," mix sex with their espionage. On the Soviet payroll are many beautiful, unscrupulous women who extract secrets between kisses. One bejeweled beauty, Irmgard Margareth-Schwidt, wooed her way into the confidence of top American intelligence officers in Germany. At one time she managed to keep up a romance with an Air Force colonel and an American civilian at the same time with neither man knowing about the other. She succeeded in getting from them the Western defense plans for West Berlin.

Buxom, blonde Margarethe Pfeiffer, an ex-model who graduated from a communist spy school in Thuringia, Czechoslovakia, practiced her wiles on enlisted men. She was caught after she picked on the wrong GI: Private Robert Eicher, who turned her in after she asked him for one of the Army's secret infra-red tank telescopes. Charged the West German police: "She devoted much energy and time trying to seduce American soldiers and luring them into her net." In South Korea a languid beauty named Kim Soo became the mistress of an American colonel. She not only slipped secrets out, but smuggled her communist husband into the Colonel's home.

[illegible] TO
THE SECRETARY OF STATE
[illegible] D. C.

DEPARTMENT OF STATE
WASHINGTON

July 19, 1960.

My dear Clare,

It is with pleasure that I inform you that your report on the Congo created a most favorable impression here, including the Secretary of State and the President. I share their opinion and hope that your work in Africa will continue to be as successful as it was in the beginning. Concerning your suggestions, all of them were agreed upon with the exception of several minor items which you should have received by the time this letter reaches you.

Although I am fully convinced that you are aware of the seriousness of the situation and have familiarized yourself with all our instructions, I take this opportunity in an unofficial capacity to remind you of the necessity to be as careful as only you can be and tender some friendly advice.

Limit your contacts with Lumumba's political opponents to a minimum, especially with Tshombe's people, although they should not be discontinued for even a moment. We of course are certain that after what he received in Washington, Tshombe will not go back on us, at least of his own free will. God only knows what these blacks are likely to do. It would be difficult to find more mercenary creatures in the whole world! At present, we here do not envisage a more suitable candidate for the post of Prime Minister of the Republic of Congo. At present he seems to be the only suitable replacement for the high-handed postal clerk who stands on the pedestal as the "Liberator of the Congo".

It is desirable that you choose more or less stable candidates for the posts of Tshombe's republican cabinet. However, he has his own ideas on this matter which he sent us a week ago with a postscript indicating that the duplicate had been sent to you. I do not think it expedient that we follow his advice on this matter. I recommend that you should see to it that at a decisive moment Tshombe's government could at once begin functioning effectively.

Best wishes for your continued success. I will only be too glad to hear from you in both an official and private capacity.

Sincerely yours,
Douglas Dillon

His Excellency
Mr. Clare H. Timberlake,
Ambassador of the United States of America,
Leopoldville.

An example of Communist forgery exposed by the Central Intelligence Agency. Copies of this faked letter were used to undermine American policies regarding new African nations.

But the most celebrated case is that of the girl with the alluring telephone voice, Urszula Discher, who caused the downfall of the first American foreign service officer ever caught in a treasonable act. For giving secret documents to the Polish communists, Irvin Scarbeck was rushed to trial and sentenced to 30 years in jail. He was quietly released in May, 1966, after serving two years of his sentence. Scarbeck's attorneys have given me some ironic facts about the case which didn't come out at the trial.

When Scarbeck first arrived in Warsaw, it turns out, he was specifically warned to beware of phone calls from strange women. It was a favorite approach used by lady spies. But he took precisely such a phone call one night when he was working alone at the American Embassy. It was a woman's voice—a rich, whispery voice—and Scarbeck was hooked. He met her on a nearby street corner and began a 14-month romance which ended in tragedy. On December 22, 1960, four Communist agents broke into Urszula's Warsaw apartment and photographed her and Scarbeck together in bed. When the Polish Reds threatened to jail her on charges of being an unregistered prostitute, he caved in and began giving classified information to save her.

Scarbeck still refused to believe that Urszula was a Polish agent who had deliberately trapped him. After he traded more secrets for an exit permit for her, she flew ahead of him to West Germany and went straight to a boarding house which was used by Red agents as a secret rendezvous. Microphones planted in Scarbeck's office by two American counter spies helped produce enough information to put him under arrest. He testified at the trial that he had betrayed his country only to help Urszula escape from Poland. Yet shortly after the trial, she quietly returned to Warsaw.

Soviet agents gather their information from a thousand sources in a thousand ways. *They pick up vast amounts in this country without violating our espionage laws, simply by a careful checking of our scientific and business publications.* They attend conventions of such vital industries as aeronautics and electronics. Consider the case of two Soviet citizens who turned up at an electrical convention in Los Angeles. They collected such a vast amount of literature that they had to check some of it with a hat-check girl while they went back for more. They finally departed with an estimated 250 pounds of technical publications. An assistant attache at the Russian Embassy purchased "The Pilots Handbook" for the East and West coasts. Two days later a chauffeur for the Soviet Air Attache bought "The Pilots Handbook" for Canada and Alaska. These books contain diagrams for all the principal airfields and approaches.

Russia's mass espionage effort dredges up tons of raw information. "I would guess 90 percent of it is worthless," estimates an American official. "But it's the remaining 10 percent that worries us." Soviet agents regularly visit the Patent Office, which publishes invention blueprints, and the Interior Department, which publishes maps. Large-scale purchases are made by the Four Continent Book Club, a New Cork group which fronts for the Soviets.

Back in 1961 two Soviet diplomats, Sergei N. Stupar and Aleksandr N. Izvekov, started attending the monthly meetings of the American Society for Metals. They struck up a friendship with John Huminik, a sprightly young scientist of Russian ancestry, who was working on a highly secret study of rocket motor failures. The two Russians eventually got around to asking him for unclassified but hard-to-get materials. Huminik discreetly checked with the FBI which encouraged him to string the Russians along.

Thus began a spy saga that was to last five years. When Stupar was recalled to Moscow in 1964, he lugged a going-away gift from Huminik, several pounds of rare chemicals, in a diplomatic pouch. From a handy hiding place, FBI agents filmed the goodbye scene. Stupar's place was taken by Vladimir P. Boutenko, an assistant commercial counselor, who was accompanied by Vladimir M. Zorov. It was Boutenko who first hinted, over hamburgers at a Hot Shoppe drive-in, that "our country is willing to pay for certain kinds of information." He requested copies of the various forms an applicant must fill out to get a government job, useful for planting Soviet agents inside the government. After clearing with the FBI, Huminik delivered the documents. But he still received nothing more than incidental gifts from the Russians.

Then, unexpectedly, another Soviet diplomat, Valentin A. Revin, telephoned "greetings from Dr. Stupar in Moscow." At a subsequent meeting he also brought a gift from Stupar, an expensive, intricately designed black jewelry box. In his next move Valentin offered cash for secrets. He handed Huminik a roll of $20 bills and instructed him to buy a Contaflex Zeiss camera. Huminik spent many nights photographing "doctored" documents for the Soviets. Usually he would walk with the film to a drug store, browse through the magazines until Revin showed up. Then Huminik would leave and Revin unobtrusively would follow. When they reached a dark spot, Revin would catch up, and Huminik would slip him the films. The Russian paid him several thousand dollars, which he turned over to the FBI. In return, Hoover's agents gave Huminik bare expense money, carefully counted out to the last penny, for which he signed receipts with a code name.

Huminik submitted regular reports to the FBI in handwriting. He kept no copies because he was warned that the Russians might "bomb" him—which, in spy parlance, means search his home for evidence that he might be a double agent. Recently I managed to obtain access to these reports.

Of Revin, Huminik wrote: "Would move faster with me but his boss would scorch him good if I turn out to be an agent of some kind. He probably feels that I am a big catch and would build his career considerably. I am probably the most important contact he has ever tried to recruit. His technical knowledge is a little weak, and I would expect that he does not like to be wrong in class and was very cocky when he came out with a good answer.

"He is punctual in his activities and would like to discuss things for a longer time period when he meets me, but his associate is waiting for him. He has a knowledge of photography, probably likes to bowl. He likes to travel and see the sights of this country. He likes American women and would welcome an affair briefly if he could get away with it. He probably enjoys his work and thinks he is good at it and feels if he converts me, he will be well on his way . . .

"He will no doubt try and find a weakness in me to blackmail me into continuing to work for him, because he knows that if I feel it's getting dangerous, I will quit and he must keep me going. He wants to know where I travel so that he can keep some kind of record and perhaps have me perform tasks in other cities."

The Russians, ever suspicious, kept grilling Huminik to see if they could trip him up. The G-men guiding Huminik from behind the scenes asked him to report his feelings. "I am tense for at least a day after the meetings," he wrote, "trying to recount all comments in terms of all meetings before . . . I know that the debriefing is not complete. I am forgetting some of the conversations and then recalling it a week later. With the kind of third degree I have been getting lately, I wonder if I can keep walking on this wire for much longer. Then I think that I must exert all effort to wreck some segment of the activities they engage in."

If Revin had any ideas about blackmailing Huminik, the thought also had occurred to Huminik. He proposed to the FBI that an attempt be made to recruit Revin. "To defect him is probably not possible but to blackmail him into some safe cooperative situation is possible if it is handled correctly," he suggested. "We must not be lazy about the preparations so that all of this effort to date will have been worthwhile. If we have to keep him on the hook for another few months to finish preparations, then it must be done. The reward will be great if he will cooperate . . .

"I must assure him that no one else but a high official will know of his cooperation—his name will never be used. We will give him a code name. He will meet with no one but me (at least for a time). . . .

"To get him to cooperate we must show him physical evidence which will convince him that embarrassment to him will be so great that his inability or unwillingness to cooperate will totally ruin his image and will embarrass his government to such a degree that the President of the USSR will consider him like the plague. This is the key and this is where we must not be lazy in preparations.

"This evidence must be newspaper proofs showing his espionage activities with pictures and captions which are embarrassing to him. He must be called a blundering spy playing into the hands of the Americans.

"The evidence must appear as if ready for immediate press release and in fact, we must be ready with something for the press in case he does not go."

While the FBI pondered this plan, it was working with another double agent, Frank J. Mrkva, a State Department courier of Czech ancestry, who had been approached by Czech diplomat Zdenek Pisk in 1961. A replacement, Jiri Opatrny, paid Mrkva $3,440 for a series of FBI-cleared documents. Mrkva's last assignment: to plant a listening device in the office of a high State Department official.

At the same time, the FBI had been keeping William Whalen, a puffy, shambling retired Army colonel, under surveillance. After his retirement, he had been reduced to taking a $1.79-an-hour job as a park-litter picker and tree-man for the Fairfax County Park Authority in Virginia. Allegedly, however, he supplemented his income by spying for the Russians.

Suddenly in July, 1966, J. Edgar Hoover was confronted with the greatest crisis in his 42 years of matchless press relations as FBI Director. The Supreme Court had demanded full details on the bugging of Washington lobbyist Fred Black's hotel suite. Over Hoover's bitter protests, then-Attorney General Nicholas Katzenbach submitted a memo to the Supreme Court, naming Hoover as the official who directly authorized the bugging, also acknowledging that the FBI had engaged in additional eavesdropping "in the interest of internal security or national safety." In all cases, Hoover had approved the wiretaps under loose authority from successive Attorneys General.

The day this memo was prepared, July 12, 1966, Hoover abruptly ordered Whalen's arrest, though the case had dragged on for seven years and the FBI had obtained 12 signed statements from Whalen 22 months previously. The next day, when the embarrassing memo to the Supreme Court was made public, Hoover broke the Mrkva case. The spy headlines dominated the news, all but smothering the unfavorable publicity.

At the same time, Hoover also sought to break the Huminik case; a July 11th memo to the Attorney General suggested closing the case. But a July 27th memo urged a delay to attempt Huminik's plan. The double agent was encouraged to feel out the possibility of blackjacking Revin into defecting. At his next meetings with the Russians, Huminik pretended to be frightened over Whalen's arrest. "I don't want to be another Colonel Whalen," he told Revin firmly.

Elaborate new precautions were taken. First, a gum signal was worked out. In case either became aware of danger, he would stick a wad of gum on a specified mail box. Both would inspect the mail box every day for gum. Revin also agreed to forge phony papers for Huminik in case he had to flee the country. A Dominican passport was chosen, and Huminik flew to the Dominican Republic to get authentic passport pictures taken.

Though the FBI's Soviet section was anxious to get the forged papers from Huminik and to reverse the play on Revin in a maneuver to persuade him to defect, someone on high abruptly blew the whistle on the case on September 3. Revin was thrown out of the country—though Boutenko, who had also obtained documents from Huminik, was permitted to remain.

Huminik simmered for a while, then angrily wrote the FBI on September 11: "I get a telephone call which, in effect, says there will not be any drop on the 20th of September, no new passports, no chance to see if Valetin will work for us; only a guillotine end to all the work we put into this thing. I would not have been as disturbed if we tried to defect him and failed, or if I had been consulted about the required rapid ending.

"I do feel that after working at this thing as intensely and with all sincerity as I have, that some last comment would have been sought . . . For example, I could have immediately sought Valentin and suggested that we have a serious discussion regarding his career; and if for the smallest reason he would have cooperated, then we would have helped tighten our overall security tremendously. If for some political reason it was necessary to throw someone out, then perhaps another Russian could have been selected for a trip home."

It can only be speculated whether the country would have gained from prolonging these spy cases. But for J. Edgar Hoover the rash of stories produced a publicity triumph, reassuring the nation of his prowess at an awkward time for him.

The security problem is worse in spy-infested Europe. Our bombs and warheads are kept in scattered stockpiles at the

I am tense for at least a day after the meeting — trying to recount all comments in terms of all meetings before — years before. I know that there must be "trip" reports on every contact I had ever had with any of them.

I know that if we succeed in trapping them they are going to be very mad because of the similarity to a previous ASM. Chaining, and I would not be welcome in the USSR.

I believe that I spend quite a lot of time thinking about the situation and should write down these thoughts and pass them down for analysis. I know that the debriefing is not complete, I am forgetting some of the conversation and then recalling it a week later. With the kind of 3rd degree I have been getting lately I wonder if I can keep walking on this wire for much longer then I think that I must exert all effort to wreck some segment of the activities they engage in. I dont feel that I am so much a patriot that I do it for the count

A portion of the report double agent John Huminik gave to the Federal Bureau of Investigation. As a result of his revelations Russian diplomat Valentin A. Revin was expelled from the U.S.

mercy of friendly but foreign governments, located in some areas where every fifth pair of eyes belongs to a communist. The move was a calculated gamble. We have built up enough nuclear power in Europe to reduce Russia to radioactive rubble. This should discourage the Soviets ever from overshooting Europe and striking only American targets. They must knock out all our retaliatory forces, as the Japanese tried to do at Pearl Harbor, or we would bounce back with devastating counter-attacks. Our atomic bases in Europe multiply the number of Pearl Harbors the Russians must destroy.

By law, we can't even show our allies the nuclear weapons they permit us to keep on their soil. We equip their planes with "atomic kits" (A-bomb racks complete with electrical connections); we also train their crews to handle the weapons. To all but our own select crews, however, the actual bombs and warheads remain invisible. But a high Defense Department officer recently confessed to me: "Let's not kid ourselves. These governments know where our nuclear fireworks are hidden. They may not know the exact buildings, but they know the locations." The security problem boils down to one key question: can we trust our allies? At least one top American thinks not. "Information we give our allies," he claimed, "has a habit of leaking to the Reds."

To keep these stockpiles secure, we continually rotate them. We might ship some atomic warheads, say from Point A to Point B. Before they reach B, secret orders may be flashed to shift them instead to Point C.

"We never leave nuclear weapons in one place for long," explained an official. "We assume every hiding place will eventually be discovered. By shifting and shuttling, we hope to keep a few days ahead of the communists." All atomic documents are classified "For U. S. Eyes Only." Then only officers with an absolute need to know are given atomic information. Thereafter, they are carefully watched and their travel is restricted. They aren't even permitted to visit Yugoslavia, a friendly but communist country.

Nevertheless, there is uncomfortable evidence that the communists have cracked the security of our North Atlantic alliance. Not long ago a courier left Paris for Bonn with a padlocked brief case chained to his wrist. It contained the secret military "force levels" NATO had assigned to West Germany. Before he reached Bonn, the Reds tauntingly broadcast the exact figures. Swiss authorities trapped a notorious Red spy known to the West only as "Lucy." He turned out to be Rudolf Roessler, a Czech communist, who had used Switzerland as a "mail drop" for stolen documents. His Swiss contact, Dr. Xavier Schnieper, confessed they had smuggled 160 secret NATO reports behind the iron curtain.

Unfortunately, these are not isolated cases. *Europe is crawling with spies, who breed on the international friction caused by two hostile worlds rubbing together.* They may be tipsters who trade in tidbits or "class five" agents; but if they work for the Russian ruble, they're after our atomic secrets. The main Soviet espionage base in Western Europe, of course, is the Communist Party. In each country, the party dispenses politics and propaganda out of the front office, conducts espionage in the basement. The underground machinery is run by doctrinaire communists who take their orders from Moscow. For eyes and ears they use party members scattered from the top of Norway to the tip of Italy.

Another source of spies are Iron Curtain refugees who have fled from Red tyranny. Coercion and blackmail are favorite Red recruiting techniques. One French operative, Mme. Raymonde Douhine, became a double agent for the Czech Secret Service for the sake of her husband and son in Czechoslovakia. In Hungary, two French embassy officials,

Jean Philip and Roger Dubois, chose to spy for the Reds rather than go to jail for smuggling. Usually a coerced spy is required to sign a formal contract with Russia. This contains an ominous clause warning that he is subject to Soviet military law and can be punished accordingly. The contract also stipulates that he must keep his activities strictly secret from family and friends.

The Soviet shotgun system has pumped so many spies into Western Europe that allied intelligence can't possibly cope with them all. For each one caught, a dozen more are turned loose in the NATO community. Some are graduated from quickie "spy schools" behind the Iron Curtain. Others get no training beyond their secret instructions. But what they lack in finesse, they make up in sheer numbers. Russia holds a mortgage on so many prying eyes that they are bound to see something.

Although Soviet spies have suffered less public humiliation than the CIA, they have had their Waterloos. Our agents still chuckle over Kalman Gabris, an American-employed janitor in Vienna, who rummaged through wastebaskets for discarded secrets. Unhappily for the communist cause, he had one glaring deficiency: he couldn't read English. He filched many a crumpled document that looked important but contained nothing more vital than the latest directive on coffee breaks. Eventually Gabris was caught with his hand in the wastebasket. A six-man surveillance team began watching his movements. On Saturdays he would sneak off to the border town of Schattendorf, cross into communist Hungary, and turn his wadded wastepaper over to a Red major named Gyorgy Csergo.

For a while the agents planned phony documents in the wastebaskets. Their final note was stamped "Top Secret" and burned around the edges to make sure it would catch Gabris' eye. *"Dear Maj. Gyorgy Csergo," it read. "The boys you send over here are an impossible bunch of stumble bums. I am proposing a gentleman's agreement. Since most of the information you want is available in our daily newspaper, I will enter a subscription for you if you agree to send over no more drunks, half wits, or juvenile delinquents. This offer may win you a promotion, the Order of the Red Flannels and an eventual vacation trip to Siberia."* Gabris dutifully plucked the singed letter from the trash and delivered it behind the Iron Curtain. He never came back.

Russian agents in this country are often heavy-handed and thick-tongued. They seem to be fascinated, for instance, with the name "George." Leonid Pivnev, an assistant air attache, said "just call me George" when he approached a Virginia photographer to make aerial maps of Chicago. The fact that he didn't sound a bit like "George" with his thick Russian accent served, of course, to arouse the photographer's suspicions. Later "George" gave himself the surname "Tinney" in an attempt to obtain a Washington business address as a mail drop. Pivnev never got his photographs of Chicago, but the FBI took his photograph.

Four years later another man called "George" was still trying to get aerial photographs of Chicago. His real name: Kirill Doronkin, a Russian UN employee. The informant he picked happened to tip off the FBI. At their rendezvous in a parking lot outside the Scarsdale, N. Y., railroad station, Doronkin showed up with his wife. She strolled around looking about as casual as Mata Hari while the contact was made.

Soviet fascination with Chicago is puzzling. Probably no other American city is more open, more photographed, more flown over. The Russians can buy all the city maps, aerial views and picture postcards they want without risking a single spy.

Still another "George," better known around the UN as Vadim Kirilyuk, tried to subvert an American student who had applied for a Soviet scholarship. He urged the young man to use his knowledge of cryptography to get a Pentagon or CIA job and pass on information. Explained friendly, reliable George: "You would have more to offer us by way of cultural exchange. Education in our country is a serious matter, not like in the United States. Persons must undergo severe tests to gain admission to our universities. This is your test."

The Russians show little discrimination in making contacts. Example: a Soviet first secretary held 15 meetings with Roger Foss, a henchman of the self-styled, crackpot American Fuehrer, George Lincoln Rockwell. They show even less finesse. They choose obscure little restaurants (although they would be far less conspicuous in a crowded place) and invariably ply their victims with liquor to loosen secrets.

One American double agent informed me about meeting a Russian for cocktails. Typically, the Russian arrived early and ordered martinis. When the time came for a new round, he took elaborate pains to point to his glass and ask for another of the same. "I've spiked the drinks of too many girls to be caught by that old trick," the agent told me. "When he wasn't looking, I sniffed his glass. He was drinking sauterne with a twist of lemon peel, which looks like a martini but lacks the knockout punch." Another time, they met at the Red Fox in Middleburg, Virginia, in the hunt country. Not only was the Russian's accent more conspicuous in this setting, but the Inn served only wine and beer. Undaunted, he produced a couple of pints of vodka from his car. His strategy backfired; the American made sure they both drank from the same bottle; the Russian got drunk and ran through three red lights driving back to Washington.

Perhaps the most amusing story is that of the U. S. double agent who was invited to a Russian's apartment for a cozy dinner. They hadn't gotten past the soup before the American spotted two out-size brogans sticking out under the floor-length window draperies. "They were flap-over, button-down shoes like granddad used to wear," chuckled the American. "You couldn't miss them. As the evening wore on, the man behind the curtain became hot and tired. In the end he was panting so loudly he could be heard across the room."

On an espionage mission, a Russian will almost never follow a straight line from point A to B. He invariably takes a devious, twisting, tortuous route—a useless waste of time for both shadowed and shadowers. It is almost impossible to shake the FBI, which will use a squad of men and a fleet of automobiles to keep one man under surveillance. A favorite Soviet trick is to duck into a crowded department store, ride up and down the escalators and try to get lost among the hustle of shoppers. But while the Russian is wearing himself out inside the store, the FBI patiently watches every exit and quietly resumes the tail when he emerges.

One Soviet operative arranged a tryst in a cheap dive near the Baltimore railroad station, less than an hour's train ride from Washington. Although the appointed hour was 7:15 p.m., the Russian set out for Baltimore at 9 a.m. He wandered around Washington, ducking in and out of eateries and art galleries, ordering ham and eggs at five different luncheon counters, until 3 p.m. Then he caught the train to Baltimore where he repeated the same pattern. "If only they would go directly to their appointments," complained a G-man wearily. "It would save us all a lot of trouble."

Moreover, the Russians are surprisingly inept at shadowing people. "Even the most rank amateur would know he was being tailed after the first block," says one who has been followed. The Soviet gumshoes are almost always grim, glum, plodding characters in blue serge suits. Sometimes the Russians will follow a man on foot by automobile, driving a few paces behind in slow, grinding gear. "They are so obvious it becomes embarrassing," an American told me. "You are not only aware of their presence but soon discover that the trailers are themselves being trailed by another set of snoopers."

Some Soviet spies have a careless habit of turning up in different disguises. One who appeared at a Washington cocktail party in Army uniform forgetfully showed up next time in a Navy uniform. Such a man of multiple identities was M. I. Krievashekov, a lowly Russian interpreter, whom the Americans at the UN nicknamed "Baby Face" because of his blond, blue-eyed, guileless face. But the FBI had seen the same unmistakably baby face elsewhere, once as a Red Army officer, another time as a Naval officer. Naturally the FBI tightened its surveillance. "Baby Face" evidently realized he was being watched; he suddenly disappeared from the United Nations without bothering to turn in his credentials.

It is typical of Soviet spies to pose as lowly flunkies. They are treated with such deference by their supposed superiors, however, that their status becomes painfully evident. A favorite front is that of chauffeur. One who was kicked out of the country for spying was Vassili Molev, who also put in time as custodian in the Soviet Embassy. He contacted an American undercover man the first Tuesday of each month on New York City's West 58th Street with all the usual mystery and drama. For his pains, he was declared persona non grata by the U. S.

The Communist spy apparatus, like the octopus it resembles, is bound to pick up some secrets with all its weaving, twisting, slippery arms. In the hands of a professional, seemingly unrelated facts can be woven into a clear picture. Our own operatives are equally expert at piecing together an intelligence jigsaw. They pay particular attention to economic activity. We know Russia cannot start World War III without shifting industrial gears several weeks in advance. Generally our espionage network behind the Iron Curtain is dependable enough to prevent surprises.

Communist espionage has been livened in recent years by the appearance of Chinese spy rings in the shadowy world of intelligence. In their effort to take over the leadership of the world communist movement from the Russians, the Chinese are creating rival espionage rings, front groups, and guerrilla uprisings—as well as stirring up their own separate trouble in Africa, Asia and Latin America. Sometimes the rival spy rings inform on one another; more often, they merely add to the West's headaches.

I recently stumbled upon a typical Red Chinese spy set-up in Mexico. It was run by a Chinese master spy, Wu Chu, who had gained admittance to Mexico as a correspondent. In a matter of months he built up a formidable underground that began smuggling dope into the U. S. and defense secrets out. In the hot border town of Mexicali he took over a sleazy gambling joint and turned it into a sinister spy trap. To operate it, he sent in Francisco Ham-cheen, Jr., a darkly handsome fellow who could pass for a Mexican but is actually Chinese. Planted on the U. S. back door stoop, he was assigned to pry open the door.

The Red Chinese have sought for years to infiltrate Mexico. The Mexico-U.S. border plunges for hundreds of miles across desolate, broken country—difficult to patrol, ideal terrain for international hide-and-seek. Wu Chu, a slender, slippery sort with shifty eyes, a pointed chin and black hair tinged with gray, came to Mexico from Cuba. He was usually seen in baggy tweeds, though he had more than enough pesos to keep pressed and pomaded. But he disbursed his funds with greater political effect for gifts and parties.

Wu was Mao Tse-tung's man in Havana—a backstage boss with authority far beyond his credentials—until he wangled Mexican accreditation as a correspondent. Though he ostensibly ran a small news bureau in Mexico City, Red China's visiting trade and cultural missions always checked in with him and cleared appointments through him. *The ex-*

planation: this strange man was a lieutenant colonel in the Chinese Communist secret police.

Francisco Ham-cheen, who took his orders from Wu, was a different sort. Hale and handsome, he came to Mexico as a student in 1942 and quickly acquired a Latin flamboyance. In 1957 he returned to the Chinese mainland for six months training as a spy and agitator. On his return to Mexico he was jailed briefly as a Communist party organizer. He slipped into the U. S. in 1958, reportedly hid out at a Chinese restaurant in New York, though the owners denied knowing him. After immigration agents picked him up for questioning in 1959, he returned to Mexico City to become caterer for a Chinese gambling house frequented by Communists and leftists. Through Mexican officials, I found a record of his registration as an alien—identification card No. FM 2-47774. The U.S. Narcotics Bureau has in its files a confidential report stating that he was getting heroin from Red China through associates in Hong Kong. My own sources said Colonel Wu sent Francisco to open a gambling dive in Mexicali, an ideal spot for trafficking in spies or drugs.

American tourists and servicemen who pour across the border every night for "kicks" provide a protective cover for the movement of agents across the border. A heavy loser would find friendly Francisco willing to excuse his debt in exchange for a small favor. If he came back to gamble again, the favors became more exacting. A businessman induced to taste of the other excitements Mexicali had to offer—and Francisco knew them all—would find himself being blackmailed. Once ensnared, the victim usually was drawn deeper into the web. The technique is as old as espionage.

Francisco was so successful in making American contacts that he brazenly traveled to Peking in 1964 for the 15th anniversary of the Chinese Communist revolution by way of the U. S. He managed to get papers that let him slip past immigration controls and fly to the Far East from California. A passenger on the same plane reported that Francisco stopped in Honolulu, ultimately landed in Hong Kong. Other sources traced his movements to Macao, then through the Bamboo Curtain to Canton and Peking.

Shortly after Francisco's stopover in Honolulu, by a curious coincidence, an American airman was transferred from Hawaii back to the mainland. He immediately wrote a letter to Mao's master spy, Wu Chu, giving his new location. Through confidential anti-communist contacts in Mexico's Chinese community, who were reading and photographing Wu's mail before he got it, I obtained a copy of the strange letter. In careful language, the letter inquired about Wu's assistant, Cheng Pien. It read:

"I recently learned that a gentleman, Mr. Cheng Pien, who I heard a great deal of while in Hawaii, has been assigned to your staff.

"Since Mr. Pien's reporting and research for your News Bureau includes much that I am familiar with, and since I am so close at this time, I thought perhaps if he would visit me here to write me, we could very well co-operate to a suitable advantage to both of us and all concerned. (The airman then gave his new Air Force assignment and U. S. address.)

"My mutual interest in Mr. Pien's research would be in the field of philosophy and history of the Oriental in Western culture. My regards also to Ya Lou and his prediction of May 1958."

I turned copies of the letter over to the FBI and the Air Force. The airman was placed under secret surveillance. He turned out to be a clerk in the public information office at Chanute Air Force Base, Illinois. Airman First Class Joe Krzympiec, in his late 30s, was surprised when at last he was called in for questioning and confronted with his letter to Wu Chu. At first, Krzympiec claimed he had only read the names of Wu and Cheng in a newspaper. Finally, he admitted he knew they were spies, but said he was hoping to win their confidence to aid the U. S. Of the "Ya Lou prediction" reference, the airman explained he was referring to a statement by Chinese General Liu Ya-lou that his country would explode an A-bomb.

Air Force intelligence officers could find no evidence that Krzympiec, son of Russian immigrants, had ever engaged in espionage. He had no access to secret information. Associates described him as moody and mixed-up. After mental observation in a hospital, he was quietly discharged from the Air Force "for the good of the service."

As for Wu Chu, Peking made hasty changes in spy assignments, and he left in a hurry for London. His place in Mexico City was taken over by a wily Cantonese called Wu Chi-gan, who arrived from Chile. Today, Red Chinese espionage continues to thrive in Mexico.

Peking has only a handful of agents in the United States. A few rabid Communists have split off from the American Communist Party into dissident groups that look to Peking for inspiration. So far, however, they haven't been whipped into a united, disciplined underground.

One of these groups is the Progressive Labor Movement, which calls itself "Marxist-Leninist" rather than Communist and reportedly has a membership of approximately 1,000. Its leaders are Milton Rosen and Mort Scheer, both of whom were expelled from the orthodox Communist Party for endorsing Mao's views. However, they maintain they have no affiliation with China. According to Rosen and Scheer, most of the membership is younger than 40. Many are college students, including some of the beatniks who defied the State Department to visit Castro's Cuba, then returned to create an uproar before the House Un-American Activities Committee. This group was so Peking-oriented that they refused to visit the Soviet Embassy while in Havana.

The Reds have small undergrounds and propaganda organs in the great Chinatowns of New York, San Francisco and Chicago. The China Daily News is published in a dingy, musty office above a cheap clothing store in New York. Its late publisher, Eugene Moy, was sentenced to a year in prison in 1955 for trying to induce Chinese in this country to send money to the Peking regime. Since his death in 1960 his wife carries on. The paper now appears only twice a week.

Mao's agents appeal to the Chinese-American's sense of pride in his ancestry. They have encouraged at least a few Chinese scientists, technicians and students to return to the "motherland." Attempts have also been made to establish contacts between American-educated scientists now in Red China and the scientists they used to know here. They have suggested exchanging information for the sake of "pure science."

There have been darker undertones: the peddling of opium and the age-old evil of extortion. Opium from the mainland, most of it transshipped through Hong Kong, has reached this country through underground Chinese channels. At least one opium seizure, traced back to Red China, was smuggled into Florida by way of Cuba.

Families with relatives still in China are pressed for money, food, clothing and medicines. A stranger arrives with an appeal from the relatives, asking for help. To the family-minded Chinese, this is difficult to resist. It becomes more difficult still when the stranger hints that failure to comply could have unfortunate results for the clan in China.

The American people have the haziest of views into the shadowy, subterranean world of espionage. Now and then, a light breaks through the murky darkness. It may shine briefly on a love nest, the confession of a refugee, a softening of will or skill. At best the public catches only an occasional, fleeting glimpse into its dramatic and deadly operation.

17

TORTURE AND TREASON

As dusk crept across the sky like a closing eyelid, an emaciated man hesitated nervously before his front door in the Montgomery, Alabama, suburbs. The door was unlatched, but he made no move to enter. Instead he pressed his finger against the doorbell and waited, hanging back in the shadows. His wife answered the ring. She gasped one word, "Andy!" and threw her arms around his thin shoulders. It was Andrew Evans' homecoming after six months in a communist nightmare. An Air Force colonel and jet ace, he had been a prize prisoner of the Korean War. He rang his own bell, like a stranger at the door, because of a sudden stage fright at presenting to his wife the man he had become.

His shyness resulted partly from his gaunt appearance, partly from the stutter that made every word a pain to speak. But worse, he was still unsure whether he had brought back the same brain. He couldn't be sure, because he had been brainwashed. He had been ground down with psychological pressure until at last he had signed a false confession admitting germ warfare against the North Koreans.

Evans is now sure of himself again, and the Air Force is sure of him. He has been promoted to Brigadier General and holds a key post in the Pentagon. But the intervening years have not been easy. Most difficult has been facing the question his friends politely never ask: "But why did you sign a confession for the communists?" There's no simple answer, but there is an answer. *It is important for Americans to understand Andy Evans' story, to learn what happens to a man reduced to a state, half animal, half human, battered with lies until the truth is wholly unreal, tormented by evil men whose morbid genius is almost beyond belief. For this may explain some of the alleged American confessions coming out of Vietnam today.*

It isn't an easy story to understand. Andy Evans can't say he was tortured in the accepted sense, because he wasn't. He puts the matter this way: "We think of giving our lives for our country as the ultimate sacrifice. That's not so. Death would have been the easy way out." Three times during his ordeal, Evans faced execution. Once he was prodded in the back with a gun and ordered to confess or die. He answered: "I won't sign." Given 24 hours to reconsider, he was again hauled before the executioners. This time the gun was pressed against the nape of his neck. "I prefer to die," he declared.

He was granted another 24-hour reprieve to think it over. The guards came for him in the middle of the night. They asked if he had decided to confess. Again he said "No." He was marched up a hill and stood against a tree facing a Chinese firing squad. Then he was offered one final chance. "Confess or you'll be shot," he was warned. "I knew it was my last night, and I was glad," Evans told me. "I said, 'No, get it over with'." But the firing squad never fired; without comments, his tormentors led him to a fate even worse than death.

General Evans' eyes had a faraway stare as his thoughts wandered painfully back. "Many times I would have preferred to be strung up by my wrists, to have been beaten into unconsciousness. These were luxuries I was not allowed. We Americans only understand what we can see and feel. It is hard for us to imagine torture of the mind. But I have been through it. Believe me, death is preferable."

Andrew Evans was already a hero before he left for Korea. A West Point graduate, he was a World War II ace of whom a superior said: "I would place Andy Evans in the highest 10 percent of all officers I have known." Among his postwar assignments, he served as executive officer to the late Air Force chief, General Hoyt Vandenberg. He was a coming young officer in the best military tradition. At Maxwell Field, Alabama, where he was stationed before going to Korea, he and his wife, Claire, were attractive additions to the Air Force set. They played golf, entertained friends and reared healthy, happy children—Jay and Dick, two boys, and Susan and Kathy, two girls.

It was a good life, but Evans begged for a combat assignment. When he got it, he couldn't be kept out of the air. In three months he chalked up 67 combat missions—371 combat hours. "Andy was such an eager beaver you'd almost think he was trying to win the Korean War single-handed," says Lieut. Col. Dave Henderson, jet pilot who flew under Evans. With enough World War II medals to open a pawn shop, he won several more, including the Silver Star for leading a mission against a heavily-defended rail bridge in northernmost Korea on March 14, 1953—a mission almost identical to that dramatized in the movie, "The Bridges of Toko-Ri." Two weeks later he fell into enemy hands.

March 27, 1953, was a day like any other. Col. Evans flew two missions in the morning, had to pull his rank to lead a third. Over the target, enemy ground fire chewed holes in Evans' F-84 thunderjet. He pointed the nose toward South Korea, hoping to crash land in friendly territory. He remembers flame and smoke swirling around the cockpit. Then he must have blacked out and somehow tripped the seat ejector. He woke up 500 feet from the ground, still sitting in the ejected seat and drifting gently down by parachute.

Freeing himself from the plane gear, he landed on marshy ground—barely 100 yards from U. S. lines. His first act was to call over his emergency radio for the disposition of enemy troops and directions to the nearest friendly position, but Chinese troops were already swarming down on him. He emptied his pistol at them, got a stern reply from a Red machine gun. So he raised his hands in surrender and was led off through a system of trenches. As he disappeared behind the Bamboo Curtain, artillery shells burst around him. U. S. troops were attempting to hold off the Chinese while he escaped. They were just a little too late.

The interrogation began almost immediately. Evans was a buoyant, cocky guy, mentally agile, morally sure of himself. "I rather enjoyed matching wits with my hosts," he says with a wry smile. He breezed through the first ten days of grilling. He was even called down for grinning saucily at a Chinese WAC. He was so successful in building a network of lies about himself that he almost had the interrogators convinced he was a person of little consequence. He was simply an administrative officer, shot down on his fifth mission, he insisted. To questions about military operations, he brashly told them "to read it in the newspapers."

The cockiness went out of him, however, when his interrogators marched into his cell, grinning, and hauled him gruffly to attention. Cursing him as "a dirty filthy liar," they gave him a complete report on himself taken from an American radio broadcast. Evans was totally unprepared for what was to follow. "I had been advised that the days of name, rank and serial number were over," he says. "In case of capture, I was told to play it by ear, to rely on my own judgment."

He was given 24 hours to admit the truth about himself. Caught with his tongue exposed, he saw no harm in acknowledging what they already knew. He agreed to sign the statement prepared for him. "This insignificant statement seemed innocent enough," he says. "I was completely unaware that the enemy wasn't after military information from me but after something unreal—an admission of germ warfare. I had a childlike innocence of communist techniques and objectives." Not until later did he realize that securing his signature on an ostensibly harmless statement was an important first move in the drive toward a "confession." He was being slowly adjusted not to mind signing his name to a communist statement.

Evans was still not mistreated in the usual way. The Chinese even brought him two colored eggs for Easter and boasted of their kindness. They also loaded him with communist literature, which he read to occupy his time. Once they sent a doctor around to see him when he became ill. The medic looked down his throat—a futile gesture because the room was almost pitch-black—and prescribed porridge. The porridge never arrived.

Meanwhile, the pattern for the months ahead began to emerge. He got no rest from his interrogators. They would take turns hurling questions at him, barrage after barrage, without let up. Day or night the grilling continued, intensively, incessantly. *Bouncing off at first, the questions soon began to pound against his brain like the constant drop of water on the forehead until he felt his brain would burst.* But he kept dodging and twisting away from giving military answers.

Evans' mental browbeating was accompanied by a deliberately erratic schedule. He never knew whether he would be questioned for 4 hours or for 24. He never knew whether he would meet pseudo-sympathy or ferocity. He never knew from one day to the next when he would eat, when sleep, when he could sit, when lie down. "There was never an opportunity for me to develop a routine," he says, "where I could sort of bunch my muscles for what was coming next."

To help break him down, he was also subjected to periods of starvation, jammed into cramped, infested quarters, shut off from daylight and fresh air (during his entire captivity he saw only two days of daylight). At no time during the day was he allowed to rest, recline or close his eyes. His sleep at night, when permitted, was sadistically interrupted. Not the least of his misery was caused by lice that multiplied in his beard, vermin that crawled over his body, rats that raced around at nights. "The lice," he recalls with a shudder, "were terrible." He fought a losing battle against them, nipping them one at a time between his fingers.

Combined, the constant harping, the disruptive schedule, the perpetual darkness, the close, vermin-ridden cell became almost unbearable torture. The accumulation became an erosive process that rapidly wore him down. "One thing followed another in an amazingly well-planned pattern which I was constantly trying to fathom but never could grasp," explains Evans, thinking back. For a while he was questioned alternately by a team of inquisitors by day and a smiling, solicitious Chinese officer at night. His interrogators asked particularly about a giant pincer movement they expected. "They would hammer for hours on a high-level military subject," he says. "Then, after getting no satisfaction from me, they would slip into a seemingly harmless personal question which I must admit came as sort of relaxation. Sometimes I told them the truth about myself." He realizes now they were trying to learn more about him—"how big a fish I was, how much propaganda value I would be."

Evans had been advised to pack a picture of his family in his wallet; it might get him sympathy in case of capture. One interrogator kept coaxing him to pull out the picture and look at it each day. He would ask patronizing questions about Evans' family: whether the children were doing well in school, how their health had been. "Carrying this picture was one of the worst things I could have done from a psychological viewpoint," Evans admits. When he realized the communists were using it to torture him with loneliness and homesickness, he tore the cherished picture into tiny pieces.

His constant desire was to become a "regular" prisoner of war; and the communists played on this desire. About six weeks after his capture, he was promised he would be taken to a camp to join other prisoners. Thankfully, he dreamed of a sort of Stalag 17 where comradeship would erase the nightmare. He was driven northward at night, stretched out on a truck floor with six armed guards hovering over him. Enroute, an American B-26 dropped a flare, followed by three bombs that barely missed the truck. Afterward he wished the bombs had killed them all, particularly himself.

At the end of his truck ride, he was thrown into a damp, filthy cell the size of a packing crate. It reeked of a stench that had no outlet. There were no windows and the door was closed tight. For furniture, a pile of urine-saturated straw was strewn on the floor. The room had one improvement over the past accommodations: an electric light. But this turned out to be a dubious blessing; it was used to shine in his face during question periods. The scraggly Evans brought a nest of lice with him in his hair, but he found other vermin waiting for him—bedbugs and rats. His every movement was watched by two guards who didn't take their eyes off him. They weren't worried about an escape attempt, they just didn't want to lose their prey through suicide.

For a few days, surprisingly, Evans found politeness and cultural conversation. A saccharin Chinese officer with courtly manners and manicured fingernails offered him hot tea and discussed aesthetic subjects in an Oxford accent. Along with the gentle talk were props. Once, off in the distance, Evans heard a group of Americans singing "Way Down Upon the Swanee River." Again he heard two men, obviously Americans, stroll by his cell chatting about a Hemingway book. Homesickness became more acute than ever. Inevitably, the Chinese Beau Brummel turned off the charm, and the browbeating routine began again, reinforced by two American-educated inquisitors who put him through a mental wringer. They would damn "the dirty white race," then exhort him to "trust us, have faith in us."

"How," Evans finally retorted, "can I trust anyone who goes around spreading this germ warfare stuff?" That started the final stage of his mental anguish. One interrogator, he recalls, "came back with a snarl and accusation that I was one of those most involved in germ warfare. Thereafter, the questioning never varied. It was either my personal biography or germ warfare."

By repetition of the same grueling techniques, Evans mind was so cruelly tortured that he longed for physical punishment as a relief. Sometimes he argued with his tormentors, even insulted them, hoping to provoke them to violence. But except for being kicked, slapped and spat upon, his person was not touched. "I was filthy, exhausted. I felt like a cornered animal," Evans says. "I thought no one could be forced to sign something against his principles unless he was drugged. I simply didn't know."

One day he was led to a room where he found himself before a somber tribunal. In an atmosphere of judicial dignity (complete with three Chinese judges), a functionary elaborately unfurled an official document and began intoning. It was an indictment charging Evans with conducting germ warfare and having innocent blood on his hands. If he begged forgiveness, it added with a verbal flourish, the good hearts of the Chinese and Korean people would permit mercy. Otherwise he would be executed. He had 24 hours to decide.

The colonel was stunned. The germ warfare hoax, which to him was utterly preposterous, would cost his life. "This may sound melodramtic," he says, "but the day was May 12, my daughter's birthday. I went back to my cell and, for the first time, cried. Within a few minutes, my chief interrogator was on me like a hound dog." The officer was all sympathy. Evans would feel so much better, the officer urged, if he would get his guilt off his chest and confess. "I told him to go to hell."

At the end of 24 hours he was marched back before the tribunal and, with a pistol jammed against his back, was asked for his decision. It was the first of his three brushes with the executioners. After his final midnight drama before the firing squad, he was starved for 12 days. Throughout the siege questioning never stopped; he was not allowed to sleep, except when he passed out for a few minutes. "I was stood at attention for hours; I was placed under a bright electric light bulb for more hours," he reports. "I was sat at attention on a hard stool for hours while I was tormented, bullied, brow-beaten."

Evans watched himself die by degrees from lack of food and rest. All the while, his captors kept drumming lies into his brain, lies about germ warfare and his participation, lies he heard so many times they almost became realistic. Some lies stuck, temporarily etched in his groggy mind. "In the end," he says, "I no longer knew what truth was. What they said couldn't be true. But after having it pounded into my head, I began to wonder. I just prayed to be left alone."

Once the guards looked away momentarily. He grabbed the lightbulb, shattered it and started slashing his wrists. He tried to complete what the firing squad had failed to do. But the guards pounced on him before his suicide attempt could succeed. Then, abruptly, the communists appeared to give up. They promised to send him to join the other POW's. There was just one minor detail: would he write out his full personal history? Evans, numb and worn, agreed. "They got no military information," he said, "but I gave them the minutest details about my personal life. I told them my father's income, my grades at school, even the names of my teachers. If I had know then what I know now, I would have realized they wanted the information to beef up a later confession. As it was, I kept hoping that by giving them unimportant details they would make me a regular POW."

More than two months had now passed since his capture. Once again, Evans was moved through the night. *His new cell was the worst torture chamber of all. It was a tiny storeroom on the side of a hill. It would have been 6 by 6 feet, except it was half filled with hugh earthenware crocks of grain.* For the next 12 weeks he lived like an animal in a space three feet square. He could neither lie down nor stand up. He sat continuously, leaning against one of the crocks to sleep. For exercise in this suitcase posture, he could only try weakly to push one muscle against the other.

Daylight was shut out by mud plastered over the windows; only an occasional glimmer stabbed through chinks in the door. The grain attracted more vermin and rats than ever. One rat became friendly and provided Evans company. The animal seemed like his last link with sanity. At least it was normal; it behaved like a rat. Added to these intolerable, inhuman conditions, a little thing like a leaky roof can be a crushing experience. It admitted enough of the summer rains to multiply his misery and create what he describes as "an atmosphere of dampness and despair."

Evans ate, drank and washed out of a bowl not much larger than a cup. His tormentors even devised a quaint torture involving the bowl. They would fill it with water, but before he could drink, his food would be brought. To make room for the food, he would have to pour out the water. He seldom could have both. By this time his chestnut brown hair had grown down to his shoulders; his shaggy beard flowed over his chest; all his hair was crawling with lice. To eat, he had to lift his straggly, filthy mustache above his lips.

His emotions went through several metamorphoses during this ordeal. At first, he was bitterly angry at the communists and all they represented. "I vowed," he says, "never to give them what they wanted." But, he adds, "their treatment never let up. I was not permitted to stand up, recline, lie down. I did not see the sunlight or feel the fresh air; I was never allowed a full day's rest or a complete night's sleep. I was unclean, infested with lice and bugs. After you're reduced half-way between the human and the animal, something begins to tarnish."

Then his emotional control began to go. He recalls having

tears in his eyes during the incessant questioning. "I kept begging them to kill me," he says. But they threatened to keep him forever in that cramped space unless he changed his mind about confessing. "At this point," recalls Evans, "I resigned myself to spending the rest of my life there, and I hoped it would be a short life." Despair gradually gave way to apathy. "I reached an absolutely impassive state. I showed no emotion whatever during the rest of my capture. I was purely animal, living from meal to meal and not really caring whether I got the meal. I would eat because it was something to do."

In his mind, he became muddled, unsure. "I began to wonder why a false signature was so important," he says. "Suppose you were captured by a group of escapees from an insane asylum. They kept tormenting you, but all they wanted was one thing—that you sign a statement saying you were the crazy one, not them. That's the way I began to feel. I rationalized that if I got back to sane people, back to Americans, they would understand. They would laugh at the ridiculous confession."

Only one thing throughout the ordeal gave his spirits a lift: the sound of American planes. One day even that stopped. Then, eight days after his straining ears no longer heard American engines, he was dragged before another tribunal. *The pathetic, bedeviled American was told that the war had ended, the United States had surrendered, all prisoners would be repatriated—except him.* Next day the tribunal offered further arguments. They handed him a letter, addressed to him by name, from North Korea's puppet premier, Kim Il Sung. The letter urged him to sign the confession, so he could be repatriated with the others. He was given 24 hours to decide.

When he expressed doubt that the war was over, he was shown a copy of Chinese newspapers printed in English. The news fitted in with the absence of planes overhead. Still at the end of 24 hours he held out against signing. "I don't want anyone to think I am an iron character," he now says. "I was just numb. Anyhow, my 'no' wasn't as decisive as it sounded. Within, I was beginning to doubt the value of struggling on."

Then came the final blow. The Reds showed him many American "confessions." One day they brought in a tape recording. He recognized the tired, halting voice of his best friend—an officer of outstanding character, bravery, and honor—telling lies about germ warfare. "To be sitting in a stupor half out of this world, as I was, and to have your senses shocked into reality by the words of your best friend," says Evans, "has a tremendous psychological effect. Also knowing that the war was over, that my country had quit fighting, that I was left in the hands of those madmen, I had begun to waiver in my own mind."

He returned glumly to his cell and for the second time sobbed. Describing his mental state, Evans explains his brain was "a confused glob of thoughts without pattern." He had lost much of his reasoning power and common sense. Only with the greatest effort could he distinguish propaganda from truth. Yet at no time did his captors convince him communism was right or he should atone for his "germ warfare crimes." He doesn't doubt that they could have done so. Continuing, unrelenting brainwashing, he is sure, would have turned him into a communist zombi. This was his mental condition as he sobbed in his tiny cubicle. His chief interrogator stood by, consoling him and exhorting him to sign, rather like a preacher at a revival trying to convert a sinner. On the 11th hour of his last reprieve, he agreed to sign.

"Probably to most people," says Evans, "to break down means utter collapse, a slobbering of words and complete abandonment of resistance. I know this is not the case. Near the end of this experience, for instance, there was another moment when I backed out on the whole deal. They kept trying to get me to backdate my confession to May. For some reason, I went into a state of obstinancy and refused to do so. But I accepted the date of August 18, though it was then September 3. My condition at that time might best be described as only half man. I could still gather my energies to fight them on some subjects, but I was completely impassive on others." Philosophizing for a moment, Evans adds: "I think we must decide whether a person's life is more valuable to us than a communist propaganda lie. I believe our men should be instructed to hold out to the limits of their endurance, but we must recognize such limits do exist."

The moment Evans relented, he was issued clean clothes and transferred to a large room with a comfortable cot. He was doused with DDT to kill the lice and was allowed to bathe in the river. A guard, still not trusting him with a razor, shaved him. For a week he was showered with treats: sacks of sugar, beer, cigarettes, malted milk, stacks of candy. Then he was ordered to write out his confession. He composed one so exaggerated that it was ridiculous on its face. The Reds, seeing its preposterous wording, became furious. But the defiance hadn't yet been drained out of Evans. He haughtily announced he had changed his mind about signing. Back to his cell he went for another 12 hours.

All the old horrors, the miseries, the soul aches, returned with a rush. He had a vision of himself disappearing forever behind the Bamboo Curtain. It wouldn't take much more brainwashing, he realized for him to lose his identity. He would be physically the same person, but mentally someone else. His captors had also convinced him that a confession would mean forgiveness. He believed they would let him go home once he signed it, so he decided to go through with it.

This time the Reds wrote the confession out for him. The 20-page document cleverly interweaved lies about his germ warfare raids with truth about his personal history. But even in surrendering, Evans tricked the communists. He had given them, as dates of his principal missions, 10 days he spent on leave in Hongkong. Unwittingly, the Reds incorporated these dates into his confession. What he really signed was a confession that he dropped germs at a time when he wasn't even flying. After signing the document, he was forced to read it into a tape recording machine. *His stutter by this time was so bad and he broke into sobs so often that it took him 18 hours to read the 20 pages.*

Three days later he was prettied up and shipped off to Panmunjon for repatriation, joining other prisoners on the way. Once a Chinese cameraman took movies of them. Another prisoner still remembers how the brainwashed, emaciated, browbeaten colonel turned defiantly and thumbed his nose at the camera. "We were deathly afraid we would be punished, maybe even denied repatriation, for Colonel Evans' impudence," recalls this witness. Fortunately the Chinese pretended not to see what had happened.

On the journey to freedom, Evans' first thought was to proclaim his confession as false, expose what the communists had done to him and thwart their propaganda scheme. Five minutes after he had been turned backed to American hands, he started in naive triumph to get his revenge on the Chinese by exposing them. He revealed to reporters that he had signed a germ warfare confession. But instead of sympathy, a horrified hush fell over the group. He tried lamely to explain the circumstances—how he had been tortured into signing—but they didn't seem to understand. He said no more.

The doctors and nurses who examined him showed little more sympathy. With casual bedside interest, they would ask whether his treatment had been rugged. When he started to tell them, they seemed indifferent, even hostile. No one appeared to care about his terrible ordeal. Result: he withdrew into the company of other brainwashed victims; he would talk to no one else. "I felt no one understood except those who had been through the experience," he explains.

Although saturated with communist lies, Evans hungered for the truth. He had an insatiable desire to reorient his mind, so he stacked magazines and newspapers high beside his bed. He discovered for the first time that many communist claims he had accepted in his mental stupor were untrue. He also learned to his shocked resentment that, for confessing germ warfare, he was considered a traitor by many. He had tried to die for his country but had been denied the luxury. He had signed a false statement when it seemed useless to go on fighting. But he had fought.

"I had signed under circumstances that I thought any American should understand," he recalls his feelings. "Under our system, no statement obtained by coercion or duress can be used as evidence against a man. I came to resent people, because they didn't try to understand. I resented anyone who looked healthy and unconcerned. Most of all, I resented the articles suggesting we, who signed confessions, were traitors." He came to this conclusion: *"Human behavior cannot be judged by a yardstick, used against suffering people by those who have never suffered."*

So it was in bitter disappointment and dismay that Col. Andy Evans later stood on the front porch of his home and waited for his wife to open the door. Only Claire—a petite, pretty blonde with sparkling blue eyes—greeted him that first night. Too self-conscious to face the children, he had phoned from San Francisco for her to have them in bed. Next morning the children came to him, one by one, to avoid noisy confusion. Each had been briefed not to mention "how daddy looks," but Kathy, then three, didn't understand. When she saw him, she squeaked: "Daddy, you don't look the same." But she looked good to daddy, who grabbed her up in his arms.

For months Andy Evans couldn't sleep more than two hours at a time. What sleep he got was haunted by nightmares. He also refused to see anyone except Claire. He would spend hours just sitting and staring into space, occasionally breaking his silence with a few stuttered remarks to Claire.

"He had a strange, far-away look in his eyes," Mrs. Evans remembers. She suspected, deep down, that he wanted the companionship of his Air Force buddies. But it took three months for her to persuade him to attend a party. Then he stayed only 15 minutes. "Andy was very concerned about that first party," his wife says. He watched jealously to notice which friends would avoid him. Except for two, everyone gave him a warm welcome. Thereafter he began to loosen up. He played golf with a few friends; others, secretly encouraged by Claire, dropped by the house. They worked hard to draw him out of his protective shell.

Still Evans remained pretty well holed up at home. He preferred to putter around the yard or play with the children. Surprisingly, they could never become too noisy or naughty to upset his shaky nerves. "He told me the little things the children did weren't really important," Claire recalls. "I couldn't get him to discipline them for over a year." The first Christmas, he took the two boys in the car and personally delivered dozens of food baskets to needy Negro families. He explained to Claire: "I want the boys to be thankful for their blessings. I think maybe this will help teach them gratitude."

Evans still has trouble restraining himself from teaching others the same lesson. If someone at a restaurant gripes about the food, he has to fight to keep from bursting out in resentment. Or, if someone complains about his quarters, he thinks of his three-by-three square and is irritated. "We don't know how lucky we are," he says, "I want to shout it from the housetops. I have to fight back resentment against those who don't appreciate what America is."

Even while still under medical care, Evans had a driving desire to get back in the air. Though underweight, he was finally granted a special waiver to fly again. As luck would have it, he was caught in a severe thunderstorm over Mississippi. His radio went dead and his fuel ran out. Heading his plane for a wooded area, he triggered the ejection seat. As he floated gently down, he couldn't help recalling another parachute landing in Korea. And he thanked God it was Mississippi beneath him.

Today Andy Evans is completely his old self again. He is a slight, thoroughly alive officer with a ready smile and a look of vigor. Lithe and agile, he is a champion golfer. But beneath his mental scar tissue, his memories are still a festering sore. He can't keep his mind from wandering back to Korea. Yet his outward attitude toward his experiences is amazingly detached and philosophical.

General Evans' career with the Air Force is unmarred by the events in Korea. An Air Force Board heard his story in secret and ruled: "It is the recommendation of this board that this case be closed and that the officer's name be removed from any possible prejudice for his acts as a prisoner of war." One board member, a high-ranking General, commented afterward: "*The cases we investigated fell into three general categories—the stinkers, whom we got rid of; a considerable number to whom we gave the benefit of doubt because we weren't sure of the facts; and a few who deserved a great big medal.* In my judgment, Andy Evans' name heads the list of the few who merited medals."

Evans' ordeal, and his articulate account of it, has helped the armed forces prepare our men for communist capture. The pilots who parachute into North Vietnam today are better braced at least for the mental torture that a few select victims may have to endure. And in the Pentagon, though many brass-bound Generals still cling stubbornly to the name-rank-and-serial-number concept, there is more tolerance for those who break under the strain.

Less understood are the Americans who voluntarily cross

over to the communist side. Consider the strange case of Captain Alfred Svenson, the Army's highest-ranking defector, who on May 4, 1964, drove up to the East German border, climbed out of his jeep, and walked behind the Iron Curtain. His superiors, who knew and respected him, were completely baffled. His mother, Mrs. Antonia Svenson of Washington, D. C., was stunned. Exactly a year later the Russians returned him under even more mysterious circumstances.

The tall, blue-eyed,easy-smiling Army officer was an ardent anti-Communist by background. As a youngster he fled his native Lithuania to get away from the Russians. His mother taught him to lie motionless in the snow, suffering intense cold in silence, as the patrols passed within yards. His father was killed trying to escape through Latvia. This strengthened the bond between mother and son, who made their way to the United States, alone and friendless.

Alfred was brought up to hate communism and to love freedom. Graduated from Pennsylvania's Scranton University, he eagerly joined the Army and was proud of his military career. From Germany, where he was stationed, he wrote to his mother enclosing the orders, underscored in red, promoting him to Captain. "You won't recognize me," he wrote. "I left as a second lieutenant, and I'm coming home as a Captain." He expected to arrive home in the Spring of 1964 after a holiday with his fiancee in Spain. He dreamed of retiring in Colorado after 20 years in the Army; he would still be young enough, he wrote his mother, to start a new career in psychology.

Then, one day in May, Alfred Svenson deserted, leaving heartbreak and bewilderment for those behind. Why did he decide to go back to the tyranny from which he had fled as a boy? "I know my son," the mother told me. "He would never have crossed the border except under the most terrible pressure." His German fiancee wrote to Mrs. Svenson that his action was "a horrible surprise." Reporters who saw him in

East Berlin said he seemed to want to come home. *He claimed he had been drugged before he defected.* Once he showed up at a Reuters News Agency office in East Berlin, his face swollen, lips bruised, shirt bloody; he had been manhandled, he explained, by border guards who had caught him in an escape attempt. But later he told a news conference in East Berlin: "I hope some day I can say I am a communist. I don't want to return to the West."

Then the Soviets, without explanation, abruptly returned Svenson. Indeed, they appeared to want to get rid of him. "He showed himself unworthy of the asylum offered him," was all they said. He came home not the proud Captain but a deserter facing court martial. He was found guilty of desertion and stealing a military vehicle and sentenced to four years at hard labor, dismissal from the service and forfeiture of all pay and allowances. *He has never fully explained what drove him to defect; the awful secret is locked inside him.* Captain Alfred Svenson, a man fascinated by psychology, must remain a psychologist's case.

But if the authorities don't understand Svenson, they are more worried about the "psychos," men like Lee Oswald, the misfit ex-Marine who decamped to Russia then returned to assassinate President Kennedy. *How many more potential Oswalds are there: military defectors who one day will come home, men trained in the use of weapons and explosives, who for dark reasons none but they can understand, may be capable of murder?* Certainly, a man driven by a tortured mind to desert his country is capable of a desperate act against his country.

Commanders with men near communist countries have been warned to be on the watch for potential Oswalds and to weed them out, discreetly moving them back stateside, away from the lures and traps that might be set for them. The military services have been warned to keep their eyes peeled for men with twisted personalities—bitter loners; men resentful of orders and discipline; above all, the kind of men who run away from their problems.

Communist authorities have handed back many of the mental misfits who have defected. How many are now human time bombs waiting to explode? Only three defectors are safe in asylums. Others who have been given routine turncoat treatment—court martial, prison term, then dishonorable discharge—are now loose in the country, taking orders from no one, serving their own peculiar purposes.

Army records describe a San Francisco youth, who stayed behind the Iron Curtain only a few days, as "paranoid and schizophrenic." Yet the Army turned him loose after three months of imprisonment. A defector from Old Landing, Kentucky, who had a history of mental illness, was given one year of hard labor, then set free. Another mentally-distressed GI, who barged across the East German border to negotiate peace with the Soviets, was quietly retired for "disability."

The Army, which has had the most trouble with defectors, boasts that none of its men have passed through the curtain for purely ideological reasons. To say otherwise would be to confess that the Generals have been lax with security. Secret files indicate, however, there has been at least an occasional slip-up. For instance, Stephen Wechsler of New York City, a Harvard graduate, defected on August 17, 1952. His Army record shows that he was a Communist Party member and that his motive for desertion was purely political. He is now working for the Reds in East Germany.

In July, 1960, Sergeant Joseph Dutkanicz of Tujunga, California, took off with his wife and three children for a three-week vacation in Germany. They were never seen again by those who knew them previously. But Izvestia, the official Communist Party paper, printed a letter from the sergeant claiming he had defected because of the "deprivation" he had suffered in the United States. Dutkanicz was known to be fluent in Russian, and his confidential Army file indicates he may have been a Soviet agent since 1958. Last heard of him was a report that he had died in Russia in November, 1963.

A month later Vladimir Sloboda, a Russian-born U.S. citizen defected from an Army intelligence unit in Germany. His wife, a British woman, told newsmen he had lost money gambling. An Army report suggests that all along he may have been a lieutenant in the Soviet Army. There is also the case of a New York enlisted man, identified in Army documents as a communist who had enlisted illegally under an alias. When he was found out, he vanished behind the Iron Curtain—only to be greeted by secret police who sent him to the Verkhne-Uraisk concentration camp. He was delivered back to the U.S. several months later, his reason shattered. "He is a mental wreck," his sister told me.

Many defectors have been servicemen on the run from the provost marshal, men enticed across the border by girl friends, or men blackmailed for debts and moral misdeeds. As a favorite bait to lure defectors, Soviet agents have become adept at tempting girl-hungry GIs with seductive sirens. They set up date bureaus, arrange sex traps. Then comes blackmail. Or the girl may plead with tears in her eyes that only by slipping behind the curtain can the GI help her and her family escape to freedom. But when the modern Pimpernel responds and reaches the secret rendezvous, he is met not by his beauty in distress but by the Communist police. More often than not, he never sees her again. She has gone back for a new assignment.

Charles C. Lucas of Xenia, Ohio, was enticed into East Germany by a girl who immediately deserted him. He stayed on, miserable, despondent, finally to die by his own hand. One seducer persuaded George W. Stabley of Jersey Shore, Pennsylvania, to go behind the curtain by having him father her child. Once on the other side, she coldly dropped him. He was afraid to return, and eventually took up with another East German girl.

Some men who fell into the girl trap have come home to face the music once love's bloom has faded. Kenneth D. Miller of Modesto, Calif., lured into East Germany by a girl friend, found he preferred love at home. He paid for his romance by going to prison for two years for desertion. Bobby F. Holland of Rockmart, Georgia, who eloped into East Germany, made his way back forlornly without his bride; he went to prison for three years. But at least a dozen others who were sweet-talked into defecting have vanished without a trace. Raymond S. Hareld of Providence, Rhode Island, deserted his Japanese wife and disappeared into Czechoslovakia with a German woman named Margita Schlotta. Others lured by love into East Germany are James W. Pulley of Norristown, Pennsylvania; Jack C. Hillie of Harrisburg, North Carolina; and Leon M. Baker of Pittsburgh.

Tall, blonde Robert Webster, sent by a Cleveland plastics firm to demonstrate plastic boats at a Moscow exhibition, fell for a Russian waitress named Vera. He deserted his wife and two children whom he left behind in Ohio. His defection provided a temporary propaganda triumph for the Russians, but now they have lost interest in him. He is eking out a poor living as a Leningrad factory worker.

Another victim of the Kremlin sex school is Sergeant James McMillan, former clerk at the Moscow Embassy, who defected with a propaganda blast. He gave ideological reasons, all phrased in stilted communist style, for his action. In fact, he had been wooed and won by a buxom agent named Galina Dunaeva. Once he had served his propaganda purpose, she walked out on him. McMillan found another Russian bride the following year; they now live in a cheap Moscow flat.

Annabelle Bucar, one-time information clerk at the Moscow Embassy, has earned the dubious distinction of being the only

American girl to fall for communist-style romance. A musical comedy singer, Konstantin Lapshin, induced her to desert the U.S. She married him and moved into a two-room flat. To curry favor with her new rulers, she wrote a book, "The Truth About American Diplomats," loaded with fictitious scandal about members of the Embassy staff. For this slander on her old friends, Annabelle was rewarded with a three-room flat. She now works for Radio Moscow as an announcer, also makes frequent anti-American speaking tours.

But the strangest love story involves Madame Sun Yat-sen, widow of the founder of the Chinese Republic and most beautiful of the famous Soong daughters (one sister is now Madame Chiang Kai-shek). A U.S. Army officer, ruggedly handsome Captain Gerald Tannebaum, gave up his commission and his country for her. Madame Sun, who was only 23 when she married the Chinese George Washington, met Tannebaum in Chunkging where he was stationed during World War II. A Lenin-leaning idealist and intellectual, he was captivated by Madame Sun's cultured charm and Marxist mind. Gradually a romance developed between them. In his love notes he called her "Susie"; she sometimes replied by sending him records of Chinese love songs. After his discharge, he went to work for the China Welfare Institute which she headed. At last report he was still in Shanghai working for her.

Others have fled into communist arms to escape punishment. They have ranged from Marvin Betty of Brunning, Nebraska, who skipped into East Germany to evade a murder charge; to Heinrich J. Newton of the Virgin Islands, who defected rather than face discharge and disgrace for homosexual behavior. Most who have made the jump have found the Soviet fire far more uncomfortable than the U.S. frying pan. While awaiting trial for robbing and assaulting a German taxi driver, Sidney Sparks of Wrightsville, Georgia, escaped from an Army guardhouse and beat it into East Berlin. He asked for "protection", expecting to be welcomed. Instead, he drew a 15-year sentence for "espionage" and served three years in the notorious Soviet camps at Vorkuta and Vladimor. Subsequently shipped back to the border and handed over to the U.S. authorities, Sparks was glad to get a 10-year sentence in a comfortable American prison.

Henry Kierman of Philadelphia crossed into East Germany to escape punishment but found life behind the curtain unbearable. Word has been received that he committed suicide on February 26, 1964. William J. Peterson of Beaufort, North Carolina, simply got drunk one night and staggered across the East German border. After three years in a communist jail he broke under brain-washing, asked for political asylum, and then committed suicide. William Verdine of Starks, Louisiana, a GI who hated Army life, concocted an elaborate plot to get out. When he crossed into East Germany he fully expected to be arrested and turned back to U.S. authorities. This, he thought, would get him a discharge. Instead, he was flung into a Soviet labor camp for six years.

Even for those who do communist bidding, life behind the Iron Curtain isn't all caviar and vodka. Many are rewarded with menial jobs at meager wages and a life of constant uncertainty, always scorned, always watched. Of 67 Army defectors, 21 have managed to return though they knew they were coming back to prison terms. They tell of others who would like to come home. *All have had their fill of a society of sweat, hunger, fear, and slum living.* One mixed-up young idealist, Bruce F. Davis of Rome, New York, who had doubted his country's desire for peace, got back to freedom after attending school in Russia. Just before his court martial, he told his mother: "I know I have to be punished, but all the hell I ever needed I had in Russia." He described the bleak, bitter life, the lack of privacy, the constant surveillance. He recently completed a year at hard labor for desertion.

Of those remaining behind the Iron Curtain, intelligence reports claim some have been recruited as spies and saboteurs for the communists. They are as curious a collection of misfits as ever have been brought together. Few started out to be traitors when they slipped across the border, but they ended up training for treason in the bleak factory town of Bautzen, East Germany.

Only one has come back from Bautzen: Gayther L. Turner of Montgomery, Alabama, who told Army authorities of joining a bizarre band of deserters sworn to overthrow the U.S. government. I tried to locate him for questioning but found he had been turned loose after serving a two-year sentence for desertion. His parents have also lost all trace of him; their last word came from a Chicago mental hospital which was about to release him. It can be presumed that the Red-trained deserters he left behind—home-grown sons who could pass in any American crowd, men skilled in the use of weapons and explosives—may be smuggled back into this country some day on secret and sinister missions.

What makes Americans turn traitor and choose to live in slave states? *Most are emotionally unstable; some are homosexuals and undesirables.* All defectors are treated with suspicion, often with contempt by their communist masters. They are subjected to severe psychological tests designed to trip up "double agents." These tests determine whether they will be packed off to concentration camps or allowed to work for starvation pay. Most end up living in hovels and working much harder than at home for low salaries.

Only the turncoat scientists, whose brains are needed, escape the bleak life of most traitors. Three prominent western scientists live in Moscow today: Dr. Bruno Pontecorvo, Italian-born atomic expert, who left London to become one of Russia's top nuclear experts; Dr. Lajos Janossy, Hungarian-born cosmic ray specialist, who fled from Ireland to join the Soviet space program; and Dr. Leopold Infeld, mathematical genius, who skipped out of Canada to work on Russian space projects. They enjoy luxuries that are available only to top communists: apartments in Moscow, villas in the country, new automobiles. Their children attend schools reserved for the sons and daughters of Soviet aristocracy.

Worst off are those defectors who live under the harsh rule of the Communist Chinese. Because of savage hate propaganda, Americans are unpopular and shunned in Red China. They live in varying degrees of loneliness and misery. Only those who lick the Chinese boots are given grudging privileges.

Anna Louise Strong, the brittle, old, grand dame of communism, is allowed to attend official functions. For this privilege, she churns out Peking-brand propaganda. (Recent example: an article entitled "Women of the Communes," extolling the joys of these slave labor camps.) She heads a group of six or eight American expatriates who prepare radio scripts for the Chinese propaganda mill. Among those reportedly working with her are Sidney Rittenberg and Talitha Agnes Gerlach.

Of the turncoats who refused repatriation after the Korean War, 21 have been permitted to return home. Those remaining either cannot get away or fear the consequences awaiting them in the U.S. One, Rufus O. Douglas of San Angelo, Texas, is reported to have died recently. The Chinese decided to make an example of him for failing to cooperate. He was forced to stand at attention in bitter cold until he dropped dead. The men with the lowest IQs, who had been unable to master the difficult Chinese language, have suffered worst. They are wandering from province to province doing menial work. Some have been thrown into filthy jails for stealing food or malingering on their job. Even those who live halfway decently have found Chinese Communist society stifling.

Fidel Castro has lured a few American defectors to Cuba. The most notorious is Robert Williams, who has starred on both Radio Havana and Radio Peking. A soft-spoken ex-

Marine, he once headed the Monroe, North Carolina, chapter of the National Association for the Advancement of Colored People. He preached armed resistance to the Ku Klux Klan in Monroe and once blocked a caravan of robed invaders who tried to drive through the colored section of town. He threw up a sandbagged barricade, positioned his followers behind it, and ordered them to fire on the approaching Klansmen. With a great flapping of white sheets, the Klansmen, though armed themselves, fled in panic. During a race riot, Williams held a white couple in his home. Charged with kidnapping, he escaped to Havana in August, 1961, just a jump ahead of the FBI. Now a hero to Negro firebrands, he has been beaming his broadcast alternately from Cuba and China to American Negroes, inciting them to violence.

Radio Havana also stars Barbara Ines Coradini Collins. Known to her listeners as "Beardless Barbara," she left her husband and a $65-a-week job with a Miami tire firm in 1961 and packed off for Cuba with their baby daughter. Mrs. Collins is the daughter of an Elizabeth, New Jersey, Methodist minister. Ilah Warner, a former South Dakota hillbilly radio performer, delivers vicious anti-American tirades over Radio Station CMCA in Havana. "The time is now ripe for the American people," she shrilled recently, "to take power into their own hands."

As they castigate their country, these turncoat broadcasters, might pause to reflect on what happened to their World War II predecessors. "Tokyo Rose" (Iva Toguri d'Aquino) was found guilty of treason and sentenced to 10 years in prison; "Axis Sally" (Mildred Elizabeth Gillars), also guilty of treason, was sentenced to 10-to-30 years.

Doubts must darken the days of all defectors. Even the luxury-living scientists cannot be sure that there will not be a knock at their door one midnight and a concentration camp at the end of a short ride. For Americans in communist countries live under constant suspicion.

18

THE RADICALS OF THE RIGHT

Almost any evening, Robert Welch, the high panjandrum of the John Birch Society, can be found in the quiet of his booklined study in Belmont, Massachusetts, his feet sheathed in slippers, his gray head bent over a map of the world. The map presents the nations in varying shades of reds and pinks, denoting the degree of communist control. Even the most reactionary dictatorships are colored light pink. *Welch regards it as his Messianic mission to change the map to a politically pure white, which unaccountably he now assigns only to Western Samoa.*

To achieve the communist-free world he envisions, Welch is spreading the John Birch gospel across and beyond America. Already missionary work has begun to pay off; new recruits are signing up in record numbers in this country, and converts are taking the bait overseas. Chapters reportedly are organizing in Australia, Brazil, and South Africa.

Welch seized upon an event that had demoralized most other deep-dyed conservatives—the smash-up of Barry Goldwater's presidential bandwagon. The day after the 1964 election, Welch began grinding a new slogan through his propaganda mill: *"Now will you join the John Birch Society?"* He capitalized on the despair of the conservatives, offering them an outlet for their frustration and a goal for the future. To those who harkened to the call, he peddled his politics of conspiracy. He has one simple answer for all setbacks: *"Treason's the reason."* He sees this country (a deep pink on his map) as virtually taken over by the communist conspiracy. To combat this menace he has launched an intensive counter-conspiracy which he has broadened in order to bring in respectable conservatives. Out of the ashes of the 1964 debacle he has built a militant movement that is far more powerful than the public is aware.

To attract conservatives less extreme than himself, Welch has been busily refurbishing the public image of the John Birch Society. His new line of persuasion has become more plausible, less frantic. He no longer suggests that "Milton Eisenhower is actually Dwight Eisenhower's superior and boss within the Communist Party." This passage has now been amended to read "boss within the whole Left Wing establishment." Where once the Birchites shunned publicity, they now seek the limelight. The press, once beyond the pale, is assiduously courted. The society has been buying newspaper ads, including a sixteen-page color supplement which has appeared in some of the nation's largest newspapers.

Local leaders are also coming out of seclusion and defending their views in public. During a Kansas City debate, the Rev. Robert Hatch, a local Birch bigwig, declared that while the society "is extremist—extremely patriotic—it is not a hate group but a love group." This brought from the Rev. Allen Hingston a skeptical retort that the John Birch Society is a "one-man" group dominated by Robert Welch. "If Mr. Welch tomorrow decided to wage war on marshmallows," Father Hingston said, "the members of the society would have no choice but to follow."

Has public relations surgery changed the face of the John Birch Society? Not at all.

Robert Welch, the retired candy manufacturer, is still a sweet mannered little man with a sour soul. He goes through the motions of consulting an executive council, but his word is still the unchallenged dogma of the society—on politics or marshmallows. "Welch pulls all the strings," an insider told me. "He decides, for example, whether a Senator or Congressman should be defeated. A discussion might follow, but it will concern only the ways and means. Welch makes all the decisions."

There is room at the top for no one else. Welch's own writings have put the matter bluntly: "The John Birch Society will operate under completely authoritative control at all levels. No collection of debating societies is ever going to stop the communist conspiracy . . . . The men who join the John Birch Society are going to be doing so primarily because they believe in me and what I am doing and are willing to accept my leadership."

Welch scoffs at democracy, which he has called "a deceptive phrase, a weapon of demagoguery and a perennial fraud." He believes the only way to fight communism is to get down to the communist level, to fight plot with counterplot, to oppose one monolithic society with another. He regards the United States as a vast "insane asylum" over which the "worst inmates" are in charge. Only the two percent who agree with him are really sane.

He explains away contradictions, as the communists do, with twisted logic. "You are going to see men," he warns, "who are recognized by informed students as communists suddenly taking some strong anti-communist line; projects that will damage communists being promoted by communist agencies; men who have built up a following as anti-communists coming out at long last in support of communist positions." This gives Welch license to decide for his followers which anti-communists are really anti-communist and which are communists in disguise.

Welch commands disciplined followers who—like the Reds they profess to hate—blacklist shopkeepers, intimidate school boards, decide what books shall be on library shelves, bully local editors. A Birchite pressure campaign has persuaded some retail chains to drop products made behind the Iron Curtain. A Fort Wayne, Indiana, store was prevailed upon to burn its communist-produced goods in the middle of Main Street.

However, another campaign failed to persuade the Xerox Corporation to withdraw its sponsorship of a television series on the United Nations, though the company was deluged with more than 10,000 angry letters. Nobody knows how many Birchite boycotts have succeeded, or how many lives and careers have been damaged by the Birchite technique of the smear letter and the deadly whisper—a technique borrowed from the communists.

For, despite all the efforts to appear respectable, extremists continue to dominate the John Birch Society. Two years after the 1964 election, the New York Times still referred to this group as "a semi-secret, authoritarian, anti-democratic, crypto-Fascist, anti-minority organization."

In keeping with the new look, Welch has welcomed Jews and Negroes into the John Birch Society, has even announced a series of scholarships for Negro college students. He drummed out one of the society's founders, Revilo P. Oliver, in July, 1966, partly for seeking to broaden the executive council but also for his too open anti-Semitism. Oliver had challenged the findings that millions of Jews had perished in Nazi concentration camps. "If only by some miracle all the Bolsheviks, or all Jews were vaporized at dawn tomorrow," he said on one occasion, "we would have nothing more to worry about." Yet the new look really amounts to little more than a sort of Kosher anti-Semitism, an integrated Negrophobia. Sheves of JBS offices remain stacked, for example, with anti-Semitic and segregationist literature. The Jewish Anti-Defamation League, in its 1966 report on the John Birch Society, charges that notorious anti-Semites are regular contributors to the society's publications. And it is reliably reported that the Society has forged an alliance in Alabama and Georgia with the United Klans of America, largest of the splintered Ku Klux Klans.

It's true that Welch has foresworn violence, but how far under the surface does violence lie? He has sluffed off asso-

CONFIDENTIAL

JOHN BIRCH SOCIETY MEETING
Friday, April 24, 1964

The local chapters of the John Birch Society sponsored a joint meeting on April 24, 1964. This meeting convened in the Park Room of the Shoreham Hotel at 8:00 p.m. Although the Park Room has a seating capacity of 250 people, there were only an estimated 100 persons present. Those making up the audience mainly ranged in ages from their late-teens to middle-age, with only a few oldsters. The Hotel bulletin board listed this as "American Opinion Meeting." General admission was $2 and student admission, $1. A check with the Hotel management indicated that the usual charge for a Friday night meeting is $150. Hence, since more than half of the audience was obviously not eligible for the student admission, I assume the admission fees totaled more than the cost of the room; however, everyone may not have registered.

Dr. Melchior Savarese, chairman of a local chapter, presided and opened the meeting with a few remarks. The John Birch Society district coordinator from Stamford, Connecticut - Thomas J. Davis - gave a short talk before the main speaker was introduced.

Most of the time which was allotted for introductions and preliminaries was spent explaining the latest statement of Cardinal Cushing of Boston, Massachusetts. Cardinal Cushing had earlier repudiated his support of both the John Birch Society and its leader, Robert Welch. Last week an elaborate explanation appeared in the newspapers claiming that Cardinal Cushing had received a hoax telegram supposedly from a foreign correspondent for an Italian or a Swiss newspaper. Both Dr. Savarese and Mr. Davis claimed the name and address of the correspondent was believed to be fictitious. A supportive letter from Cardinal Cushing was read in which he apologetically explained that he had been a victim of a hoax telegram and that he felt that all anti-Communists should work together and that he welcomed opportunities to work with organizations fighting Communism along with the Catholic Church. Nothing was said specifically indicating that Cardinal Cushing had renewed his support of the John Birch Society or Mr. Welch.

The guest speaker of the evening was Scott Stanley, editor of American Opinion and a former student of Dr. E. Merrill Root at Earlham College in Indiana. Mr. Stanley changed the topic of his speech as was printed, "No Substitute for Victory," to "Right-Wing Extremists I Have Known." Mr. Scott commended Cardinal Cushing saying, "I would have done exactly the same thing, if I had been under the same pressures. It was all an attack on us by the left-wingers." Mr. Stanley then spent 15-minutes castigating the U.S. State Department; the Roosevelt, Truman, Eisenhower, and Kennedy administrations; the "misled" liberals and "satisfied" conservatives. In his attack on the State Department he claimed that in 1956 the State Department was retaining the services of some 800 individuals who were security risks - major and minor. He further stated that of the 800 security risks there were 250 serious menaces in the State Department and about half of these were employed in positions of extra-ordinary security. According to Mr. Stanley, these 800 security risks were Communists, fellow-travelers, homosexuals or liberals. Mr. Stanley indicated that during the Eisenhower administration less than 150 security risks were removed and most of the others transferred to other positions; however, since then some have been reinstated to their former positions. He mentioned two persons in particular - William A. Wyland (alias Arturo Menegro, sp?) who was a leftist before

Extract from an investigator's confidential report on a John Birch Society meeting in Washington, D. C.

ciation with such armed crackpot commandoes as the Minutemen, California Rangers, and Soldiers of the Cross. Yet these gun-packing groups are still led by men who are Birchers in every essential sense. Robert de Pugh, head of the Minutemen, was a JBS member until 1964. An inside report claims he is now trying to organize an underground guerrilla group as an armed auxiliary of the John Birch Society.

In St. Petersburg, Florida, Birchnuts have circulated a document calling on "patriots" to arm themselves and form into secret cells. The appeal, also mailed to other John Birch chapters across the country, recommends the types of weapons for adult males and females, for teen-agers and younger children. It urges the stockpiling of 300 rounds of ammunition per family, plus another 200 rounds for target practice. "The fight with the enemy" the document adds, "will require total dedication and personal sacrifice from each of us if the Constitutional Republic is to be saved."

The extremist guerrilla groups, disavowed by Welch, present an even more chilling specter. Thousands of fanatics, their minds twisted with hate, have been attracted to them. In their bigoted, tormented propaganda President Kennedy's martyrdom was cheered in 1963. Now their ravings are directed against President Johnson. This raises a disturbing question: could another fanatic, lurking behind a window with a rifle, assassinate a future President?

A former leader of the Minutemen, Jerry Milton Brooks, has told a Kansas City grand jury that at one meeting he had heard talk of assassinating Senator J. William Fulbright (D-Ark). Many with a grudge against society seem to be drawn to the nation's capital, the better to brood or to unloose their venom. Some make it their headquarters. Across the Potomac from the White House, for instance, a gang of Hitler-heiling rowdies wear pistols at their hips and drill with rifles. For target and bayonet practice they use "Jewish" dummies.

PROSPECT REFERRAL

To *Mark Anderson* Date *11-19-65*

Name *John Knowley*

Address *1220 McClelland St.*

City *Salt Lake City* Home Phone *487-1830*

Office Phone ______

Date Sent

☐ JHR Speech
☐ called SM office
☐ see attached letter
☐ referred to us by:

______

who is a ☐ JBS member
☐ non-member

attitude:
additional information:

☐ wanted information
☐ requested intro brochure
☐ requested Blue Book
☐ wants to attend a meeting
☒ wants to attend introductory film presentation
☒ has read Blue Book *Bought*
☐ wants Bulletin subscription
☐ wants American Opinion subscription
☐ Form Letter sent

By

Jean Lambson
3103 S. 10th East
Salt Lake City.

~~SYcamore 9-0876~~
~~2566 Mission Street~~
~~San Marino, California~~

FOLLOW-UP

Name *John Knowley* Date

☐ was invited to meeting
☐ attended meeting
☐ did not attend
☐ was contacted again and invited to other meetings
☐ attended one of these
☐ did not attend
☐ joined JBS
☐ has not joined to date
reasons:

Section Leader

Please detach and return to our office when completed.

This membership referral form reveals the thoroughness of the John Birch Society's missionary system.

Their weapons, like the $12.78 mail-order rifle that Lee Oswald used to gun down Kennedy, are easy to acquire.

Millions of guns, turned out in basement workshops overseas, have been shipped into this country and have been sold at cut-rate prices to any criminal, crackpot or child who could fill out a mail-order form. In investigating the traffic in firearms, the Senate Juvenile Delinquency Subcommittee traced several gun shipments to hate groups. After a racial flare-up in Alabama, a Senate spot-check produced records of 180 mail-order deliveries to Alabama cities at the height of the tension. Most of the purchases were made by extremists on both sides.

Across the country, hate-crazed fanatics have been linked with violence. At Nazi headquarters in Arlington, Virginia, storm troopers grabbed some taunting teen-agers and gave them the third degree. The troopers handcuffed one 13-year-old boy, dragged him into their headquarters and terrorized him by waving a lead pipe and twirling a pistol. (One of the bullies, 35-year-old Robert Garber, was later convicted of possessing a machinegun.) Another time, police found a cache of loaded pistols, rifles, and tear-gas guns at Nazi headquarters. The strong-arm men on the premises identified themselves by such code names as Trooper Gun, Trooper Pistol, and Trooper Scar.

Other groups of radicals are training for "guerrilla warfare" in their neighborhoods. Several months ago 20 showed up for maneuvers in southern Illinois with weapons ranging from recoilless rifles to mortars. A public controversy over the leadership of the Minutemen in southern California brought out that two rivals, William Colley and Troy Houghton, had been convicted of sex offenses. At one Los Angeles meeting a guerrilla "commander" called upon his volunteers to buy rifles and prepare to stand off a Chinese Communist invasion. "Our counter-intelligence units," he announced gravely, "re-

FORM 1120

U.S. Treasury Department
Internal Revenue Service

U.S. CORPORATION INCOME TAX RETURN—1965

... other taxable year beginning .... 1965, ending .... 19...
(PLEASE TYPE OR PRINT)

52-278951

Check if a—	Name	E. Employer Identification No.
A. Sole proprietorship ☐ or partnership ☐ electing under sec. 1361 to be taxed as a corporation.	LIBERTY LOBBY, INC.	53-[illegible]
B. Consolidated return. ☐	Number and street	F. County in which located.
C. Personal Holding Co. ☐	132 Third Street, S. E.	None
D. Business Code No. (see instr.)	City or town, State, and Postal ZIP code	G. Enter total assets from line 13 Sch. L (see instruction R).
	Washington, D. C. 20003	$ 53,589.53

IMPORTANT—All applicable lines and schedules must be filled in. If the lines on the schedules are not sufficient, see instruction Q.

GROSS INCOME	1. Gross receipts or gross sales .... Less: Returns and allowances	208,627.54
	2. Less: Cost of goods sold (Schedule A) and/or operations (attach schedule)	
	3. Gross profit	208,627.54
	4. Dividends (Schedule C)	
	5. Interest on obligations of the United States and U.S. instrumentalities	
	6. Other interest	212.03
	7. Rents	
	8. Royalties	
	9. Net gains (losses)—(separate Schedule D)	
	10. Other income (attach schedule)	
	11. TOTAL income—Add lines 3 through 10	208,839.57
DEDUCTIONS	12. Compensation of officers (Schedule E)	
	13. Salaries and wages (not deducted elsewhere)	79,217.71
	14. Repairs (do not include cost of improvements or capital expenditures)	
	15. Bad debts (Schedule F if reserve method is used)	
	16. Rents	8,738.59
	17. Taxes (attach schedule)	5,006.28
	18. Interest	2,665.00
	19. Contributions (attach schedule—see instructions for limitation)	
	20. Losses by fire, storm, shipwreck, other casualty, or theft (attach schedule)	
	21. Amortization (attach schedule)	
	22. Depreciation (Schedule G)	359.54
	23. Depletion (attach schedule)	
	24. Advertising	
	25. (a) Pension, profit-sharing, stock bonus, annuity plans (see instructions)	
	(b) Other employee benefit plans (see instructions)	
	26. Other deductions (attach schedule)	278,960.79
	27. TOTAL deductions in lines 12 through 26	373,750.42
	28. Taxable income before net operating loss deduction and special deductions (line 11 less line 27)	L(164,910.85)
	29. Less: (a) Net operating loss deduction (see instructions—attach schedule)	
	(b) Special deductions (Schedule I)	
	30. Taxable income (line 28 less line 29)	L(164,910.85)
TAX	31. TOTAL income tax (Schedule J)	None
	32. Credits: (a) Tax paid with Form 7004 application for extension (attach copy)	
	(b) Payments and credits on 1965 declaration of estimated tax	
	(c) Credit from regulated investment companies (attach Form 2439)	
	(d) Other (specify)	
	33. If tax (line 31) is larger than credits (line 32), the balance is TAX DUE. Enter balance here →	None
	34. If tax (line 31) is less than credits (line 32). Enter the OVERPAYMENT here →	
	35. Enter amount of line 34 you want: Credited on 1966 estimated tax .... Refunded	

FILE COPY

Under penalties of perjury, I declare that I have examined this return, including accompanying schedules and statements, and to the best of my knowledge and belief it is true, correct, and complete. If prepared by a person other than taxpayer, his declaration is based on all information of which he has any knowledge.

CORPORATE SEAL

Date .... Signature ....

Right wing extremism is a thriving business, as this income tax return of Liberty Lobby, Inc., indicates. Note that its total income in 1965 was $208,839 and that claimed deductions were $373,750.

port several hundred thousand Chinese Communist troops on the Mexican mainland."

A private detective, who infiltrated a Chicago group called the Fighting American Nationalists, reported that its members practiced with pistols in their barracks-like headquarters. Their moon-faced leader, Malcolm Lambert, preached Nazi doctrines and reportedly carried a pearl-handled revolver inside his coat. The American Nazi Party has its own storm troopers in Chicago, led by Roy James, who was awarded the party's Adolf Hitler medal for leaping out of an audience in Birmingham and pummeling Dr. Martin Luther King with his fists.

New York police found a deadly arsenal in a truck that had dropped off hecklers to break up racial demonstrations in the Bronx. At the home of one of the hecklers still more arms were found, including rifles, shotguns, revolvers, thousands of cartridges, bottles of nitric acid, machetes, and bayonets. Eight who were arrested turned out to be members of the fanatical American Renaissance Party.

Especially ominous is a drive by extremists to infiltrate the police. John Rouselot, the John Birch Society's publicity director, boasts that Birchers belong to all major city police forces. Though his claim no doubt is exaggerated, Birchers in police uniforms indeed have been found from New York to Los Angeles. Philadelphia's Mayor John Tate, who suspended twenty Birch members from his city's force, warned: "This is the way the Nazi party began, and this is the way the Communist party operated in the 1940's."

The John Birch Society also urges members to infiltrate school boards and PTAs. "Join your local PTA and go to work to take it over," Welch has instructed.

The National Congress of Parents and Teachers has accused Birch members and other extremists of attempting to emasculate both the curriculum and teaching methods in local schools, "to bar discussion of controversial ideas, and to ban certain

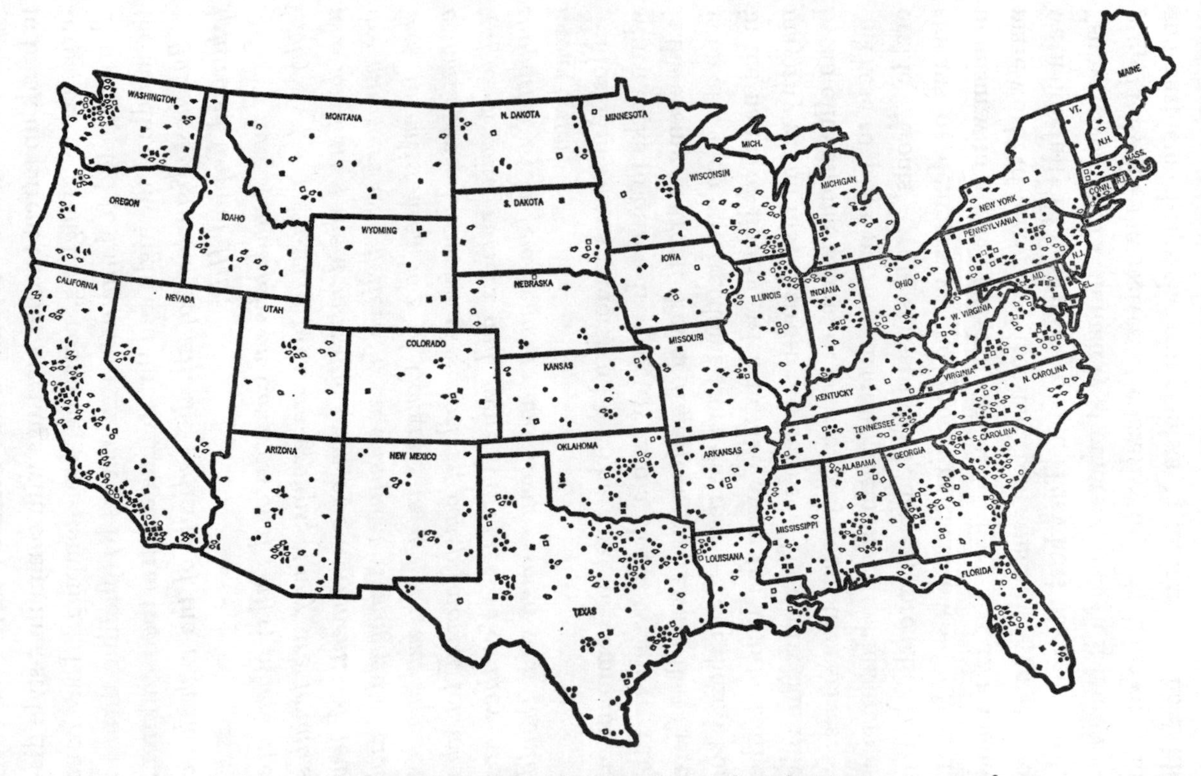

A map showing the extent of right wing radio-television propaganda.
Each dot pinpoin[illegible] where such propaganda is broadcast.

books" from the classroom. Some Birchites have even tried to break up parent-teacher meetings with communist-style disturbances—haranguing, coughing, foot-stomping. They have also attempted to intimidate PTA officers by phoning them in the middle of the night and threatening to harm their children.

But most disturbing of all, the radicals of the right have infiltrated Capitol Hill.

Some have found jobs on Congressional staffs; others are lobbyists for right-wing pressure groups. They are fanatics who don't trust the democratic form of government. A few are ministers who believe in an imminent Armageddon and seek to enlist Members of Congress in a holy war against communism. They are a humorless, conspiratorial lot who traffic in wild rumors and weird intrigues. Yet they are supported by a few Senators and Congressmen who should know better.

Most Americans understand the challenge of communism, which seeks to turn a free society into a closed tyranny. This is the enemy in front. Fewer Americans are aware that there is an attack on our freedoms from the rear—from those who, in the name of liberty, wish to take away the liberty of the majority whom they distrust and despise. They advocate rule by an elite among whom, of course, they count themselves.

These soapbox patriots disguise themselves behind innumerable "fronts" with star-spangled names, preach all the slogans of democracy, and proclaim their hatred of communism with a great gnashing of teeth. They live in a nightmare world of terror and treason, from which they emerge to warn dolefully of impending doom. They hurl the ugly word, "subversive," indiscriminately at others, although it more appropriately fits themselves. Generally their doctrine of hate and suspicion helps the communists to undermine the faith of Americans in their government.

It is one of the paradoxes of our time that the fanatics of the right and the left, who profess to be bitter enemies, often find themselves dancing together around the May Day pole. Consider the testimony of Arthur Larson who, as director of the U. S. Information Service under former President Eisenhower, made a close study of the communist line: "It is more than a coincidence that the communists and the right wingers are usually found on the same side of major international issues. It is also an historical fact that the communists' bitterest hate has always been reserved for the progressive moderates." They backed "peace" candidates against liberal Democrats in many districts, for example, in the 1966 election.

Similiarly, the right wingers' bitterest hate has been directed against conservatives. They talk loudly against communists but work against conservatives. In state after state, the extremists campaigned against conservative candidates in 1966. They even put up a John Birch tub-thumper against Senator Karl Mundt, (R-S. D.), who has endorsed many right-wing causes but is too genuine a conservative to suit the fanatics. In the secrecy of their own circle Scott Stanley, editor of the John Birch Society's official magazine, *American Opinion,* recently directed his fire against the very conservatives whom the group is trying to recruit, against what he called "the comfortable, well-fed, travel-happy, cigar-smoking conservatives whose main accomplishment is an anti-communist sticker pasted on the rear bumper of their cars."

Some right-wing groups are still flourishing on funds collected for Barry Goldwater's presidential campaign. The Citizens Committee for Conservatives alone inherited $200, 000 of unspent Goldwater contributions. Though Goldwater personally appealed to them to turn the money over to the Republican National Committee, they have used it instead to promote right-wing candidates and causes. In some areas the Young Americans for Freedom have supported extremist candidates against the GOP incumbents. Example: the YAF backed a John Birch Society coordinator, William Flax, against Congressman Robert Taft, Jr. in Ohio. In New Jersey the Republicans drummed out of the party some YAF leaders, known locally as the Rat Finks, who sang anti-Negro and anti-Semetic songs at a Young Republican convention.

Liberty Lobby, whose policy board reads like "Who's Who" in the right wing, has issued strident propaganda attacking Republican leaders. One pamphlet, professing to reveal "How the GOP Leadership Sells Out the Voters," called Senate Republican Leader Everett Dirksen "slippery" and derided former House Republican Leader Charles Halleck as lacking backbone. However, Liberty Lobby has called upon right wingers not to desert the GOP but to fight for control. "A Party-within-a-Party should be built in every state where control of the GOP is not already in Conservative [meaning right-wing] hands," urges a Liberty Lobby memo.

Thus the truth is beginning to dawn that the radicals of the right are not conservatives at all; their only desire is to dominate. They give lip service to conservative ideals, just as the communists have counterfeited the language of the liberals. If communists speak of dictatorships as "peoples' democracies" and aggressors as "liberators," so do the right-wing extremists promise "more individual freedom" and "less government" at the same time that they plot to restrict the freedom of those who do not agree with their warped views.

The inroads these fanatics have made on Capitol Hill should be a matter of national alarm. With plenty of money to spend, they have attached themselves like limpets to powerful men in the Senate and the House. One nest of right wingers gathers on Saturday afternoons, usually in the office of some Congressman, for grim bull sessions. There is tortured talk about the State Department's "plot" to turn the country over to the communists, the "infiltration" of the Central Intelligence Agency by communist spies, the secret and sinister hold that mysterious "Fabian Socialists" have achieved on the White

Bartlesville, Okla. Examiner Enterprise, Wednesday, October 28, 1964

COMMUNIST PARTY U.S.A. SUPPORTS PRES. JOHNSON

The Worker
WEEKEND EDITION

The Worker declares that only under a Johnson Administration will the United States remain a fertile field for the continued growth of socialistic ideals leading to a Soviet America. The Editors warn that the election of a Goldwater-Miller Ticket would "wipe out" all the gains of Communism!

—The Worker, July 26, 1964

Gus Hall, Secretary General of the Communist Party, U.S.A., Said The Communists Fronts NOW Active In The U.S.A. Are Operating Almost Wholly "Within The Orbit Of The Democratic Party!"

Scare propaganda disseminated during the 1964 campaign.

House. The conspirators of the right even profess to know the target date for the complete communist take-over of America.

Sometimes the paranoia reaches absurdity with epithets like the Liberty Lobby's reference to "Political Zionist Planners for Absolute Rule via One World Government." Beneath the surface is a witches' brew of hatred against Jews and Negroes. Seldom is it spoken; most of it is subliminal. Attacks are directed against "wrong" thinkers rather than "wrong" races, but disclaimers of prejudice invariably reek of malevolence.

Typical is Richard Cotten who delivers a radio commentary called "Conservative Viewpoint," which the Anti-Defamation League has charged is defamatory and anti-Semitic. Cotten professes to hold pious feelings for all mankind, Jews and gentiles alike. In this spirit of brotherly love, he condemns organized Jewry as "the international and satanic hidden hand," and singles out prominent Jews for personal attacks. No less zealous are such men of the pulpit as Carl McIntire, a defrocked Presbyterian minister, and Billy James Hargis, a former Disciples of Christ pastor, who preach a gospel of hate-thy-neighbor which must sound grotesque to the Maker they profess to serve.

If these hate specialists lack evidence for their smears, they simply conjure it up. Frank Capell, a right-wing pamphleteer convicted of an ugly smear against Senator Thomas Kuchel (R-Calif), has surpassed even that vicious attack. He has produced a pamphlet, bound in red, accusing the communists of murdering actress Marilyn Monroe in order to cover up an alleged affair with Senator Robert Kennedy (D-N.Y.).

Yet these twisted souls appear to have the free run of certain Congressional offices. Capell was put in touch with the Teamsters Union, for example, by the office of Congressman Michael Feighan (D-Ohio). But not even the Teamsters, who have no love for Bobby Kennedy, would help circulate Capell's bizarre pamphlet. Cotten, who virtually makes himself at home in Rep. Feighan's office, actually featured the Congressman on one of his notorious broadcasts. This was the same program that the Federal Communications Commission had been asked to bar from the air. The majority of Commissioners, though expressing "the strongest personal feelings against the views represented," voted not to interfere with Cotten's freedom of comment. Dissenting, Commissioner Kenneth Cox accused Cotten of broadcasting, "with reckless disregard of its truth or falsity, viciously defamatory matters."

The right-wing infection has turned Congressman Feighan, once an engaging Irishman, into a suspicious old man. He recently rose on the House floor to charge that the Central Intelligence Agency and State Department were communist-infiltrated. At a 1965 immigration conference in Switzerland, he suddenly assailed the memory of the late President Kennedy for "his left-wing attitudes and his softness on communism." Life magazine reported that Feighan also called the slain President "a nigger lover." It is no mere coincidence, of course, that the right wingers have brought their influence to bear on poor Feighan. He is next in line to suceed 78-year-old Congressman Emanuel Celler (D-N.Y.), as chairman of the powerful House Judiciary Committee.

Those Saturday right-wing bull sessions on Capitol Hill, incidentally, have been attended by no less a person than Speaker John McCormack, No. 3 man in line for the presidency, who is dominated by an intense hatred of communism. He has been careful not to lend his name to right-wing causes, but I can find no evidence that he ever registered his disgust at the nonsense he has heard.

Admittedly, the peril on the right is more difficult to perceive than the communist threat. It isn't likely anyone in Congress could be persuaded to attend a communist front meeting. But with an anti-communist war going on in Vietnam, with Red China exploding atomic bombs, with Russia still blustering in Europe, the right wingers seem to be saying things that appeal to unthinking prejudice. *Result: a disturbing number of legislators have endorsed right-wing causes. Like the ultra-liberals of the 1930's who allowed their names to be used by communist front groups, some ultra-conservatives are now allowing their names to be used to give respectability to the right-wing fanatics.*

None has been more permissive than stern, erect Senator Strom Thurmond (R-S.C.). A legislator who literally stands on his head to keep in physical trim, he has a weakness for reactionary doctrines so long as they are wrapped in red, white, and blue. Thurmond has taken part in more far-right events, touted more far-right groups, and endorsed more far-right publications than any other Senator.

Thurmond's Senate office has been headquarters for almost every big-name right winger who visits Washington. He has arranged rooms for them to hold meetings right under the Capitol dome. He has signed letters urging financial support for the Liberty Lobby and the Young Americans for Freedom. He has advocated that all Americans read "Human Events," a right-wing publication that once advised American mothers to discourage their daughters from joining the Girl Scouts because of the organization's "subversive nature."

Senator Thurmond led the Senate defense of Major General Edwin Walker, who resigned from the Army under fire after he had tried to indoctrinate the troops under his command with John Birch Society propaganda. The Senator has also joined Carl McIntire, the right-wing evangelist, in sponsoring "Christian" youth conferences that are more like right-wing rallies.

Indeed, half of the South Carolina Congressional delegation have been infected with the radical right virus. Congressman L. Mendel Rivers of Charleston, chairman of the House Armed Services Committee, has extolled the John Birch Society on the House floor as "a nationwide organization of patriotic Americans" although he has denied being a Birch member. Congressman Albert Watson of Columbia, who

This is the Symbol of
MY FAITH

The CROSS is the symbol of Western, Christian civilization.

I believe America was founded as a CHRISTIAN Nation, and nobody has a right to destroy that tradition of the majority.

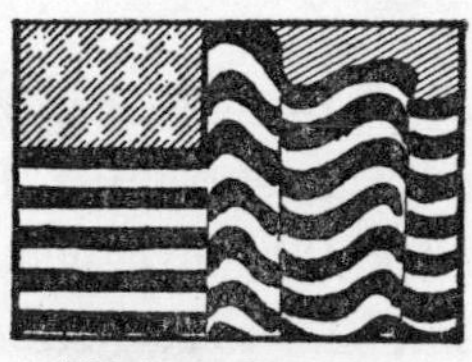

This is the Symbol of
MY COUNTRY

My ancestors fought and died to establish our blessed American Constitutional REPUBLIC.

I believe we have the right to KEEP it a REPUBLIC, not a race-mixing Democracy as the Reds preach.

This is the Symbol of
MY RACE

....My WHITE Race. The swastika was first used by the White Conquerors who brought civilization to India, the Aryans. Because I love my WHITE RACE, it does not mean I hate other races. But I DO hate what some "minority" groups are DOING to my White Christian America. Forced and hypocritical race-mixing helps NOBODY but the Communists, who want chaos and upheaval

FOR INFORMATION WRITE:
AMERICAN NAZI PARTY
POST OFFICE BOX 1381 • ARLINGTON, VA.

PRINTED IN U.S.A.

Examples of racism trying to sink its roots into American soil.

AT THE REQUEST OF
Mr Robert Welch
The Union League Club of Chicago
HAS THE HONOR TO EXTEND TO
Mr Mark E Anderson
THE PRIVILEGES OF THE CLUB
FROM June 3rd TO June 6th 1966
NUMBER 11006 [illegible] SECRETARY
OVER

This guest card was issued by John Birch Society leader Robert Welch to one of his western organizers. Chicago's exclusive Union League Club is composed of wealthy businessmen who are supposedly selective about whom they will admit.

switched to the GOP after the Democrats stripped him of his seniority, has plugged the extremist Liberty Lobby. In a letter mailed out to 100,000 prospective customers of the group's "Liberty Letter," he urged subscriptions as "A good way to keep abreast of these perilous times on Capitol Hill . . ." Congressman W. J. Bryan Dorn of Greenwood, is the recipient of a citation from the Liberty Lobby proclaiming him a "Statesman of the Republic." He was also a featured speaker at a so-called "Coalition Conference" attended by far right leaders who sought to unite but couldn't overcome personal rivalries.

In addition to Dorn, the Liberty Lobby has bestowed its "Statesman of the Republic" awards on Congressmen E. Y. Berry (R-S.D.), John Dowdy (D-Tex.), James Utt (R-Calif.), Joe Waggonner, Jr., (D-La), and John Bell Williams, (D-Miss.).

The Liberty Lobby carefully inspects the voting records of Senators and Congressmen for "communist" tendencies. Only three—Representatives Berry, Utt, and Waggoner—have consistently qualified as this extremist group's idea of 100 percent Americans. Ironically, Senator Thurmond averaged out as a mere 95 percent American, though no doubt it will startle him to discover anyone could be more patriotic than himself.

Like Watson, Congressman Utt has permitted his name to be used to sell subscriptions to "Liberty Letter." Here's his sales letter pitch:

"Liberty Lobby consistently works in the halls of Congress to oppose the international socialist takeover. Its 50,000 Conservative activists form a letter writing brigade which has already made its influence felt in several crucial votes . . . To be able to exert maximum effectiveness, Liberty Lobby needs the support of every concerned and conscientious American. That is why I am writing you. I strongly urge you to send in your subscription to Liberty Lobby's legislative report,

HONORARY CO-CHAIRMEN
HON. WARREN R. AUSTIN • HON. JOSEPH C. GREW
STEERING COMMITTEE
SEN. PAUL H. DOUGLAS, HON. CHARLES EDISON, REP. WALTER H. JUDD, SEN. KENNETH B. KEATING, HON. H. ALEXANDER SMITH, REP. FRANCIS E. WALTER
TREASURER DR. B. A. GARSIDE • SECRETARY MR. MARVIN LIEBMAN

THE COMMITTEE OF ONE MILLION

Against the Admission of Communist China to the United Nations

SUITE 909 • 79 MADISON AVENUE, NEW YORK 16, NEW YORK • MURRAY HILL 5-0190

NON-CONGRESSIONAL MEMBERS

(Partial List)

Mr. Robert S. Allen
Mr. Murray Baron
Gen. Lewis H. Brereton
Mr. George Bucher
Mr. Wm. F. Buckley, Jr.
Mr. James Burnham
Miss Taylor Caldwell
Mr. John Chamberlain
Gen. Lucius D. Clay
Fr. Dennis J. Comey, S.J.
Adm. Charles M. Cooke
Bishop Fred P. Corson
Mr. C. Suydam Cutting
Mr. Cleveland E. Dodge
Mr. John Dos Passos
Dr. Paul F. Douglass
Mr. Max Eastman
Mr. Christopher Emmet
Mr. James T. Farrell
Mr. Bob Feller
Mrs. Geraldine Fitch
Hon. Ralph E. Flanders
Mr. J. Peter Grace, Jr.
Mr. Albert M. Greenfield
Dr. Magnus I. Gregersen
Adm. J. L. Hall, Jr.
Gen. E. N. Harmon
Rev. Frederick Brown Harris
Adm. Thomas C. Hart
Gen. John R. Hodge
Mr. Sal B. Hoffmann
Prof. Sidney Hook
Hon. Stanley K. Hornbeck
Gen. Robert W. Johnson
Prof. Horace M. Kallen
Mr. H. V. Kaltenborn
Gen. George C. Kenney
Hon. Wm. F. Knowland
Mrs. Alfred Kohlberg
Mr. Victor Lasky
Dr. Emil Lengyel
Mr. Marx Lewis
Mr. Eli Lilly
Mr. William Loeb
Adm. Leland P. Lovette
Gen. Frank E. Lowe
Mr. Henry R. Luce
Mr. Eugene Lyons
Mr. Arthur G. McDowell
Fr. F. A. McGuire, C.M.
Bishop Leslie R. Marston
Mr. Adolph Menjou
Mr. Frank S. Meyer
Hon. Robert Morris
Mr. Norbert Muhlen
Mrs. Robert B. Patterson
Rev. Norman Vincent Peale
Col. Bruce Pirnie
Rev. Daniel A. Poling
Miss Katherine Anne Porter
Adm. Arthur W. Radford
Mr. Serafino Romualdi
Mr. George S. Schuyler
Mr. Leslie R. Severinghaus
Bishop Bernard J. Sheil
Mr. Igor I. Sikorsky
Bishop John M. Springer
Dr. Robert G. Sproul
Adm. William H. Standley
Adm. Emory D. Stanley
Dr. Wendell M. Stanley
Hon. J. Leighton Stuart
Prof. George E. Taylor
Archbishop Theodotus
Mr. Ralph de Toledano
Gen. James A. Van Fleet
Gen. Albert C. Wedemeyer
Bishop Herbert Welch
Mr. William L. White
Dr. W. Carlos Williams
Dr. Karl A. Wittfogel
Dr. Max Yergan

TO: CITY EDITORS
EDITORIAL WRITERS
COLUMNISTS
COMMENTATORS

FOR RELEASE TO ALL PAPERS
MONDAY, SEPTEMBER 24, 1962

259 CONGRESSMEN URGE DEFENSE OF QUEMOY

OPPOSE "TWO CHINA" POLICY AND ADMISSION OF RED CHINA TO U.N.

New York, New York: 36 Senators and 223 Representatives joined in issuing a Declaration which called for the defense of Quemoy and Matsu and opposed any "two China" policy which would seat Red China in the United Nations. The Declaration was circulated by the Committee Of One Million (Against the Admission of Communist China to the United Nations) which is headed by Warren R. Austin, former U.S. Senator and first U.S. Ambassador to the U.N. and Joseph C. Grew, former U. S. Ambassador to Japan and Under Secretary of State. The group's Steering Committee include Senators Paul H. Douglas (D., Ill.) and Kenneth B. Keating (R., N.Y.); Representatives Walter H. Judd (R., Minn.) and Francis E. Walter (D., Penna.); Charles Edison, former Governor of New Jersey and Secretary of the Navy; and H. Alexander Smith, former U.S. Senator and Special Assistant to the Secretary of State.

The Declaration said: "The President of the United States and his Secretary of State are publicly committed to a sound and firm policy toward Communist China. This position has the support of the American people and the Congress. Recently, there has been renewed pressure on the part of some American publications, organizations and individuals calling for drastic changes in this line of action through offering various and substantial concessions to Communist China. We, therefore, believe it appropriate at this time to reemphasize and to reiterate our support of United States policy toward the Peiping regime.

A spin-off of Chiang Kai-shek's China lobby, the "Committee of One Million" is composed largely of right wingers determined to keep Red China out of the United Nations.

Liberty Letter, without delay. The cost? Only one dollar per year. . . . The battle is on here in the nation's capitol and the call is to every real patriot."

A more cautious letter touting Liberty Letter has been mailed out to 100,000 people under the signature of Congressman Otto Passman (D-La.). The self-styled "Louisiana country boy" declared: "I am not a member or supporter of the Liberty Lobby, but I like some of the things they stand for. This is the first time in my 18 years in Congress that I have recommended that anybody buy anything or subscribe to anything."

Two of the most enthusiastic endorsers of radical right causes are Congressman John Ashbrook, (R-Ohio), a flaming young militant, and Congressman Berry, a more stodgy ultra-conservative. If a right-wing promoter needs a speaker, patron, or patsy, he can usually count upon Ashbrook or Berry. They seem ready to lend the dignity of their office to anyone who shouts loudly enough that he is anti-communist. They fail to recognize that, while all good Americans are anti-communists, unfortunately, not all anti-communists are good Americans.

Another who seems unable to distinguish between good and bad anti-communists is Congressman Durward Hall (R-Mo.), a physician with a severe bedside manner. If his medical diagnoses were as indiscriminate as his political disgnoses, he would be treating everyone for cancer. Though he is not a member of the John Birch Society, he considers it a "fine" organization. The only reason he has not joined, he says, is because "I haven't been asked." His logic: "I think anything that comes out against communism is a good thing." This reasoning would put him on the side of the American Nazi Party, the Ku Klux Klan and the Black Muslims, to name a few.

The far-right extremists have money and plenty of it. Not a few Texas oil tycoons, including billionaire H. L. Hunt, have wide-open check books for almost any organization that claims to be anti-communist. These are the greenest of pastures for the hate peddlers and pamphleteers. The freedom of any American to express an opinion, no matter how wild, is basic. But it is also a duty of sane Americans—men of influence, above all—to be on guard against the fanatics of the right as well as the left.

In their campaign to influence Congress, the infiltrators of the right are supported by a spate of hate which pours in through the mails. *Of the thousands of letters, postcards, and telegrams that swamp Congressional offices, about 10 to 15 percent are devoted to vitriol.* What disturbs most members of Congress is the sickness it reveals in our midst. "Malice in wonderland," humorist Bill Mauldin calls it.

A Senator who catalogs and studies his hate mail believes the letter writers are paranoic. They seem to be obsessed OVER PLOTS!! to OVERTHROW AMERICA!! They also rave about the failure of the press to tell the PEOPLE the TRUTH!! They make their points by using capital letters, writing them in red ink, or underscoring them many times. Some are savage in their denunciations, threatening death or torture. Yet a sampling of 600 letters received by Senator Thomas Kuchel (R-Calif.) reveals a surprisingly high standard of literacy. Many are written in the shaky handwriting of the elderly. (Little old ladies in tennis shoes?) But one pattern runs through all the anguished letters; they are characterized by an almost complete lack of logic. The statements are overwrought, over suspicious and over-aggressive. They may advocate causes for which there are legitimate arguments, but these points are ignored in a flood of hysteria. *Generally missing are the simplest elements of reason.*

Senator Kuchel gets 60,000 letters a month and estimates that at least 6,000 of them are paranoic. He calls them "my fright mail." They are written by fanatics with feverish imaginations, who have reported such memorable "plots" as these: *"Some 35,000 Communist Chinese troops bearing arms and wearing powder-blue uniforms, are poised on the Mexican border about to invade San Diego. The United States has turned over—or will at any moment—its Army, Navy, and Air Force to the command of a Russian colonel in the United Nations. Almost every well-known American leader is, in reality, a top communist agent. A U. S. Army guerrilla-warfare exercise in Georgia, called Water Moccasin III, was in fact a United Nations operation to take over the country."*

My own survey of hate mail indicates that most of it comes from the far right, from people who are convinced that the nation is in the grip of a vast communist conspiracy. The recurrent theme is that the government is hopelessly infiltrated by communists. The only wonder is, if this is believed, that the Kremlin hasn't taken over formally. Many letter writers claim to have a mysterious, intimate knowledge of the communist timetable. "Time is running out," they warn. An Arlington, Virginia man with inside information warns that the Reds will complete their takeover in exactly 18 months. "The 1964 election," he declares darkly, "was our last free election." But further down, his letter maintains that even the 1964 election was manipulated by the communists.

An Illinois writer, also claiming access to Kremlin secrets unavailable to others, goes even further. He holds that the late President Kennedy was a communist tool and was shot for falling behind schedule. The writer continues: "The effective capture of the United States was supposed to have occurred in 1963."

Of course, some extremist mail comes from the lunatics of the left. In one week Senator Gale McGee (D-Wyo.) received threatening letters from fanatics of opposite ideologies. A Seattle peace-monger, in the name of non-violence, threatened violence against the Senator. A Washington, D. C., war-monger, in the name of Christianity, called him some decidedly un-Christian names. The peace-monger threatened: "Mc-

Gee, we are warning you if we get in a big war we will kill you just as sure as the sun sets in the West. All war-mongers like you will be killed, and we mean what we say. Any man who wants war is a maniac and must be lynched, and put out of the way down in the ground where he won't harm anybody, and that is the place where you belong." The war-monger cursed: "It is bastards like you that have torn up the Federal Constitution and collaborated with the enemy in a cowardly scheme to destroy Christianity from all the face of the earth. Now you propose to finish the job by suppressing the right to bear arms. How in the hell the decent people of Wyoming ever elected a screwball like you to the Senate is one for the books."

After surveying the hate mail of two Senators—some 3,000 letters and postcards—the Anti-Defamation League concluded: "The two dominant things in the mail are sadism and smut. Not only is the great proportion of the mail insulting and vituperative, but it tells the Senator to drop dead, take poison, hang himself, drown himself, etc. The terrific amount of misinformation and illogic is a sad commentary on our educational system and on our newspapers."

The fright mail includes a startling number of letters from doctors, men who no doubt are completely competent in their profession. Yet in other areas they seem to be somewhat abnormal. They refuse to face established facts; their release for hidden frustrations is to spew out hate. For whatever interest it may be to psychiatrists, virtually no letters from attorneys turned up in the hate samplings.

It is a paradox that the sicker the writers may be, the more often they accuse their victims of being sick. Typical is this letter to Senator McGee, which starts: "You poor demented sick devil!!! Get *out* of *our* country or we will have you put away in a mental institution where you *rightfully* belong. You poor demented idiot, Americans who have never heard of you before now *hate* you with a *violent,* white hot hate!!!! We never realized such a devil, such an *animal* existed as you, and to think you even walk on legs, with your tail between your legs to be sure!!! You're no man, you sick, demented fool!!! Get yourself in a mental institution before you are put there *bodily* by decent God-fearing loyal Americans."

The hate samplings collected on Capitol Hill reveal that most come from California: 23%; the Midwest and Deep South account for 19% each; Texas is next with 11%; followed by Florida with 9%. The West Coast, not counting California, mailed in 8%, the East Coast only 4%.

Those who are accustomed to receiving fright mail have found the answer lies in the waste basket. *But the spate of hate is spreading. When it extends to the families of soldiers on the battlefield and to neighbors who have voiced a sincere view on a local issue, then this becomes serious.* What can be done? It is almost impossible to legislate against crackpots without impairing the rights of sane citizens. For in a free society, the crankiest crank must be allowed the right to air his views.

The poor souls, tormented by nightmares, are less to blame than the hate merchants, many of them opportunists, who feed the fears of the fanatics. Much of the hate literature, running through the sewers of America, is written less to spread the word than to extract dollars from the disciples. For the writers and promoters have discovered there are huge profits to be made from prejudice. Fanatics will dig deep into their pockets for money to buy literature that fans the fire within them. Men of affluence, fearful of socialistic seizure of their property, will donate heavily to right-wing causes. Shortly before this book went to press, the John Birch Society received two individual bequests of $250,000 and $1 million.

Extremist pressure groups, like the JBS *and the Liberty Lobby, have mushroomed almost out of nowhere into sizeable, big-money operations.* Rare is the right-wing project that

WHY I JOINED THE JOHN BIRCH SOCIETY

Some day, when people are able to look at themselves dispassionately, perhaps the true history of these times can be told. However, until that day the world will always need honest, stout-hearted men to interpret the times correctly. Hence, I have taken it upon myself to lay the WORD on my friends and neighbors in the hopes that they will consequently be able to see, and aid me in the good fight!

My interest in political activity started some years ago when I was still in college. At that time I was with a fast crowd. You know, freethinkers, perverts, dope-fiends. I was eventually sickened by all this dissipation and later found myself in a great state of psychologico-philosophico-economico-religico-metabolico-politico depression. In my darkest moment I was found and led to light by a member of the Birch Society. I vowed from that moment I would serve only the Society, and no other false gods.

I later discovered that my former friends (now my detractors and taunters) were actually all a part of the vast, dread communist conspiracy that has come within sight of grandma's prayers of taking over the country. (It is a known fact that the communists fear nothing. They are audacity impersonalized.)

With these facts I issue a challenge to all Americans. Crawl out of your air-conditioned bomb shelters and fight! Smash your stores of canned water and cookies! Make your action irreversible! The liars who wrote our American history have so confused you that we doubt if you understand half of what you read. (Even WE are sometimes confused!) You most likely are still under the impression that full-page ads like this were probably paid for by kooks and fanatics, when really I (and the other five fellows in the cellar with me) are the only real patriots left in a country which has drifted so far left it may soon drop off the edge of the world. (It isn't advised to be too hasty about accepting that subversive foreign doctrine that says the world is round. All the statistics aren't in yet!)

A major symptom of the communist disease is that we do not recognize traitors when we see them, when actually we are surrounded and nearly swamped by treason! treason! easoneasoneason sonsonson! My friends! Do you know that many of the "great Americans" whom we admire were really infiltrators sent by the Kremlin! The enormity of the thought! The control exerted by our Liberal, Socialist, Communist masters is based on the lie that the Russian Revolution took place in 1917. The FACTS are quite different. It really happened one hundred years earlier, in 1817, but its existence was the best-kept secret of that century. Ivan the Terrible was really named Barry Ivanovitch Giltwasserski, and his persecution and mutilation of the starving Russian peasantry was simply a deceptive technique which proves he was nothing more than a tool of the class revolution. Throughout his reign the slow, insidious infiltration of top government positions took place until on the eve of the centennial of the rise of "Ivan" the actual revolution was nothing more than a push-over. There wasn't even a fight; the soldiers of the Republic had been steeped in propaganda from their own state department. Americans! Heed the warning!

With the Bolsheviks already active in 1817, seventeen cells were immediately dispatched to America, where one of them joined the march of the pioneers to Central Illinois. (About their activities in the G.A.R., more later.) It is enough now to mention that approximately 55% of the early settlers carried RED bandanas next to their hearts!

I should like to ask at this point if ever, as a small child on the farm, you attended a barn-raising? This is a communal effort. Have you poisoned the social thinking of your children by taking them to potluck suppers? This kind of communist training in share-and-share-alike theories have so weakened our moral fiber that our nation may soon fall! Our secret tip, from sources too high to identify, is that the take-over will be accomplished by doping the potato salad with truth serum, so that all who attend potluck suppers will feel urged to rise and confess their "sins" against the Almighty State. Then the local Commissar will train the enslaved and terrorized picnicers to munch their fried chicken in unison while humming the Internationale.

I would like to point out to you that much of the alien Bolshevik way of life which has been forced on us has come about through our idolatry of a popular Republican president who was really a conscious, dedicated agent of the Communist Conspiracy for all of his adult life. This man can be proved to be a communist because he associated with people who were communists because they associated with other individuals suspected of left leanings.

This president posed as a great war leader when, as we all know, he never fired a machine gun in his life. (On the contrary he left the nation war-torn and saddled with an intolerable debt that would have enslaved the nation on the spot if it were not for our superb morality at the time.) He also claimed to have given civil rights to the Negroes and he even went so far as to use federal troops to enforce his interracial designs in the South. Is it necessary to point out that all the members of his own family were white?

We refer, naturally, to that alien traitor, Abraham Lincoln! (Few historians realize the Zionist implications of his choice of a first name.) There have been those brave few recently who have tried to "read Abe Lincoln out of the Republican Party". It was to be expected that they would meet with many a stiff arm and upper lip, which is exactly what has come about. Even the present leaders of the party are hesitant about this important point. It shows grave weaknesses and pinko concessions on their part. As I have demonstrated, it is essential that the name of Lincoln be purged from party rolls and history for all time.

How does all of this apply to the eventual take-over of America? (Note: It has been said that America is over 50% controlled at the present. I know better. Comsymps make statements like that to lull the average guy who is too busy making an honest living to study the matter. The fact is that it is more nearly something like 98%. Put THAT in your pipe.)

Simple arithmetic would show anyone caring about the matter that the communists have in fact ALREADY TAKEN OVER THE WORLD! We must fight harder than ever! How is the final capitulalation of America going to come about? By the following method, my friend:

A. The communists in the Kremlin have worked out a master plan in trade for the test-ban treaty: one out of every three persons elected to public office will be communist.

B. There will be an end to the oil depletion allowance, the mainstay of American economic life against the tide of communism.

1. Teachers will be forced to recite passages from the complete works of Marx to replace school prayer.
2. Molybdenum will be placed in all public water treatment plants to soften our brains and damage our doudenums.
3. A total breakdown in our passenger railroad service which will lead us to total chaos.
   a. The mass release of hardened criminals from our model prisons; all of whom will immediately get jobs in the civil rights movement.
   b. The raising of farm parity laws to the point where all farmers will no longer work at all.
      Sub 1. The gradual takeover of the U.S. by the communist-dominated F.B.I.
      Sub Sub 2. Hollywood's recent announcement that they will make a super spectacularscope production of "The Life and Hard Times of Karl Marx", in color, starring Tony Perkins and Ma Kettle.
      Glub. Personal attacks on me and my organization which will lead to universal conflagration and apoplexy.

All of the above facts have led me to the conclusion that all of our existing organizations are not "extreme" enough in the defense of our precious liberties. This has led me to even doubt the veracity of the John Birch Society. The John Birch Society (Jaybeez) have, through the agency of the magazine, "American Opinion" published articles on lefties such as that infamous Martin Luther King, Jr. (We had a photograph of him preaching to a group of Peace Corps youth some years ago. Among their ranks appeared none other than Lee Harvey Oswald! However, this valuable document was filched from us by a Harvard-educated CIA agent.)

"Moderation in the pursuit of ANYTHING is no virtue!"

(We now have good reason to believe that Oswald is alive in Angola training insurgents with our tax money. Justice Warren, of course, is using all his might to hide this startling fact in order to frame Jack Ruby.) These mighty truths are hidden from the public even with the Birchers. As a result, I have broken with my onetime mentor and [illegible] a path of Truth and Goodness and Right that is unparalled. (It should be realized by all my readers that the presidential hopeful for the Republicans is dragging the Birchers through the mud of moderatcism, which is only a step from socialism; and who is unaware of THAT hidden dragon in our society?) I am calling on all you right-thinking Americans to join with me! Have you truly virtue and undaunted courage? Can you unglue yourselves from the Red Menace of Teevee? Are you truly independent and aware of the grave issues? Can you break into houses when your chief demands it? Can you crawl on your belly like a reptile? Can you snatch purses in the defense of Freedom? If you have these rare, all-American qualities, then you can be admitted to the ranks of the New Organization of the Right, FFFF! Facts For Freedom Foundation!

Join with me! Send your dimes and dollars (estate management service offered free of charge) today! Since 1963, 99.44% of Americans have been inalterably contaminated. Needless, this has hamstrung the House Unamerican Activities Committee investigative efforts. This situation shall be remedied! Our Motto: An Investigator for Every Taxpayer!

DO YOU WANT MORE?

- More financial support for known Communists such as Franco, Salazar and Chiang-Kai-Chek?
- More Supreme Court decisions that give more votes to two downtown, crook-ridden Chicago acres than to 200 acres of virtuous, rich central Illinois farmland?
- More Attorney Generals who force Sensorship on their own brothers and force hateful voting rights on happy, banjo-strummin', carefree southern laborers?
- More State Department plans to abolish our universally beloved, all-American drab laws? (Ask your [illegible] about this question.) More plans to stop inter-national anarchy and war, and starve our defense workers to death.
- More deals with the Kremlin determining the number of missionaries into the Congo?
- More disease-ridden kids as a result of swimming in fluoridated public pools?
- More textbooks that teach that [illegible]
- More price increases, more taxes, more injustice, more wasted space in newspapers, more anxiety toward our future? Then don't join us! Sit on your thumbs! Our organization is for those who think young and for themselves!
- For an introductory packet on our ideas send a blank check to: FFFF!, MOSCOW, IDAHO

FFFF! MOSCOW, IDAHO

MAIL ORDER COUPON

FACTS FOR FREEDOM FOUNDATION MOSCOW, IDAHO

Dear Sirs: Please send me the following books or booklets at the prices indicated that I have checked below:

☐ **The ABCs of Winning Debates** — BY DR. W. M. SCHMALTZ
An amazing account of the author's many encounters, both public and private, with dirty commies! How he uses the correct lines of thought to win over innumerable public enemies! (Only $10.00 per pamphlet.)

☐ **THE MORTICIAN** — BY ROBERT BELCH
A biography of the hard times of the people of America under the infamous President, "Red" Kennedy. Hidden soup lines revealed for the first time! Accounts of Pagan Romanish activities in Washington! Revealed: The "Black Chamber" under the White House! New facts on the Assassination and the Great Foreign Plot! Get several copies for friends! Only $24.95 per copy.

☐ **Grandma Was a Comsymp** — BY PROF. REVILO BOLLIXER
The insidious growth of Communism in family life, as characterized by the [illegible] "Children, you [illegible]"

☐ **None Dare Call it Reason** — COLLECTED ESSAYS, ED. BY EVERETT McKINLEY ROWE
Rats in the Sewers of Journalism: The big plot to Prevent Freedom thru Public Poetry Programs; 99 44/100% of the Clergy Dead, Don't They? [illegible] by Nikita Khrushchev. The Cotton-picking of the Bay of Pigs, all revealed with six-color illustrations for just 29¢.

Answer These If You Can!

1) Are you really hip? If not, what are you doing to achieve hipness?
2) If you are hip, why is FFFF! Peace?
3) Do you have acne?
4) Who can defend America more favorably than FFFF!?
5) Without FFFF! All is lost! (We're in debt up to our ears for WW II bomb shelters [illegible] Argentina.)
6) What is your income bracket?
7) Tautological. See question #1.
8) Do you want to see the [illegible], God, motherhood, the flag, [illegible] apple pie under Communist shackles? What are you doing to prevent this irreversible trend?
9) Ref. question 1 again. Are you willing to force (Reads Police Brutality) your neighbors to [illegible] truth? What are you, a pansy?
10) We pledge not to stand fast! Will you join us, or [illegible]?

For further information about FFFF! Send $15 for a special whopping truth-packed folder [illegible] FFFF! MOSCOW, IDAHO

FFFF! MOSCOW, IDAHO

Robert Belch, President
H.L. Runt, Finance Chairman
General Balker, Drill Corps
Revilo Bollixer, Philosopher

THIS PRESENTATION WAS MADE POSSIBLE BY THE GENEROSITY AND SIMPLEMINDEDNESS OF THE EDITOR, WHO LEFT THE OFFICE UNLOCKED AND FORGOT TO PROOFREAD THIS PAGE!

Ridicule of this sort has been an effective means of showing up extremists. This appeared in the Prairie Post (Maroa, Illinois).

doesn't have its price tag. The first thing a fanatic learns, once he's hooked by one of the outfits, is that it costs to defeat the communists. There is literature to buy, paraphernalia to pay for, memberships to maintain. To hasten the impeachment of Chief Justice Earl Warren, for example, the John Birch Society sells a "Warren Impeachment Packet" for $2.45. And a $1,000 contribution, which will get a person into the President's Club and entitle him to the LBJ family album, is otherwise good for a life membership in the JBS for those who esteem Robert Welch above Lyndon Johnson.

In most right-wing patriotic societies, raising funds has priority over fighting communists. Nothing, for example, will galvanize the self-proclaimed American fuehrer, George Lincoln Rockwell, into action like the scent of the green. A defector from his Nazi barracks recently described one of Rockwell's financial forays for me.

The fuehrer and several aides left their Nazi headquarters in Arlington, Virginia, with elaborate secrecy in the eerie gloom before dawn. Slouched low in the automobile, Rockwell wore dark glasses. He kept peering through the rear window to see whether they were being followed. One of his officers, Captain Robert Lloyd, tried to give the appearance of dozing. Nobody took the slightest interest in them.

Once on the highway, Rockwell, who considers it Nordic to keep the temperature frigid, rolled down all the windows and started a tape recorder going full blast with Nazi march music and Hitler's rantings. Possibly he was disappointed at not being followed and sought to attract attention. The Commander, as he prefers to be called, broke into the racket with occasional outbursts about his plan to remold society. In an aside to one of his aides he fulminated against the "scum" he was obliged to accept as troopers (a not inaccurate description, since they are mostly ex-convicts and homosexuals). "They are," he explained, "temporarily necessary." As for the sort of men he sought, he cited Captain Lloyd, who is florid-faced, pimply and pudgy—but blonde. "Ah," said Rockwell, pointing at the Captain, "If I could only breed a race of men like this!"

Their destination, which he had kept secret from his own traveling companions, proved to be an abandoned farmhouse near Nicholasville, Kentucky, deep in the tobacco country, where they met with a conspiratorial little group—some farmers, some ex-military officers who had fought the German Nazis but who were now so filled with petty hatreds that they had turned to Rockwell. The musty old frame house had belonged to the father of their host. Though the conference room had been carefully prepared, Rockwell was not satisfied. He complained about the single air conditioner and insisted that a second be purchased to get the room down to the proper Nordic climate. He also forbade smoking because it might heat up the room.

In that freezing room with all shades drawn, the conference dragged on for three days. Rockwell was in his element, playing the role of the new fuehrer to the hilt. In describing the Nazi Party, he compared it to the body of an octopus, whose tentacles were front organizations reaching out across the nation. The purpose of the meeting was to add another tentacle, he said, to be called the United White Christian Majority. Rockwell didn't mention a more pressing purpose: to squeeze money out of the embittered old men he addressed, four of whom abandoned the cause before the end of the session. But the remaining seven coughed up $1,000 apiece to found the new front. One, a portly retired officer with white, crew-cut hair, declared solemnly: *"The Nordic race originated on Mars, so it is different from the races indigenous to earth."*

Once the contributions were safely in his pocket, Rockwell flew off to a vacation in Maine. His comrades were obliged to drive back to the barracks where they found discipline had completely collapsed in the Commander's absence. Officers and troopers alike had gone on a glorious, week-long binge. One got so drunk he shot up the place, adding bullet holes to the decor. A lieutenant brought a new-found friend to the barracks who, during the alcoholic camaraderie, was rash enough to say: "You don't really believe in Rockwell, do you? Nobody can be that much of an ass." Troopers fell upon the luckless man, punching and kicking him. He ended up in the hospital with a skull fracture and other injuries. The lieutenant was picked up by the police and booked for assault and battery.

On his return, Rockwell held a solemn, Nazi-style court martial, stripped the offenders of their rank, and transferred them to Chicago. He also seized upon the opportunity to get rid of another lieutenant, who had no part in the revelry but who had beaten him at chess. He drew up 30 charges against the lieutenant, then proceeded as the prosecutor. In true Nazi tradition, Rockwell also told the "judge", Lieutenant Colonel Alan Welch, what evidence to admit, what verdict to bring in, and what punishment to mete out. The lieutenant made an impassioned plea: "I am a leader of men. Let me organize the backwoods resistance. I know guerrilla warfare . . ." But Rockwell turned a deaf ear to his chess opponent. The "leader of men" was reduced to the ranks.

After the "judge" intoned the verdict, Rockwell's favorite, Captain Lloyd, addressed the "court". Stumbling for words, he blurted in a voice chocked with emotion: "There's another charge that hasn't been mentioned. The lieutenant has said that the only reason I was made a captain was that my father had contributed to the party." Lloyd declared his honor had been impugned, demanded satisfaction, and marched into the yard to do battle.

Lloyd was a big blonde bruiser, bulging with muscles. The lieutenant, thin, sallow, and older, quietly disappeared. No one blamed him; it looked as if a massacre was about to occur. The captain, red in the face and strutting about like a turkey

(Paid Political Advertisement) (Paid Political Advertisement) (Paid Political Advertisement) (Paid Political Advertisement)

The price of the Presidency... smear lies and slander!

Every President of the United States must suffer in silence the abuse and slander that comes his way.

Why? Because no great leader could possibly take public notice of smut, because no President would dignify lies and slander in court. From George Washington to Lyndon Johnson, each President has silently had to bear malicious rumors and smut.

OF GEORGE WASHINGTON IT WAS SAID:

"I know your administration to have been deceitful; the interest of the disbanded soldier was sold to the speculator and the Chief of the Army became the patron of fraud."

Washington was accused of stealing money from the government . . . of having committed murder . . . of being soft on Britain. His enemies demanded impeachment.

OF JEFFERSON IT WAS SAID:

"Do you believe that a spendthrift, a libertine, an atheist is qualified to govern you and your posterity?"

The personal attacks on Thomas Jefferson in the election of 1800 were the most vicious of any Presidential campaign—until today!

OF EISENHOWER IT WAS SAID:

"With regard to this . . . man Eisenhower, it is difficult to avoid raising the question of deliberate treason. For his known actions and apparent purposes certainly suggest a possibility of treason to the United States, no matter how he may rationalize it to himself, as loyalty to an international dream." —Robert Welch, President of the John Birch Society.

NOW IT'S PRESIDENT JOHNSON'S TURN:

Some of the most violent and slanderous campaign literature in the history of American elections is currently being circulated in every section of the country. The mongers of hate and villification have permeated every state and city, every county and rural area.

Two infamous examples of this vicious hate material are J. Evetts Haley's "A Texan Looks at Lyndon" and John Stormer's "None Dare Call It Treason." Almost fifteen million copies of these two diatribes have been published this year.

Commenting on the use of these books, Republican Governor John Anderson, Jr., of Kansas, called it "... dirty politics."

Governor Robert E. Smylie of Idaho, Chairman of the Republican Governors' Conference, has termed "A Texan Looks at Lyndon" and similar books as "smut" and urged that they not be used in the campaign.

A LOOK AT THE MAN WHO LOOKED AT LYNDON:

J. Evetts Haley, author of "A Texan Looks at Lyndon" is an "ultra-conservative," an embittered and frustrated politician who, in the 1936 gubernatorial race in Texas ran a distant last in a field of four. In 1962 Haley was involved in another Texas gubernatorial election . . . this time as a supporter of arch-right-winger, Major General Edwin Walker.

Haley is the Chairman of a vigilante group called "Texans for America" which was created to spearhead a move to examine and censor school textbooks. One of the kinder comments used in reference to this organization was "crackpot" by Life Magazine.

J. Frank Dobie, the noted Texan historian, who had known Haley personally said, "He is a mean fighter and will kick you where it hurts. He believes the end justifies the means. He hates, hates, hates."

Let us not think for one minute, however, that Lyndon Johnson is Haley's only victim. Haley has accused former President Eisenhower of "extending regimentation (and) socialism." He has also called for the hanging of the Chief Justice of the United States.

A. C. Greene, Editor of the Dallas Times Herald, said of "A Texan Looks at Lyndon": "So outrageously, surreptitiously wrong that it is almost impossible to isolate the heavy, thick aura of wrongness and define it. The result is a book which will appall decent men. The only fit word I can find for it is evil. A more candid subtitle might be 'A Study in Unhospitalized Paranoia'!"

Haley's book purports to be documented history, and Haley proclaims his credentials as a historian. But, in writing his book, Haley violates all the rules of a respectable historian and uses as authority rumor and gossip, enhanced with fiction and an occasional fact—when it fits his purpose.

In discussing Haley's use of rumor, fiction and gossip, Ronald Dugger, Editor of the Texas Observer, points out: "Haley's way of using footnotes disguises the slipperiness of his methods. Instead of footnoting each of his assertions of vital new fact, or ostensible fact, he specifies groups of sources that he says undergirds long passages. Released from precise documentation by this method, he asserts as facts contentions that have not been established and builds rumors into interpretations that would collapse without them. Rumormongering Haley uses these phrases: 'The story is told that . . .' 'It was reported that . . .' 'There is a persistent but completely unconfirmed story that . . .'"

Haley even admitted in an interview with the New York Times that he made liberal use of rumor, but contended that "rumor is a psychological phenomenon in the public mind, the existence of which is a historical fact."

Meg Greenfield, writing in the Reporter Magazine, finds factual mistakes running throughout Haley's book and concludes that Haley "sums up every primative discontent that has made itself heard in this election year."

The Dallas Times Herald best characterizes Haley, his book and its alleged authenticity when it says: "Haley deserts historical principles and takes up personal hatred as his guide."

NONE DARE CALL IT REASON.

The author of "None Dare Call It Treason," John Stormer, is the thirty-six-year-old former chairman of the Missouri Young Republicans. Stormer denies that he is a member of the John Birch Society, but admits that his wife is a member and he recommends membership in the Society to his readers.

Stormer also recommends in "None Dare Call It Treason" that the reader subscribe to the Christian Beacon. This extremist publication once commented that Roman Catholicism is the "greatest enemy of freedom and liberty that the world has to face today" and that "one would be much better off in a Communist society than in a Roman Catholic Fascist setup."

As the New York Times points out the theme of ("None Dare Call It Treason") "is the familiar right-wing message that the nation is perilously close to total subjugation because of its leaders' conspiritorial failure to deal effectively with Communism." Stormer is non-partisan in his indictment for he expends as much vitriol on Republican Eisenhower as on Democrats Johnson and Kennedy.

The National Committee For Civic Responsibility, which has done an exhaustive study of "None Dare Call It Treason," was formed last year in Cleveland. The Committee is led by Thomas Westropp, Vice President of the Federal Savings and Loan Association of Cleveland. Members of the Ethics Committee include a monsignor, a Presbyterian minister, a rabbi and a Republican judge.

Many have expressed awe at the elaborate "documentation" of "None Dare Call It Treason," yet few have seen the NCCR study on the book in which the NCCR states: "Since this book contains 818 references supposedly substantiating the material contained therein, it gives the appearance of being the well-documented study which it claims to be. Nothing could be further from the truth!

"The reader has a right to expect that references set forth by Stormer as documentation will at least say what Stormer claims for it. In case after case, the author has subverted these references to give a totally erroneous impression and even to say precisely the opposite of what his own reference claims."

The NCCR Report also finds that "the word 'subcommittee' does not apply to ... Stormer's sources." Many sources which Stormer cites are statements of the John Birch Society or are statements made in various extreme right-wing publications. The NCCR finds "many and obvious distortions of fact, historical and otherwise." The NCCR concludes: "To the average reader (Stormer's) documentation seems impressive and few will take the time to discover that it cannot withstand even the most cursory examination. In summary, the book is at best an incredibly poor job of research and documentation, and at worst a deliberate hoax and a fraud."

WHO IS SPREADING THIS MATERIAL?

The New York Times has reported that: "Among the first organizations to buy, distribute, and promote the books was the John Birch Society. They also have been purchased by the hundreds of thousands by individual Goldwater supporters and mailed free to friends and strangers alike. They are now stocked and prominently displayed at general bookstores from coast to coast. In some cases right-wing pressure was applied to get stores to stock the books."

Right here in Richmond with its heritage of fair play, courtesy, and gentlemanly demeanor, both of these books are being eagerly distributed by those who would hope to gain from the spread of fear and mistrust.

THE SOUTHERN BAPTIST SUNDAY SCHOOL BOARD

"Dr. E. S. James, editor of the Baptist Standard in Dallas, Texas, announced that... A Texan Looks at Lyndon had been ordered removed from Baptist Book Stores carrying it.

"Dr. James L. Sullivan, executive secretary-treasurer of the Southern Baptist Sunday School Board, said the board had acted September 23."

Richmond Times-Dispatch, October 13, 1964

The people of Texas looked at J. Evetts Haley in 1956.

They resoundingly rejected him.

The people of Texas have looked at Lyndon Johnson for over thirty years.

They sent him to Washington to represent them in the House of Representatives, the Senate and as Vice President of the United States.

Senators Byrd and Robertson have looked at Lyndon Johnson.

They elected him majority leader of the Senate and supported him for President in the Democratic Convention of 1960.

The American people looked at Lyndon Johnson.

They elected him Vice President in 1960 and on November 3rd they will elect him President of the United States.

The choice is clear.

Do you believe in the responsible choice of our citizens and leaders or the distorted voice of the radical right?

CHRISTIAN CENTURY.

Of A Texan Looks at Lyndon-- "a smear biography of the President of the United States... sewer history."

Of None Dare Call It Treason-- "A package of political poison."

THE AMERICAN LEGION

"After receiving the NCCR report, the American Legion in Cleveland canceled plans to distribute (None Dare Call It Treason) as part of a fund-raising activity."

New York Times, October 4, 1964

VIRGINIANS FOR JOHNSON

Robert R. Merhige, CO-CHAIRMAN | C. Braxton Valentine, Jr., CO-CHAIRMAN | Jerome Gumenick, SECRETARY

Extremist attacks on President Johnson were answered in this advertisement, published in the Richmond (Virginia) Times-Dispatch during the 1964 campaign.

cock, was about to claim victory by default when the lieutenand suddenly materialized. He was stripped to the waist, wore tights, and was bare-footed. Gravely, he appealed: "Captain, we are Nazis. We should not be fighting each other. We should be fighting our common enemy, the Jews."

But with a roar, the captain rushed forward like an angry bull. "Kill him, captain!" yelled Rockwell. At the same moment the emaciated lieutenant stepped deftly aside, and delivered a kick to Lloyd's groin. The blonde bruiser came to an abrupt halt, the belligerence suddenly drained out of him. Slowly, he turned and gathered steam for a new charge. He was stopped again with a kick to the midsection. Only once or twice did he succeed in getting his paws on the older man, who easily slipped out of his grasp and kept landing those terrible barefoot kicks. Rockwell's cries of "Kill, him captain, kill him," had now died to an astonished silence. The last kick felled Lloyd, who sat in a daze, legs spraddled, bleeding from the mouth, nose and ears. The victor explained that he had not worn shoes to avoid killing the man, then walked away.

It is worth a few words to describe George Lincoln Rockwell, extremist extraordinary. Anyone less like an Aryan superman would be hard to imagine. Dark-haired, he has schooled his features into a dark, brooding look, accentuated by the heavy pout of his lower lip. In his quarters at the Nazi barracks, he can usually be found slouched glumly in an old stuffed chair, unwashed and unshaved, dressed in faded blue slacks and a seedy T-shirt. Tufts of black hair poke through holes in the shirt, and his paunch bulges over a cowboy belt. He sucks a long-stem corncob pipe but rarely smokes it; he uses it as a character gimmick, an idea he apparently picked up from the late General Douglas MacArthur.

Like a true Nazi top dog, Rockwell avails himself of top-dog privileges and orders private meals served in his room. He partakes of such fancy fare as turtle soup, lobster and steak while his men eat hash. For *bonne-bouches,* he enjoys sucking kumquats. He is also the only one in the barracks allowed to have feminine company. Living among those American Nazis is a lone woman, Barbara von Goetz, a tall, fading blonde, who has a room across the hall from his, but more often can be found in his room. She too is fed lobsters and kumquats. Even more astonishing, the records reveal that a baby daughter also lived with her in the barracks for several months. She gave birth to the child, according to records at the District of Columbia General Hospital, on December 8, 1961. The baby's name is recorded as Laurie Gissela Mappffi; the last name is taken from Miss von Goetz's former husband. At the Nazi barracks, little Laurie caught a bad cold, possibly from the icy atmosphere Rockwell maintains. A doctor was called in, but the child died on October 25, 1962. A coronor's report claims she "choked and gagged" to death.

Though Rockwell may appear to be more extreme than some other right-wing leaders, they all operate on the same wave length. The same names show up on the letterheads of far-right groups; the same phrases appear in their propaganda. Some of the nation's most notorious anti-Semites, for example, have served on the Liberty Lobby's Board of Policy. One former board member, J. Evetts Haley, has produced a smear biography of President Johnson entitled "A Texan Looks at Lyndon." He was assisted with the research by Thornton Dewey, owner of a ranch six miles from the Haley spread near Canyon, Texas. Dewey has contributed to the American Nazi Party and has entertained Rockwell on his ranch. The Liberty Lobby, however, has disavowed Rockwell.

If I have emphasized the radical right above the lunatic left, it is only because the danger on the right is less understood. I have frequently pointed out that the extremists, both of the right and left, use the same methods to achieve the same end. They seek to discredit democracy at the same time that they pay lip service to its ideals and institutions. The most effective weapons for this sort of ideological sabotage are hate and suspicion.

The common purpose of these extremists is nowhere more evident than in the civil rights movements. Communists and Ku Klux Klansmen, Minutemen and Black Muslims, working at opposite ends of the civil rights struggle, have fanned the flames of violence. While Klansmen dynamite churches and murder civil rights workers in the South, communists whip up the mobs during race riots in the North. An inflammatory tract recently handed out to rioters by Red agents declares: "Once again the cops have murdered one of our children. They have been killing about one black person a day in New York City."

When I pointed all this out in a series of columns, the communists complained with an injured air that I had tarnished their reputation. G. A. Meyers, speaking for the Communist Party, wrote an aggrieved letter to the Washington Post: "Mr. Anderson claims to have uncovered 'some strange Communist-Klan-Muslim links that suggest at least a unity of purpose.' That purpose, according to Mr. Anderson, is to stir up racial conflict in America, 'apparently for the sheer sake of chaos.' The Communist Party completely abhors the Klan, and while we are aware of the frustrations that bring such organizations as the Black Muslims into being, we do not identify ourselves with their philosophy." It was the old story of the pot calling the kettle black.

The best way to fight the extremists, no matter at which end of the spectrum they may be found, is to challenge their hate propaganda wherever it bubbles up from the sewers below. Men and women of reason, who all too often remain silent rather than get embroiled with cranks and crackpots, must stand up and speak up. What is needed today, though it may sound like a contradiction of terms, is more militant moderation.

19

NAZIS IN AMERICA

The ghost of Adolf Hitler, if it has been exorcised from Germany, still stalks the back alleys and catwalks of South America. After the torch was put to his corpse, as his mad empire crumbled under Allied attacks, thousands of his most fanatical followers fled across the South Atlantic. Their escape organization developed into a Nazi underground which still operates today, tied by a grapevine that spans the South American continent and reaches into the remotest parts of the pampas and jungle.

Guided by confidential contacts, I followed the Nazi trail through South America. I met former SS men, Nazi functionaries, and Hitler toadies, most of them small fry, too inconsequential to trouble the world's conscience. But they led me to the fringe of the world's most secret and sinister coterie: the society of mass killers. Between them, these artists of atrocity, these masters of massacre have accounted for millions of innocent lives. The kidnapping of Adolf Eichmann, who was whisked off the streets of Buenos Aires by Israeli commandoes, jolted them, and sent them deeper into the underground. Suddenly those who had hunted Jews for Hitler became the hunted; the terrorists became the terrorized. I found one—Herbert Cukurs, who had 32,000 massacred Jews charged against his conscience—holed up in a lakeside home near Sao Paulo. The avengers, it turned out, weren't far behind me.

Tracking down the men who belong to this macabre social circle is no easy task. Those who know them and their whereabouts are frozen-tongued. Within 24 hours of the Eichmann kidnapping, for instance, a tall, handsome greying businessman sometimes seen in Eichmann's company dropped out of sight. His friends responded with blank stares to inquiries about his forwarding address. He is Dr. Josef Mengele, described by the little Jewish girl Anne Frank in her now-famous diary as "the angel of extermination" at Auschwitz concentration camp.

With a wave of his cane, Mengele decided which Jews should go to the gas chambers, which should be used for medical experiments, which should be worked to death. If he was in a bad mood, he would not hesitate to wave a whole contingent of Jews to the death chambers. He was known as a fanatic on racial-biological research with particular interest in the hereditary basis of twins. Children who resembled each other would be put together and coached to identify themselves as twins. Then Mengele would spare their lives—so long as they suited his experiments.

Thanks to family wealth, he acquired a small chemical plant in Buenos Aires, lived comfortably, moved in good society, enjoyed deep discussions on history and philosophy. For security's sake, he did not practice medicine, but he never bothered to change his name. One of his last discussions with a friend was about the communists' ability to develop brilliant scientists who, away from their work, were political morons willing to obey unthinkingly. *He told how Stalin had sought to create perfect police by crossing Lithuanians with Kirghis—the first known for strength and fearlessness, the second for cunning, cruelty, and indifference to human life.* Mengele said that not only Stalin, but the Nazis, too, had made medical studies along these lines.

Another elusive member of the macabre society is Eichmann's former boss, the darkly handsome Gestapo chief Heinrich Mueller, last seen in Hitler's bunker on April 29, 1945. He came to Buenos Aires for a short stay, then moved south to Patagonia where he lived for awhile in the mountains. The

Eichmann kidnapping scared him, too. His trail has now disappeared.

Eichmann's counterpart in the Nazi foreign office, Franz Rademacher, is also in South America. His name appears on many documents relating to Jewish executions and deportations. While awaiting sentence as a war criminal, he escaped to Argentina, then crossed the La Plata River into Uruguay. He was last seen in Montevideo, where he once served as secretary in the German legation.

Most fascinating of all are reports that Martin Bormann, Hitler's private secretary and heir apparent, is still alive in South America. My search for him triggered excitement that led Argentine police to pick up his double, one-armed Walter Flegel, who turned out to be merely a minor German refugee. Bormann was with Hitler and his mistress, Eva Braun, during their last hours in the Berlin bunker. After their double suicide, Bormann sent a telegram saying he was on his way to join Admiral Doenitz, then negotiating surrender. Bormann never reached Doenitz. According to Hitler's chauffeur, Rich Kempka, Bormann was killed when a Russian bazooka hit the German tank he was following through the Ziegelstrasse. This testimony was given at the Nuremberg trials and was repeated by Nazis I met in South America. But I found the assertion so pat it was unconvincing. Other sources contend that Hitler's heir planned his escape for months. When the end came, they say, he commandeered two submarines for a top-secret voyage to Argentina. One was U-530, which he reportedly boarded with his family.

My pursuit of the Bormann rumors led to a Milton Canto, introduced to me as a completely responsible person. He told me he was positive he had seen Bormann, flanked by two bodyguards, at a settlement called Xavantina in Goias State, Brazil. He claimed Bormann's features were still recognizable, though aged. When Canto made inquiries about the person he believed to be Bormann, he was told the man's name was Herman Meng. Brazil's efficient political police discounted this story. They described Xavantina as an airstrip on the edge of the jungle and said only Indians lived around there. Whoever Herman Meng was, he has now vanished as if whisked to the moon. Attempts to track him down got nowhere.

Another reliable source, who asked not to be identified, has seen papers said to be written by Bormann. These papers were shown to Bormann's son, Martin, Jr., who became a Catholic priest in Austria in 1958. He identified the handwriting positively as that of his father.

I tracked down one war criminal outside Sao Paulo—Herbert Cukurs, a stocky, muscular Latvian. Eye witnesses charge that he took a leading part in the massacre of 32,000 Jews in Riga in 1941. They claim he was the right-hand man to Viktor Ajars, chief of the pro-Nazi Perkonkrust (Thunder Cross) Party. Ajars and Cukurs were reportedly given the job of liquidating all Jews when the Germans moved into Riga. The ghetto was cordoned off, and the city's blue busses were used to haul Jews to a nearby forest for execution.

Witnesses assert that Cukurs barricaded and burned Jews in their own synagogues. Their affidavits charge that they saw him throw children into the flames. At nights, they say, he also barged into the homes of defenseless Jews and abused their daughters. The affidavits give names, details, dates. Max Kaufman in his book on the extermination of the Jews in Latvia describes Cukurs as a "murderer".

It was in a neat blue-and-white Spanish bungalow in a fashionable lakeside resort area that I came face to face with the scourge of Riga. He was wearing a leather jacket and the barrel of a pistol peeped from a hip pocket. He operated three seaplanes on the Paulista Riviera, offering transportation to vacationers. But a former SS major confided to me that the planes were also used for whisking nervous Nazis into the interior where Cukurs owned two small ranches.

Cukurs escaped from Latvia with the retreating German

army, set up his family in a villa on the Rhine, then established himself in a Berlin apartment near his work as an aircraft engineer. When the end came, he made his way to Marseilles, then to Rio de Janeiro. He probably chose Brazil because no survivors of the Riga massacre were known to be in that country. But if his purpose was to avoid recognition, he failed. Less than four months after his arrival in November, 1945, Jewish leaders in Brazil were tipped off about his presence. "According to statements of responsible refugees arrived here from Latvia," a cable advised, "Herbert Cukurs leader ghetto Riga reported in Brazil. Tortured sadistically camp inhabitants himself killed children." It was three years, however, before the Jews found Cukurs operating a pleasure boat concession on a lake in Rio. Jewish youths picketed the place. When Cukurs applied for Brazilian citizenship, the Jewish community successfully blocked him. Then he dropped out of sight again.

Curiously, Cukurs saved a Jewish girl's life and brought her out of Latvia with his family. Her name is Miriam Keitzner, now married to a Jewish doctor in Rio. Cukurs cited this as evidence that he could not have been guilty of atrocities against the Jews. Yet in light of the scores of affidavits against him, the obvious question is: did Cukurs save Miriam's life as insurance against Jewish retribution? That he is capable of this kind of cunning is suggested by an equally curious fact. He and his wife, both in their sixties, suddenly produced a Brazilian-born child after their other children (two sons and a daughter) were grown. *The suspicion is that Cukurs may have picked up the boy from among Brazil's homeless waifs and claimed him as his own.* The Brazilians are sentimental about native-born children and would be less likely to extradite Cukurs if he could claim a son born in the country.

I reached Cukurs' home on the Paulista Riviera after a hot and dusty jeep ride over dirt roads. I caught a glimpse of him studying me carefully from the backyard; then he strolled to the gate. "So," he said after examining my credentials, "you have come to see the great war criminal?" His smile was defensive, pleading, like a silent whine. Then he demanded: "Are you Jewish?" When I said I was not, he grunted "All right," and waved me through the gate. In broken English, nervously fingering his heavy black-rimmed glasses, he launched into a rebuttal of the charges against him. He pulled out tattered yellowing documents which he claimed proved his innocence.

It was the Jews, not he, who had committed atrocities. When the Russians first overran Latvia, he charged, the Jews had helped them to massacre Latvians. Most Latvians had looked upon the Germans as liberators, and he himself had led a band of Latvian partisans to help the Germans, he claimed. Later, he insisted, he became both anti-German and anti-Russian. He did not explain how, if he were the simple refugee he claimed to be, he managed to acquire from the Nazis a villa on the Rhine plus an apartment in Berlin.

Cukurs' manner was amiable enough, though always defensive. He made no attempt to hide his bitterness against the Jews. Finally, he declared: "I do not have the blood of Jews on my hands." He said he had been too busy repairing trucks "for politics and Jew killing." But the affidavits against him, impressive in their details, tell a different story. The most moving and prophetic, written by a woman, Iona Rodinov, states: "Jews from the labor concentration camps saw how Herbert Cukurs took their mothers, sisters, fathers, and children to their deaths. They swore over the bloody streets of the ghetto in Riga that they will never forget and much less forgive."

If Cukurs was unaware of the affidavit, its message was etched on his conscience. For he was clearly a frightened man. Perhaps the avengers were already on his trail. Perhaps they read in Parade the story I wrote about my visit with him. But on February 23, 1965, vengeance caught up with Herbert Cukurs. His bullet-riddled body was found in a trunk in Montevideo, Uruguay, where he had been decoyed to his death. Greed had turned Cukurs into a Nazi thug, and greed led to his downfall. A lucrative travel agency contract was evidently the bait that tempted him to Montevideo.

Nobody knows who was responsible for the execution—it is hard to call it murder—of Cukurs, except that it was carried out by a group calling itself "Those who can never forget." Apparently there were at least two executioneers: a tall, thin man in his late 60's who spoke French, and a shorter, younger man who spoke Spanish. They rented the Casa Cubertini villa in a fashionable suburb of Montevideo. One day they were seen lugging in a large crate and were heard to say: "At last the refrigerator has arrived." That was on February 20, three days before Cukurs arrived in Montevideo from Sao Paulo with an airline ticket to Buenos Aires. He never got further than the Casa Cubertini.

Cukurs had fled across half the world, and from across half the world vengeance had reached out for him. The first clue to his death came in a note addressed to the Associated Press office in Bonn, Germany. It announced that Cukurs, who had been named in absentia at Nuremburg as a war criminal, had been tried, found guilty and executed. His body, said the note, would be found in a trunk at the Casa Cubertini, Calle Colombia, Balnearlo Parque Carasco, Montevideo.

At first the note was considered a grisly prank. But after a follow-up phone call, the AP cabled its Montevideo office, which in turn notified the Uruguayan police. The mysterious tenants of the Casa Cubertini had vanished. *Cukurs was there—dead in the trunk.* On the body was an airline ticket in his name and a small gold medallion with a Nazi air force insignia and a tribute to Cukurs engraved on it. The avengers clearly had gone to some pains to make sure that everyone would know Cukurs had been punished.

How did notorious Nazis manage to escape Germany? Adolf Eichmann, overlord of the gas chambers who scoffed at God and man, was helped by Catholic priests. The good fathers, of course, didn't know they were assisting the murderer of five million Jews. They regarded the slight, slim man with the flop ears, drooping nose, bandy legs, and apologetic manner as just another refugee from war-torn central Europe. As such, they passed him on to the Vatican's Displaced Persons Relief Department, which certified him as a refugee without a country and helped him obtain Red Cross identification papers.

This man, who once bragged that he would "leap into my grave laughing" over his role in the great Jewish slaughter, turned up in Buenos Aires as meek "Ricardo Klement." He pretended to be a lowly, simple man—a role that was neither new nor strange to him. For at the height of his diabolical career as the head of the Gestapo's Jewish section, he concealed his murderous mission from the German people by posing as a minor bureaucrat who never rose above the rank of Lieutenant Colonel. But in the company of his Nazi cohorts in Argentina he was a different man, given to hard drinking and boastful talk. Of course, they knew his true identity. Some who worked with him in the Buenos Aires office of Mercedes-Benz referred to him respectfully as "Herr Obersturmbannfuehrer." Once he lost his temper with a colleague, dropped his mild manner, and snarled: "You dirty Jew!"

Toadying to Eichmann by Nazis in Buenos Aires did not extend to financial help. His home on a lonely road 15 miles outside the city was modest in the extreme—"built with his own hands," his friends claim. It had no electricity, no water except for an outside hand pump.

When he was kidnapped in broad daylight off the Avenue General Paz, his wife and four sons disappeared into the Nazi underground, later reappeared. My contacts put me in touch with the oldest son, Nicolas Eichmann (he prefers "Nick" to "Klaus," the German form). For three weeks, I stayed close to him, listening to his life story, studying his reactions, seeking an insight into his thoughts. I saw the legacy Adolf Eichmann had left; the son who vaguely resembles him bears the deep and grotesque imprint of a hideous past.

Most people like Nicolas the first time they meet him. He seems like a perfectly normal young man with curly dark hair, blue eyes, jughandle ears, and a long nose like his father's. He is friendly, has a boyish expression and a ready smile. He speaks fluent English he learned from GIs after the war. He likes to ogle girls, watch TV westerns, and talk about cars. Mention his father, however, and a chip pops up on his shoulder. He is defiant, defensive, full of bitter wisecracks. "My father?" he once responded. "He used to eat Jews for breakfast." Again, while watching the television show "Have Gun Will Travel," he blurted: "I should have cards printed, 'Have Gas Chamber Will Travel.' "

Nicolas claims to know little about Hitler's Germany, insisting his father rarely discussed the subject. However, he admits that Adolf Eichmann was proud he had been an SS officer, sometimes sang military songs, and described how he had taken the Nazi oath in a great Munich outdoor rally. "I have never violated that oath, and no one has asked me to withdraw it," Nicolas recalls him saying. When his sons pressed him for details about his wartime experiences, he dodged. "We are living in peace," he would say piously. "Let us be grateful and not talk of war." Nicolas says that although his father was raised a Lutheran, he roundly condemned Martin Luther, brushed off the New Testament as "full of nonsense," and ridiculed his wife, a devout Catholic, for reading the Bible. Nicolas wears a religious medal, but he seems embarrassed if you mention it.

In the eyes of his sons, Adolf Eichmann was a brave man.

"He obviously knew he was being hunted, otherwise he would have used his real name," Nicolas told me. "Yet he never carried a weapon, and he never seemed to be nervous. Once or twice he talked about death, but in a way that a man might tell you where he kept the insurance policies." In some ways, Nicolas admits, he would like to model himself after his father. "He was very strict with us and my mother, which is the way I think a man should be!" the youth says.

Ever since Adolf Eichmann's kidnapping on May 12, 1960, Nicolas has been fascinated with the whole subject. He avidly clips every newspaper article on the subject and reads it again and again. As he pores over them, he mutters, "How stupid!" about his father's detractors. Notoriety has given Nicolas a bad dose of the small-man syndrome. He boasts and swaggers, but obviously fears he is a marked man. At home, the Eichmann boys pack revolvers.

Nicolas is tortured by the possibility that he may have caused his father's capture. One reason is that Lothar Hermann, a blind Jewish attorney in Buenos Aires, claimed the reward for "fingering" Eichmann. Hermann is the father of a girl who dated Nicolas some years ago. The son has retraced the kidnapping route again and again. He repeatedly questions anyone remotely connected, seeking to know exactly where and how the whole thing happened. He has concluded that the capture did not take place on a main street in daylight, but in a field near the family home. He even believes he might have saved his father, except for a quirk of fate. On most Wednesdays, Nick took the mail to his father's home, which was beyond delivery routes. But on the Wednesday of the kidnapping, his daughter Monica had a cold and Nick stayed home. According to the timetable he has figured, he and his father would have been on the same bus, and Nick would have had his .45. "Then what would they have done?" he asks. "What if I had started shooting? Maybe none of of this would have happened."

מלון לב-הכרמל

Lev Hacarmel Hotel

Mt. CARMEL, HAIFA - TEL. 81406-7

BANKERS: KUPAT-AM LIMITED

TELEGRAMS: LEVACARMEL HAIFA

HAIFA, 19.Marz 1961

Nach Diktat:

Lieber Dieter, lieber Horst, lieber Klaus!

Ich freue mich, dass ich über Euch Gutes höre, seid brav und haltet wie Pech und Schwefel zusammen.

Ich habe heute von Herrn Dr.Servatius mitgeteilt ... Anzug, ... Euch ... zu tragen. ... sonst ... für den Prozess hier von amtswegen mit ... Behör- ... Man bekommen ... nötigen versorgen.

Euer Papa

A montage showing portions of the last letters Adolf Eichmann sent to his family from captivity in Israel. The notorious mass murderer signed his letters "Papa." The letters were obtained from the Eichmann family while Jack Anderson was investigating the Nazi underground in South America.

After his dramatic capture and appearance in Israel, Adolf Eichmann wrote only rarely to his family. His few personal letters, signed simply "Your Papa," were written in German. Nick translated them for me. What advice did he have for the sons who carry on his name he made infamous? He called upon them to "be brave and stick together like cement." What were his last words to the wife who had kept his terrible secret? He admonished her to keep out of debt: "I had a further thought that you might be forced one day to borrow money. I warn you not to do that, never lend money and never borrow money."

Eichmann reminisced about his last Easter at home: "I think in silent joy of our Easter celebration when Hasi [his pet name for his 5-year-old Argentina-born son, Ricardo] busily looked for Easter eggs and then gave them to his mama. Little Hasi laughed and laughed and was excited over such a good Easter rabbit. In this way, a human being lives in joys of the past, like drinking from a spring which never runs dry."

Ironically, the man who callously marked six million Jews for death railed against the unfairness of his own accusers. He declared his innocence to his loved ones: "On the eve of my monster trial, I will repeat once again: I assure you by the eternal peace of my dead parents and of my late father-in-law, their fathers as well as our brothers killed in the war, that I: (a) never have killed; (b) never have given a command for killing." Concerning the accusations made against him he said: "I cannot defend myself against lies and falsifications, against discrimination and meanness."

Eichmann claimed to be unconcerned about his fate, at peace with himself: "Rarely was there an accused man who regarded his immediate fate with as little concern as I do. Rarely was there an accused man who has had to take as little refuge in lying and betrayal as I have. I really praise the quietness of my imprisonment. This has to me the value of gold."

Writing from his cell, he boasted of his loyalty to the SS: "Several persons asked me in Israel, and especially the interrogating captain of the Israeli police, whether I have been a good SS officer. I answered this question: 'I have done my duty, and I was obedient to the orders of my superior SS generals. I was always conscious of my vow which I have sworn to the flag. As an SS lieutenant-colonel, my honor called for as much loyalty as that of every last SS man.' I have kept this vow until exactly May 8, 1945, and not one day less. If that which I have done according to my vow to the flag during the war and which I was obliged to do is punishable today, then I will not bargain. Then I have to take the consequences as a former SS officer."

On April 17, 1961, as Eichmann was about to face the angry accusations against him, he wrote his family: "On the eve of the beginning of my trial, I wish to speak once more to all my loved ones. First I thank all of you for your sincere greetings which have really given me much joy. If I had needed reinforcement, they would have done it." Of his trial, he wrote bitterly: "I think that the sensations and lying propaganda around my person will suffer a defeat in this trial independent of how the trial might end. One certainly does not know how far certain notorious twisters of the truth will be able to twist my own words right from my mouth."

As the condemned man listened to the evidence against him, his bland attitude was reflected in a letter he wrote his family on June 10th. "Seldom has there been an accused man," he declared, "who could say that the court as well as the accusations were the very opposite of distasteful to him." Then he penned a postscript in Spanish to Nick's pregnant wife. "My dear little Martita," he wrote, "many kisses for you and for Monica. I hope in the next few days there will be hearty congratulations and a second little girl."

Eichmann's letters reveal that there is something human in the most inhuman of us. They show that even a mass murderer is wrapped up in familiar, everyday concerns. They also show that this former SS officer and mass murderer remained an unrepentant criminal, a stiff-necked Nazi who believed to the end that allegiance to the Fuehrer was more important than six million innocent lives.

What of Eichmann's family? His sons have not stuck together; quarrels have been frequent. They have turned to the only people who would befriend them, the diehard Nazis. The last I heard from Nicolas was a 1965 Christmas letter in which he told me that his wife had divorced him and that he had gone back to Germany to live. There was bitterness in his words and a hint that he may be conspiring with the modern neo-Nazis. Thus it would seem that Adolf Eichmann destroyed yet another family after the gas chambers were closed and the last moan came from the concentration camps.

Eichmann was not the only Nazi war criminal to use the priestly escape route through Italy. Thousands of Nazis, big and small, passed through Catholic monasteries which offered them temporary haven in their flight to the German communities of Argentina, Brazil, Chile, and other South American countries. Some even disguised themselves in clerical garb. One notorious example: the Croat leader and Nazi puppet Ante Pavelic, whose record of butchery was less wholesale but more savage than that of Eichmann. In robe and sandals, this unlikely "father" arrived in Argentina aboard the Italian liner SS Andrea Gritti.

During his reign over Croatia, now a part of Yugoslavia, Pavelich sent his Ustashi stormtroopers, almost as ruthless as the hordes of Atilla the Hun, to exterminate not only Jews but the Serbian minority as well. The victims had their limbs torn off, eyes gouged out, skulls crushed with hammers. The wounded were sealed in caves with the dead. The Italian author Curzio Malaparte reports visiting Pavelic in his palace in Zagreb and noticing on his desk a wicker basked filled with what appeared to be shelled oysters. When Malaparte asked whether they were Dalmatian oysters, Pavelic replied grimly: "It is a present from my loyal Ustashis. Forty pounds of human eyes."

Pavelic's friends, whom I met in Buenos Aires, do not deny that some eyes were gouged out, but they insist Malaparte went too far in claiming their chief collected them by the basket. These friends describe him as a hearty, good-natured fellow with a robust, Khrushchev-like sense of humor. Pavelic used to delight in introducing Eichmann as "my old Jewish friend." Although Pavelic has gone to answer a Higher Judgment, his devoted followers still maintain a headquarters in Buenos Aires. His picture occupies the place of honor just inside the door, easily seen from the street.

To the monks who helped these Nazi fugitives escape, any man or woman knocking on their gate with a story of persecution deserved succor. Throughout the war they had hidden political and Jewish refugees fleeing from Hitler. Since it was impossible to check each individual, the guilty mingled with the innocent. That was how Eichmann and Pavelic got through.

While searching South America for war criminals who have eluded justice, I was able to piece together the pattern of the great Nazi get-out. A former SS major, who told me about the Nazi escape route, insisted it was neither organized nor financed on a grand scale, but I found considerable evidence indicating that the underground organization was highly efficient. In Rio de Janeiro, I examined the entry documents of several Nordic-looking priests with Italian names. I compared these papers with the alien registration documents of the same period. *The photos still on file revealed that some "priests" had abruptly changed status on the day of their arrival.*

The same faces appeared on the alien identification cards, but the priestly garb had been replaced by civilian clothing. After discarding their black robes the "priests" posed in a borrowed suit for their identification photos. Each was photographed in the very same suit; even the tie and lapel button were exactly the same in the separate photos. Clearly what had happened was that the "priests" were met by friends who hastily dressed them in suit, shirt, and ties for their phony identification papers. Then they returned the borrowed clothes for the next arrival to use. Once their new identities were established, the "priests" simply vanished overnight.

Although most Nazi refugees changed their names fast and often, many managed to keep in touch with their families. Even the much-hunted Eichmann received regular letters from him family in Austria addressed to "Uncle Ricardo." Later his wife and four sons joined him in Buenos Aires. A number of Nazis re-married their wives under their new names. Some kept their new names; others after the heat was off returned to their old ones. In the majority of cases these fugitives had no need to flee at all. They would have been perfectly safe back home in Germany.

For most Nazis who fled after the crash of the Reich, Argentina was the goal. Dictator Juan Peron, who had plotted with the Nazis throughout the war, was in power. His private press secretary, Rodolfo Freude, was the son of Ludwig Freude, named by the U.S. State Department as "the leading Nazi in South America." Ludwig championed the Nazi cause while the war was on. After the Nazis were beaten, his son took over the work of rescue. He had extraordinary powers which he did not hesitate to use. Such a small matter as fixing up phony identification papers was easy for him. As a cover and contact point for his activities, he set up a small bookshop and haberdashery in Buenos Aires called the "Durer Haus". It became a headquarters and clearing house for ex-

Nazi leaders. Here they could contact each other, arrange jobs for newcomers.

Luftwaffe pilots and engineers, including General Werner Baumbach and Adalf Galland, were welcomed with open arms by Peron's state-run aviation industry. On the same payroll appeared the names of Colonal Hans Ulrich Rudel, Hitler's No. 1 air ace; SS General Otto Skorzeny, the paratroop commander who rescued Mussolini from prison; Willy Tank, one of the Hitler's top airplane designer. *Four Gestapo specialists*—Dr. H. Theiss, Dr. F. Adam, H. Richner, and J. Paech—*were hired to teach Gestapo methods to Peron's secret police.* Wilfred von Oven, former aide to propaganda boss Goebbels, and Robert Kessler, ex-SS colonel, began publishing a Nazi newspaper called "Freie Presse". Mussolini's son, Vittorio, was a welcome guest.

After Peron's fall, there was a scattering. Some Nazi returned to Germany. Some went to Egypt and took jobs under Nasser. Others headed for neighboring countries or disappeared underground. Vittorio Mussolini went home to Italy. The Nazi clubs and veterans' associations which had sprung up in Argentina began to fade out.

Today only three major Nazi organizations remain there: the Kameradenwerk, a "friendship society" believed to be active in aiding war criminals; the Scharnhorst, an ex-servicemen's association which still distributes neo-Nazi literature; and a Croatian society built around the late Ante Pavelic. Robert Kessler still puts out the "Freie Presse", but its tone is now tame.

The Eichmann kidnapping was the second big jolt for the Nazis in South America after Peron was forced to flee. Fear that Israeli agents may at any time make another raid on their ranks continues, but these men will not be easy to capture now. Like the Jews who once fled from them, they have become experts in hiding. South American countries also have a long tradition of political sanctuary. They resent Israel's invasion of their territory for purposes of vengeance.

Finally the Nazis in South America have their own network and their own curious code of honor. They are in touch with one another; they seldom talk to strangers. They have hideouts in the jungle and on the pampas. Perhaps the only consolation to the world that suffered their crimes is that they will live out their lives in fear.

20

THE POLITICS OF CRIME

Back in 1945 a stranger got off the train from New York, sauntered into the Bank of Commerce and Savings in Washington, peeled off $10,000 in large bills and opened a new account. He signed his name as Murray Olf. He was a dapper fellow with blue eyes, apple cheeks and brown wavy hair. FBI file No. 364802 also notes that he has a telltale scar under his right eye, a slight lump on the edge of his left ear, and a full set of false teeth. Olf was a big-time racketeer, a four-time loser, a key figure in the organized underworld. *He was sent to Washington by a crime syndicate anxious to protect its interests and to keep the federal heat turned down.*

For more than a decade, Olf lived in the shadow of Capitol Hill hobnobbing with Congressmen and lobbying for underworld enterprises. Now retired, he lives at a discreet distance from his former Congressional haunts and collects a weekly "retirement" check from a mob-controlled newspaper. He has been replaced by other quiet fixers who work the shady side of Washington for the crime syndicate.

I personally know three men-about-Washington who pull political strings for gamblers and gangsters. One operates out of a plush penthouse that looks as if it were designed in Hollywood. A rich red canopy is suspended over his desk, which is sleek, shiny, and uncluttered except for a miniature TV set. Another has a downtown Washington office, tastefully appointed; and the third operates out of his hat, using a midwestern Senator's office as his base. I don't intend to name these three underworld lobbyists, because I couldn't prove in court what I know about them. But there is no question that they count among their clients some of the nation's top manicured and monied mobsters.

All three use pretty much the same modus operandi. They deal largely in cash, which they pass out as if they were campaigning for the Presidents whose pictures appear on the greenbacks. They seem to have an equally unlimited supply of wine and women. They have also opened the glittering doors of Las Vegas for those few members of Congress who will allow themselves to be lured to the gaming tables. It has been said that a Congressman, no matter how reckless, can't lose at the Las Vegas games.

The overlords of the underworld also seek out legitimate Washington representation. Most desperate are, of course, those gangsters who have had the misfortune to be born abroad. A particular word gives them the nervous tremors: *deportation.* One after another, they have been snatched from their neon-lit lairs and shipped back to their native lands, a fate regarded as worse than an income tax rap. To escape exile, the racketeers scoured Washington for the best immigration lawyer available. They found bald, benign Jack Wasserman, whose soft voice, gentle manners, and angelic glow give him more the appearance of a clergyman than an underworld mouthpiece. Yet in recent years, this brilliant lawyer has represented more than a dozen of America's most feared gangsters.

Much to the distress of the Italians, most gangsters who get separated from the American fleshpots end up in Italy. After canvassing Italy's 92 police districts, the authorities recently came up with the names of some 400 derelicts from the U.S. underworld cast upon their shores. Some, like Frank Frigente and Ralph Liquori, are small fry trying to look big. They get by on the few lire they can make hustling American tourists. Frigente, deported for murdering his mother-in-law, boned up on detective magazines and gave himself a phony background as an intimate of big-name racketeers. Once, he tried to organize the deported racketeers for a march on the American Embassy in Rome to dramatize their plight.

In contrast, the big-name deportees live in mysterious luxury. They still keep their manicured fingers in American crime, but they miss the bright lights and fast pace of New York, Chicago, Miami, Las Vegas. Such is their obsession that some who have been kicked out have actually taken great risks to sneak back in again. Sooner or later, those who face deportation turn up in the modest offices of Jack Wasserman. Among his clients have been Frank Costello, the retired elder statesman of organized crime, and Russell Bufalino, the gray, sallow Pennsylvania racketeer who is credited by federal agents with setting up the ill-famed Apalachin crime conference. "Big Bill" Lias, the Wheeling, West Virginia, gambling czar, was sent to Wasserman by the late Pennsylvania Attorney General Charles Margiotti, who, himself, had been a front man for the mob. Two of Wasserman's first clients were Settimo "Big Sam" Accardo and his brother, Joe. The heavy, graying "Big Sam"—described in federal files as "a very important top echelon Mafia leader"—jumped $92,000 bail bond and fled to Italy.

Around Wasserman, so he says, the underworld czars behave like gentlemen. "The only strong-arm stuff I've seen has been pulled by the government," he told me, smiling benignly. He referred to two of his clients, the notorious Mike Spinella and Carlos Marcello, who were both bundled out of the country unceremoniously. Spinella, fat and arrogant, looks like the Hollywood stereotype of a racketeer. He was picked up in Washington's Willard Hotel and hustled off by Immigration agents to Italy, where he arrived squawking loudly that he had been shanghaied. *It wasn't long before the outraged outlaw was back in the U.S. without benefit of passport.* When the word leaked out that "Spinella is back," more than 100 federal agents staked out his old haunts. But somehow he eluded them and got word to Wasserman that he would be contacted by a "representative."

Later, a stocky character sporting a trim Van Dyke showed

up at Wasserman's office and introduced himself as Spinella's cousin. The mild-mannered attorney, who gave him advice to take back to the fugitive, didn't learn until later that the "cousin" was actually the racketeer in disguise. But despite the advice, Spinella finished up back in Italy. He spends his time lying in the sun on the Isle of Capri. There, he cultivates his paunch with rich food, smokes big black cigars, imports former girl friends from Miami, and complains about his "raw deal." His parting words to Wasserman: "You can reach me any time. Just address the letter to Mike Spinella, Capri, Italy."

Carlos Marcello, the brutal boss of the New Orleans underworld, was whisked off to Guatemala in the same brisk fashion as Spinella's departure for Italy. Though born in Tunisia, Marcello was deported to Guatemala, presumably because that's the only country that would take him. Except for three Immigration men, he was the sole passenger on the government plane that flew him to Guatemala City. "They had orders that they couldn't even talk to me," he later lamented to me. The nas an after thought, he added: "One guy offered me a cup of coffee."

But Marcello grew weary of the drowsy, dolce vita in the banana republic and, like Spinella, sneaked back into the United States. When the feds got wind of his return, they descended in force upon all his known haunts, using two-way walkie-talkies to keep in touch with one another. *Despite this massive surveillance, Marcello casually walked through their midst, undetected, into his house.* He put through a telephone call to Wasserman at a nearby motel, which was also being closely watched. At five o'clock on a Sunday morning, Wasserman managed to slip past the drowsy agents. Later he invited them to the Marcello home where he surrendered the racketeer.

To beat the dreaded deportation rap, some mobsters have induced members of Congress to introduce private bills on

September 13, 1965

CABINET REPORT FOR THE PRESIDENT

FROM : The Attorney General

SUBJECT : Campaign Against Organized Crime

You have frequently expressed your interest in removing what you have called the cancer of organized crime from this Nation.

During the past fiscal year, the Federal Government's efforts to combat organized crime have been carefully reviewed, and significant new directions and continuing accomplishments can be reported.

1. We have determined that quality as well as quantity of racketeer prosecutions should be a major goal. Thus we have aimed specifically at one of the most important areas of organized criminal activity--the corruption of local officials by racketeers. Among the convictions in fiscal 1965:

--the mayor and four councilmen of a midwestern city, charged with extorting money from a contractor doing business with the city;

--a lawyer, charged with perjury for denying he had bribed a judge;

--the rackets' boss and mayor of an eastern city, charged with conspiracy to extort money from firms selling parking meters to the city.

2. We have concentrated our efforts on breaking the "conspiracy of silence" in organized crime. We have called leading crime syndicate members before grand juries in several cities. In some of these cases, in endeavoring to secure vital testimony on syndicate operations, witnesses have been granted immunity. Those who still refused to cooperate have been convicted of contempt, and as a result leading national figures in the Cosa Nostra have been sentenced to jail terms.

3. We have placed new emphasis on the more complex and sophisticated racketeer activities. The success of the federal organized crime battle over the past several years has served to drive many racketeers out of the more obvious forms of organized crime, such as narcotics and gambling. Thus, the racketeers are searching for new fields of operation in activities difficult to ferret out from legitimate business and financial endeavors. In anticipation of this development, we are concentrating especially on investigating usurious loan schemes, devious factoring arrangements, fraudulent bankruptcies and labor racketeering. These

Extract from a Justice Department report to President Johnson. Often reports of this type seem to be more designed to impress the public than to inform the President.

their behalf. It takes no small persuasion to coax a politician out on a limb to save the skin of a notorious gangland figure. Still, a few racketeers have managed, ever so quietly, to arrange Congressional intervention. These have not been obscure hoodlums who could pass themselves off as aggrieved constituents. They were big-time, big-money racketeers with international police records.

Representative Mike Kirwan, the tough, twinkling Irishman from Youngstown, Ohio, introduced a private bill to save Frank Cammarata from exile. The Sicilian-born Cammarata, lean and mean, is a graduate of Detroit's infamous Purple Gang. In the Justice Department's rogues' gallery he is described as "a killer, holdup man and narcotics distributor." Congress failed to share Kirwan's benevolent attitude toward the mobster, who finally skipped to Cuba in order to avoid deportation to Italy.

Cammarata soon fell into the clutches of dictator Fidel Castro who had him arrested for possessing cocaine. According to U.S. narcotics officials, however, the racketeer's real offense was smuggling drugs without giving the Castro government its cut. FBI files give a fascinating account of how the bearded Cuban dictator tried to take over Cammarata's operation. He used two renegade American hoodlums to try to trick Cammarata into disclosing where he got the stuff and how he disposed of it in the United States. One of the hoods, who used the alias of Carl Weston, actually was planted in Cammarata's cell to win his confidence. But the wily racketeer was too experienced at keeping his mouth shut and didn't tumble for the ruse.

Another private bill to stop the deportation of New Orleans mobster Silvestro Carollo was introduced by handsome, happy-go-lucky Congressman Jimmy Morrison (D-La.) who, until Murray Olf's recent "retirement," was one of the underworld lobbyist's boon companions. On at least one occasion

Morrison also arranged a good time in Las Vegas for a group of Congressional secretaries.

Carollo, a darkly menacing fellow with black, thinning hair and a long curving face, is currently No. 34 on the international list of narcotics violators. "This man," says the confidential government report accompanying his photo, "is a dangerous man and has been connected with narcotics traffic for many years." His arrests go back to 1933 and encompass everything from swindling to the attempted murder of a narcotics agent. Fortunately, Congress learned the truth about him in time to pigeonhole Morrison's bill. Carollo was duly deported to his native village of Terrasini, Sicily, where he now operates the biggest bar in town.

The late Senator Olin "The Solon" Johnston (D-S.C.) somehow was persuaded to introduce a private bill for the special benefit of Nicolo Impastato, a slight, thin-faced, shy-looking man who wears rimless glasses and resembles a college professor more than the crime czar he is. Beneath his photo in the federal rogues' gallery appears this statement: "Has been known to use violence, including murder to maintain his organization; though deported, he still has an income from rackets in the United States." When Johnston's bill failed to save him, Impastato slipped across the border into Mexico to continue directing his operations. However, the Mexican authorities caught up with him and deported him to Italy, saving Uncle Sam the trouble. He now operates a farm outside the same village of Terrasini where Carollo also lives in exile.

Congressman George O'Brien (D-Mich.), before his recent retirement by his Detroit constituents, placed a private bill into the House hopper to keep racketeer Ralph Cannavo in this country. The slender blue-eyed, fair-haired mobster actually has been deported three times but keeps bouncing back. His niche in the underworld's hall of infamy is assured by this caption beneath his photo: "A hardened criminal who has never had a legitimate source of income; has engaged in counterfeiting and narcotics trafficking for many years."

These are strange constituents, indeed, to be on friendly terms with men who make the laws they break. No less strange is the convivial relationship between the underworld's Washington lobbyists and a few Congressmen.

Take the case of Murray Olf. For a man who has made a career of law breaking, he has managed to keep on surprisingly intimate terms with law makers who have attended his parties, drunk his liquor, and lounged in his plush suite. There have even been whispered reports of pay-offs to Congressmen. One played errand boy for Olf and contrived to get a confidential Senate crime report for him. The Congressman's secretary, Senate investigators learned, received "loans" from the racketeer. Word also got around that Olf was good for a fat campaign contribution to any Congressman not too choosey about his support. The only contribution traced to him was a political ad which appeared in the printed program at a Republican rally in Maryland's fifth congressional district. It read simply: "Compliments of Murray H. Olf, General Merchandise."

Before Olf moved from the Congressional Hotel, across the street from the old House Office Building, to the Woodner apartment three miles away, I got hold of the switchboard records which showed he was telephoning Capitol Hill a dozen times a day. He also loaned his phone freely to the lawmakers. Congressman Chester Gorski (D-N.Y.) charged most of his long-distance calls to Olf's bill. An attractive secretary to Representative Phil Welch (D-Mo.) borrowed money from Olf and also charged long-distance calls to Olf's bill, though she made them from her own phone.

Olf also used to gather legislators around him in the Filibuster Room of the Congressional Hotel to sing lusty songs. On Fridays, he often entertained them at intimate luncheons in his suite. *At the same time he was consorting with Congressmen, he was also in close touch with gangland chiefs around the country.* His telephone calls to Capitol Hill were interspersed with calls to such notorious mobsters as Frankie Costello in New York, Jake "Greasy Thumb" Guzik in Chicago, "Dandy Phil" Kastel in New Orleans, Morris Kleinman in Cleveland. Once racketeer Joe Adonis hid overnight in Olf's apartment while a Senate committee was searching for him with a subpoena. Another night a stranger parked his car in the hotel garage and charged the bill to Olf. The New York license plate was later traced to the notorious mobster Myer Lansky.

Confronted with these findings, Olf bantered about his activities, claimed with an amused twinkle that he was in the juke box business. "But business is bad," he said sadly. "All the bars have television sets." All he ever did on Capitol Hill, he said, was visit the Congressmen's barbershop. "I can get my haircuts cheaper there," he told me solemnly, flipping his $15 necktie. "They think I'm a Congressman."

Olf was less flippant when he was caught by a surprise Senate subpoena ordering him to report with all his records before a special subcommittee investigating crime in the District of Columbia. He showed up with a paper package which he claimed contained all his records. But he refused to let the committee open the package on the grounds that it might incriminate him. *The committee cross-examined him behind closed doors about his lobbying activities, but never published the official transcript because the names of prominent Congressmen were dragged into the hearing.* Here, however, are excerpts from the secret transcript:

"Did you entertain any Congressmen at the Congressional Hotel?" asked Counsel Arnold Bauman.

"I don't know exactly what you mean by 'entertained'," replied Olf.

"Let me make very clear what I mean," snapped Bauman.

"You used to throw little shrimp luncheons for Congressmen on Friday afternoons, did you not?"

"At the hotel I had a kitchen," Olf acknowledged. "On some Fridays I would cook shrimp. And as it so happened while maybe in the lobby talking, I would say that I was cooking shrimp and whoever dropped in would be welcome." These stray guests, he admitted, included mostly Congressmen.

"Have you ever told these men that you have been convicted of various crimes from grand larceny to mail fraud on four different occasions?" demanded Bauman.

"Mr. Bauman," whined the racketeer, "there was never any occasion for me to mention those things."

Bauman then went down a list of Congressmen whom Olf had entertained. "Personally I don't see why you should bring up men who are members of Congress, gentlemen whom I was honored to be with," protested Olf. Bauman questioned the unhappy gangster about lobbying with Congressmen against bills that would curb gambling. At first Olf tried to shrug off the whole thing, then abruptly retreated behind the Fifth Amendment. He also refused to tell whether he had received $60,000 influence money from crime czar Frankie Costello.

Olf refused, of course, to discuss his own criminal background, which included a boyhood on the sidewalks of New York, graduating from juvenile delinquency to bootlegging. As early as 1928 he was on intimate terms with Costello. Real estate records show that Costello's wife, Loretta, transferred a parcel of land to Olf in 1928. After a few brushes with the police, Olf drew a five-year term at the Lewisburg Penitentary where his cell mate was none other than Jake Guzik, one of Chicago's most sinister racketeers.

During a gambling raid, police once confiscated Olf's little black book and turned it over to federal authorities. In it they found the phone numbers of the nation's top mobsters, a few

Congressmen, Army generals and one federal judge. Many of the names were traced to Olf's girl friends, scattered throughout New York, Chicago, Cleveland, Baltimore, and Washington. Though in his 60's and married to a white-haired, grandmotherly type, Olf apparently was a swinger. His wife, a former bit actress in silent movies, lives by herself in Flushing, Long Island, in a five-room apartment cluttered with antiques, clocks, and bric-a-brac.

Of all the gangland-Washington links the most startling is the strange friendship that ex-Senator Barry Goldwater formed with some of the underworld's most unsavory characters. I dug into the story while Goldwater, during his 1964 presidential campaign, was pounding on the lawlessness issue, blaming President Johnson for the soaring crime rate. Goldwater was close to at least two notorious mobsters, Willie Bioff and Gus Greenbaum. Both left this world in classic gangland style. Bioff was blown to bits by a bomb attached to the starter of his pickup truck; Greenbaum's throat was expertly slit by underworld killers as he lounged in bed in beige silk pajamas.

Among the sheriff's confidential reports on the Bioff murder is a summary of a police interview with Phoenix jeweler Harry Rosenzweig, whom Goldwater has called his "closest friend." This report, No. 87-218, signed by Lt. R. W. Edmundson, declares: "Harry Rosenzweig stated that on Oct. 7, 1955, he made reservations for Sen. Goldwater, the Senator's wife and daughter, and the daughter's boy friend to stay at the Riviera Hotel in Las Vegas, Nev. He stated that he made reservations at 10:15 p.m. Oct. 7 on the Bonanza Airlines to go to Las Vegas, and Bioff stated that he and his wife would like to go along. So Bioff, his wife, and Rosenzweig went to Las Vegas and stayed at the Riviera Hotel . . . It was Rosenzweig's opinion that it was very possible that Bioff could have been recognized during their recent trip to

Las Vegas by one of his old cronies and followed to Phoenix."

Rosenzweig admitted to me that Bioff flew back to Phoenix with the Goldwaters in their private plane. It was the racketeer's last plane ride.

As for Gus Greenbaum, the Phonix newspapers of December 6, 1958, decribed the mobster's gala funeral. "Among the mourners," reported the Phoenix Gazette, "were Senator Barry Goldwater and his brother Bob, president of Goldwater's Department Store; jeweler Harry Rosenzweig, and other community leaders."

The same brother mentioned in the newspaper item, Robert Goldwater, made a deal with gangster Moe Dalitz to open an apparel shop in Las Vegas' fabulous Desert Inn. Dalitz is boss of the former Cleveland crime syndicate that has taken over the Desert Inn. The Las Vegas shop, like the family store in Phoenix, was to bear the Goldwater name until the Senator got caught up in presidential politics. Then the name was hastily changed to the D. I. Distinctive Apparel Shop.

The Senate's No. 1 crime crusader is Senator John McClellan, (D-Ark.), who has turned over a compost pile of underworld rackets. He has investigated gambling, white slavery, narcotics, labor racketeering, and other underworld enterprises. It may be worth recording, parenthetically, that he has overlooked one sin center in his own home state. *Gambling and vice flourish in Hot Springs, Arkansas, without the slightest interference from McClellan's investigators.*

McClellan's greatest coup, stage-managed by the Justice Department in the middle of the Senator's embarrassing investigation of the TFX contract, was the appearance before his committee of Joe Valachi, the underworld's most celebrated squealer, who testified about life inside the Cosa Nostra. His revelations rocked the dreaded underworld society, whose bosses promptly placed a $100,000 price on his head.

Valachi's gravel voice earned him the nickname "The Canary who Sang Like a Crow" but he told the McClellan Committee only part of his extraordinary story. Scribbling away in his two-cell suite at the District of Columbia jail, he began writing his life story. In a crude, sprawling hand, he filled 20 to 30 pages a day of a saga he calls "The Real Thing" but might better be titled "The Memoirs of a Stool Pigeon."

The prison authorities, taking a dim view of Valachi's literary attainments, banned its publication. The Justice Department overruled the prison censor and turned the manuscript over to a professional writer for "polishing." This produced an outcry from the Italian-American community, whose leaders suspected the book would be, as one wag put it, "anti-Semitic against the Italians." Attorney General Nicholas deB. Katzenbach, a most nervous fellow who tests the political winds before making a decision, hastily retreated and ordered suppression of the manuscript.

I have managed to obtain a copy of the controversial manuscript from my own confidential sources. Since the Federal Bureau of Investigation has been trying to find out how I managed to smuggle the manuscript out of the Justice Department, I won't elaborate on this aspect of the story. However, I checked Valachi's bizarre confessions against the findings of federal investigators. Out of this material has emerged a story so shocking it is hard to believe, a story that certainly should be published to alert the public to the savage, sordid jungle of organized crime.

Joe Valachi, alias Joe Cago, is no author. Until he learned to write while serving a stretch in Sing Sing, he couldn't read the street signs in his native Bronx. But he acquired an education of a different sort, and became one of New York City's most feared and deadly gunmen. He once boasted to a cellmate that he was responsible for more than 20 murders. Federal agents who have traced his career believe he was being modest for once. Like many illiterates, he has a fantastic memory. It is his last remaining weapon against his underworld enemies—most of all against his old boss, the notorious

Vito Genovese, who ordered his murder and gave him the "Kiss of Death" while they shared a cell in the Atlanta penitentiary.

Valachi writes pretty much as he talks—in almost pure Runyonese—but takes care to shield his readers from the profanities which spice his conversation. As a substitute he uses "Gee!" throughout his manuscript. He vows, of course, that every word is the whole truth and nothing but the truth. "I have no reason to lie," he writes, "I am telling you the truth and I must tell you the truth or I will look bad and I ain't aiming to look bad. After all I ain't the dumbest guy in the world. Thank you people as you have been swell to me as I received a couple of hundred fan mail."

Though Valachi may distort an occasional detail, federal agents have verified the general truth of his revelations. The picture he draws of the underworld, its curious code and its ghastly vengeance on those who break it, seems incredible.

Valachi has lived all his life by the fist and the gun. The wonder is that he has survived so long. Now in his sixties, he is reconciled to spending his life in jail, alone save for the company of his guards, for he would be less than safe among other inmates. The arm of the Cosa Nostra is long, its memory even longer where a squealer is concerned. Yet given a shotgun and some triggermen to back his play, the unrepentant Valachi would willingly battle it out with his enemies in the streets. When a government agent asked him what he would do if he were freed, Joe growled: *"I'd kidnap some mob guy for $100,000 ransom and use the dough to hire me some 'soldiers.' Then I'd get a shotgun and go after those blankety-blank rats!"*

Valachi grew up in the streets of the Bronx and Brooklyn, maturing into a seasoned gangster in the best tradition of "The Untouchables." Squat, heavily muscled and ruggedly handsome, he was known for his quick temper. He shot or slugged it out with cops and fellow crooks alike in dozens of

THE REAL THING

THE EXPOSE AND INSIDE DOINGS OF COSA NOSTRA
BY JOSEPH VALACHI, MEMBER SINCE 1930

To begin with, I must say that I came from the poorest family on earth -- at least that was the way I felt when I was a little boy. As a boy I went barefoot most of the time. Never did I receive anything at Christmas time. I believed in Santa Claus and hung my stocking up every Christmas, but never ever found an apple, all I would get on Christmas was being awakened and having my father try to give me a glass of whisky, which I used to refuse -- it was too strong.

One night when I was about eight years old my brother and I were awakened about 1:00 o'clock in the morning. What woke us was my Mother and Father were having a fight. It was about a dispossess. At this time the rent was about seven dollars a month. My brother told me to dress up. He was three years older than I, so I dressed up and he took me on Park Avenue around 114th Street. By this time it was about 2:30 in the morning, so we broke into a store. I don't remember what kind of store but all I know we took two bags of Fairy soap. We found the bags in or around the cellar as

A reproduction of the first page, typed by government stenographers, of the manuscript that underworld informer Joe Valachi scrawled out in long hand. The Justice Department has refused to make the manuscript public.

scrapes. He wore flashy clothes, squired gaudy girls, hung out at bars, bistros and race tracks. In the ranks of the Cosa Nostra, he was known as a tough "soldier" but hard to handle. During the height of his criminal career, he commanded a small murder squad which killed by "contract."

In recounting the grisly details of gang murders, Valachi goes far beyond his public testimony before the McClellan committee. He gives a more heroic account of his own actions, however, than federal agents might do. As Joe tells it in "The Real Thing," he was all heart when fulfilling a "contract" to rub someone out.

There was the time, for example, that he set up an ambush in an empty Bronx apartment for a racketeer called Joe Baker. When the victim showed up with his wife, big-hearted Valachi waited for her to kiss him and get out of the way. As he recalls it: "Baker came out of the office and as he reached the corner his wife met him and she handed him something and they kissed and he went the other way and the wife just stayed there and was watching him go when Buster had to shoot. It all happened so fast . . if we could have had another chance at Joe another time we would have done nothing this time. We had no choice as this was our first and last chance. . . . As I said before, I liked Joe Baker. Solly said that he saw the dust come out of Joe's coat as the bullets hit him in the back."

Another time, Valachi went to his Mafia chieftain, Vito Genovese, to plead for the life of a friend marked for murder. "I want to tell you now Vito I said if I can't do him any good I'll do him no harm," writes Valachi. "I must explain to the readers that sometimes a guy goes to the front for someone and he winds up by getting the contract for shooting him. So I went down prepared for such a thing." In this case, the doomed man was allowed to live.

But Joe was unable to save another crony in crime, known as the "Gap," who returned from an Italian trip suspected of squealing. Since the two had been close pals, Valachi got orders to watch for him. In time, "Gap" turned up at a Bronx bar owned by Valachi and greeted his friend with a fraternal kiss. Relates Joe: "I said Gap things changed around here since you were deported to Italy. Yes, he said, so I heard. Then he hesitate and he said in a very low voice that he and I are going to Cuba. So I whispered go to Cuba tonight but he was so drunk that it went over his head. Well I was trying to help him as I owed him a favor as he saved me once in Brooklyn in 1931. I give him a hint and he is too drunk to catch it. After the Gap left I made a call."

Tipped off by Valachi's phone call, other gangland killers caught up with the Gap in another bar. Joe learned from an eye witness of the Gap's last words. "So he tells me that the Gap realized you were trying to tell him something. He said that you told him to go to Cuba . . . He the Gap mentions Cuba a car pulled up. To tell you the truth he said his [the Gap's] brains were shot out of his head."

Valachi also relates how he set up the famous, heretofore unsolved murder of mobster Eugenio Giannini, who was shot before dawn on September 21, 1952, in front of a Bronx athletic club. Police found only an elderly Italian tidying up the sidewalk, but he hadn't finished cleaning up a red splotch which police identified as blood. Later, Giannini's bloodied body was found face up in a gutter several blocks away. Valachi got the contract from his immediate superior in the mob, Tony Bender. "He said," recalls Joe, "that Charlie Lucky Luciano had sent word that Gene had been an informer for the past 17 years and Tony told me that Charlie Lucky said that Gene is the smartest stool pigeon that ever lived. Kill him and whoever comes and fronts for him." In describing their first confrontation, Valachi says:

"Gene walked in the bar and the first thing Gene told me was that he felt he was going to die. . . . So I give Gene a pat on the back and I told him to have a drink and stop the nonsense. In the meantime there was a girl at the bar that used to work for me. I called her over and I invited her to have a drink with us. I told Gene why don't he grab her and go out and have a good time and forget about this feeling of being killed. Gene said he had no money in his pocket and he showed me that he had only twenty dollars so I hand him two more twenty dollar bills and I told him that he had enough to take her out. I remember her name and I don't think it is proper to mention her name as it is so long ago and she may be married and why should I start trouble."

Shortly after staking Giannini to a last binge, Valachi and his killers began stalking him. "When it was two o'clock in the morning I got tired as Gene did not show up so I asked one or two of the guys to drive me up to the Lido and they drove back. In about an hour or more I don't remember Fiore calls me and tells me that he just got there, but he Fiore meant Gene as we did not want to mention his name on the phone. I tell Fiore to go ahead and see him and he knew what I meant. About half hour later or more I really did not check, Fiore calls me and he tells me that they saw him and that they are going away for a couple of days."

By "see" him, they meant, of course, "shoot" him. But Valachi later got called on the carpet for the careless handling of the body. He recalls that the top boss, Vito Genovese, was furious: "Now when Vito did arrive the first thing that he said was that he wanted to get the first punch and he made a fist as he said it. Then he told me those guys claim that they took Gene's body away from 112 Street to save the game [a crap game going on there]. What do you say Vito asked me. I said that I only could tell you what the kids told me . . . The carpet was because I ordered Gene to be killed in front of the crap game as if I did it on my own. First they tell you to do something of which I can't refuse then they make believe that they don't know anything after its done."

Valachi was constantly being disciplined by the mob. "He

had a cut in every beef," explained an agent who has followed Joe's career. To keep the hoods from fighting among themselves, the mob had a rule against assault and battery. This was the rule that the tempestuous Valachi most frequently violated. In an account of a typical altercation, he tells about tangling with his partner over the profits from their bar and describes the underworld hearing that was called to settle the dispute. Relates Valachi: "So I pulled him in the back room away from the bar and I tell him put up your hands I'm going to swing on you. He tried to block his face but I pulled his hands away from his face and I rap him on his left and right eyes. I got so angry that I was dragging him down the cellar from the kitchen because there is where he landed as I was hitting him the pie man stopped me."

Concerning what happened when he was summoned before an underworld court or "table," Joe is quite frank: "We are all called in the restaurant room and there was Tony Bender [Joe's boss], Frank [the plaintiff], Charley Brush, who represented Frank, Albert Anastasia who was the boss. Albert Anastasia started to do the talking and he started with me. He first said to me you know that you could start a war by what you did and there is no excuse for a guy like you. You know all the rules and you know what will happen if you take the law into your own hands. Frank tried to talk at this moment but he was told to keep his mouth shut. I was told not to talk no matter what Albert says. But Albert said well lets not make a long story out of it."

Both sides, represented by their underworld mouthpieces, told their story. The verdict: "Albert looked at me and said give him a couple thousand dollars and Frank tried to say something and Albert said take what I say or you don't get nothing."

For the edification of his public, Valachi explains: "Of course the reader must know by now that a table is a carpet just like a trial that is held in any court room. I wanted to tell the readers as to make them understand how the mob handles carpets almost every day if it ain't one thing it's another and they are always having tables."

What are the laws governing this strange subterranean society of cutthroats? *"The very first and most important rule," according to Valachi, "is not to expose the secret of the Cosa Nostra—it means death without hope of ever being forgiven.* If the Cosa Nostra calls for a member he must drop everything he's doing, no matter how important it is . . . If he is ordered to go into a police station he must go, of course, that never was done, it is only to explain the importance of the order. *Death is the penalty for violating another member's wife. Death is the penalty for telling wives anything about the Cosa Nostra.* It has been a long standing rule that no kidnapping is allowed in the Cosa Nostra. It is against the rules to hit another member with your hands. Another rule—orders passed from lieutenants to the soldiers have to be followed without question. Death is the penalty for disobeying such an order. There is a rule against procuring but this rule was violated frequently within the Cosa Nostra."

Never one to take kindly to discipline, Valachi was disgruntled over all the rules. "Now," he writes, "as far as rules are concerned there are so many of them that it is impossible to mention them all." Joe's infractions were so frequent that he was forever appearing before "tables." This left him with a sour attitude toward underworld chieftains: "Most of the bosses stink. There is a few good ones but not many. I'm sure that when the soldiers read this what I'm saying most of them will agree if not out loud at least to themselves."

No. 1 on Joe's "stink" list is Vito Genovese. Addressing himself to this underworld top dog, Joe says: "You didn't care how anyone feels you are the power but I hope to take care of your power and throw it in the river and I'm going to try my best to break up the mob of yours. Now I want to warn Anna that was Vito's wife and as she stood up for me when I was married and I find her a wonderful person—I want her to know that Vito is having her tailed so be careful. Anna he loves you but he ain't got the guts to come out and let you know how he feels. He is worried as to what the mob might think. He must keep his pride. He asked me in Atlanta if I ever heard anything about his wife. I told him I did not. He was happy to hear it. Anna and he was crying. Anna what did he do to you? I remember when you told me that night when we went out the four of us that if Vito tells you that it is raining and you know the sun is out you will believe him. You loved him so much what happened Anna, did he kill your love the way he killed mine."

Valachi spread his own affections among a number of mistresses, most of them blond and brittle. Indeed, he wrote poetry to his favorite, a young chick named Carol Jacobs. Federal agents discovered several tender verses among the pistols and brass knuckles at his hideout. What these poems lacked in rhyme, they made up for in bizarre sentiment. Example: "Do you love your Joey boy? If you don't love your Joey boy, he is going to die." Being such an affectionate fellow, Joey boy had enough love left over for his wife, whom he used to address as "Mommy." But whatever feeling "Mommy" (formerly Mildred Reina) has had for Valachi apparently has faded. Alone in his cell, Joe now writes: "My wife was a saint, even if she is mad at me. I must tell the truth there isn't a woman on earth that is better than her they could equal her but not better—a lot of class—God bless her."

Joseph Valachi gives a surprising account of how he started his life of crime: "One night when I was about eight years old my brother and I were awakened about 1:00 o'clock in the morning. What woke us was my Mother and Father having a fight. It was about a dispossess. At this time the rent was about $7 a month. My brother told me to dress up. He was three years older than I, so I dressed up and he took me on Park Avenue around 114th Street. By this time it was 2:30 in the morning so we broke into a store. I don't remember what kind of a store but all I know we took two bags of Fairy soap. At this time Fairy Soap was 5c a bar. We went from house to house and sold the soap for two bars for 5c."

Three years later, Joe did his first stretch. "When I was about eleven years old I went to the N.Y. Catholic Protectory for throwing stones at the teacher. I didn't mean to hit her—I meant to scare her but I happened to hit her in the eye. I felt real bad about it so I went away for two years." He started out a model inmate, reciting his catechism and abiding by the rules. Thus he attained what he describes as "a state of grace," probably the only period of this sort in his life. Whatever good fortune he enjoyed thereafter, he attributes to this brief period of piety: "I became one of the rough boys at the NYCP. But as I go on with this story I will explain time and again how I was saved in the underworld life that right now I believe that this state of grace helped me along in the life at least I believe, as you will see as I go on, how many times I was saved by mere luck."

Valachi unquestionably had a number of narrow escapes. During one hold-up, police shot him in the head at point-blank range. After managing to elude the police, his accomplices dumped the bleeding Valachi on the street and fired some shots into the air to attract help. The hoods came back about an hour later, found him still lying on the street. Charitably, they hauled him to the office of an underworld doctor. Somehow he survived to philosophize: "So the ones that got caught sleeping slept forever I was just lucky and again I thought of the state of grace that I kept in the Catholic Protectory."

Along with his peculiar state of grace, Joe had at least one Cosa Nostra rule going for him. Had it not been for this rule, federal agents say Valachi would have been bumped off half-a-dozen times by his own superior in the mob, Tony Bender,

NAME	:	Joseph VALACHI
ALIASES	:	Joe Cago, Joe Cargo, Joe Kato, Joseph Siano.
DESCRIPTION	:	Born 9-22-1903, NYC, 5'5", 195 lbs, brown eyes, grey hair, dark complexion.
LOCALITIES FREQUENTED	:	Resides 45 Shawnee Avenue, Yonkers, NY, frequents the Belmont Ave. section of Bronx, NY, & Yonkers (NY) Racetrack.
FAMILY BACKGROUND	:	Wife: Mildred; son: Donald; father: Dominick; mother: Mary Casale; (both deceased); girl friend: Carol Jacobs Cuccuru.
CRIMINAL ASSOCIATES	:	Anthony Strollo, John Stoppelli, Vincent Mauro, Arnold Romano, Salvatore Santoro, John Batista Salvo, John Ormento, Giuseppe Doto, Fiore Siano and Giacomo Reina.
CRIMINAL HISTORY	:	FBI #544 NYCPD #B-58458 Record dating from 1921 includes arrests for concealed weapon, burglary, robbery. Pleaded guilty to Federal Narcotic Law violation (1960).
BUSINESS	:	Formerly owned Lido Bar, 1362 Castle Hill Ave., Bronx, NY. Has part interest in juke box firm and in several race horses.
MODUS OPERANDI	:	A trusted Mafia member and part of the Anthony Strollo narcotic smuggling and distributing organization. Wholesales heroin to major Mafia narcotic traffickers on the Upper East Side of NYC.

Property of U. S. Govt — For Official Use Only
May not be disseminated or contents disclosed
Without permission of Commissioner of Narcotics

This confidential data about mobster Valachi is taken from the rogues gallery kept by the U.S. Bureau of Narcotics.

who became impatient with him. Joe's description of the rule: "They made a council of six, meaning they made a new board. It was to protect the soldier, in other words it meant that a boss or under boss or anyone else cannot have one of his soldiers killed just because he did not like him. It meant that if a soldier did anything wrong he will get a trial and be judged by seven men. Everyone was glad to hear about the council. They know soldiers were being killed for nothing through the years."

Newspaper headlines have told the story of how Valachi, sent to the Atlanta penitentiary and given the "Kiss of Death" by cellmate Genovese, bludgeoned an inmate to death by mistake, thinking he was the underworld enforcer Joseph "Joe Beck" di Palermo. What hasn't been told is how Valachi, who had killed his share of informers for the mob, happened to be branded as an informer himself. Once he was questioned for four hours while other inmates waited in the bullpen, wondering why Valachi was spending so much time with the agents. Relates Valachi: "So I tell the agent what do you think I don't know what you are up to. You know well enough that there are other boys in that bullpen and you want it to appear that I am telling you something. Why are you bothering me? I have nothing to tell you and if I had something I won't tell you anything—even if I get a hundred years."

Government agents confirm that Valachi refused to talk, but he was right about the suspicions planted in the minds of the other inmates. "I did not say anything I was in a daze," he writes. "I did not know if I was going or coming. I went and sit in a corner." Then he panicked, asked to be sent to Atlanta alone in a car. When he was put aboard a bus with other prisoners, an agent told me, tough guy Valachi "cried like a baby."

The whispers quickly spread that he had squealed. In his distress, Valachi tried to send a message to George Gaffney, then boss of the New York City narcotics office. Unaccountably, the prison authorities never contacted Gaffney. But Valachi claims that word of his attempt to contact Gaffney reached Genovese. Joe tells of his panic before he finally broke: "I was in such a state of mind that I did not know if I was coming or going but one thing I had in mind that I am not going to die alone. I'm going to take someone with me. I did not know who—there were so many of them so I was thinking of the worse one. . . . I would not want Vito himself because I wanted him alive so that I can do just what I am doing and what I'm doing would kill him. Now Vito must live . . . he got to find out that he caused me to do what I am doing. I'm being a rat the way he wanted me to die branded a rat. Well Vito I said to myself this would put an end to the things that you have been doing all your life to avoid being brought before the councilmen. He just has them killed and then he yells Rat."

Regarding the day Valachi left his cell the last time, he recalls: "I was waiting for everyone to leave until Vito and I remained alone. He stood about five minutes with me and as I was leaving I called him and I waved with my hand and I said to him Good Bye Coupe Good Bye Coupe. I just looked and said nothing and went out of the cell block."

The rest is history. *If there is a moral to Valachi's story, it is that the underworld is real and not just a figment of crime writers.* No crime is too vicious for the lords of the Cosa Nostra and their hirelings. They are creatures of darkness. Or, as Valachi himself puts it: "I hope that some day the American people would benefit by what I have been telling them as far as the mob is concerned. I am alone in this world. I write to no one of my family as the world knows they disown me and I don't blame them. I would had been dead two years now and I would had the same name as I have now so what is there to lose. Mr. Vito Genovese you tell me."

It is a rare month that some notorious underworld figure doesn't turn up mysteriously murdered in New York, Chicago, Detroit, Pittsburgh, Los Angeles. For a while, Youngstown, Ohio, was known as Murdertown; gangsters fighting to control its $15 million annual gambling rackets carried out more than 75 bombings before reformers cracked down. Most unsolved slaying are the work of underworld executioners, men so skilled in their grisly profession they rarely leave behind evidence the police can use against them. To the proliferation of corpses must be added an even greater number of underworld "disappearances." Typical, for example, is the case of Joe Valachi's superior in the Cosa Nostra—Tony Bender alias Anthony Strollo, identified in federal files as "one of the most powerful racketeers in the U.S.," who vanished about the time Valachi started singing. Agents have little reason to doubt the underworld whispers that he was killed and dumped into the Hackensack River.

In gang slayings, arrests are rare; even rarer are convictions. *Yet the truth is that most of the murderers are known. A federal agent has told me that he knows one man, still walking free, who has been responsible for 32 "hits"—the underworld euphemism for killings. The agent has heard of others, longer in the trade of death, who have notched up as many as 50 murders.* "These men kill," he said, "as casually as you would swat a fly." They are not casual, however, in their methods. They may study a victim for weeks before they go after him with gun, knife, or bomb. Though some are more skilled than others, they seldom leave any clues at the scenes of their gruesome work.

Lacking the evidence to convict, I can't give full names. But a few brief descriptions will serve to draw a composite of the men who live by murder. The top professionals are seldom young; most are over middle age, some in their sixties. In the main, they are quiet mannered, soft spoken, well dressed. Some are alumni of Murder Incorporated who escaped prosecution and resumed their chosen profession after the heat subsided. Typical are "Dandy Jack," in his late sixties, a doy-

NAME : Vito GENOVESE

ALIASES : Don Vitone, "The Old Man"

DESCRIPTION : Born 11-21-1897 Roccarainola, Naples, Italy. 5'7", 160 lbs, brown eyes, black-grey hair, wears glasses. Naturalized 11-25-36, NYC

LOCALITIES FREQUENTED : Resides 68 W. Highland Ave., Atlantic Highlands, N.J. Frequents Greenwich Village area of NYC, Old Orchard Country Club and Piano Bar, Atlantic Highlands, N.J.

FAMILY BACKGROUND : Separated from wife, Anna Petillo; son: Philip; step-daughter: Mrs. Anna Simonetti; brothers: Michael and Carmine; father: Felice; mother: Nunziata (both deceased).

CRIMINAL ASSOCIATES : Frank Costello, Tony Strollo, Tom Lucchese, Joe Biondo, Joe Stracci, Joe Doto, Lucky Luciano.

CRIMINAL HISTORY : FBI #861267. NYCPD B#59993. Extensive arrest record since 1917, including burglary, concealed weapons, auto homicide and murder; has conviction for violation of Federal narcotic laws.

BUSINESS : Has interests in Colonial Trading Co., Waste Paper Removal Co., Erb Strapping Co., Tryon Cigarette Service Co. and many night clubs, all in N.Y.C.

MODUS OPERANDI : Attended Apalachin Mafia meeting 1957. Financial backer for international narcotic smuggling. Is reputed Mafia head of N.Y.C. rackets, shares in gambling and other interstate rackets with deportee Lucky Luciano.

Property of U. S. Govt — For Official Use Only
May not be disseminated or contents disclosed
Without permission of Commissioner of Narcotics

Note that this confidential dossier states that Vito Genovese has "interests [financial] . . . in many night clubs."

en of death dealers, who left Murder, Inc., in Brooklyn to become a labor racketeer around Hazelton, Pennsylvania; "Willie Potatoes," in his fifties, Chicago free-lance killer with a reputation as a torturer; "Cockeyed Phil," in his late fifties, pint-sized, sallow-faced, with a crossed left eye, who is known in the New York underworld for his violence.

The younger killers favor Ivy League style and deportment. Among them are the coldly suave "Cirino" brothers and "Benny the Cringe", partners in murder for the New York mob; "Joe the Blonde," slim, neat, ruggedly handsome, with cold blue eyes, known as a ruthless enforcer in the Flatbush area of Brooklyn.

Today's gang killings are not so raw as they were when Al Capone's reign of terror in Chicago was climaxed by the notorious St. Valentine's Day massacre. *The age of the "pineapple" tossed into a speakeasy, of the speeding black car, and blasting tommy-gun is over.* The underworld has learned to shun the headlines; a professional killing today is accomplished quietly and expertly. Chicago, for example, has a Murder Council of four leading mobsters who are responsible for pronouncing death sentences. They have a staff of 13 executioners, all well known to the Chicago police. When an underworld character gets out of line—by welching, cheating, or squealing—the council meets like a Supreme Court to decide his fate. Once the verdict to "hit him" has been handed down, reprieves are rare.

It is a Cosa Nostra tradition that a man marked for death should receive a gift of white roses as a warning of his fate. These may be sent to him, or he may receive the gift symbolically in the form of a whispered message mentioning white roses. One man who got a white-rose warning went to his friends and pleaded with them in tears that he had been wrongfully accused. The friends succeeded at the last minute in persuading the Murder Council to reverse its decision.

The white rose gesture, though it may seem flamboyant, serves a highly practical purpose. It usually isolates a man from any help he may hope to get. Eyes go blank, ears deaf, faces stoney, hideouts closed. He becomes a man alone, scurrying down one dark alley after another with killers stalking him.

Sometimes the killers with grisly goodwill may invite the victim for a night on the town, as Joe Valachi did before stalking Giannini. If the victim happens to be lucky, he will get a quick ride to some remote spot and a clean, swift bullet or knife thrust. If he is to be made an example, he may be slowly tortured to death. The word of his fate will get around. Men have been dumped into tubs of cement, given drinks and cigarettes while it hardened, then dropped into a river or lake still alive. Contrary to general belief, the cost of underworld murder does not come high. Sometimes it is done free, as a favor for a friend, as a gesture by a young man eager to get ahead in the rackets, or by a man on the run to pay for his hideout. The fee may be as low as $100.

The execution of an important hoodlum, one who has his own bodyguards, might cost as high as $10,000. When the time to "hit" him comes, he will be "hit." Nothing will stand in the way of the sentence, not even the lives of innocent people. Take the case of Charles Cavallaro, a Youngstown racketeer who was known as "Cadillac Charlie" because of his taste for expensive cars. He was blown to eternity outside his home when he switched on the ignition of his automobile. Along with him died his son Tommy, 11. An older son, Chuckie, 12, had his left hip torn off and was crippled for life. Ironically, Cavallaro did not die in the car that gave him his nickname. He was blown up in a Ford. The murder remains a mystery.

The underworld bosses are worried, almost as much as the police chiefs, by the new rise in gang murders. It signifies a collapse in their authority, dating back to the 1957 "summit conference" at Apalachin in upstate New York, when the nation's top mobsters got together to plan policy. They rolled up in sleek Cadillacs, flashed huge rolls of greenbacks, and otherwise made themselves conspicuous in this out-of-the-way spot. Later they were rounded up pretty much by one lone state trooper. Some tried to flee through the woods but were picked up, their expensively tailored suits snagged by brambles and burrs. This display of panic and folly made a bad impression on the rank-and-file gang members. One small-time mobster told a federal agent: "If we had done that . . ." Then, expressively, he drew his finger across his throat. The young racketeer made it clear that he had less confidence in a high command he no longer respected.

To add to the breakdown in underworld discipline, federal racket-busters have kept the top gangsters under such close surveillance that they haven't been able to hold any more Apalachin-style meetings. They have gathered a few times in Hot Springs, Miami, and Acapulco, Mexico, but they were so nervous about the federal watchdogs that they could only manage a fleeting exchange. When they tried to meet in crowded New York City in September, 1966, cops swooped down on them and arrested 13 top bosses. Result: underworld disputes are settled less often around a conference table. Ambitious young men, coming up in the rackets, are grabbing new territory. In this clash of ambitions, the specialists in assassination are getting more "contracts" to kill.

The Justice Department's organized crime section, a top flight unit of crackerjack agents, has been putting together the story of muscle and murder from the reports of 24 federal enforcement agencies. It adds up to a picture of underworld savagery that makes the wildest TV blood chiller seem fare for tiny tots; the truth is sometimes more terrifying than any fiction. Some killers-for-hire have been jailed. A few have been persuaded to defy the Mafia code of omerta (silence or death) and talk to federal agents. In exchange for their information, they have been guaranteed protection. Two or three have been given whole new identities, enabling them to escape the implacable vengeance of the gangs. Planted informants are also passing out information from inside the murder rings.

Most of the victories against the Cosa Nostra must be credited to the Treasury's Narcotics Bureau. It was the first law enforcement agency to infiltrate the underworld's most closely guarded citadel. The bureau moved into the Cosa Nostra 20 years ago in a long battle against organized dope smuggling, fought from the inside. How successful it has been is evident from the decrease in the narcotics trade. Significantly, although only two of every 100 government agents are N-men, they are responsible for 15 of every 100 convictions. As undercover men, federal narcotics agents learn to look like gangsters, talk like gangsters, think like gangsters. Sometimes they also die like gangsters—shot, knifed or strangled in some dark alley. They work across the world, for the traffic in illicit drugs knows no frontiers. The shadowy figures they trail may lead them into any city. And always death walks with them.

During a recent nine-month period, N-men engaged in seven running gun battles with drug smugglers—three in this country, four in Turkey. Agents have been run down by automobiles. One was thrown through a window. Some have died under torture. They face addicts who are wildly unpredictable, racketeers who will stop at nothing to defend their huge revenues. Often the men against them are equipped with speed boats, planes, radios—and, above all, cold cash to buy silence, to hire killers, to appear respectable.

Inside Cosa Nostra, one small slip can mean an N-man's death. For those who have taken the Mafia blood oath are the world's most sinister cutthroats. Their mood can switch in a moment and they kill without warning. Agent Wilson Shee, for example, had an appointment with an informer who had been furnishing him information for several months. Suddenly the squealer whipped out a gun and shot Shee to death, then killed himself.

Narcotics officers have been responsible for the arrest and conviction of the Mafia's most notorious ringleaders. Prize of the bag: Vito Genovese. Others put behind bars include such delegates to the infamous Apalachin crime conference as chunky Carmine Galente, who has a reputation in the underworld as a sadist; big, booming, 240-pound "Big John" Ormento, who has unhappily exchanged his diamond stick-pins and flashy clothes for prison garb; and barrel-chested Vincent Mauro, a surly customer who is described in Narcotics Bureau files as a "vicious killer."

Not long ago an agent called on Mauro in prison and tried to pump him for information. The mobster spurned a warning that he would be wise to cooperate. "You're the one who has to worry, not me!" he snarled at the agent. The Narcotics Bureau later learned from underworld tipsters that Mauro's threat was no mere bluff. According to the bureau, the imprisoned Mafia lords, alarmed over the demoralization of their mobs, had marked five agents for murder. Such a dramatic gesture was needed, they decided, to show their defiance of the government and to impress rank-and-file mobsters. Mafia leaders on the outside feared the scheme was too dangerous. "You kill five federal agents, and they won't be above framing all of us," was the reaction of one racket boss, as quoted by an informer. Genovese reportedly decided it would be enough to bump off one key agent. The last word was that the murder "contract" had been issued.

Federal enforcement files portray an underworld so hideously grotesque as to seem unreal. The shocking and sinister truth, however, is that the dark domain of the Cosa Nostra is all too real.

MAFIA LIST INDEX

Name	Page
ABATE, Antonino	199
ABATE, Onofrio	281
ABATI, Michael	3
ABBATE, Anthony @	199
ABBRESCIA, Angelo	329
ABBRESCIA, Arcangelo @	329
ABRUSCIA, Angelo @	329
ACCARDI, Sam @	282
ACCARDO, Anthony J.	121
ACCARDO, Settimo	282
ACCAROBI, Giuseppe @	282
ADAMO, Charles @	547
ADAMO, Giuseppe	4
ADAMO, Joseph @	4
ADAMO, Vincent @	547
ADONIS, Joe @	789
ADRAGNA, Gaetano @	27
AFFRONTI, Leonard	243
AFFRONTI, Lonnie @	243
AGA KHAN @	746
AGATO, Emmet @	325
AGRESTA, Ippolito P.	73
AGRESTO, Paul @	73
AIDA, Giuseppe @	308
AIELLO, Gasparo	681
AIELLO, Joe J. @	681
AIELLO, Joseph @	349
AIUPPA, Joseph	122
ALAIMO, Dominick	699
ALAIMO, Salvatore	700
ALAIMO, Sam @	700
ALBANESE, Philip J.	330
ALBANO, Alfonso @	104
ALBASI, John	331
ALBATE, Charles M.	332
ALBERO, Charles	333
ALBERTI, Andrew	334
ALBERTINI, Charles A. @	743
ALBERTINI, Dominique	743
ALBERTO, Frank @	630
ALDERISIO, Felix A.	123
ALDERISIO, Phillip @	123
ALEX THE OX @	425
ALFANO, Joe @	376
ALFONSO, Don @	104
ALIAMO, Dominick @	699
ALIAMO, Sam @	700
ALIMAO, Nick @	699
ALIMO, Dominick @	699
ALLEGRETTI, James @	157
ALLEN, Albert @	108
ALLEN, James @	336
ALLEN, Jerry @	299
ALLEN, Tom @	27
ALLOCCO, Dominick	335
ALO, Vincent	336
ALTIMARI, Michael P.	337
ALTROAD, L. L. @	348
AMALFITANO, Vincent	338
AMARENA, Salvatore	79
AMARI, Filippo	283
AMARI, Philip @	283
AMAROSA, Alexander	339
AMATO, Angelo A.	682
AMATO, Frank	701
AMATO, Pietro	761
AMELI, Salvatore @	479
AMELI, Sam @	479
AMELLA, Santiago @	325
AMENDOLA, Frank	340
AMOFRIO, Lanolli @	3
AMOROSA, Alexander @	339

Property of U. S. Govt – For Official Use Only
May not be disseminated or contents disclosed
Without permission of Commissioner of Narcotics

The first page of the Narcotics Bureau confidential index to the world's most notorious Who's Who—the leaders of the Mafia.

21

WASHINGTON WITHOUT WHITEWASH

Washington may not have the ancient architectural splendors of Paris or Rome, the grim, grimy majesty of London, or the sinister, sullen beauty of Moscow as an early snow begins to silver the golden onion domes of the Kremlin. But Washington has a magic of its own. The tranquil beauty of its shaded avenues and curving shorelines, its many circles and squares set like oases among the brick and cement casts a quiet spell upon visitors. The sun splashing on white marble and granite, pricking through the foliage of Rock Creek Park, flickering over the ripples in the Tidal Basin adds to the serenity.

But the aura of peace is deceptive. Deep in the granite and sandstone compounds of government, beyond the stares of the sightseers, a civilian-suited army is constantly at war. They not only direct the hot war in Vietnam and the cold war in China. They are also engaged in a hundred other wars—wars against crime and congestion, disease and drudgery, hatred and hunger, poverty and pollution. Some soar into space seeking conquest of the moon; others would be content to conquer the mundane fruit fly.

They are the bureaucrats, those unsung soldiers of the swivel chair, who wage their wars largely on paper. Behind their red tape entanglements, they bombarded one another with memos in septullicate. They can produce answers on almost anything from the habits of the hagfish to the habitat of the hackmatack. At the end of each day, more than 80 tons of wastepaper are picked up off the battlefield.

More often damned than praised by the citizens they serve, the bureaucrats man the cumbersome machinery of government. Elections are held, opposite political parties take power, administrative heads come and go. But the bureaucrats remain to guide each new appointee through the marble maze. He soon finds himself caught up in the petty rivalries and ancient animosites of the Balkanized bureaus, which encroach on one another's authority and raid one another's appropriations.

Even the strongest of Presidents have found themselves but small dogs wagged by a giant bureaucratic tail. They have differed only in how they have described their frustration. Franklin D. Roosevelt, after trying to impose his policies upon the Navy, compared the experience to boxing a featherbed. Dwight D. Eisenhower said he felt like a driver who had taken the wheel of a ten-ton truck hurtling down a steep grade. There wasn't much he could do, he found, except hold it on the course it was already traveling. John F. Kennedy's brief struggle with the federal bureaucracy, he once remarked, was like wrestling a whale. He never could seem to get a firm hold on the blubber.

On a typical day, coded messages flood into the State Department by pouch and cable from diplomatic posts all over the world. The most urgent telegrams are attached to clipboards beneath the appropriate wall maps in the Operations Center. A digest of overnight intelligence reports already has been delivered to the President. Hovering in his shadow is a warrant officer, unobtrusive but omnipresent, ready instantly to spring to his side with a slim black case. This contains the world's most secret code, which only the President can use to order a nuclear attack.

If the terrible order should ever come, it would be flashed to a central command post 45 feet underground near Omaha, Nebraska. Coded instructions are ready in a red box to send B-52 bombers and intercontinental missiles thundering into action. An airborne command post, code-named the "Looking Glass," is also on constant alert seven miles above the American landscape. It is mother hawk to a flock of B-52s, hovering on high, ever ready to retaliate in case of a nuclear Pearl Harbor. In the bomb bay of each B-52 is packed more destructive power than all the explosives used in all the past wars of human history.

Pondering this power in the Pentagon below, civilian technicians manipulate the buttons and knobs on a complex computer. Colored lights, blinking rapidly, signify the destruction of an "enemy." It is a new kind of war game that largely baffles the brass hats brought up on Clausewitz. The complexities of modern warfare, however, are no more staggering than the costs. On this typical day, it will cost the taxpayers no less than $145 million to run the Defense Department, more than they spend on cancer research in a year. Yet ten times more Americans will die of cancer this day than will fall on the Vietnam battlefields.

On Capitol Hill, Congressman George Mahon (D., Tex.), the powerful House Appropriations chairman, recommends a million-dollar military expenditure on the basis of a one-line budget request. Later he angrily demands more justification for a $73,000 slum clearance project, though it is explained in full-page detail. Congressman Charles Jonas (R., N. C.) delivers a ritualistic little speech about the dangers of federal spending. His reasoning seems to be that children are better off in a firetrap financed locally than in a modern school building constructed with federal help. He implies that federal funds might somehow corrupt school boards. Gravely nodding their agreement, committee members turn next to a shipping subsidy, which they apparently feel would have no such harmful effect on shipbuilders.

Across the Capitol grounds, in the Corinthian temple that houses the nation's highest court, nine black-robed men behind a mahogany bench listen in various stages of boredom to the oratory of a pompous attorney. Two lady tourists pick out Justice William O. Douglas and share hushed giggles. Earlier, his name was stricken from the Washington social register for his offense against society when, at 67, he married his fourth wife and second 23-year-old. He not only was unconcerned but one friend suggested he took perverse pleasure in "imposing his young wives on the old crones" of Washington society. The friend described the ruddy, heavy-boned, six-foot jurist as "something like a great old grizzly bear at the end of his trail."

Not far away, the National Aeronautics and Space Administration, its eye on the unexplored, and the Health, Education and Welfare Department, its eye on the unemployed, occupy buildings across the street from one another. NASA officials prepare to present two astronauts, just back from orbit, to the President. Humped over a desk at HEW, a scientist who had stopped the sale of a dangerous liver extract, thus saving thousands from debilitating sickness, continues his daily grind in obscurity.

On one side of Capitol Hill, Public Health officials spend the taxpayers' money on a campaign to persuade people to stop smoking. On the other side, Agriculture officials spend ten times more to subsidize tobacco crops and to promote tobacco sales. Within the white marble Agriculture building, itself, Secretary Orville Freeman struggles to reduce the bulging farm surpluses at the same time that he recommends millions for research to make farmland more productive.

In the Executive Office Building, an architectural horror adjacent to the White House, Vice President Hubert Humphrey discusses high policy with National Security Council members. Around a corner, a budget official pores over an ant bed of figures. "Effective budgeting," he says "is the uniform distribution of dissatisfaction." At the Government Printing Office, another official ponderously prepares the paperwork necessary to replace the pamphlet, "Bed Bugs: How to Control Them," with an updated version, "How to Control Bedbugs."

As the day wears on, the bureaucrats are absorbed in matters both weighty and weightless. They save lives, waste money, alleviate suffering, cause headaches. At nightfall, an army of moppers and scrubbers invade the government buildings, armed with 12-quart buckets and two-pound mops. Others with suction cups mounted on long poles change the light bulbs that have burned out during the day.

As the city adorns her neon jewelry and the mad beat of the go-go rooms blends with traffic noises, unescorted ladies hurry to their apartments and bolt the double locks. State Department secretaries, working overtime, are cautioned not to enter the elevators alone but to seek company as far as the front door where a cab can be hailed.

An attorney, unable to flag a taxi, boards a bus in downtown Washington. Three young Negroes block the aisle. He squeezes past two, but the third stretches out his arms to stop him. Wearily, the lawyer ducks beneath an arm. The Negro whirls around and rasps viciously: "How would you like a knife in your side?"

Chief Justice Earl Warren directs his limousine to stop at a supermarket where he hurriedly searches for items on a crumpled list. He asks for trading stamps to take home to his wife. The eight Associate Justices, compelled to share a single official car, hail cabs for the trip home. They are passed on the way by sleek government limousines carrying minor functionaries.

Television commentator David Brinkley, driving over the speed limit to keep an appointment with President Johnson, spots a flashing police light in his rear-view mirror. He is taken on a detour past the third precinct where he counts out $10 collateral on the way to the White House. Not far away, a man springs out of the shadows, slams British correspondent Donald Ludlow to the sidewalk and escapes with his wallet. All through the night, yoke victims shuffle into hospital emergency rooms.

In fashionable northwest Washington, a matron is attacked

by a man who barges into an elevator with her and jams all the buttons to stall the car. She fights him off with judo jabs, learned for precisely such an occasion. He is still cowering in a corner, warding off the blows, when the police arrive. While they wait for firemen to break into the stalled elevator, they shout instructions to the attacker concerning his constitutional rights.

Some 200 Negro youngsters, many of them teen-age girls, gather rocks, bottles and debris to repel an invasion of their territory by a rival gang. When the intruders fail to appear, the disappointed youngsters start hurling their ammunition at passing motorists. Police cars, rushing to investigate, also are battered. Two false fire alarms bring firemen who are greeted with a fresh barrage of debris. A police captain hustles his beleaguered patrolmen behind a building, orders them to discard their night sticks and avoid trouble. In their place, Negro social workers are dispatched to plead with the young lawbreakers.

Anti-poverty officials, emerging from a late conference, stop at the Embers, a fashionable cocktail lounge beneath their offices. Gulping down dollops of whisky, vodka and gin, they deplore the islands of poverty in the American sea of affluence. Not far away, a woman pregnant with her sixth illegitimate child tries out car doors. When she finds one unlocked, she beds down some of her children for the night. Evicted from their home for non-payment, the family had spent three nights sleeping on the floor of a friend, a "wine-head," who began to take liberties with the 12-year-old daughter. Indignantly, the mother led her brood into the streets.

Long, gleaming limousines roll up to the Canadian Embassy, disgorging starched and sabled passengers for a formal affair. Less than two blocks away at Dupont Circle, a man clad only in shorts and daubed with red paint goes through a ritual at each of the four corners of the central fountain. At each stop, he ceremoniously dips a cup in the fountain and drinks of the polluted water. He is ignored by guitar-strumming beatniks who conduct an impromptu rock 'n' roll session around the fountain.

Over in a corner of a Georgetown apartment, a pair of bongo drums throb and sob. In the center of the dimly lit room, hazy with smoke, two couples dance as if in a daze. Other boys and girls in beatnik garb, eyes glazed, sprawl on the floor, some in close embrace. One girl stands on her head, unkempt hair screening her face, slim legs braced against the wall. Nobody seems to think her behavior the least unusual. She is the hostess, a daughter of prominent parents listed in the social register. Attending private school by day, she goes beatnik at night. For refreshments, she serves "acid" (LSD) and "pot" (marijuana). Occasionally, a guest will take a shot of "bam" or "hash" as more potent drugs are called by the initiated.

As the darkness deepens, the streets begin to empty and an eerie stillness settles over the city, broken now and again by lone footsteps or the rumble of a passing car. Washington will sleep a few hours before it springs to life again at daybreak with a snarl of cars and buses.

INDEX